UNDERSTANDING CANADIAN SCHOOLS

UNDERSTANDING CANADIAN SCHOOLS

AN INTRODUCTION TO EDUCATIONAL ADMINISTRATION
SECOND EDITION

Jon Young
Benjamin Levin

University of Manitoba

HARCOURT
BRACE
CANADA

Harcourt Brace & Company, Canada

Toronto Montreal Fort Worth New York Orlando
Philadelphia San Diego London Sydney Tokyo

Canadian Cataloguing in Publication Data
Young, Jonathan C.
    Understanding Canadian schools : an introduction to educational administration
2nd ed.
Includes bibiliographical references and index.
ISBN 0–7747–3537–6

1. Public schools—Canada. 2. School management and
    organization   Canada. I. Levin, Benjamin Ruvin, 1952 II. Title.
LA412.Y68 1998   371'.01'0971   C97–930978–6

Acquisitions Editor: Joanna Cotton
Senior Developmental Editor: Laura Paterson Pratt
Production Editor: Stacey Roderick
Production Co-ordinator: Sheila Barry

Copy Editor: Claudia Kutchukian
Permissions Editor: Elizabeth Edwards
Cover Design: Gillian Tsintziras
Interior Design: The Brookview Group Inc.
Typesetting and Assembly: Carolyn Hutchings
Technical Art: Carolyn Hutchings
Printing and Binding: Webcom Limited

Cover Art: *Cottingham School After the Rain*, 1969, Christiane Pflug, 1936–72.
          Oil on canvas, 126.6 x 100.2cm. Reproduced with the permission of
          Michael Pflug.

This book was printed in Canada.

2 3 4 5   02 01 00 99

PREFACE

Everyone has some understanding of what schools are about. The purpose of this book is to build on and extend readers' understanding of the way Canadian schools have come to operate, and to challenge our thinking about why they are the way they are.

Two basic ideas have driven the writing of the book. First, we are fundamentally more concerned with ideas and issues than with facts (although the two are obviously mutually dependent). Second, we believe that the design of schools should not be left only to those people referred to as "administrators," but is an important concern of everyone interested in education, including teachers, students, parents, and many others. Attempting to incorporate these ideas in a text that is broad in coverage, combines a broad overview with sufficient detail, has a Canadian focus, and is also interesting to students and teachers has taxed our skills!

Acknowledgements

No book can be written without the participation and assistance of many people. So many people have helped with the book, or influenced the ideas that are found in it, that a list of thanks will inevitably miss someone who was important; we can only apologize for any oversights.

Among those we particularly want to recognize are our colleagues in educational administration at the University of Manitoba: John Long, J. Anthony Riffel, and John Stapleton. Many discussions with them about educational administration are reflected in these pages. Nancy Buchanan provided valuable research assistance. Heather McWhinney of Harcourt Brace first suggested this project and provided support throughout. All the staff at Harcourt Brace, listed on the previous page, were helpful and professional to work with. Several reviewers made many valuable suggestions to improve the text — W. Rod Dolmage, University of Regina; Donald Diubaldo, University of Windsor; Andrew Effrat, York University; Noel P. Hurley, University of Windsor; Graham Kelsey, University of British Columbia; David MacKinnon, Acadia University; Keith McLeod, University of Toronto; Mary Nixon, University of Victoria; and Dennis Treslan, Memorial University of Newfoundland. Many colleagues also provided encouragement for us to do this book. We hope that our efforts have met their expectations, at least in part.

Special thanks go to our students in 116.301 (school organization) and other courses at the University of Manitoba. Every time we teach a course our students end up teaching us about learning and education. We thank them.

Finally, we express our thanks and our love to our families, Nancy Read, Andrew and Ian Young, Barbara Wiktorowicz, and Clare, Anna, and Ruth Levin. We can never do so enough.

A Note from the Publisher

Thank you for selecting *Understanding Canadian Schools: An Introduction to Educational Administration*, Second Edition, by Jon Young and Benjamin Levin. The authors and publishers have devoted considerable time to the careful development of this book. We appreciate your recognition of this effort and accomplishment.

We want to hear what you think about *Understanding Canadian Schools*. Please take a few minutes to fill in the stamped reader reply card that you will find at the back of the book. Your comments and suggestions will be valuable to us as we prepare new editions and other books.

INTRODUCTION

This book was written for those who want to know more about educational administration and school organization. We see the book having two main audiences. The first includes those who are studying educational administration and school organization as part of an undergraduate or graduate program in a university. The second audience consists of noneducators, such as school board members, school advisory council members, or interested parents who have come to be involved with school administration and want to develop a better understanding of this subject.

Many students regard the study of school organization as a subject that has little connection with the everyday realities and needs of teaching. This is probably particularly true of those in preservice teacher education programs, who may be inclined to regard this course as another requirement unrelated to what they want and need to know to become a teacher, such as how to manage a classroom. However, as we try to illustrate throughout the book, matters of school organization are important precisely because they have such an enormous influence in determining the nature of teachers' work. Learning about school organization is important not just as an intellectual exercise, but because such knowledge gives all those involved in public education the ability to understand and be more effective in their work environment.

Another important purpose of this book is to help readers become critical learners and thinkers. When we use the term **critical thinkers**, we mean people who ask questions about why things are as they are, who evaluate practices and ideas based on careful analysis, and who are committed to trying to change things for the better. This requires that people think carefully about schools and how they work.

We do not regard education at any level as being a matter of learning some set of essential facts. Rather, we believe education should focus on central ideas and questions that are more important than particular pieces of information. Facts have their place — any worthwhile idea or opinion must be supported by reason and evidence. One cannot have an informed opinion without some knowledge about the matter at hand. At the same time, however, formal education too often consists of memorizing discrete pieces of content without placing them in a larger framework or connecting them to each student's own understanding of the world.

In this book, we try to stress ideas and questions. We do so because the questions will remain, even though the facts may change. For instance, we might have listed — and students might be asked to learn — the law regarding home schooling in all ten provinces. But that law will change over time, while the central questions concerning home schooling (those that have to do with the ability of the state to compel behaviour) will not change. Learning the current law may be important for a particular purpose or for thinking about the larger questions, but by itself it is not enough.

Consider also what it means to "know a fact." Take the fact, well supported by research, that in most classrooms boys speak more often than girls, are called on by teachers more often, get more attention from teachers, and interrupt girls quite regularly. Does being able to repeat this sentence on an exam mean that we know it? Or do we truly know it only when we have internalized it to the extent that it affects our behaviour as teachers and students? Furthermore, could we say that a young girl in elementary school, subject to being ignored and interrupted, "knows" this fact even though she could never articulate it? In other words, there are various forms of knowing, and our interest is in the form that means more than the ability to repeat something—namely the integration of that knowledge into our ideas and behaviour.

This sort of knowing depends much more on the students than it does on teachers. Of course, teachers can play an important role in showing students connections among ideas, in asking probing and challenging questions, in pushing students to articulate the full implications of their ideas, and in treating students with respect and consideration. But in the end, it is the students who must determine the meaning that ideas have for them, and who must integrate new knowledge with their existing ideas, beliefs, and values.

To make this statement is to describe a socially constructed version of knowledge. By this we mean that knowledge is something people make for themselves, whether individually or, more often and more powerfully, in groups or social settings. Our sense of what the world is and how it is to be understood comes from the collision between each of us as a person—our ideas and experiences—and the events of our lives, many of which are beyond our control. People can and do disagree vehemently on what seem to be straightforward matters. Is education improving or getting worse? Are teachers dedicated professionals or overpaid baby-sitters? We disagree because our own predilections, life experiences, and social context have pushed our thinking in different directions.

There is, then, no single right way of looking at the issues raised in this book. Indeed, we hope and expect that there will be debate about many of these issues in and out of class. Readers should treat the material in the book not as something to be written down in notes and memorized, but rather as a basis for debate, what is sometimes called "interrogating the text." Discussing differing perspectives and learning to understand how others see the issues (and why) is to us a critical part of education at all levels.

On the other hand, we do not believe that one opinion is as good as another. Anyone who truly did believe this statement would be unable to maintain any opinions of his or her own because there would be no basis for preferring them to any other opinion. It is important to test our ideas and opinions against those of other people, against data or evidence on the matter in question, and against the ideas of scholars in the field. We should strive always to develop an informed opinion (i.e., an opinion that can be supported or justified based on careful, reasoned argument and the best available evidence).

Critical thinking and informed opinion, however, are not sufficient in themselves. They must be directed toward some goal or objective. Fundamental to our writing this book was our wish to foster in readers the desire to make schools better places. The essence of teaching is trying to move students from their current state to another, more desirable state. The same goal should apply to schooling itself—to move it from its current state to one that is better. This task requires an understanding of schools as they currently exist, and of the factors that have shaped and continue to shape them. It also requires a moral commitment to particular values. But just as importantly, it requires that people be prepared to work to have those values realized. If the earlier two elements are difficult, this last is even more so.

The goal of improvement means that schools are places of struggle. People will disagree about what schools can and should do, and about how they should do these things. Such disagreements can and will occur between teachers and administrators, between teachers and students, between teachers and parents, and among people in each of these groups. Individual teachers are often themselves struggling with what they mean by schooling and education, and with how best to achieve their goals. Schools, like all human activities, are, in a sense, re-created every day by the actions of people who choose to do things differently, to learn from experience, and to try something new. Far from seeing this struggle as a problem to be overcome ("if only we could agree once and for all"), we see it as a fundamental condition of human existence. The struggle can be frustrating and difficult, but it can also be invigorating and tremendously rewarding. It is the opportunity to make the world a better place that makes teaching such an important and potentially rewarding activity. As Foster puts it, "We, as teachers and administrators, are engaged in a profession whose purpose is to make a difference. The joy of being an administrator or a teacher is to recognize and understand that each life makes a difference" (1986, p. 70).

The Organization of the Book

In writing this book, we tried to keep in mind issues of design and organization as well as content. Features such as case studies, real examples, and current Canadian data are intended to make the text both more interesting and easier to understand.

Order

The book begins with broad issues of school organization, while later chapters focus more on the school and the classroom. Recognizing that there are numerous interrelationships among the elements in the various chapters, and that the ideas are interconnected, we have done some cross-referencing in the text but have tried to avoid making the practice annoyingly frequent. The order in which the chapters are studied can certainly be altered, with the exception of Chapter One, which should be read first.

Themes

The chapters have been organized around a number of central questions or issues, which are introduced at the beginning of each chapter. In addition, the chapters begin with a prologue — a vignette intended to illustrate some of the links between the practice of teaching and the ideas presented in the chapter. We have left it to readers to make these, as well as their own, connections between the text and the realities of daily life in schools.

Examples

The book has an explicitly Canadian focus. To that end, we have included examples, statistics, excerpts from documents, and other data drawn from various parts of Canada. The reading lists and references draw extensively from Canadian sources, though we also include relevant sources from elsewhere. These materials are intended to promote class discussion or debate, and may form the basis for written assignments in a course. We also encourage you to include, where appropriate, material from your own province or local area.

Terms

Throughout the book we use **boldface text** to indicate a term that is being defined. We use *italics* for emphasis.

Exercises

The exercises at the end of each chapter are intended to focus attention on many of the key points made in the chapters. They range from the relatively simple to the complex, and can be used in various ways. Some are appropriate for use as course assignments, depending on the instructor's wishes. Others can be used as class activities to promote discussion, and still others can be done by students independently as a way of expanding their understanding of the issues raised in the book.

Readings

Chapters Two to Ten conclude with suggestions for further reading that relate to some of the main issues. Additional reading is fundamental to education. No book can possibly contain everything a reader might want to know. Moreover, we regard it as particularly important for students to seek out other points of view on the issues we raise, and not simply to accept our version. The references at the back of the book and further readings provide some sources and suggestions, but there are many other worthwhile readings for students to discover.

Our approach to references and further readings has been to try to focus on what we consider to be the most important work in a given area, with special attention to current Canadian scholarship. However, we have undoubtedly omitted work by Canadians and others that another author might see as vital. Again, we urge readers to look for themselves, and to approach all readings critically.

Sources of Current Information

Although we have endeavoured to provide the most recent available information, many aspects of education in Canada are changing rapidly, and it is quite likely that some of what you read will be outdated by the time you read it. For example, as this book is going to press, Ontario is planning to make major changes in the organization and funding of schools.

It is important, then, for readers to seek out the most current information on their own situation by looking at materials produced by provincial governments, teacher and school board organizations, school districts, and others interested in education.

The Internet and the World Wide Web provide other important vehicles for finding current information about education. More and more organizations have "home pages" that include access to documents, or at least information about current documents and issues. These include most provincial departments of education and most national organizations, such as the Council of Ministers of Education (CMEC), Canadian Teachers' Federation, and Canadian School Boards Association, as well as many school districts and schools. University faculties of education may also have online information on current research. As Web sites and search engines change rapidly, we suggest you look for a university or other training session that can help you make use of electronic sources of information.

Sources of Scholarly Work on Education

The Handbook of Research on Educational Administration (edited by N. Boyan; Longman, 1988) is a one-volume U.S. review of scholarly work in the area. The *Third Handbook of Research on Teaching* (edited by M. Wittrock; Macmillan, 1986) is a similar work that deals with research on many aspects of teaching, again with a largely U.S. focus. Revised editions of both works are now being written and may be available in 1998.

The main source of information about scholarly work in education is the ERIC system, which is available in most university libraries and contains information about more than 700 000 works, all searchable by computer on CD-ROM or via the Internet. ERIC itself is largely American, but International ERIC is a thorough index of Canadian, British, and Australian work. MICROLOG is another source of Canadian information that includes many government documents on education that are otherwise hard to find.

Among the main sources of Canadian academic writing on the issues in this book are *The Canadian Journal of Education, Our Schools/Our Selves, Journal of Educational Administration and Foundations,* and the *Alberta Journal of Educational Research.* Canadian publications aimed primarily at educators and policy-makers include *The Canadian School Executive, Education Canada,* and the *Newsletter* and occasional monographs of the Canadian Education Association.

The World Wide Web has also changed the process of academic research. Many sources are available in one form or another on the Web, sites are often linked to related sites, and up-to-date information and reports are frequently available for reading or downloading.

Much of the statistical information in this book is drawn from Statistics Canada sources. Statistics Canada provides a range of sources, including published reports (which can be found in libraries), analytic studies such as the *Education Quarterly Review,* offices in many Canadian cities that can be visited in person, and electronic data sources such as E-Stat. E-Stat, available in many university libraries, makes census and other data available for easy computer analysis — for example, to determine the economic or demographic characteristics of a school district. Statistics Canada maintains a World Wide Web site with up-to-date information about its services.

CONTENTS

Chapter Four
Law and Education   91

Chapter Five
Resources for Education   131

Chapter Nine
Teachers, Students, and Teaching   247

Chapter Ten
Prospects for Education   279

Appendix
Canadian Charter of Rights and Freedoms   309

References   313

Index   325

CHAPTER ONE

Making Sense of Public Schooling

▼ PROLOGUE:
The Staff Room, 8:15 A.M.

Linda Chartrand arrived at school at her usual time: 8:15 A.M. Getting her own children ready for school and to the neighbour's for preschool care was hard, but she found that she needed at least half an hour before the students arrived to review her plans for the day and make sure that she had all the materials ready. She also used the time to chat with colleagues in the staff room, to find out whether there had been any important developments since yesterday, or to check on which resource people might be in school that day.

"By the way, Linda," Pat, the office secretary, said as she came through the staff-room door, "don't forget that your class will be going to the auditorium at 3:00 P.M. to practise for the school concert. And could you make sure that all the money is in for the book orders? Oh, and Mrs. Koslowski is looking for you. She wants to ask if she could send the kids back ten minutes early from Phys. Ed. so she can make a meeting with the divisional consultant. Is that OK?"

"Sure," Linda replied. As an experienced teacher at both the junior high and elementary levels, she knew that there would be days requiring last-minute changes in her schedule. She had intended to get into a new unit with the class toward the end of the day, but that would have to wait, and she would have to find something else for them to do for the half hour between 2:30 and 3:00 P.M. As she was pondering what this might be, the resource teacher, Eric Sigurdson, asked if he could take three of her students for an extra half hour that morning. "The parents I was going to meet with had to cancel, so I'd like to give your kids the time." Again, Linda agreed to the change. She didn't like the model of resource withdrawal very much, preferring a collaborative, in-class approach, but there was no doubt that Eric was a help to the students he saw; she had a hard time finding the time to give them the individual attention they needed, even in her relatively small class of 23.

Linda checked her staff mailbox and pulled out an agenda for an upcoming in-school, professional-development day. At the first staff meeting of the year, the principal had asked the staff to spend the year reviewing the school's mission statement and reaffirming their collective vision and goals for the school. This was to be the focus of the day's meetings.

Linda had been through a comparable process in her previous school, and she smiled to herself as she thought of the similar reactions to the request among the two staffs. Some teachers had asked what was wrong with the existing mission statement that had been written by the previous principal when the school first opened fifteen years ago. Others expressed surprise that the school *had* a mission statement, because they'd been working at the school for several years and had never seen it. A few wondered why it would take a year to do this. Surely, they argued, a small subcommittee could draft something fairly easily, working from the old statement and from a few other schools' goals. This, they maintained, would allow time for the rest of the staff to focus on some of the pressing and practical issues that needed to be dealt with, like a new conflict-resolution program for the children and the co-operative learning initiatives that the Grade 6 teachers were working on.

But the discussion that had followed had been a good one, and by the end of the meeting most of the staff were supportive of the project. The principal had emphasized that she wasn't interested in simply producing a public-relations document full of all the right phrases and current jargon. She wanted the staff to talk through their different views of the school's goals and priorities, and to come up with a statement of purpose that the staff as a whole would feel was their own, and that would relate to daily school practices as well as set a direction for future initiatives. Some teachers began talking about their dreams for — and frustrations with — the school, and how they thought it had changed over the years. Despite the differences in the concerns and ideas expressed by the teachers, when the meeting ended there was an air of excitement about the project, which had carried over into the ensuing weeks.

Now, as the bell rang for the first class of the day, Linda was still thinking about the process of developing a mission statement that would actually capture what the school was all about. She thought of the mixed group of students she had in her class. They were good kids and she liked them all, but she was always being reminded of how different they were, from her and from one another. It wasn't that their reading levels ranged from Grades 2 to 8; that was normal. It was just that there were so many other differences. The two new immigrant children were just starting to learn English, and couldn't yet speak very much to the other kids. She hardly noticed Rose's wheelchair anymore, since Rose was so much a part of the class now. But Tommy still had occasional severe outbursts of rage that were hard on her and the students, although he'd improved since the year began. The full-time teacher aide helped, but Linda wondered how much Tommy was really learning. And there were so many others, the quiet ones for example, who raised questions in her mind about her teaching strategies and effectiveness.

Yes, she thought, it was going to be a good exercise to step back a bit from the everyday demands of the classroom and to think through what the school's priorities were, and what kind of balance it wanted to establish among what seemed to be an unending set of demands and expectations. What *were* the goals of the school? ■

The purpose of this book is to help readers understand how and why the organization of schooling is important. It begins with the story of Linda because organizational matters shape in fundamental ways the nature of teaching, the work that teachers do, and their level of success and satisfaction. This chapter sets the stage by discussing some important underlying aspects of schooling in Canada. We begin with the importance of an analysis of education that goes beyond the status quo to ask why things are as they are and how they might be different. We then turn to a discussion of the purposes of education and the goals of schools, followed by a discussion of the main features of public schooling and some central tensions and dilemmas that are embodied in the organization of Canadian schooling. Taken together, this examination provides important background to the various more specific issues in later chapters.

Limitations of the Status Quo

Many people may take for granted the organizational aspects of schools, assuming that schools are the way they are for good and sufficient reasons, as people do with much of the world they encounter every day. But because schools have the potential to be much better places, for both teachers and students, we regard it as very important for everyone involved with education to understand the way in which our schools are organized and operated so that they can ask questions about, and propose changes to, current practices. One approach to developing this understanding is to embark on a description of the existing constitutional, legal, and administrative structures that currently exist and give direction to administrators, teachers, and students in the daily routines of school life. This has become, in a sense, the official or taken-for-granted version of school organization. It is important because no one who is to be involved in schooling can afford to ignore the power exercised through these structures and processes. As a result, this text gives considerable attention to them and attempts to demonstrate concretely how they affect, on a daily basis, the work of teachers and what it means to be a teacher.

However, this approach is not a sufficient introduction to school organization, because the context for Canadian schooling has been shifting in important ways, and from many points of view the status quo is no longer seen as adequate. Whereas twenty years ago schooling was an unquestioned positive and Canada was busy expanding its education system at all levels, today there are many questions about what schools are for and how well they are meeting their goals. Changes in policy and practice are frequently announced by governments and school districts. A variety of lobby groups press for changes of one sort or another. Newspapers and other media ask questions about whether our schools are good enough, too costly, well run, and so on.

The reasons for the current climate of uncertainty are varied, but are largely connected to changes in Canadian society generally. Changes in the nature of work, in the structure and functioning of families, in gender roles, in technology, in the age profile of the population, in the role of government — all of these affect the schools (Levin & Riffel, 1997). Practices that used to seem effective may no longer seem so, not because schools have changed, but because the practices are no longer seen as consonant with what people feel they need (Hargreaves, 1994). For example, rising unemployment may call into question the value of secondary schooling. Information technology can change how, where, and when people learn. Changing roles for women and changes in family structures mean that the traditional school day and year don't work as well as they used to. And so on.

In a climate of change, critical re-examination of school organization is essential. Rather than viewing current practice as somehow natural or obvious, we want to examine why things are the way they are, how they came to be the way they are, who benefits most from them, and how they might be otherwise.

We also believe that one must approach school organization from a moral and educational perspective as well as from a technical perspective. In other words, questions of "how to" cannot be separated from questions of "why." Nor is it possible to detach the discussion of school organization from a broader discussion of the purposes of schooling and its place in Canadian society.

Another way in which we have sought to extend the official version of school organization in this text has been to recognize the real world in which students, teachers, and administrators live and work on a daily basis. The official image is often a pale reflection of the complexity of real classrooms and schools. It is important to pay attention to the uniquely human nature of schools and to human behaviour with all of its idiosyncrasies, its intertwining of personal and professional lives, its dreams and disappointments, its friendships and hostilities, its egos and ambitions. Often all of this is underemphasized in administration texts as being too messy for neat theories, lectures, and organizational charts of the way the world ought to be. We attempt to incorporate this reality into our discussion.

School organization and administration must be seen as concerning not only those people who occupy positions termed "administrative" (e.g., policy-makers, directors, superintendents, and principals), but everyone who is engaged in, and affected by, the educational process. As Baron notes, "[V]iewed in its widest sense as all that makes possible the educational process, the administration of education embraces the activities of Parliament at one end of the scale and the activities of any home with children at the other" (cited in Saxe, 1980, p. 14).

The Purposes of Education

In everyday language, people slip easily from "education" to "schooling" as though the two words, if not synonymous, were at least mutually supportive, with schools as the formal institutions of education. This blurring of concepts is not always helpful. If we are to examine thoughtfully the organization and administration of schooling in Canada, then it is important to think about the meaning of education, the purposes of schooling, and the significance of public schooling.

Questions of what it means to educate, or to be educated, have long been the subject of intellectual debate. In the Western liberal tradition, education is inextricably bound to ideas of self-knowledge or identity, as well as to empowerment, which means "becoming more than we are." In describing the relationship between education and self-knowledge, Symons (1975) argues that to be educated means to know ourselves: who we are, where we are in time and space, where we have been and where we are going, and what our responsibilities are to ourselves and to others. Nor, he suggests, can self-knowledge be separated from an awareness of the social context in which we live our lives, the two kinds of knowledge being not merely interdependent, "but ultimately one and the same" (p. 14).

For this process of acquiring self-knowledge to be considered educative and not simply socialization into existing ways of thinking, people must play an active and critical role in creating their knowledge. It must be an active and purposeful endeavour that informs our actions and provides the understanding, skills, and dispositions that enable people to grow and to exercise more control over the ways in which they live their lives within their social, communal, and ecological contexts. This view of education, although simplified in its presentation here, would not be acceptable to everyone. Traditionalists, for example, might argue that it does not give adequate attention to absorbing the central lessons of the past and the best of our collective cultures. Furthermore, when we speak of "control" we need to pay very careful attention to the interrelated nature of our social lives, and to the global devastation that has resulted from the pursuit of control over the environment.

This definition of education is still too broad to be confined to the formal process and structure of schools. Indeed, the great bulk of what people know, believe, and can do is not learned in schools (Resnick, 1987). We learn many of the most important things in our lives before we begin our schooling, and over the course of our schooling we continue to learn many things outside of schools as a result of our experiences, our reading, and our contact with other people. Even institutional education extends well beyond the school system. Programs ranging from day care to courses for senior citizens, and including the vast gamut of adult education activity in Canada, are also clearly educational in their focus.

At the same time, for many people there is a clear connection between these general ideas of self-knowledge and their expectations of public schools in Canada. We expect schools to be places of learning and development for students. Yet this rhetoric masks the multiple functions that have been assigned to public schools since their establishment as compulsory institutions in Canadian society. The problems and tensions facing schools can be seen by considering their official goals and their actual purposes.

The Goals of Schools

Why have formal education at all? We tend to take the goals of schooling as being relatively self-evident, but they are actually quite problematic. To understand the operation of schools, we need to go beyond formal statements of goals and ask about the functions schools actually perform. Schools have purposes that are rarely talked about in the official statements. Holmes (1986) describes six such purposes for Canadian secondary schools — allocative, custodial, intellectual–vocational, socializing, aesthetic, and physical. The allocative function has to do with determining who gets what—for example, who qualifies to go to university. Custodial refers to the child-care function of the schools. Intellectual–vocational includes what are usually thought of as school goals — developing knowledge and skills. The socializing function refers to inculcating desired values and behaviours. The aesthetic purpose has to do with developing appreciation for arts, culture, and beauty. And the physical function involves the training of the body — sports, exercise, and so on. Educational philosopher Robin Barrow (1981) identifies a similar list — critical thinking, socialization, child care, vocational preparation, physical instruction, social-role selection, education of the emotions, and development of creativity.

There are several important questions to ask about any statement of educational goals:

- Are the goals mutually compatible?
- Are the goals achievable?
- Do the goals have a commonly shared meaning?
- Do the goals affect what schools do on a day-to-day basis?

Before discussing these questions more fully, consider the list of goals in Box 1.1. Although this particular set is drawn from Prince Edward Island, most provinces and many school systems would have quite similar goal statements.

Box 1.1
Statement of Goals for Education in Prince Edward Island

The goals of public education are to enable the student to:
- develop an appreciation for learning, an intellectual curiosity, and a desire for lifelong learning;
- develop the ability to think critically, apply knowledge, and make informed decisions;
- acquire the basic knowledge and skills necessary to comprehend and express ideas through the use of words, numbers, and other symbols;
- develop an understanding of the natural world and of the applications of science and technology in society;

(continued)

(continued)

- acquire knowledge about the past and an orientation to the future;
- develop an appreciation for one's own heritage and a respect for the culture and traditions of others;
- develop a sense of self-worth;
- develop a respect for community values, a sense of personal values, and a responsibility for one's own actions;
- develop a sense of pride and respect for one's community, province, and country;
- develop a sense of stewardship for the environment;
- develop creative skills, including those in the arts, and an appreciation of creativity in others;
- develop skills and attitudes related to the workplace;
- develop good mental and physical health and the ability to creatively use leisure time;
- acquire a knowledge of the second official language and an understanding of the bilingual nature of the country;
- develop an understanding of gender equity issues and the need to provide equal opportunities for all;
- develop an understanding of fundamental human rights and an appreciation for the worth of all individuals.

Source: Prince Edward Island. (1989). *A philosophy of public education for Prince Edward Island.* Charlottetown: Government of Prince Edward Island. Reproduced with permission.

Compatibility

There is no guarantee that all the goals on any list can be achieved at the same time. It may be that achieving one purpose will necessarily be at the expense of another. There is only so much time, energy, and money. If one of our goals is to make students physically fit, the time spent on fitness cannot also be spent on, say, reading.

Most sets of school goals are very ambitious, and it is reasonably clear that doing them all at a high level would take more time and energy than is currently available. Thus, a school is always faced with the problem of having to decide *which* goals should get *how much* emphasis. For instance, does it place its energy into improving mathematics, expanding multicultural awareness, improving students' behaviour, or emphasizing critical thinking?

More fundamentally, purposes and goals may be logically inconsistent with one another, such that pursuing goal X means, by definition, not pursuing goal Y. For example, one common goal of schools is to teach students to think critically and to make their own decisions, while another common goal is to teach students to appreciate some of the basic values of our society, such as patriotism or respect for others. But what if a student, after thinking about it, decides that he does not want to be patriotic or to respect others? Are educators prepared to say that, because the student has formed an independent opinion, he is free to disregard social conventions? Probably not. A 12-year-old student who, after careful thought, decided that she would gain more benefit from reading at home than from going to school every day would not be allowed to exercise her critical-thinking skills; she would be compelled to attend school anyway. One of the basic tensions in schooling is between our desire to help individuals learn to think for themselves and our desire to have those individuals develop the same basic attitudes and values as everyone else in our society. It is not possible to maximize both of these goals at the same time; the same logic applies to numerous other mutually conflicting school goals.

Achievability

It is one thing to write down a goal, and quite another to be able to accomplish it. It is doubtful that schools can achieve all the goals set for them, even if there is agreement on what those goals are. As you will see later in the book, knowledge about how people learn and about how to teach them is limited. There are many things schools would like to do, but we don't know how. As an example, consider the very basic skill of learning to read. A great deal of a teacher's time and effort goes into developing reading skills in children. Yet some children learn to read almost effortlessly, while others learn only with considerable difficulty and still others do not learn to read well at all. All of us can recall this variability in learning from our own elementary-school experience. Learning differences exist not because teachers or students aren't trying, but because we do not fully understand how people learn to read and are therefore only partially successful in teaching them.

If teaching students to read presents difficulties, it is even harder to teach values like an appreciation of the worth of all individuals or love of learning. Of course, just because educators aren't sure how to accomplish something does not mean they should stop trying. It is important to set our sights high and to expect a great deal from ourselves. But setting many goals we do not know how to achieve is likely to create considerable frustration.

Shared Meaning

A statement of goals is an attempt to generate agreement among many people as to what schools should do. In education, there is currently much talk about creating a "common vision," which also requires agreement on aims and purposes. But there may be quite a bit of disagreement among and between parents, students, teachers, and others as to what the schools should do. Students, especially in secondary schools, place high value on preparing for jobs or for postsecondary education, while teachers and parents place far more emphasis on goals such as developing positive personal habits and attributes. Some parents want a great deal of emphasis placed on reading and writing skills, while others want more emphasis on the arts or sciences. Some parents want their children to be exposed to many different ideas, while others want schools to reinforce the values of the home.

Such different priorities have significant implications for the way schools and teaching are organized. To place more emphasis on preparing for jobs, for example, schools could increase the amount of vocational and co-operative education, add staff to provide vocational counselling, or provide work-experience opportunities for students, in addition to courses in job-seeking skills. On the other hand, placing more emphasis on academic skills might involve cutting back in the above areas and allocating more time and resources to areas dealing with reading, writing, library use, and so on. Different goals should lead to different kinds of activities.

One way schools try to cope with the differences in people's desired goals is to smooth them over with language. Thus, a statement of goals can be worded in such a way as to generate agreement, even if people would not agree on what the statements mean in practice. As long as the discussion stays at the level of words, the disagreement can be hidden. Often this approach works reasonably well in allowing people to move ahead with their work instead of spending endless time debating purposes.

Impact on Practice

It is one thing to espouse a goal and quite another to be able to put that goal into practice. For instance, many studies have concluded that the overwhelming emphasis in secondary schools is on preparing students for further education, and particularly for university studies, even though most high-school students do not go on directly to postsecondary education (Radwanski, 1987; Canadian Education Association (CEA), 1995). Despite many calls for changes in the priorities of the secondary schools, this academic emphasis has persisted for many years.

The gap between goals and practices does not usually exist because people are malevolent or stupid, but because it is so difficult to align our behaviour with our ideals. At a personal level, how many people are always able to behave in the way they think and feel would be most desirable? The same discrepancy between thought and action is true in organizations, including schools.

The fact that goals are hard to define and difficult to achieve should not be taken to mean that the effort to do so is fruitless. Important decisions about education are made every day by students, teachers, administrators, school trustees, and others. These decisions need to be based on some sense of direction and purpose, despite all the difficulties in doing so. The goals may evolve, and they may never be fully achieved, but they remain a beacon in our day-to-day efforts.

Tensions and Dilemmas in Canadian Education

One way to think of public education is in terms of a series of characterizing attributes or elements. For example:

1. *Public accessibility.* All persons of school age should have a right to free access to schooling.
2. *Equal opportunity.* All children should receive equal opportunity to benefit from schooling, regardless of factors such as their culture, gender, ability, and so on.
3. *Public funding.* The costs of schooling should be borne by government so that the quality of schooling received by a student is not related to the ability of the student or the parents to pay for that schooling.
4. *Public control.* Decisions about the nature of public schools are made through public political processes, by persons who are elected at large to carry out this responsibility.
5. *Public accountability.* Public schools act in the interests of the public and are answerable to the public for what is taught and for the quality of the experiences provided to students.

Most people would probably agree with these characteristics in principle, but what they might mean in practice is much less evident. As Canadians have struggled with them in specific situations, a number of ongoing tensions or dilemmas have arisen — areas where trying to recognize one reality leads us away from another that may be equally important. Much of the history of Canadian education can be seen as an effort to find an appropriate but always temporary balance between these competing objectives. Three tensions are particularly important: uniformity and diversity, stability and change, power and equality.

Uniformity and Diversity

The first tension is between the desire to have a common education system for all, and the recognition that students and communities are quite different from one another and may therefore have different educational needs.

In many ways, despite the variety of school systems, present-day schools in Canada are remarkably similar to one another in their internal appearance: rows or groups of classrooms full of desks or tables, generally empty hallways, libraries, gyms, administrative offices, and almost always groups of students of about the same age who are engaged in some activity that is directed and supervised by a single adult.

Students everywhere in Canada study quite similar material, which is divided into subjects. They have to learn certain material on which they are tested, and their progress through the system depends largely on how well they do on various assessment measures. Children are judged individually, and do the vast bulk of their work as individuals. Students have very little say in shaping the nature of their education and classrooms tend to be dominated by teacher discussion, with students playing a largely passive role in the whole process. The school day is about the same length and covers about the same hours of the day almost everywhere.

While these similarities are quite consistent, even to the point of crossing national boundaries, schools are found in diverse settings. Consider a school in a very small community in the high Arctic. The community has a few hundred people. It is very isolated, and transportation in and out of the region is entirely by airplane, with limited service. There is continuous darkness for about three months each winter, and continuous sunlight for three months each summer. The school has a few dozen students, from kindergarten to Grade 9, and a couple of teachers. Most of the children are Inuit, and they come to school speaking Inuktitut, while the teachers are probably white, come from southern Canada, and often leave after three or four years. Resources for the school have to be flown in from outside, as does much of the community's food. Many of the children have never been in another community, although through satellite communications they do have access to television. Everyone in the community knows everyone else, and many of the students are related to half or more of the people in the community. They rely heavily on one another for almost everything.

Compare such a community with a school in a new suburb of Montreal. There may be 400 or 500 students and about 30 teachers in such a school. Nobody has lived in that community for more than a few years because the homes and school were built only a few years ago. Most but not all of the children speak French. Many also speak English. The school is officially Catholic, and includes religious exercises in its program. A significant number of students are members of visible minority groups. Many of the children have travelled quite extensively with their families and are used to books, libraries, museums, and all the other amenities of a large city. They also face the pressures of commercialism and isolation that inundate our cities. Many of them do not have any close relatives living in, or even near, the same community.

Or consider a third setting—an inner-city school in Winnipeg. Here, many of the children are from non-English-speaking families. Many families are Aboriginal or immigrant. Many of the families are subject to frequent unemployment and are unable to afford adequate food and housing, let alone holiday trips or the latest trend in athletic shoes. Some children move to different schools two or three times in a school year. Their parents have limited education and are intimidated by the school system. After years of unsuccessful struggle, some may feel powerless to influence their situation and live very much on a day-to-day basis.

It is clear from these limited descriptions that the conditions of learning and the job of teaching vary across settings, even though the schools themselves may be structured in quite similar ways. There can be no single right way to organize schools and schooling. Different students and communities may well require different educational approaches. There will be substantial disagreement about how best to organize and conduct schooling to meet these needs. It is also possible to conceive of ways of conducting schooling that are quite different from those in common use. Yet there is surprisingly little debate about many basic aspects of schooling that are shared by all kinds of schools and communities.

Stability and Change

The second tension concerns the degree to which schools should change to meet changing needs or should remain constant to a set of educational ideals and practices. Most of us tend to think of schools as having always been the way they are now. There is much in schools today that is easily recognizable to the student of 50 years ago. But in other respects, schools, like other institutions, have changed in significant ways, just as the society around them has changed. Until the last century, there was no mass public education; schools were primarily private or church affiliated, and they charged fees that only the wealthy could afford. In the mid-nineteenth century, however, a number of countries began to introduce free and universal public education. Historians have different views about why this occurred. Some see the development of schooling as part of societal progress. Others believe that mass schooling was developed in order to ensure that the new factories and industries had an adequate supply of workers who were both skilled and trained in habits of obedience to authority.

As recently as 50 years ago, however, schools were different from those of today in some important respects. In many areas, the church remained a key provider of education. Most communities were rural, and each rural community had its own school. As new communities developed, people formed a school board, built a school building (often with their own hands), hired a teacher (who typically taught eight or more grades in a single room), and operated the school. Control was very much in the hands of the local parents, or more particularly the fathers, since most school trustees were men. Teachers, usually unmarried women, were not well trained and were very poorly paid.

Gradually, these conditions have changed. Power has shifted away from local parents and communities. Small school districts have largely disappeared in Canada, usually as a result of government legislation, and have been replaced by much larger school districts, which are generally run by professional administrators. Manitoba, for example, had more than 2000 school districts in the early 1950s but has only about 60 today, with pressure to reduce the number further. While school boards still exist, many are now responsible for running large and complex organizations that may have hundreds or even thousands of teachers, as well as huge budgets. For example, the Peel Board of Education in Ontario, one of the largest, has 100 000 students in more than 150 schools and an annual budget of more than $700 million, and Ontario may soon have boards much larger than that. In this kind of setting, each school trustee may represent many thousands of people. Schools are also larger. Thus, schools have changed from being small and local to being large and bureaucratic in their organization, though they may still be administered largely by males, still be staffed predominantly by women, and still give almost no meaningful role in governance to students.

Another important change has been the amount of schooling most people receive. More people are getting more years of formal education than ever before. Not so many years ago, Grade 8 was the common finishing point for many people and the mark of someone with a reasonable level of education. Now those with less than Grade 9 may be classified as being functionally illiterate (although one might well question the accuracy of such a standard). Formal education and its credentials have become much more important elements in the organization of modern society.

Most of these changes, significant as they were, are now taken for granted. We seldom ask ourselves whether they have produced the desired results, or whether they imply that we ought to change the way we conduct formal education. For example, as parents become more educated, they may well have more views about how schools should operate and be less willing to assume a passive role.

Power and Equality

Schools, like all organizations, are shaped by power relations. Some people have more influence over what happens than do others. Final authority over most aspects of schooling rests with elected officials in the provincial government or school board. Within any given school, administrators typically have the most official power. Principals can give instructions to teachers, students, and (sometimes) parents. Teachers have considerable power over students, but not very much over administrators. And students have almost no official power, although they can exercise quite a bit of informal influence when they want to. Where power exists, so does the potential for unfairness and abuse. It is important to ask at all times whether power is being used in the right way, and to guard vigilantly against its abuse, no matter who the perpetrators or victims might be.

Much of the history of schooling in Canada has been marked by struggles over power and control from which enduring questions have emerged. How much authority would be held by laypeople (parents and community members) and how much by professionals (teachers, principals, and superintendents)? How much authority would rest at the local level in a community, and how much would rest with provincial governments? An important distinction can be made between *representative democracy* and *participative democracy*. The former implies that legitimacy is conferred on a central authority, such as Parliament, by the population and then held accountable to the population through the electoral process. The latter implies a quite different form of civil life: self-government by an active citizenry, "where self-government is carried on through institutions designed to facilitate ongoing civic participation in agenda-setting, deliberation, legislation, and policy-implementation" (Barber, 1984, p. 151). Currently the move to school councils and local school management is consistent with participatory democracy, but the simultaneous move to give more power to provincial ministers of education is quite in the other direction. (More is said about these points in Chapters Two and Three.)

Schools also are marked by inequality. Some schools are better staffed and equipped. Some teachers get better teaching assignments or more resources for their courses. Some students have more access to computers, reference materials, or field trips. Some students get better marks, enjoy school more, and are treated better by staff. Again, where there is inequality, there is the potential for abuse. We are not suggesting that everyone should be treated precisely the same at all times; that is both impossible and undesirable. Rather, it is important to ask whether the kinds of inequality that exist in schools are justifiable. Is it right (and if so, why) that some students get to learn much more than others? Such questions are important in analyzing the way in which schools are organized and how that organization affects those who come into their orbit.

Inequalities in schooling are not accidental. One job that schools have been expected to perform is allocating social roles, determining who will go to work for low wages and who will get professional training. How is it possible to reconcile this purpose with the desire to have every student develop all the skills and competencies listed in the goals statement in Box 1.1? Indeed, some believe that failure is part of the mission of schooling:

> Imagine what would happen if ... the goals that educators and reformers officially seek were actually accomplished. All students would become top performers. All of them would make ... perfect A records throughout their schooling. Chaos would ensue. Colleges would not have room for all, but would have little ground on which to accept some and reject others. Employers looking for secretaries, retail salespersons, waiters, busdrivers, and factory workers would have jobs unfilled as every student considered such work beneath his or her accomplishment.
>
> As long as education is used to rank young people and sort them into occupational futures that differ substantially in the money, status, power, and intrinsic rewards they can yield, good education, or students' success at education, must remain a scarce commodity (Metz, 1990, p. 85).

The fact is that schooling in Canada and in other countries does produce unequal results. Some people do well, go on to higher education, earn higher incomes, and attain greater access to societal rewards, whereas others do not fit in with the school, fail or drop out, and end up in low-paying jobs. Worse still, societal rewards are not distributed only on the basis of talent. The kind of family you come from, and particularly your parents' income and occupations, have a great deal of influence on how much education you receive, what kind of job you have, and how much money you earn (Tepperman, 1988). For example, university students in Canada (and in other countries) are much more likely to come from families with higher education and income levels than are community college students or those who leave school without any postsecondary experience (Levin, 1990).

This tension between the allocative and educative functions of schooling is another example of the point made earlier in this chapter about the problems schools face in attempting to develop creative, critical individuals while at the same time passing down the basic values of the culture. The conflict between these purposes is of enormous importance in understanding what schools do and how they are organized.

The Moral Nature of Schools and Teaching

A final complication in the discussion of the goals and purposes of schooling has to do with its moral nature. Schooling is not simply a matter of teaching skills to students, although this is how it is often described. Rather, schooling is essentially concerned with introducing young people (and, increasingly, adults) to the nature of the world as we understand it, and equipping them to live in that world—what we earlier called the development of self-knowledge. In this process, moral and ethical considerations are of fundamental importance, for students learn as much from *how* they are taught and treated in schools as they do from *what* they are taught. Every day, teachers and school administrators are acting as moral examples to students and one another, and are creating a community that embodies particular concepts of ethical behaviour. If students are treated as unimportant, as people whose ideas and feelings are of no consequence, then they are more likely to see the world as one in which some people matter while others do not. If teachers embody respect for students, for one another, for their subjects, and for the development of knowledge, then students are more likely to develop and prize these qualities. According to Gary Fenstermacher,

> Teaching becomes nearly incomprehensible when disconnected from its fundamental moral purposes. These purposes are rooted in the moral development of the young ... moral qualities are learned—acquired in the course of lived experience. If there are no models for them, no obvious or even subtle pressures to adopt moral qualities ... the moral virtues may be missed, perhaps never to be acquired. ...
>
> What makes teaching a moral endeavor is that it is, quite centrally, human action undertaken in regard to other human beings. Thus, matters of what is fair, right, just, and virtuous are always present. ... The teacher's conduct, at all times and in all ways, is a moral matter. For that reason alone, teaching is a profoundly moral activity (1990, pp. 132–33).

There are some important technical skills to be learned about teaching. Student teachers are understandably anxious about their ability to manage classes, maintain order, and create reasonable learning experiences for students. But these skills are not meaningful unless they are tied to an ethical and moral view of teaching. Think back to the teachers you had, and you will probably see that the example set by good teachers had more impact on you, and is more vivid in your memory, than the subject matter they taught.

Moral issues are not only embedded in the fabric of teaching, they are also integral to school organization and administration. Such matters as the division of schools into classes, grades, and ability levels, the assignment of work to students, or the awarding of marks and credits also have important moral dimensions.

Conclusion

The inconsistencies and tensions discussed in this chapter raise important questions. How do we work in an institution whose goals are uncertain, sometimes in conflict with one another, and perhaps unachievable? How do we decide what is worth our time and effort? Even more significantly, the idea that schools might actually *require* some students to fail—that this is a built-in part of what schools do—is a difficult one for many teachers who see their job as helping students to succeed. The shock value of the quote on page 15 lies in making us ask ourselves whether this quest for educational quality and equality can ever be totally successful, and whether the institution in which we work could survive if it were.

Some teachers probably don't think about these issues very much. They just go on doing their daily work, help students as much as they can, and try to avoid the contradictions in the system. Other teachers come to the conclusion that they cannot do the things they value in schools as presently constituted, and they leave teaching. Some combine their teaching with active involvement in larger educational and social issues, whether through their professional association or through other kinds of volunteer work and public service. Others make up their minds to live with the frustration and inconsistencies because they continue to believe that their work is important, and that they can make a difference, even if only in their own classroom. In taking this position, teachers are embodying a concept of schools as institutions that are based fundamentally on moral considerations. A vision of the good school is intimately connected with a vision of the good society and the good life.

Exercises

1. Briefly state your view of the purposes of schools. Compare your view with those of Holmes or Barrow as cited in this chapter. Do their arguments modify your initial ideas? Why or why not?

2. Find a goal statement from your province or a local school district. Compare it with the statement in Box 1.1. Does it embody the same sorts of problems noted in this chapter? Why or why not?

3. Reread the goals statement in Box 1.1 while thinking back to your own experience as a student. Which of these goals would you say were regarded as important in your school? Which were de-emphasized, ignored, or even contradicted?

4. Consider one of the goals in Box 1.1 (e.g., developing critical thinking). Write a brief statement indicating how a school might be organized to achieve this particular goal more effectively if it were suddenly given top priority. How might these changes affect other purposes of the school? Would you advocate the changes? Why or why not?

5. Interview three or four people involved with schools either as students, teachers, or parents. Ask them what they see as being the most important purposes of schools. Compare their answers. How much agreement is there? What disagreements occur? Why?

6. How are schools in your community accountable to the public? Talk to people in the schools about this issue, and compare your perception with theirs.

7. Conduct an informal survey of people in your community as to the relative power held by teachers, principals, school trustees, and parents on such matters as the curriculum, teaching methods, or school rules. Analyze and try to explain the agreements or disagreements among your respondents.

8. Do a survey of your university class to assess the occupations of your classmates' parents. Compare their distribution with Canadian census data. Is your class broadly representative of the Canadian population? What are the differences?

9. Write a brief description of a teacher you remember as being particularly good. What made him or her a good teacher? Are these qualities that any teacher could develop? Why or why not?

CHAPTER TWO

The Structure of Canadian Schooling

▼ PROLOGUE

Trustee Norman Wright sat reviewing the materials sent by the superintendent in preparation for the evening's special meeting of the school board called to discuss the establishment of an Aboriginal* high school in the division. It was nearly two years since the first formal approach had been made to establish such a school. Since then, discussions among trustees, senior administration, and the board's Aboriginal advisory committee seemed to have progressed slowly, always surrounded by controversy. Now, as a new school year was about to begin, the school was going to open its doors — the building was ready, the principal and her staff had been hired, and approximately 100 students had registered at the school.

Yet much remained to be done if the school was to flourish, and there seemed to be little agreement among the different parties on several of the outstanding issues. One goal of tonight's meeting was to try to hammer out an agreement on the governance structure for the school that would define explicitly the powers and responsibilities of the school board, the Aboriginal community, the school principal, and the parents in setting policy directions for the school and for its day-to-day operation. Far from being a technical detail, this question seemed to go to the heart of the purpose of the school.

* Aboriginal peoples of Canada are defined in the *Canadian Charter of Rights and Freedoms* as including Indian, Inuit, and Métis people of Canada. According to *The Report of the Royal Commission on Aboriginal Peoples* (Canada, 1996) the Aboriginal population of Canada in 1991 was between 626 000 and 1 000 000, depending upon what definitions and data sources were used. Based upon their analysis of different data sources, they estimate the Aboriginal population in 1991 at some 727 700, of whom some 438 000 were registered North American Indian, 112 600 were nonregistered North American Indian, 139 000 were Métis, and 38 000 were Inuit. A full discussion of these figures can be found in Volume 1, Chapter 2, "From Time Immemorial: A Demographic Profile" of *The Report of the Royal Commission on Aboriginal Peoples*. While the funding of education for registered/status Indians on reserves is provided by the federal government, providing education for the children of nonregistered/nonstatus, off-reserve Indians and Métis people is normally a provincial responsibility. As this latter population has become increasingly urban, the educational needs of Aboriginal students have become increasingly important issues for many urban school divisions.

The term "Indian" is used in this chapter as primarily a legal term to refer to those people who have the status of registered Indian as defined by the *Indian Act*. Beyond this legal distinction the term has little utility: used by Europeans to identify Aboriginal people of America, it homogenizes an ethnically and linguistically diverse group of people. For political identification, the term "First Nations" is preferred by many Aboriginal people to refer to the various governments of the Aboriginal people of Canada. The Assembly of First Nations (1988, pp. 45–46) uses "First Nations" rather than "Indians," "tribes," and "bands" (terms used extensively by the federal and provincial governments), and as a noun-adjunct instead of "Indian" in phrases such as "Indian education."

In the initial proposal prepared for the school board, the Aboriginal advisory committee had documented the lack of success experienced in the district's schools by many Aboriginal students (both the children of Aboriginal families living in the city and students from reserve communities across the province who came to the city to attend high school). A school controlled by the Aboriginal community, embodying Aboriginal values in all aspects of school life and drawing on community members for instruction related to cultural practices, was seen as one vital element in reversing this pattern of failure. On the principle of control, the proposal was explicit: Aboriginal control meant equal partnership between the school division and the Aboriginal community in all aspects of running the school.

In the months since the submission of the original proposal, the advisory committee had devoted a lot of time to the development of a joint management model that would balance the school district's legal responsibility for education and the Aboriginal community's desire to have direct input into the education of its children. The model to be voted on at this evening's meeting called for a contract to be drawn up between the school district and a legally constituted Aboriginal community society, open to all Aboriginal people over 16 and living in the province, which would delegate authority over the school to a joint management committee consisting of the school's principal, a teacher, one nonteaching member of the school's staff, two students, and two community group members.

When this proposal was first presented to the school board, the reaction was mixed. Some trustees questioned the merits of a school that they saw as segregated along racial lines and therefore running against their commitment to a public school system based on the ideal of a common school for all. Some argued that as duly elected trustees they represented the legitimate vehicle for expressing parental and community interests, and that other creations were not only unnecessary but would subvert that legitimate authority. Furthermore, they questioned whether the Aboriginal community group would in fact represent the interests of the entire Aboriginal community, including the Métis population. Probably the majority, Norman estimated, were generally supportive of the proposal, yet there were concerns even among the supporters as to whether the proposed delegation of authority could be legally made by the board without contravening their responsibilities as laid out in provincial legislation. After some lengthy discussion, the proposal had been referred to the superintendent for evaluation.

Now, as Norman read over the superintendent's evaluation, he let out an audible groan. It was the district's legal opinion that the school board could not delegate such sweeping powers over the running of one of its schools to the sort of management committee suggested in the proposal. The responsibilities of any school board were clearly laid out in the province's Public Schools Act, and while the legislation did allow school boards to delegate their powers in certain circumstances, these circumstances were clearly specified and related to the delegation of authority to an existing legal entity operating a school facility, such as a neighbouring school district offering special programs. Furthermore, making the school principal accountable to such a management committee would appear to contradict the regulations under the province's *Educational Administration Act*, which stated that "the principal is in charge of the school in respect to all matters of organization, management, discipline and instruction."

Norman wondered about a system that established public accountability through the trustee system and then so bureaucratized the operation of the system that trustees were often left dependent on the advice and instructions of the professional administration. He had spent his whole career as a teacher, senior administrator, and university professor, and he still found himself in this dependent position — and he didn't like it! Nevertheless, as he ploughed on through the documentation and struggled to plan for the meeting, he maintained a deep-seated conviction that it mattered, that these painful debates over governance and administration were central to the kind of school that was being created, and to the quality of the lives of the children who would go there. ■

This chapter presents an outline of some of the main structural forms that characterize Canadian school systems and examines some of the ways in which they were developed and continue to evolve, as well as the purposes and interests they serve. No attempt is made to provide either a comprehensive survey of each of the different school systems across the country or a chronological history of their development. Instead, the chapter highlights a number of issues related to the organization of public schooling and places them within a particular social and historical context.

A central concern in performing this task is to explore issues of power and authority in Canadian schooling—who is allowed to participate in educational decision-making processes and whose experiences have been legitimized within the school system. Throughout the chapter, attention will be given to:

1. contradictory pressures for centralized authority and local control in education;
2. the ongoing debate between advocates of professional versus public authority across a range of educational decision-making situations;
3. the conflicting expectations that public schools should provide common experiences for all students while at the same time accommodating diversity; and, as a key part of this,
4. the place of religious interests in a public education system.

Wrapped up in these interconnected tensions are unavoidable questions of purpose, quality, and costs that relate to the goals of education—as well as to issues of bias and equality of educational opportunity, national unity, religious and linguistic diversity—and the role of technical expertise in the improvement of schooling. Such issues have been the subject of much controversy in the 1990s, and they have very pragmatic implications for teachers' careers. More profoundly, they inform a teacher's evolving professional identity. Being an effective teacher means understanding the nature of the networks that make up one's professional context, and the values and interests they represent, so that one can make critical choices about how to work within that context.

An Overview of Canada's School System: Who Goes Where?

Since the introduction of compulsory attendance legislation in Quebec in 1943, young people have been required to go to school everywhere in Canada (although across the country there are different legislative provisions relating to compulsory school ages, definitions of what constitutes a school, and grounds on which one might be exempted from attending). As a consequence, provision has to be made annually in Canada for the schooling, in one form or another, of some 5 million young people.

The predominant vehicle that has been developed for this task is a publicly funded, provincially controlled school system. It is this system, prescribed in the *British North America Act, 1867* and detailed in the various education or public school acts and regulations of the provinces, that houses some 95 percent of the country's student population (see Table 2.1). The remaining student population is to be found in private schools (which are also a part of the provincial design of education in as much as they are regulated by provincial legislation) and in federally or First Nations–controlled schools (primarily for Aboriginal students or for children of military personnel).

The constitutional basis for this current arrangement is to be found primarily in Section 93 of the *BNA Act* (re-enacted and retitled the *Constitution Act, 1867* by the *Constitution Act, 1982*), which, it is important to note, incorporated an already well-established distribution of authority in education rather than creating a new one.

The limitations of provincial authority as they relate to separate and dissentient schools (discussed later in this chapter) provide an important element in the structure of Canadian public schooling; these limitations, it should be noted, serve to shape the various provincial systems rather than create an alternative to provincial control of education.

In exercising their constitutional authority in education, most provinces have created some form of local educational body, usually called school boards or school districts, with legally defined powers delegated to them by the province. These bodies, however, exist only at the discretion of the provincial government, and final authority over most areas of educational decision making remains at the provincial level, with a minister of education.

Table 2.1

Elementary and Secondary School Enrollments by School Control and Province, Canada 1992–1993

Province	Public schools (% of total)	Private schools (% of total)	Federal schools/First Nation schools (% of total)	Total enrollment
Newfoundland	118 273 (99.8)	274 (0.2)	—	118 547 (100)
PEI	24 242 (99.0)	196 (0.8)	48 (0.2)	24 486 (100)
Nova Scotia	164 722 (98.1)	2 100 (1.2)	1 137 (0.7)	167 959 (100)
New Brunswick	138 686 (98.9)	797 (0.6)	895 (0.6)	140 378 (100)
Quebec	1 039 690 (90.5)	103 520 (9.0)	5 742 (0.5)	1 148 952 (100)
Ontario	2 039 709 (96.0)	74 850 (3.5)	10 275 (0.5)	2 124 834 (100)
Manitoba	195 761 (88.4)	11 826 (5.3)	13 895 (6.3)	221 482 (100)
Saskatchewan	198 331 (93.3)	3 200 (1.5)	11 146 (5.2)	212 677 (100)
Alberta	512 255 (94.8)	19 209 (3.6)	8 932 (1.7)	540 396 (100)
BC	568 668 (91.3)	49 334 (7.9)	4 695 (0.8)	622 697 (100)
Yukon	5 762 (99.7)	15 (0.3)	—	5 777 (100)
NWT	16 252 (100)	—	—	16 252 (100)
Overseas	—	—	613 (100)	613 (100)
Canada	5 022 351 (94.0)	265 321 (5.0)	57 378 (1.1)	5 345 050 (100)

Source: Statistics Canada. *Education in Canada, 1995* (Cat. no. 81-229), pp. 38–39. Ottawa: Ministry of Industry, 1996. Reproduced with permission.

The Development of Provincial Control over Schooling

The development across Canada of a system of school administration in which legislative and regulative power is concentrated within a centralized provincial bureaucracy — responsible to a minister of education working in Cabinet and answerable through the provincial legislature to the electorate — has many of its roots in the well-documented political struggles of Upper Canada/Canada West in the first half of the nineteenth century, and in the work of Egerton Ryerson, Superintendent of Schools in Canada West/Ontario from 1846 until 1876. During this period, heated debates over the organization of elementary education were at the heart of a broader discussion concerning the role of the state in Canadian society. Attention to this historical context is important not only for an appreciation of how contemporary arrangements came into being, but also in order to understand the grounds on which alternative versions of how state schooling should be organized were advanced and justified by different interests.

According to educational historians Gidney and Lawr (1979), there was general agreement in Upper Canada in the early nineteenth century that the state should play a major role in the provision of education. However, there was no agreement either on the form that support should take or on the degree of supervision and control that was to accompany it. Instead, fundamental issues in the organization of an emerging school system (e.g., the role of the church; the place of elected versus appointed officials in the system; the location of taxation powers; authority over the curriculum and textbooks; and responsibility for the training, certification, and inspection of teachers) underwent a prolonged educational debate in both the press and legislature.

At the heart of much of this debate was a political struggle over what was to constitute "responsible government," which contrasted American models of republican democracy with British models of a monarchical system of colonial administration. Responsible government to members of what was then called the Reform Party implied electoral responsibility, the championing of local electoral democracy (in the narrow and patriarchal sense of local property), and a decentralized school system. For Upper-Canadian Conservatives, such a vision of local democracy was seen as being far from responsible; rather, they predicted, this form of representative government would be "imperilled by local ignorance" and seriously undermine the social fabric of the colony. Instead, responsible government to them meant government by men deemed "responsible" on the basis of "technical competence and worth" (Curtis, 1988, p. 52).

The ebb and flow of these struggles is evidenced in the series of education acts introduced into the legislature between 1836 and 1850. Some of these bills were defeated, while others were vetoed by the Executive Council; but those passed into law by 1850 detailed a provincial system of schools that in many important ways foreshadowed the contemporary structure in most Canadian provinces.

Prior to the 1840s, state involvement in education was prescribed primarily by the *School Act* of 1816, which allowed local property owners to meet, select three trustees from among themselves, and hire a teacher who, if approved by the appointed District Board of Education, was eligible for a grant-in-aid from the state. However, in the aftermath of the 1837 rebellions in the Canadas, the victorious Conservatives in Upper Canada came to view this localized autonomy as a contributing factor to the insurrection. From this perspective, Republican sentiment had been allowed to spread throughout Upper Canada, in part because the central authorities had permitted communities to hire American teachers and to use American textbooks—a combination that served only to alienate the population from the British monarchical form of government (Wilson, 1970). In the interests of ensuring that these destabilizing influences were contained, many believed that a central authority was needed to monitor and provide direction to local schools.

In Lower Canada, the 1837 rebellion had greater intensity, was of longer duration, and was perceived to pose a more obdurate threat to the British connection than the hostilities in Upper Canada. Lord Durham wrote in his famous *Report* that he was perplexed to find there "two nations" warring in the bosom of a single state ... a struggle not of principles, but of races" (Craig, 1990, p. 315). It was his conclusion that French Canadians, whom he viewed as unprogressive and obstinate in the face of British cultural and material superiority, should be assimilated, and to do this he recommended, among other things, that the two colonies be joined in a single political entity. This was done through the *Act of Union* in 1841.

Given that colonial officials in both sections (Canada East and Canada West) of the newly united colony were anxious to undertake the task of remaking the political and cultural character of the respective populations, it is not surprising that educational legislation should have been among the earliest considerations of the freshly constituted Canadian government. The *Common School Act* of 1841 created, for the first time, a central administrative authority, establishing the post of the chief superintendent of education, an officer appointed by the governor to oversee the operation of elementary education in both sections of the colony. This position was abolished two years later when it became apparent that the historical development of school systems in the Canadas made a single bureaucracy inoperable. French-Canadian politicians were not about to submit to a policy of forced assimilation in any case, and so an assistant superintendent was appointed for each section. The 1843 *Education Act* gave these officers responsibility for allocating the common school fund, collecting and reporting information on local educational organization, and instructing other education officers in matters relating to "the better Organization and Governance of Common Schools."

The 1841 legislation also stipulated that local property assessments should match the contributions of the colonial government; the responsibility for raising these funds was removed from locally elected trustees and given to the more broadly based elected township Board of Commissioners. The absence of well-developed government at the municipal level led to the repeal of the 1841 *School Act* in 1843 and the reinstatement of the local elected trustees. These boards resumed responsibility for maintaining the schoolhouse, calculating and collecting the school rate, hiring teachers, selecting textbooks, and overseeing the courses of study. They did not act alone, however; positions of county and district superintendents were created. The county superintendents were assigned the task of examining and certifying all prospective teachers and re-examining practising teachers at their discretion. In addition, they were required to visit all schools at least once a year, to advise trustees and teachers on the operation of their schools, and to submit annual reports to the colonial superintendent.

Neither the 1841 nor the 1843 legislation radically altered the practical powers of local educational self-management, which remained substantially located with local property. What the legislation did do was contribute significantly to the development of a modern education bureaucracy by establishing what Houston and Prentice (1988) refer to as "the paperwork principle"; written reports on forms provided by the provincial authorities were now required as essential to the working of the system (p. 110). The significance of this new development in terms of the relationship between local and provincial jurisdiction and between lay and professional authority is noted by Curtis (1988):

> The administration of the 1843 Act produced a marked shift in the relations of knowledge/power between the central authority and the local schools. ... The central office increasingly had a corps of paid and respectable educational investigators in the field. While many teachers and other local educational participants continued to correspond with the central office, their conceptions for and interests in educational organization could, from 1843, be counterposed by central administrators to those of respectable men of character (p. 32).

If the 1841 and 1843 legislation left intact a largely decentralized school system in Upper Canada in the hands of local property, the *School Act* of 1846, introduced by a Tory-dominated legislature and revised by Reformers in 1850, served to promote a shift of much of this local power to centralized administrative structures. Under the provisions of the 1846 act, the chief superintendent of education, advised by the newly created General Board of Education, was made answerable not to the legislature but to the governor-general-in-council. This meant that Egerton Ryerson, although not himself an elected official, was, as chief superintendent, accountable to the Cabinet alone and was thus only indirectly accountable to the popularly elected legislature. In addition to the responsibility of gathering and disseminating information, the superintendent was given authority to prepare whatever regulations were deemed necessary for the improvement of schooling, and the power to withhold grants if these regulations were ignored or broken. In the area of teacher training, the act called for the establishment of a provincial "normal school" and placed the responsibility for its operation with the superintendent and the General Board of Education.

The chief superintendent's powers were exercised energetically by Ryerson in the years following the passage of the 1846 legislation as he struggled to establish an orderly and uniform school system. As Houston and Prentice (1988) note,

The new chief superintendent of schools was determined not only that there would be adequate school law in the province; he wished also, as his title suggests, to superintend: to instruct, advise, and regulate, down to the finest detail, the schools and schooling of Upper Canadians (p. 119).

Effective central authority was dependent on an effective inspectorate. Ryerson sought, unsuccessfully, to establish this at the central level, and the 1846 act continued the existing arrangements of local superintendents appointed solely by district councils. However, the act added to this arrangement the requirement that the local superintendents follow the instructions of the chief superintendent, establishing an important supervisory link between the central authority and local trustees. These superintendents, in addition to their task of certifying teachers, were empowered to give advice to local authorities and to begin the work of actually regulating life in schools.

The revisions introduced in the 1850 *Schools Act* modified some of the centralizing powers of the 1846 legislation and, in line with Reform philosophy, reasserted the principle of electoral self-government, spelling out the powers of local trustees and adding a degree of political control to the centralized bureaucracy that Ryerson had built. The powers of the chief superintendent and the General Board of Education (renamed the Council of Public Instruction) remained largely unaltered, but they were made explicitly responsible to the ministry, which had not been the case in 1846. However, despite these concessions to local electoral autonomy, the division of power between central and local authorities had shifted significantly in favour of the former.

This system of governance has not remained unaltered in Ontario, nor was it faithfully copied in all other provinces across the country. Yet the divisions of power and the institutional forms developed in Ontario during the middle part of the nineteenth century provide a common framework for contemporary public school systems across Canada.

Separate and Dissentient School Systems

From the earliest days of state involvement in Canadian education, schools have been recognized as powerful agencies of socialization and social control, introducing the youth of the country to a particular view of citizenship and the knowledge, skills, and values needed to fulfil this role properly. In a country characterized by diversity, defining *whose* views of citizenship were to be promoted and legitimated in the public schools has been a continuous source of controversy and debate.

Today, forces such as increased interprovincial and international mobility and the development of a global economy, coupled with efforts to equalize educational opportunities and to see schools play a role in promoting and sustaining a sense of Canadian identity, have produced pressures for increased standardization of schools and curricula across the country. Yet, at the same time, countervailing pressures require schools to acknowledge the linguistic, regional, and cultural diversity of the country, and to empower individuals and communities to exert more control over the school experiences of their children.

These tensions are not new in Canadian schooling. It is important to recognize that for a large part of Canada's history since Confederation, public schools have served to suppress diversity rather than sustain it—to "civilize" and assimilate the poor, the immigrant population, and Canada's First Nations. However, Canadian schools have, at different points in their history, been required to acknowledge and accommodate differences. This recognition is to be found most concretely in the entrenchment of educational rights across the country among its most numerous populations: the English and the French. These rights originally focussed on religion, but today are increasingly concentrated on language.

In the aftermath of the American Revolution, the British government became convinced that among the causes that led to the breakup of the first British Empire, the absence of a state church in the American colonies was the most significant. Consequently, subsequent colonial policy gave emphasis to elevating the Church of England to the status of a state religion in the various colonies of British North America. The initiative was ultimately doomed by the imprecise wording of legislation (e.g., using the term "Protestant" rather than naming the particular denomination), and by the inability of the Church of England to gain a majority of adherents among the thousands of immigrants who entered the colonies around the turn of the nineteenth century. Anglicans were, however, able to dominate colonial state offices as a common church affiliation became a distinguishing feature among elites like the Family Compact in Upper Canada. Efforts to extend the Church of England's influence into the realm of state schooling were led by Bishop John Strachan of Toronto; he continued to claim that his church had special status in the colony, even after the 1830s when funds from Britain designated for the support of Anglican educational work were finally halted. Indeed, it was Anglican and not Roman Catholic lobbying that first established the principle of religious immunity (the right to establish publically funded separate or dissentient schools) in the 1841 *Common School Act* (Wilson, 1970, pp. 210–11).

Between 1841 and 1863, a series of acts created the "separate schools" of Canada West and the "dissentient schools" of Canada East, allowing Protestant and Catholic parents to establish their own schools and, subject to provincial controls over the curriculum and teachers, to receive public funding. Section 93 of the *Constitution Act, 1867* entrenched these rights in the Canadian Constitution. Thus, separate schools and school boards in Canada are not usually outside the public school system or beyond the control of the minister of education. They are subject to the authority of the provincial government, but that authority is constrained by the provisions of Section 93 (listed on page 30) and by the many interpretations of the Section's intent that have been made by the courts.

In and for each province, the Legislature may exclusively make laws in relation to education subject to the following provisions:

(1) Nothing in any such Law shall prejudicially affect any right or privilege with respect to denominational schools which any class of persons have by law in the province at Union;

(2) All of the powers, privileges, and duties at Union by law conferred and imposed in Upper Canada on the separate schools and school trustees of the Queen's Roman Catholic subjects shall be and the same are hereby extended to the dissentient schools of the Queen's Protestant and Roman Catholic subjects in Quebec;

(3) Where in any province a system of separate or dissentient schools exists by law at the Union or is thereafter established by the Legislature of the province, an appeal shall lie to the Governor-General-in-Council from any act or decision of any provincial authority affecting any right or privilege of the Protestant or Roman Catholic minority of the Queen's subjects in relation to education;

(4) In case any such provincial law as from time to time seems to the Governor-General-in-Council requisite for the due execution of the provisions of this section is not made, or in case any decision of the Governor-General-in-Council on any appeal authority in that behalf, then and in every such case, and as far only as the circumstances of each case require, the Parliament of Canada may make remedial laws for the due execution of the provisions of this Section and of any decision of the Governor-General-in-Council under this Section.

Catholic and Protestant separate schools and school boards exist in a variety of different forms across the country, reflecting in part the existing status of denominational schools in the provinces prior to entry into Confederation, and in part the outcome of legal and political challenges since then. The most serious constitutional confrontation between Catholics and Protestants concerning Section 93 occurred in Manitoba after provincial legislation in 1890 abolished the dual confessional (meaning organized on the basis of religious belief) school system that had been in place since Manitoba entered Confederation in 1870. Provincial Catholics believed that the right to operate their own system of schools had been guaranteed in the *Manitoba Act*, which became an amendment to the *BNA Act* on terms negotiated by Louis Riel's provisional government. A series of court cases and one attempt by the federal government to introduce remedial legislation all failed to move the province to overturn its school legislation during the 1890s, and no appeal to the courts has since been launched (Clark, 1968).

In documenting the development of denominationalism in Canadian public schools, Bezeau (1995, pp. 29–62) classified current arrangements into six distinct groups. In British Columbia and Manitoba, the public school system is "strictly non-denominational." Parents seeking a Catholic or Protestant education for their children in these provinces have to look to private schools, which today are eligible to receive some provincial funding. In Alberta, Saskatchewan, and Ontario, "public and dissentient separate schools" exist and are protected in law. The existing systems in New Brunswick, Nova Scotia, and Prince Edward Island are ones Bezeau described as "non-denominational with informal concessions." A series of important court challenges in New Brunswick between 1873 and 1896 denied Roman Catholics the right to separate schools, but did support the informal accommodations that had been established in the province. Today, recognizably denominational schools, owned by the Roman Catholic Church and leased to the local school board, continue to exist—without legal status—in New Brunswick and Nova Scotia.

Bezeau classifies the different groups of schools in Quebec and Newfoundland as "denominational systems" while noting that both are in the process of significant change. In Quebec an attempt by the provincial government to reorganize school boards on the basis of language instead of religion in 1983 was ruled a violation of Section 93 of the Constitution. It was not until a decade later that revised legislation to replace all existing school boards except those with protected denominational rights with either English-language or French-language boards was approved by the Supreme Court (Bezeau, 1995, pp. 50–51). Unlike any other province, Newfoundland prior to the 1990s had developed a multidenominational series of school systems. These included a Roman Catholic system, a Pentecostal system, a Seventh Day Adventist system, and an Integrated system that combined four official systems: Anglican, Salvation Army, United Church, and Presbyterian. In 1997, following a constitutional amendment to Term 17 of the Terms of Union of Newfoundland with Canada, this multidenominational system was replaced by an interdenominational system. Under this arrangement, all of the ten newly created school boards in the province became interdenominational, with trustees for each board being elected from two groups—denominational representatives and "at large"—while individual schools are designated either interdenominational or unidenominational (Pentecostal, Roman Catholic, or Seventh Day Adventist) based on parental wishes (Newfoundland, 1997a; 1997b).

Bezeau's fifth classification, "denominationalism permitted administratively," is used to describe the existing arrangements in the Northwest Territories and the Yukon, and finally the arrangements that will apply when Nunavut becomes Canada's third territory he classified as "currently uncertain."

Minority Language Education Rights

Religion was the vehicle in the *BNA Act* for protecting English and French minority rights in education. Because they are enshrined in the Constitution, the religious provisions of Section 93 continue to be important determinants of the organization of schooling in many parts of Canada, even though religion itself is generally a less important part of Canadian life than was the case a century ago. Meanwhile, in the second half of the twentieth century, this continued struggle has been recast largely in terms of language, which now has wider significance in Canada than religion.

Section 23 of the *Canadian Charter of Rights and Freedoms* (see Appendix), entitled "Minority Language Educational Rights," provides parents who speak the minority official language in their province with specific rights to public schooling for their children. According to the language provisions in Section 23(1):

> Citizens of Canada: a) whose first language learned and still understood is that of the English or French linguistic minority population of the province in which they reside, or b) who have received their primary school instruction in Canada in English or French and reside in a province where the language in which they received that instruction is the language of the English or French linguistic minority ... have the right to have their children receive primary and secondary school instruction in that language in that province.
>
> (2) Citizens of Canada of whom any child has received or is receiving primary or secondary school instruction in English or French in Canada, have the right to have all their children receive primary and secondary instruction in the same language.
>
> (3) The right of citizens of Canada under subsections (1) and (2) ... a) applies wherever in the province the number of children of citizens who have such a right is sufficient to warrant the provision to them out of public funds of minority language instruction; and b) includes, where the numbers of those children so warrants, the right to have them receive that instruction in minority language educational facilities provided out of public funds.

The above provisions establish the requirement for provincial governments to provide instruction in the official minority language. Since 1982, there has been considerable political and judicial activity across Canada to interpret these provisions and to bring existing practice into line with constitutional requirements. Provincial governments have used various strategies to defuse the political controversies surrounding issues of language. Several provinces have chosen to place the issue of how they are required to comply with Section 23 before the courts rather than risk initiatives of their own that might be unpopular with voters. Even when the courts have made rulings, in several provinces governments have appointed third-party commissions to develop implementation plans. The implementation of provisions for francophone governance of minority language education in English-speaking provinces has been very slow, even when court decisions and commission reports established a path.

One question the courts have been asked to interpret is the meaning in Section 23(3) of the phrase "where numbers warrant." Tardif (1990) notes that in Quebec this number has generally been defined as 1 student, but a Nova Scotia judge deemed that 50 students were insufficient to justify a French school, and a request in Alberta from parents of 188 children was also refused. These differences, Tardif suggests, are rooted in the distinction between "entitlement" and "demand"—that is, whether parents under Section 23 have only to show that they are entitled to minority language education, or whether they are required to demonstrate sufficient demand. Because it fails to take local circumstances into account, the courts have rejected any fixed minimum number of students as defining "where numbers warrant," and have denied the use of existing school district boundaries to define minimum numbers. However, Tardif notes that the Court of Appeal judgement in

Alberta in the case of *Mahé et al. v. Her Majesty the Queen* (1987) appears to place the burden of proof of demand on the parents.

A second critical set of issues on which the courts have been asked to rule includes the homogeneity of schools and questions of control over minority language education. Section 23(3) refers to "minority language educational facilities." Some jurisidictions have interpreted this requirement to be satisfied by the provision of distinct programs for francophones in existing educational facilities. Other jurisdictions have recognized the broader educational and cultural argument that only separate francophone schools can satisfy the spirit of the *Charter* and avoid the damaging effects of linguistic interference and assimilation that could occur in mixed facilities.

In the area of governance, the courts have interpreted Section 23 as conferring on minority language parents a right to be involved in the management and control over their children's schooling, although the courts have not specified what form that management right must take. Summarizing court cases that have addressed this topic, Bezeau (1995) notes that those in Alberta and Ontario have provided some guidelines regarding the minimum level of management required. His conclusion is that considerable autonomy is required, but not necessarily a separate school board. Provisions across the country do indeed vary. For example, Ontario has placed francophone trustees, with exclusive power over minority language programs, on the boards of districts that have significant francophone minority populations, while Manitoba has created a separate francophone school board.

These changes give recognition to the critical role that schools play in either the promotion or erosion of languages and culture, and to the struggle required to have a language and culture other than that of the official majority properly accommodated within the public school system. For languages and cultures that lack the constitutional force of the English and French, this struggle is more difficult. However, where the legitimacy of linguistic and cultural diversity is recognized, new organizational arrangements are likely to be required that may add to the complexity of both existing provisions and single, geographically coherent school boards.

Because of Canada's history and its population dynamics, religion and language will continue to play an important role in Canadian education, and will constitute one of the major political issues with which provincial governments must cope. Specific provisions are likely to continue to evolve, but the issues will not disappear whatever arrangements may be made.

The Minister of Education and the Department of Education

In each province, the Department or Ministry of Education (the term "ministry" is used in British Columbia, Ontario, and Quebec), headed by the minister of education, is the central educational authority. The minister of education, an elected member of the provincial legislature, is appointed to the education portfolio by the premier; he or she is also a member of Cabinet. In the Canadian parliamentary system, the Cabinet—responsible to the legislature and dependent on the support of a majority of its members—is the key planning and directing agency of government. It determines what legislation is brought forward by the government, as well as formulates policy and supervises its implementation in education and all other areas of provincial jurisdiction. Although the drafting and passing of new laws often receives the greatest attention, it is only one of the ways in which government affects education. Since most provinces have only a few basic laws governing education, and these have not been revised significantly very often, most government work in education lies outside the area of legislation. The distinctions among these various avenues of government activity are explained more fully in Chapters Three and Four.

The role played by a minister of education at any particular period of time depends on the overall priorities of the premier and the government, and on the ability of the minister to influence these priorities. Some ministers are important and powerful people in the provincial government as a whole, while others are much less so, and consequently less able to make education an important issue. Nonetheless, because ultimate legal authority over education rests with provincial governments, ministers do play a critical role in determining how a province sets long-term educational policy and in influencing the level of funding provided to schools (see Chapter Five). They make or approve decisions about all sorts of educational issues, from new curricula to be introduced, to rules governing the certification of teachers, to the number of credits required for high-school graduation. The minister must defend before the public the government's policies on education, even if he or she was opposed to the policy. And when parties to a local dispute at the school board or district level cannot come to an agreement, they will often call on the minister to intervene and settle the matter.

Being a government minister is an extremely demanding job. Leading a large and complex department is in itself a complicated task. But ministers must also participate in the work of the Cabinet as a whole, which means making decisions about all policy issues facing the province. Ministers are under constant pressure from various individuals and groups who wish to meet with them in order to influence what the government does. Ministers receive hundreds of such requests each year, just as they are asked to speak or appear at hundreds of public events. As politicians, ministers also have a responsibility to be in their constituency and available to the voters who elected them. Nor should we forget that ministers have personal lives and may reasonably want to spend time with family and friends.

Given all of this, no minister can possibly know all the departmental details or activities under her or his authority. Most of the work of the department is done by civil servants within the broad guidelines set by the minister, or within agreements established by past practice. A great deal of this work is fairly routine or formalized. For example, the development of most new policies and procedures for schools normally proceeds through the work of committees, with the minister being involved, if at all, only at the end of the process in approving the final result. The issuing of certificates to new teachers (or teachers new to the province), the provision of cheques to school divisions, the approval of architectural plans for new schools, the operation of correspondence courses—all of these activities are usually performed under the supervision of Department of Education staff (the special circumstances of British Columbia and Ontario and their respective colleges of teachers are examined separately in Chapter Eight). The direct involvement of ministers is usually reserved for items of great long-term importance or for those having to do with important policy directions, politically sensitive issues, or crises.

The department's civil service is headed by the deputy minister, who is a civil servant appointed by the Cabinet. At one time, provincial deputy ministers were almost always career educators, many of whom had previously been teachers, principals, and school superintendents. In recent years, however, a number of Canadian provincial governments have brought deputy ministers into education from other areas of government, particularly finance (presumably in order to control educational expenditures). Unlike most other civil servants, deputy ministers serve at the pleasure of the Cabinet, which means that they can be dismissed by a government at any time. It is common in Canada when there is a change of government after an election for the new government to replace a number of deputy ministers.

The deputy minister co-ordinates the work of the department in all its multiple functions. A typical department of education will have units dealing with areas such as planning, school finance, curriculum development and assessment, special education, language programs, and renovation/construction of school buildings. All of these tasks require full-time attention and some technical expertise; thus, departments of education today tend to be large organizations (although smaller than they were a decade ago) employing hundreds of people, many of whom are professional educators (see Figure 2.1). The enormous range of issues dealt with in a department of education includes highly complex financial, legal, and technical questions, as well as issues typically thought of as educational, such as curriculum or school regulations.

The Department of Education is a mix of political and professional authority, embodying the tension between professional and lay control mentioned earlier in the chapter. The civil servants are generally guided by their professional training and background. Their views of the needs of education are often similar to those of teachers in schools. They may be quite resistant to what they see as a partisan political direction taken by a government that wants public schooling to move in a certain way. The minister, on the other hand, is primarily oriented toward the political agenda of the government and to his or her own personal views and interests. The deputy minister and senior officials are caught in the middle; they are guided by professional values, but see their job as serving the minister and government. Under these circumstances, a sort of tug-of-war occurs in which ministers try to push their departments to move in particular directions, and civil servants try to convince ministers to see issues in the same ways that the civil service does. Usually, neither party feels entirely satisfied. Ministers feel that though they are elected to bring in certain policies, their will is often frustrated by unelected civil servants. Civil servants, on the other hand, feel that ministers do not always understand the

Figure 2.1

Alberta Department of Education Organizational Chart

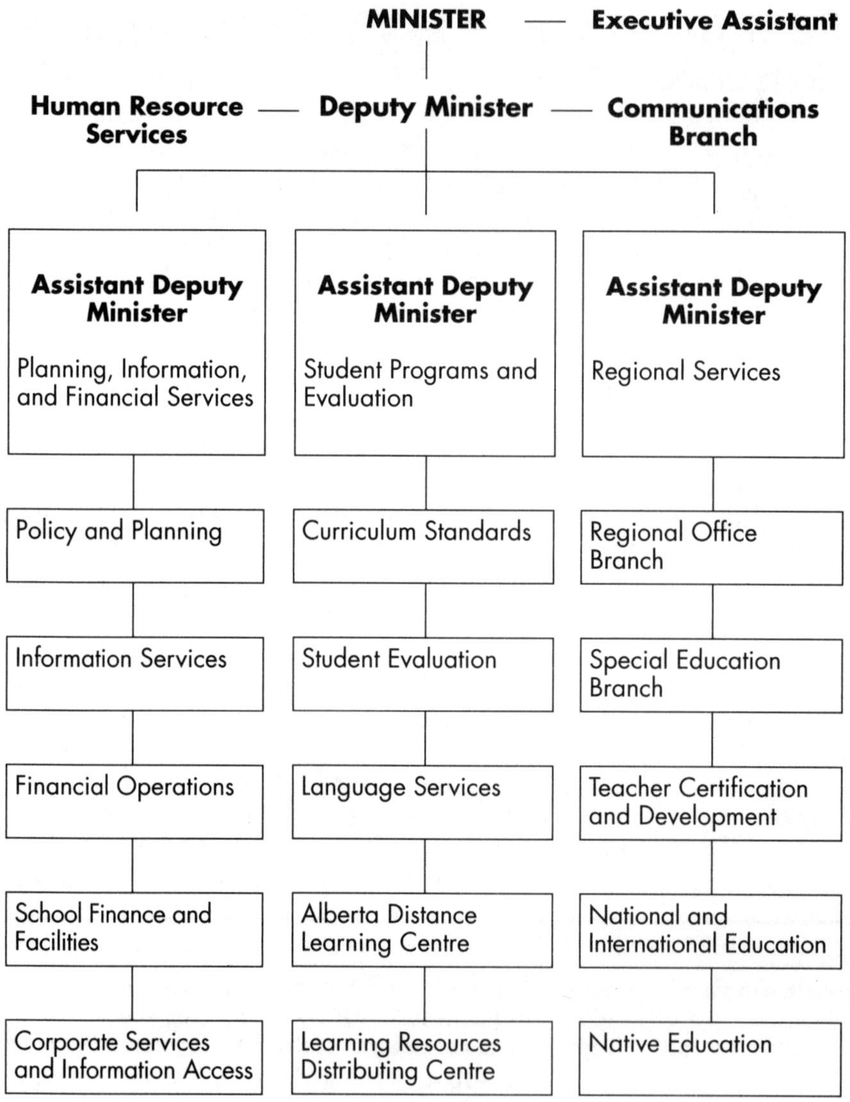

MINISTER —— Executive Assistant

Human Resource —— Deputy Minister —— Communications
Services   Branch

Assistant Deputy Minister	Assistant Deputy Minister	Assistant Deputy Minister
Planning, Information, and Financial Services	Student Programs and Evaluation	Regional Services
Policy and Planning	Curriculum Standards	Regional Office Branch
Information Services	Student Evaluation	Special Education Branch
Financial Operations	Language Services	Teacher Certification and Development
School Finance and Facilities	Alberta Distance Learning Centre	National and International Education
Corporate Services and Information Access	Learning Resources Distributing Centre	Native Education

Source: Alberta. (1995–96). *Annual report,* p. 11. Edmonton: Alberta Education. Reproduced with permission.

subtleties of education, and may be guided by short-term political considerations at the expense of long-term educational needs. These tensions are part of the process of government, and can contribute toward developing policies that are sensitive to both professional skills and public wants.

School Boards and the Local Control of Schools

School boards in Canada currently find themselves in a politically difficult situation. They are caught between the strong centralizing pressures of regional and pan-Canadian curriculum development and assessment and the contrary decentralizing pressures of parent councils and site-based management. Furthermore, they are faced with responsibility for setting school budgets at a time when provincial governments are freezing or reducing their grants to public education but public expectations for the provision of programs remains high.

In New Brunswick these sorts of pressures have led to the abolition of local school boards completely (see Box 2.1), and in virtually every other province some sort of school board consolidation has either taken place in the last few years or is currently underway. Nonetheless, local school boards remain an important element in the Canadian public school system, acting (New Brunswick aside) as the agents of provincial authority and a focal point for local input into the school system.

Working within the constraints laid down by provincial legislation and regulations, school boards are responsible for much of the day-to-day administration of schools. It is generally the boards that hire and pay school personnel and that develop transportation systems and provide physical facilities for pupils (although the costs of new schools are carried by the provinces). In times of declining enrollments, boards close schools, set budgets, and raise local education taxes (except in those provinces where education is entirely funded by the provincial government), and, in line with the discretionary powers delegated to them, boards adapt and modify the provincial curriculum.

Box 2.1
New Brunswick: Provincial Boards of Education, District Parent Advisory Councils, and School Parent Advisory Committees

---

In 1996 the government of New Brunswick announced plans to abolish its local school boards and replace them with a system that includes two Provincial Boards of Education (one French, one English), eighteen District Parent Advisory Councils, and local School Parent Advisory Committees. Provisions for these bodies is contained in the 1997 *Education Act*.

(continued)

(continued)

Provincial Boards of Education

COMPOSITION:

- 12 members elected by and from the District Parent Advisory Councils of the same official language community.

ROLES AND RESPONSIBILITIES INCLUDE:

- Overseeing plans, policies, programs, and services to preserve and promote the language and culture of that official language community.
- With the Minister, to develop an annual provincial education plan.
- To provide a link with District Parent Advisory Councils.

District Parent Advisory Councils

COMPOSITION:

- 6–10 members elected or appointed by and from parents or their representatives serving local School Parent Advisory Committees.
- 1 student elected from School Parent Advisory Committee.
- 1 Aboriginal representative where applicable.
- The Superintendent or Director of Education.

ROLES AND RESPONSIBILITIES INCLUDE:

- To advise the Superintendent and Director or Education on a district education plan.
- To provide a link with School Parent Advisory Committees.

School Parent Advisory Committees

COMPOSITION:

Each committee will have 6–12 members made up of:
- More than 50% of the committee will be made up of parents of pupils in the school or persons nominated by the parents as their representatives.
- 1 teacher elected by and from teachers in the school.
- 1 student at the high-school level elected by and from the student body.
- 1 or 2 community members appointed by the committee if they so wish.
- The school principal.

ROLES AND RESPONSIBILITIES INCLUDE:

- To advise the principal on a school improvement plan.
- To participate in the selection of the principal.

Source: Adapted from the *New Brunswick Education Act* (1977), Sections 32–41. Reproduced with permission. See also the New Brunswick Department of Education Home Page. URL: http://www/gov.nb.ca/education

The History of Consolidation

Today, the local school board in a rural area is likely to be responsible for the administration of many elementary and secondary schools, spread out over a large geographical area and enrolling several thousand students. Urban school boards may have jurisdiction over as many as 100 000 students and 200 schools.

This pattern of large local school districts is a recent phenomenon in Canada, the product of the consolidation during this century of a patchwork of thousands of small, usually single school districts that provided an earlier structure for local educational authority. In the section that follows, the process of consolidation in Alberta is briefly outlined. Alberta was one of the first provinces to begin to create larger administrative units in earnest, and this development had considerable influence across western Canada. While consolidation has since occurred in all provinces, it has not always taken exactly similar forms, and in many provinces did not take place until considerably later.

Consolidation in Alberta

By the time Alberta entered Confederation in 1905, an educational system based on small local administrative districts, sometimes referred to as "four-by-fours"—four miles long and four miles wide—was well established. Some 600 such districts existed when Alberta was incorporated as a province, and with continued settlement and development in the early twentieth century, this number eventually surged to over 5000.

While these small administrative units were in many ways well suited to the existing educational needs, economic conditions, available transportation systems, and political preferences, they also gave rise to administrative and educational problems. Their size, while facilitating student access and community input, was often perceived as an obstacle to the improvement of rural schooling. Small districts, it was argued, made it difficult to provide for education beyond the elementary grades; resulted in large discrepancies among districts in terms of their financial strength and the quality of education they provided; made it difficult to create stable working conditions and career options that could improve the professional status of teachers; and led to duplication and a related lack of economies of scale in the buying of school materials. Such concerns gave rise in the early decades of the twentieth century to a number of experiments in which local districts co-operated to create larger consolidated school districts covering up to 207 km², with students being transported to a central village or town school. This development began in Alberta with the formation of the Consolidated School District of Warner in 1913, and by 1919 there were 63 consolidated school districts in Alberta. However, this approach to consolidation lost its momentum, and after 1922 a number of consolidated districts were disbanded.

The limitations that small school districts posed to the development of secondary schooling resulted in several provinces moving to larger administrative units in two stages — the first involving only secondary schools, and the second bringing elementary schools into the secondary units to form a unified school system. In Alberta, the *Consolidated School Act* of 1921 made possible the creation of a number of rural high-school districts in which four to eight local districts combined for the purposes of providing secondary education (while maintaining their individual responsibility for elementary schools).

While a number of such districts were created in the 1920s, it was in 1936 that the largest step was taken in consolidating Alberta's school districts, when by ministerial order all rural districts were absorbed into greatly enlarged administrative units referred to as school divisions. These divisions initially consisted only of rural districts and hamlets, but they were soon joined by most towns and villages, so that by 1939 there were some 44 divisions in operation across the province, and by 1959 there were 55 covering almost all of the rural settlement in Alberta. The divisions comprised between 70 and 80 school districts and covered from 3885 to 5180 km² in area. Local districts remained in existence, but school divisions, governed by an elected board of trustees and supported by a full-time central office staff and a provincially appointed superintendent, assumed virtually all of their administrative responsibilities, leaving the district board with a very minor advisory role in matters related to religious instruction and the use of French in schools.

The 1950 *County Act* allowed for the establishment of counties in Alberta. These were to be a unified form of government that, instead of keeping separate municipal and educational responsibilities, combined them in a single administrative unit. Established in many parts of rural Alberta, they provided an alternative structure to the separately administered school divisions and municipal districts.

In the 1990s, Alberta, like virtually all other provinces, has initiated a further consolidation and regionalization of its school boards. By a process of both voluntary and mandated amalgamation during 1994, the number of operating school boards in the province was reduced from some 141 to less than 70.

The Role of School Boards

As has already been noted, local school boards are required to act within the parameters laid down in provincial legislation and regulations, and are held accountable to the provincial government through the minister of education. However, school boards are also, in most cases, subject to local election every two to three years, which obliges them to reflect the educational aspirations of their local voters.

When school boards were responsible for very small jurisdictions, the most common number of board members, called trustees, was either three or five. Today, school boards generally consist of seven to fifteen trustees, although in some provinces there are boards that exceed this size. It is normal in most provinces for trustees to be elected, either by the electorate of the school division as a whole or by individual wards; under the latter system, the division is subdivided into wards, each of which elects one or more trustees to represent its interests on the board. In recent years, an important modification to this process has been the institution of legal provisions by some provinces and territories to ensure the representation of specific minority populations on their school boards.

There are few restrictions on who can run for election. The Manitoba *Public Schools Act*, for example, states that anyone who is (1) a resident elector of the division, (2) at least 18 years old, and (3) a Canadian citizen can run for election to the school board. Once elected, it is the trustees collectively who constitute the board as a corporate body with a legally defined range of duties. This collective constitution is important because it means that the board exercises its authority only as a single corporate entity and not through the actions of individual members.

As with their counterparts at the provincial level, the elected school board members are generally assisted by a professional administration headed by a CEO, variously referred to as superintendent/chief or superintendent/director of education. The size of the board office administration is usually determined by the size of the division. Many of the same tensions that exist between politicians and professionals can also be found between school boards and their superintendents. Superintendents may feel that trustees are uninformed about education, and have agendas that are short term and much too heavily influenced by re-election considerations. Trustees may feel that their professional staff is insufficiently concerned with what the public thinks, and too unwilling to admit any criticism. As at the provincial level, this tension can be positive or negative, depending on how well the parties are able to work together to take best advantage of their different viewpoints. Trustees have the last word in that the school board hires—and can fire—the superintendent. While firings of superintendents occur regularly in Canadian school districts, it is more common for superintendents to serve for many years or leave voluntarily to pursue another job.

School boards are mandated both to ensure local compliance with provincial laws and to be responsive to community interests (which may themselves be multiple and contradictory). Their situation can fluctuate quite rapidly from public disinterest—reflected in low voter turnout at elections, acclamations, and empty board meetings—to passionate, and even violent, involvement characterized by packed board meetings and electoral defeat for trustees. Action can come as a consequence of either competing local interests or as conflicts between local and provincial agendas. The following examples describe only some of the controversial issues that school boards are likely to address.

1. *Setting budgets.* Deciding issues such as cutting or increasing budgets, laying off teachers, reducing services, and raising local taxes.
2. *Personnel.* Negotiating collective agreements in some provinces for professional and support staff. Defining working conditions in areas such as class size, preparation time, maternity/paternity leaves, and pensions.

3. *Facilities.* Deciding on school closures and school openings, as well as reorganization; selecting which schools will offer which programs; and determining how transportation will be provided.
4. *Programming.* Deciding on the provision of programs other than those mandated by the province (e.g., international baccalaureate programs, AIDS and family life education, and minority language programs).

Schools and School Councils

The processes of consolidation outlined earlier in this chapter substantially altered the balance of authority in most provincial school systems. The trend of shifting power away from the school neighbourhood or community, and away from direct public involvement, continued as the larger school divisions came to depend increasingly on the professional expertise of their superintendents and staffs. Recently, however, there have been attempts in most provinces to strengthen the role of local voices—particularly those of parents—in the education system. This has been done by giving legal status to a variety of parent advisory committees, school councils, and orientation committees at the school level, together with an elected membership and an expanded role in influencing the ongoing life of the school (Rideout, 1995).

While such initiatives have seen the inclusion of different "stakeholders" and the delegation of different degrees of authority over various elements of school life, most have sought to include a greater advisory or consultative role for parents in a broad range of school-related issues (see Table 2.2). The phrase "partners in learning" characterizes the idealized relationship between parent and teacher, family, community, and school. Justifications for such initiatives have come from at least three directions: (1) the growing research literature that indicates that parental participation has positive effects on student learning; (2) social and political arguments that support parental rights to advocate on their children's behalf over matters of education; and (3) a pragmatic argument that suggests that the availability of the resources necessary for public schooling in the future will depend increasingly on the political support of parents in the face of increased competition from other sources.

The Royal Commission on Education (British Columbia, 1988) found that there is widespread support from both the public and educational professionals for school councils made up of parents and other community members. The authors concluded that "the Commission believes strongly in the value of elected consultative committees of parents who are closely associated with schools, and who meet regularly to discuss all aspects of school policies and procedures and who offer advice to school principals and staffs, and through them, to school boards" (p. 188), and it went on to recommend that each of the province's 75 school districts provide for parent–community advisory committees at both the school and district levels. One year later, the revised *British Columbia School Act* (1989) responded, in

Table 2.2 Parental Participation in School-Level Governance in Canada

	Legislation	Structures	Description	Composition
British Columbia (1989)	Yes	Parent Advisory Council and District Advisory Council.	Permissive, advisory, non-specific.	Parents only.
Alberta (1988/1994/1995)	Yes	School Council.	Mandatory, advisory, specific, elected, flexible, functional.	Parents, principal, teachers, students, community reps.
Saskatchewan (1996)	No	School Advisory Council.	(As proposed) Advisory, elected or appointed, volunteer.	Parents, community teacher, students, and principal.
Manitoba (1994/1996)	Yes	School Advisory Council.	Permissive, elected.	Majority parents (2/3), community reps, ex officio non-voting principal and one elected teacher.
Ontario (1995)	Legislation anticipated.	Ontario Parent Council and School Council.	Mandatory, advisory, elected.	Majority parents, appointed community rep., elected student rep., principal, elected teacher rep., elected non-teaching staff rep.
Quebec (1972/1988)	Yes	School Committee, Orientation Committee.	Mandatory, functional, advisory.	Parents only.*
New Brunswick (1996)	New Education Act with provisions to be tabled Fall 1996.	School Parent Committee, District Parent Advisory Council, Provincial Board.*	Mandatory, elected.	Majority parents, teacher, and principal (ex officio) [student and community reps optional].
Nova Scotia (1995/1996)	Yes	School Advisory Council (SAC).*	Permissive, advisory, elected.	Teachers, parents, community members, students, non-voting principal.
Prince Edward Island (1993)	Yes	School Council.	Permissive, advisory, specific.	Majority parents.
Newfoundland (1996)	Proposed Bill in draft form.	School Council.	Advisory, elected/appointed.	Parents, teachers, the principal (by virtue of his/her position).
NW. Territories (1996)	Yes	Parent Advisory Committee	Permissive, advisory.	—
Yukon (1990/1996)	Yes	School Council/School Committee/Boards.	Advisory, mandatory, elected.	Composition set by regulation. Guaranteed Aboriginal reps.

* Each school has an orientation committee in addition to a school committee. While the latter comprises parents, orientation committees have representation from teachers, administrators, support staff, and students at the secondary level.

Source: Copyright © Yvonne Martin, Faculty of Education, University of Victoria, BC. Reproduced with permission.

part, to this recommendation by formally establishing the right of parents to have a parents' advisory council in each school to "advise the board and the principal and staff of the school ... respecting any matter related to the school" (Section 8(4)).

The Yukon, with the passing of the 1990 *Education Act*, has perhaps gone further than any other jurisdiction to decentralize and democratize its educational system, and to establish a broad base for local participation in, and control over, schools. Under the provisions of the new act, existing school committees, which prior to the act had only a limited advisory role, are encouraged to evolve into school councils or school boards with substantial authority over the operations of the local school. School councils of three to seven members (which may include guaranteed representation for Yukon First Nations populations) have substantial powers, subject to ministerial approval, over such matters as the selection of the school principal, approval of school rules, development of local curriculum, and evaluation and dismissal of teachers. After being in existence for at least one year, the parents in the educational area served by the council may vote to become a school board and to assume increased powers over all areas of their school's operations.

In Quebec in the 1980s and 1990s, parental participation and public accountability on the part of schools have been, along with the already mentioned reorganization of school boards, a central part of the province's educational reform agenda. To achieve this objective, provision has been made for the creation of school committees, orientation committees, and school board advisory committees. The school committee, comprising between five and twenty-five parents whose children are enrolled in the school and who are elected by other parents, is responsible for promoting parental participation in the educational mission of the school and for acting as an advisory body to the school's principal and orientation committee as well as to the school board. Quebec's orientation committees, required under Article 55 of the *Education Act* (1988), offer a unique forum for community input and a distinct approach to public accessibility, involvement, and accountability. Comprising parents, teachers, nonteaching and support staff, and, at the secondary level, students (with parents making up at least 50 percent of the group), the orientation committee is expected to play an important role in creating a school whose whole ethos is responsive to the community it serves (see Box 2.2).

Box 2.2
Quebec's Orientation Committees: Articles 77–80 of the *Education Act* (1988)

---

77. The orientation committee, after consultation with the school committee, shall determine the specific aims and objectives of the educational project of the school. The orientation committee shall give its opinion to the principal as regards the measures likely to ensure the implementation and evaluation of the aims and objectives.

(continued)

(continued)

78. The orientation committee also has the following functions:
    (1) to promote communication and coordination between the persons having an interest in the school;
    (2) to adopt, with or without amendments, after consultation with the school committee, rules of conduct and safety rules proposed by the principal;
    (3) to approve, after consultation with the school committee, the choice of educational activities proposed by the principal, which entail changes in the students' regular schedule, or which cause them to travel to places outside the school.
79. The orientation committee shall advise the school board
    (1) on any matter the school board is required to submit to it;
    (2) on any matter likely to facilitate the operation of the school and the implementation of its educational project;
    (3) on any matter that may ensure a better organization of the services provided by the school board.
80. The orientation committee must be consulted by the school board on the following matters:
    (1) the amendment or revocation of the deed of establishment of the school;
    (2) the criteria for the selection of the principal;
    (3) the application for recognition of the confessional status of the school or the withdrawal of such recognition;
    (4) the modes of implementation of the basic school regulations (régime pédagogique) in the school;
    (5) the enrichment and adaptation of the official programs of studies and the elaboration of local educational programs and programs of student services and special educational services for the school;
    (6) the organization, on school premises, of sociocultural or sports services and of day care.

Federal Involvement in Education

The role of the federal government in Canadian education is an unusual one. Canada is the only industrialized country that has no federal office or department of education. Even in other federal states, such as Germany, there is a significant role in education for the national government. In Canada, federal activity in education, while it exists, occurs almost surreptitiously. Thus, there are different arrangements in each province for curricula, teacher certification, and even grades within the school system.

While the provisions of Section 93 of the *Constitution Act* give primacy to provincial authority over education and to the structures outlined in the preceding pages, the act does not preclude federal government involvement. As education grew in importance in Canada, the federal government began to play a more important role, and today it continues to have a substantial presence in education despite the constitutional provisions of Section 93 (Hodgson, 1987; Nagy and Lupart, 1994). This involvement occurs through many federal government agencies and departments. Some educational programs are run directly by the federal government, while others are collaborative ventures run jointly with the provinces or other educational authorities. In some cases, the federal government's activities conflict with those of provincial governments. (The federal role in the funding of education through transfer payments to the provinces is dealt with separately in Chapter Five.)

A major area of federal activity arises out of attempts to address the educational requirements of those areas of federal jurisdiction spelled out in Section 91 of the *Constitution Act* (e.g., national defence, Indian affairs, the territories, prisons, external affairs, and the economy). Thus, the federal Department of National Defence is responsible not only for the education of service personnel, but also for the education of children of members of the armed forces, either through the operation of schools on military bases or through agreements with nearby school boards. Similarly, the solicitor general is responsible for education and training programs for the inmates of penitentiaries, while the Department of External Affairs, through the Canadian International Development Agency (CIDA), provides educational and technical assistance to other countries and funds programs for Canadian teachers to work abroad. In the Yukon and Northwest Territories, education remains, in part, a federal responsibility. Although in both territories departments of education perform functions generally similar to those of the provinces, they are funded largely by the federal government.

The Education of Registered Indians

The provision of education for Aboriginal people is a critical issue in Canadian education — one that is very closely related to the broader questions of the purposes of schooling that were raised in Chapter One, as well as to issues of authority and structure already introduced in this chapter.

Section 91(24) of the *Constitution Act* designates as federal responsibility "Indians and Lands reserved for the Indians." An important legal distinction has to be made here between registered (or status) Indians and nonstatus Indians. It is the former whose names are included on a register kept by the Department of Indian and Northern Affairs Canada (INAC), who fall under the legal jurisdiction of the *Indian Act*, and whose schooling is a constitutional responsibility of the federal government. However, registered Indian families living away from reserves have not generally come under federal jurisdiction. Like nonstatus Indians, Métis, and non-Aboriginal students, their education is a provincial concern. Nonstatus Indians are those who have lost their status through enfranchisement, and who are unable, or do not wish, to regain their status as registered Indians (Wotherspoon & Satzewich, 1993, p. xv).

The *Indian Act*, first introduced in 1876 and revised several times since, provides the legal framework that has regulated the federal government's relationship with registered Indians. Administrative responsibility has resided primarily with the federal Department of Indian and Northern Affairs. Sections 114 to 122 of the *Indian Act* deal specifically with schooling. Section 114 addresses the question of control over schools. It states:

1. The Governor in Council may authorize the Minister of Indian and Northern Affairs in accordance with this Act to enter into agreements on behalf of Her Majesty for the education in accordance with this Act of Indian children, with:
   a) the government of a province
   b) the Commissioner of the Northwest Territories
   c) the Commissioner of the Yukon Territory
   d) a public or separate school board, and
   e) a religious or charitable organization.

Nowhere in this list of potential purveyors of education is there recognition given to Indian consultation or to the legitimacy of Indian control of Indian education.

The early history of the implementation of the *Indian Act* saw the federal government enlist the services of the churches to operate schools among Indian communities. Over the years, a number of different institutional forms were experimented with, ranging from local day schools to residential schools that often specialized in industrial and agricultural training. Their general aim was to Christianize Indian children and to assimilate them into the lower strata of the dominant society (Barman, Hebert, & McCaskill, 1986; Wotherspoon & Satzewich, 1993).

It was not until the 1950s that the federal government began to take direct charge of Indian education and to operate its own schools. In the 1960s, under a new federal vision of Indian education, there was a movement toward integrating Indian children into the provincial school systems, either through master tuition agreements between federal and provincial governments (negotiated without Indian consultation or agreement) or through individual agreements between the federal government and local school boards. However, throughout this period the federal government also continued to operate many of its own schools, and, despite changes in the ways in which federal responsibility for Indian schooling was carried out prior to the 1970s, there was much that did not change. First, the structure and content of Indian schools and their curricula were always defined and controlled by non-Indians. Second, the definition of an appropriate curriculum considered Indian cultures, languages, histories, and identities as essentially irrelevant. Third, Indian schools were, with very few exceptions, unsuccessful by almost any definition.

Since the 1970s, First Nations communities have struggled to change the circumstances imposed on them by the federal government, asserting the importance of an education that reflects their histories, languages, values, and aspirations, and over which they alone exercise control. The National Indian Brotherhood (1972) stated clearly:

If we are to avoid the conflict of values which in the past has led to withdrawal and failure, Indian parents must have control of education with the responsibility for setting goals. What we want for our children can be summarized very briefly: to reinforce their Indian identity; and to provide the training necessary for making a good living in a modern society. We are the best judges of the kind of school programs which can contribute to these goals without causing damage to the child (p. 3).

The Assembly of First Nations (1988), in a declaration of First Nations jurisdiction over education, restated and reframed this position within a jurisdictional claim of sovereign self-government by asserting that

> [e]ducation is one of the most important issues in the struggle for self-government and must contribute towards the objectives of self-government. First Nations governments have the right to exercise their authority in all areas of First Nations education. Until First Nations education institutions are recognized and controlled by First Nations government, no real First Nations education exists. The essential principles are that each First Nation government should make its own decisions and arrangements rather than having them imposed from outside (Vol. 1, p. 47).

In 1973, the federal government stated that it was prepared to accept the principle of local control. Important steps toward that end have since been taken (Kirkness, 1992), although as the Assembly of First Nations (1988) and *The Report of the Royal Commission on Aboriginal Peoples* (Canada, 1996), clearly indicate, much remains to be done. The goal of a First Nations educational system involves not only passing authority and jurisdiction to individual First Nations and their education authorities, but also developing and implementing a curriculum that makes education relevant to the philosophies and needs of Indian people, and training Indian teachers to deliver that curriculum. In short, it is a holistic and lifelong education relevant to the contemporary needs and aspirations of First Nations people.

Today, approximately 50 percent of registered Indian students attend band-controlled or First Nations schools; a large majority of the remainder attend provincially operated schools. A few federal government schools continue to exist, and in Quebec, Alberta, and British Columbia, private schools also play a role in the education of registered Indian students, as shown in Table 2.3.

No single blueprint for Aboriginal self-government in education exists—indeed, a central principle of self-government is that local communities and individual First Nations should be free to develop their own plans without outside interference. Across Canada this has seen innovation at the local and provincial levels. In February 1997 an agreement between the federal government, the provincial government of Nova Scotia, and the Mi'kmaq Chiefs of Nova Scotia provided the first agreement in Canada to transfer jurisdiction for education from the federal government to First Nations communities. Offering a model of how First Nations' jurisdiction in education might develop into a national educational network, *The Report of the Royal Commission on Aboriginal Peoples* (1996, Vol. 3, pp. 563–65) laid out a proposal for a four-tiered system that would involve local community, individual First Nations, multi-nation organizations, and Canada-wide networks collaborating to provide a comprehensive Aboriginal education system (see Box 2.3).

Table 2.3

Elementary/Secondary Enrollment on Reserves by Type of School, 1991–1992

School type	Atlantic	Quebec	Ontario	Prairies	Yukon/BC	Total
Federal						
schools	4	2	17	16	4	43
students	243	244	2 522	3 025	146	6 180 (6.4%)
Provincial						
schools	132	174	337	517	576	1 736
students	2 086	7 286	7 924	15 077	10 719	43 092 (44.6%)
Private						
schools	2	39	0	30	91	162
students	2	260	0	464	931	1 657 (1.7%)
Band						
schools	16	29	56	136	92	329
students	1 781	4 996	6 907	28 062	3 919	45 665 (47.3%)
Total						
schools	154	244	411	699	763	2 271
students	4 112	12 786	17 353	46 628	15 715	96 594

Source: Derived from the Management Information Branch, Ottawa: Department of Indian and Northern Affairs, 1992. Reproduced with the permission of Public Works and Government Services Canada, 1997.

Box 2.3
Model of an Aboriginal Education System

Local Community

- Participates in policy making through representation in Aboriginal nation governing bodies and nation education authority.
- Makes decisions on instruction of local students.
- Implements nation policy in local Aboriginal institutions.
- Negotiates tuition agreements in accord with nation policy.
- Participates in decision making in local institutions under provincial/territorial jurisdiction.

Aboriginal Nation

- Enacts or adopts laws on Aboriginal education.
- Establishes an education authority to make policy on
  - education goals and means of achieving them in the nation
  - administration of schools and colleges within the nation
  - tuition agreements
  - purchase of provincial/territorial services
- Receives revenues and distributes funds for government services including education.
- Participates in establishing policy framework province-wide through representation in multi-nation organizations.

Multi-nation Organization

- Negotiates policy framework with the province or territory for
  - tuition agreements
  - access to provincial or territorial services
  - transfer between Aboriginal and provincial or territorial academic programs
- Develops curriculum.
- Monitors academic standards in Aboriginal system.
- May coordinate nation support of Aboriginal postsecondary institutions.
- Advises provincial ministers of education, colleges and universities, and training.
- Provides an umbrella for representation of community interests to governments administering education.

Canada-wide Networks

- Federated organization reflecting nation interests.
  - Aboriginal Peoples' International University
  - electronic clearinghouse
  - statistical clearinghouse
  - documentation centre
  - associations for standard setting and accrediting postsecondary programs and institutions.

Source: Adapted from Privy Council Office, *Report of the royal commission on aboriginal peoples*, Volume 3, *Gathering strength*, p. 564. Reproduced with the permission of the Minister of Public Works and Government Services Canada, 1997.

Federal Collaboration in Provincial Schooling

In addition to those areas directly responsible for the delivery of educational services, the federal government plays a role in representing what it sees as the national interest in the provincial educational arena. Such initiatives have taken many forms, but the common element is the provision of federal funds in their support. During the 1970s and 1980s, the Canada Studies Program, administered by the Department of the Secretary of State, represented such an initiative. In response to concerns expressed about students' ignorance of their own country, this program saw considerable resources allocated to the production and implementation of elementary- and high-school curriculum materials. Similarly, the Secretary of State continues to provide the Official Languages in Education Program, which is directed toward educating official minority language students in their mother tongue and toward promoting bilingualism. In this program, the federal government enters into bilateral agreements with the various provinces to provide money in support of minority language programs, including immersion ones. Federal funds have played a major role in expanding immersion and protecting other minority language education opportunities.

Vocational and technical training is another area in which the federal government has a long history of collaboration and conflict with the provinces. Federal activity in this area, justified by the federal government's responsibility for national economic development, began in the first decades of this century. In the 1960s, the federal government provided, through the *Technical and Vocational Assistance Act* (1960), funds for building technical and vocational high schools and departments in existing high schools. The federal government's concern with producing a better-trained Canadian labour force has continued into the 1980s and 1990s. Its 1990 Stay-in-School initiative was designed to combat high-school drop-out rates. In announcing this program, the government noted that "while education is a provincial responsibility, it is one of the federal government's main responsibilities to establish national labour market policies and programs. ... Ensuring that young people are prepared for the transition from school to the workforce is a shared responsibility" (Canada, 1990c). A recent federal initiative has been to support schools across the country accessing the Internet through the development of SchoolNet (URL: http://www.schoolnet.ca).

National Organizations

Canada has a number of organizations that are involved with education at the national level. The provinces, worried about growing federal involvement in education, created in 1967 the Council of Ministers of Education, Canada (CMEC). CMEC is made up of all the provincial ministers of education and higher or postsecondary education (a number that can be as high as twenty depending on whether these two areas are the responsibility of one or two ministers in each province). The council can act only when all of the ministers agree, and this does not happen often on matters of import. Thus, the organization has, for most of its history, had only limited impact on Canadian education. CMEC recently developed a set of pan-Canadian achievement tests to measure Canadian students' learning in different curriculum areas as part of the School Achievement Indicators Program. These tests have been administered annually in different subject areas to a random sample of 13- and 16-year-old students in all provinces and territories except Saskatchewan (Canadian Education Statistics Council, 1996) and provide an example of pan-Canadian activity by the Council of Ministers of Education.

Another significant national educational organization is the Canadian Education Association (CEA), which is made up of both individual members and organizations such as provincial governments, universities, and school districts. CEA attempts to be a nonpartisan information exchange, promoting discussion of educational issues.

Each of the major interest groups in Canada also has a national organization to lobby on its behalf. The Canadian Teachers' Federation (CTF) represents English-speaking Canadian teachers. The Canadian School Boards' Association includes school districts across Canada. The Canadian Association of School Administrators (CASA) has a membership primarily of school superintendents, while the Canadian Association of Principals (CAP) is the umbrella group for school principals. None of these organizations, however, plays a very important role in shaping provincial or national policy in education.

Conclusion

Education's "structure" consists of those more permanent sets of relationships of power that are formalized through laws, regulations, and policies, and that regulate the day-to-day operation of schools and school systems. While there is much that is relatively unchanging in these structures (as was suggested in our examination of the educational debates in Upper Canada in the mid-nineteenth century), in the 1990s there is also much that continues to change. Provincial government reforms, the contemporary struggle for Aboriginal self-government, *Charter* challenges over minority language rights, and the implications of economic globalization are each likely to require that we develop new relationships to meet the educational needs of a changing world. That these structures are neither necessarily permanent nor necessarily right, but rather a reflection of a particular set of interests expressed at a particular point in time, requires that we understand what those interests are. A central concern of this chapter was examining who exercises the power that defines the form of public schooling, and how this power is regulated and legitimated. What is clear in both a historical and contemporary context is that the "public" to whom public schools were held accountable has been a particularly exclusive group. It is to this question of the struggle for power — the politics of public schooling — that we turn in Chapter Three.

Exercises

1. The prologue to this chapter outlined some of the complexities of both school board decision making and Aboriginal education in Canada. In the prologue, Norman has to decide what to say and how to vote in an upcoming board meeting. Based on the information in this chapter, identify what you consider to be the essential issues in the case study and prepare a presentation for Norman that details what you think the board should be doing, and why.

2. This chapter has described Canada's public school system as being centralized at the provincial level. Find out more about the educational system of a country that is either more centralized or decentralized, and use your findings to discuss the advantages and disadvantages of a centralized system.

3. Some observers believe that school boards have outlived their usefulness and should be abolished. Write an argument either defending or critiquing this view.

4. Write a brief paper outlining the arrangements in your province with regard to minority language education. In particular, how are the management rights of the minority community interpreted in your province? Has the issue been controversial? Why or why not?

5. Does your province recognize separate (religious) schools? If so, in what ways? Trace the origins of separate schools (or lack of them) in your jurisdiction.

6. Interview an official of the Department or Ministry of Education in your province. Write a brief description of his or her job. How does he or she envision the role of the department? How has this role changed over the last twenty years or so?

7. Find out who the minister of education is in your province. What is this person's background? What policy positions or issues is he or she presently tackling? (You may want to undertake this assignment by writing to the minister, in which case part of your study could be what sort of response you get, from whom, and when.)

8. Interview a trustee from your local school board. Ask him or her about what the board does, what the role of the trustee is, how he or she came to the position, and what issues are of major concern.

9. Assume that your school board is opening a new school next year. It is hoped that the school will be a model of school–community collaboration. Prepare a plan for community involvement that would include deciding (1) who constitutes "the community" (parents, students, residents, businesses, and so forth); (2) which areas of school life the community would—and would not—be involved in; (3) what you mean by "collaboration"; and (4) how you would regulate collaboration.

10. School board members are meant to provide representation to the communities they serve. Yet electing trustees for large boards through a process that is based on ward systems and simple vote counts may leave many communities feeling that their interests are not properly represented on the board. Recent provisions that allow for the appointment of Aboriginal trustees to boards that serve Aboriginal students exemplify one attempt to increase representation on boards. The creation of separate French-language boards exemplifies another. Discuss how a province might attempt to increase the participation of a broad segment of its population in the governance of its schools.

11. In Canadian public school systems, the director/superintendent of education is generally a career educator with teaching and school management experience who is hired by the school board. Discuss the possible merits of (1) appointing a superintendent who was an experienced senior administrator but in an area other than public schooling (e.g., social work, business, the military); and (2) making the position of superintendent an elected position.

12. With the exception of Quebec's orientation committees, the student voice is not afforded any formal place in Canadian school governance. As yet, students are not included in the concept of "public" to which schools are accountable. Suggest ways in which students could be given a greater part in the administration of their school systems.

13. Canada is one of the few countries in the world without a federal government ministry or department of education. Is this appropriate? Why or why not? What arrangements might be most suitable for the federal role in education?

14. Using historical writings, trace the development of education for Aboriginal people from its inception to the present. What forces have driven the changes that have occurred?

Further Reading

This chapter covered a very broad range of topics, many of which have unique elements in each province and territory. Most textbooks on education in Canada provide some basic coverage, but no text can hope to cover all of these details, and there are relatively few other general works on Canadian education. Students should seek out local source materials, such as provincial legislation, Department or Ministry of Education reports and studies, reports prepared by organizations of teachers or trustees, and provincial royal commissions. *The Report of the Royal Commission on Aboriginal Peoples* (Canada, 1996) is an important source for First Nations education in Canada, particularly Chapter 5, "Education," of Volume 3, *Gathering Strength*. Also important at the national level is the Assembly of First Nations 1988 report, *Tradition and Education: Towards a Vision of Our Future*. Detailed statistics on the school experience of Aboriginal students can be found in the Statistics Canada publication, *The 1991 Aboriginal Peoples Survey (APS)* (Cat. Nos. 89533 and 89534). The Canadian Education Statistics Council, a joint undertaking of Statistics Canada and the Council of Ministers of Education, Canada, publishes statistical data on Canadian education. The Canadian Education Association also publishes a variety of reports that provide a national overview of educational issues. The journal *Our Schools/Our Selves* offers a valuable current discussion of many of the issues raised in this chapter and elsewhere in the text.

CHAPTER THREE

Policy and Politics

▼ PROLOGUE

Linda Chartrand was already quite concerned when the meeting began, and the meeting did not make her feel any better. There were ten of them, meeting in the large and rather formal committee room in the school board office. Nobody was feeling very cheerful.

Superintendent Ron Brandt began by reviewing the situation. "As you know, a number of parents in this school district have objected to the use of *The Stone Angel* by Margaret Laurence in our high-school English literature program. They have appeared as a delegation before the school board asking — no, I'd better say demanding — that we remove the book from our program because they claim it is both obscene and blasphemous. While I'm sure none of us here shares that view, we do have to take their opinion seriously. They have certainly indicated that they won't accept no for an answer; if we don't respond, they'll continue to fight the issue, perhaps running candidates in the school-board elections next fall.

"We've gathered here — the chair of the school board, myself, the two high-school principals, the English department heads, and teachers from the district's language arts curriculum committee — to decide what to do. I'd appreciate your comments. Mr. Pershanti, as chair of the board, would you like to begin?"

"Thank you, Ron," said Arvin Pershanti. "The board finds itself in a very awkward situation here. We believe that *The Stone Angel* is a perfectly legitimate book to teach in high school. It's approved by the provincial Department of Education. It was selected by our teacher curriculum committee. We've been teaching it for several years with no problems. But now we definitely have a problem.

"The trustees are wondering if we might consider temporarily taking the book off the program, at least for a year or two, until the fuss dies down."

Seta Bolissian, one of the teachers present, burst out, "How can you say that? Are we going to knuckle under to a small group of cranks? What about our academic freedom as teachers? What about what's best for our students? What about the vast majority of parents who are quite happy with the curriculum? Surely there are some principles at stake here."

"Well," said Lou Bryan, one of the principals, "points of principle are all very well, but we also have a practical problem. This may be a small group of people, but they can sure cause a big set of problems for us. We've got a good atmosphere of calm and co-operation in this district. If we let this issue get out of hand, all of that could turn into conflict, distrust, and mutual recrimination. I ask myself if one novel, however good it might be, is worth all of that. And I come to the conclusion that the board's strategy is a good one. They're not asking us to give up our principles, only to exercise some discretion for a little while. It seems like a good solution to me."

Linda reflected that this was hardly surprising. Lou Bryan, who had been her principal a few years ago, was well known in the district for agreeing wholeheartedly with whatever the board or the superintendent did.

Now Larry Tucci, the other principal, was speaking. "Can't we make this the province's issue somehow? After all, *The Stone Angel* is on their list of approved books. Couldn't we dump the issue into the lap of the minister of education?"

"I've thought of that," said Ron Brandt. "I spoke with the provincial director of curriculum earlier today. He said that he thought the minister, if the question came to her, would dodge it. After all, we aren't required to use that book; it's just one on the list from which we select. And the minister would likely point out that decisions about specific books, and about community standards, belong to local school boards. She might even say that she would never want to interfere with the autonomy of the board in making these choices. I don't think that strategy will work, I'm sorry to say."

"We can't just think about this instance, either." Department Head of English Joan Gold now had the floor. "After all, if we give in this time we will be encouraging other groups to make similar demands. We need to think of a way to deal with these sorts of issues so as to try to reach some compromise that everyone can live with. I believe that decisions about curricular materials should be made by teachers — that is our professional right and responsibility. But we do need a process in which people who are unhappy can raise their concerns and have them heard without it turning into a game of political hardball."

"Joan is right," Linda broke in. "Let's remember that 20 or 30 years ago our schools were full of books that portrayed Aboriginal people as savages and women as housewives exclusively. People who complained about those things were probably thought about just the same way we're talking about this group — as crackpots or extremists. I don't want *The Stone Angel* removed from the curriculum, and certainly not because someone demands it and issues threats. But we do need to make a serious effort to hear what their concerns are, and to try to respond to them in some way. I can't believe that we couldn't reach an acceptable compromise if we tried to debate the matter with some understanding."

"I like what you're saying," said Ed Safniuk, another teacher. "There are many kids in my class from cultures that have quite different values, and many of their parents have problems with books like this. I think we need to broaden the issue to ask what literature best serves our students' needs. That is something we can discuss with parents and students, rather than making this a power struggle."

"You're naïve, Linda, and you too, Ed," said Larry Tucci. "These people don't want a serious dialogue. They're determined to have their way, no matter what. I'd like to see the board tell them to drop dead, but I can understand why the trustees may not want to do so, and I'm prepared to live with the solution Mr. Pershanti put forward." ■

The politics of education have been changing dramatically in recent years. Governments have been increasingly active in developing and legislating major changes in many aspects of schooling, including governance, testing, curriculum, and teacher training. Parents are more involved and vigorous in expressing their views than ever before. A wide variety of external groups is also actively involved in political issues around education. Education is often a subject of political debate, and schools are in the news more than they have been for many years. Expectations are increasing and diversifying, with the result that everyone in the school system — teachers, principals, school boards, and provincial governments—is under more political pressure.

Understanding the dynamics of education politics is fundamental to understanding the nature of public education in Canada. This chapter focuses on the following questions of policy and politics in education:

1. What is policy, and why are policy questions important in education?
2. How do political processes operate to establish policies?
3. What are some of the dilemmas or tensions inherent in the politics of Canadian education?
4. What are some of the central questions that can be used to analyze and understand political and policy debates?
5. How do these questions help us understand the politics of education at the provincial, school board, and school levels?

Education Policy

The everyday world of teaching and learning in schools is greatly affected by a wide range of policies. The term **policy** is usually defined as a general guideline that shapes decisions or actions. Some people think of policies as rules, but for purposes of this chapter policy is defined as a general approach to things, intended to guide behaviour (although, as we will see later, policies have other purposes as well). A policy decision in education, then, is one that has broad implications within a particular setting, whether a country, province, or school.

Policies shape the structure of schools, the resources available in schools, the curriculum, the teaching staff, and, to a considerable extent, the round of daily activities. Policies determine how much money is spent, by whom and on what, how teachers are paid, how students are evaluated, and most other aspects of schools as we know them. The impact of policies can be illustrated by listing just a few areas of education policy. Some important policy areas — such as school consolidation, language policy, and Aboriginal education — have been discussed in earlier chapters.

What is taught is affected by provincial curriculum policies, school board curriculum policies, and school curriculum policies, all of which determine what is on the curriculum, how much of the content is prescribed, what textbooks can be used, and how much flexibility teachers have to alter curricula. For instance, how much time and attention will be given to art and music as opposed to language? How much attention will be given to labour history or women's history in social studies? How much will be taught about war and how much about peace?

Who can teach is determined by policies on teacher training and certification, and on teacher evaluation. Will people with particular skills (e.g., languages) but without teacher training be allowed to teach? Will teachers require specialist qualifications for certain positions?

How students are treated is affected by school and district policies on discipline, attendance, student activities, student evaluation practices, grading, failure, and so on. Given recent legal decisions regarding the *Canadian Charter of Rights and Freedoms*, to what extent will students be given the same protections that apply to other citizens?

How teaching occurs is affected by policies on timetabling, teacher workloads, class sizes, assignment of students to classes, availability of supplementary materials and equipment, access to field trips, and so on. How easy is it for teachers to undertake innovative teaching activities? Is co-operative learning to be supported? Are field trips seen as an important part of the program?

How schools operate is affected by policies that deal with the provision of spaces for classrooms, libraries, gymnasia, labs, music rooms, and other areas. Will all elementary schools have libraries? Where will vocational facilities be placed? Will older inner-city schools have the same facilities as new suburban schools?

Where teaching occurs is affected by provincial policies on construction of new schools, and by district policies on how programs and resources are to be divided among schools. For example, will small schools remain open? Will high-school students be placed in different courses ("tracked") by their achievement and ability? Will language programs be housed in specialized schools?

The Influence of Politics and Power

Important policy decisions, whether they occur in education or in other fields, are made through political processes. Although there are many definitions of the term **politics**, one of the most frequently cited is that politics determines "who gets what" (Laswell, 1950). In other words, politics is the process within a society (or an organization within a society) through which people determine how to distribute power, wealth, opportunity, status, and other social goods. Education politics concerns the determination of what will be taught, where, by whom, how, to whom, and under what circumstances.

Politics also involves questions of choice, although opinions about what choices are to be made will often differ. This means that politics is centrally affected by questions of power. Since not everyone can have what they want, the question is, who does get what they want and who does not? Political philosopher Glenn Tinder describes a political system as "a set of arrangements by which some people dominate others" (1991, p. 162). In Canada the rhetoric is that everyone is equal, but political influence in our country is highly unequal, and those who have the least wealth and status tend also to have the least influence on political decision making.

Every education policy decision can be seen as being, in some sense, a political decision. However, this does not mean that every educational issue will be the subject of intense public discussion and political lobbying. Indeed, most policy decisions in education are made with little or no public attention. Ministries of education, school boards, schools, and teachers are constantly making policy decisions without public outcry or concern. Sometimes these decisions are controversial within the organization itself—the department of education, the school district, or the school—and sometimes not. But even if they are not controversial, education policy decisions, because they involve questions of public choice and concern, are essentially political in nature (Manzer, 1994).

Many people tend to think of politics as the formal process of elections, political parties, and the actions of governments — the things we see on the national news or read about in the newspaper. This is an important part of education politics. But as was pointed out in Chapter Two, each level of the system has particular responsibilities and can make policy decisions within these responsibilities. There is a great deal of political activity at the federal and provincial level, as well as in school districts, not only by the elected bodies themselves but also by all of those trying to influence the direction of policy. Some of the most basic policies are cast into provincial legislation, giving them legal force and making them difficult to change. For example, compulsory school attendance is a policy that has been made into law in all Canadian provinces. Additionally, provincial Cabinets and ministers of education may issue policy statements that are supported by varying degrees of legal force. The creation of provincial examinations would be an instance of such a policy, but there are many others also. School boards may pass motions setting out various policies within their areas of jurisdiction, such as deciding which programs will be offered in which schools or what forms of reporting to parents will be used.

Politics as defined in this book includes these activities, but also extends to the actions and attitudes of every member of society. Every time an individual or group tries either to change or maintain the existing order, politics is involved; this process is part of the fabric of democracy. A school principal or staff member makes policy decisions in areas such as student discipline, teaching methods, or student evaluation. Individual teachers make many decisions about the nature of their teaching, such as how students should behave, what sort of instruction will be provided, what kinds of assignments will be given, and how certain kinds of situations will be handled. All of these can be seen as policy decisions in that they shape the actions of people in schools, even though they may apply to only a few students, or may be made informally by individual teachers.

Feminist political theorists have shown that personal matters can also be seen as political (Acker, 1994; Blackmore & Kenway, 1993; Reynolds & Young, 1995). For example, a female teacher's choice of whether or not to become a parent is affected by — and affects — public policies concerning maternity leave, working conditions, day care, relative wage levels of men and women, and so on. Politics, broadly conceived, may be defined as the way each of us, whether individually or working with others, tries to make the kind of school, community, or society that we want to have. Thus, political processes occur continuously in groups and organizations at all levels. The actions of a group of parents in urging a new program in their school, or of a group of students protesting changes in extra-curricular programs, or of a First Nation taking over the administration of its own schools are all political actions in the realm of education.

Central Dilemmas in Canadian Education

Several ongoing tensions or dilemmas characterize Canadian education politics.

Centralization versus decentralization has to do with where authority over educational decisions will be located. Will it be at the local level — the school or school district — or will provincial governments or even the federal government take on a greater degree of control? This general issue shows up in a great number of decisions about schools. Should curricula be set locally or provincially? Should students be evaluated within the school or through provincial examinations? Should schools be able to hire whomever they want as teachers, or must all teachers meet certain provincial requirements?

Professional authority versus lay authority deals with the amount of control over schooling exercised by teachers and administrators as opposed to parents and community members. Examples of this tension include debates over the degree of freedom teachers should have to control their own subject matter and teaching style, over whether hiring decisions should be made by school boards or by superintendents and principals, over whether parents should have a role in evaluating school programs, and so on.

The tensions between *uniformity and diversity* concern whether the school system will be standard in its operation across communities, regions, and even provinces, or whether schools will vary across settings because the Canadian population is so diverse. Historically, *language and religion* have been particularly prominent aspects of the struggle over diversity. Some of the most vociferous debates in Canadian education continue to revolve around the issue of how and to what degree we are prepared to accommodate different linguistic and religious views. The varying arrangements across Canada in regard to minority religions and languages show how differently these questions have been answered depending on circumstances. And now Canadians face new issues concerning diversity. Do we provide separate Aboriginal schools in our cities? Do we teach non-English-speaking primary students in their mother tongue? Do we produce textbooks and teaching materials in languages such as Italian, German, and Ukrainian as well as French, English, Inuktitut, and Cree? What does it mean to provide equal opportunities in schools for girls and women in areas such as science and technology? How do we safeguard the rights of minorities while seeking to maintain a common education?

The above tensions run through many aspects of educational policy-making and politics, as will be illustrated in the remainder of this chapter.

Elements of Political Analysis

Within the broad sphere of political activity in education, there are many differences in how particular issues are handled. Some are the subject of legislation, others of informal bargaining. Some are written down for all to see, while others are dealt with through implicit bargains. Some issues come to a clear resolution, others linger on indefinitely. In all cases, we can achieve a better understanding of any particular political issue by considering the following five general aspects:

1. What is the issue and how is it being defined? (*Issues*)
2. Who is involved in making the decision? (*Actors*)
3. Through what decision-making process will a decision be made? (*Processes*)
4. What factors might influence the decision? (*Influences*)
5. What are the outcomes of a political process? (*Results*)

Although we will consider each of these aspects separately, it is important to realize that all five operate simultaneously and are intimately connected with one another.

What Is the Issue?

Because politics centres on conflict, a policy or political issue will be seen differently by different people. Political debate has as much to do with determining what the exact question is as it does with providing an answer. Consider the decision by a provincial government to introduce provincial testing. This decision might be seen by various groups of people as: (1) an issue of maintaining standards of achievement; (2) a way of controlling teachers; (3) an unwelcome distraction from attempts to meet the varying needs of students; (4) a waste of money or a public-relations ploy.

A school board's decision to recruit more female administrators could be seen by some as a long-overdue attempt to redress biases in our hiring practices, and by others as an inappropriate challenge to the merit principle in hiring. Offering heritage language courses might be seen by some as building the multicultural ideal in Canada, and by others as detracting from Canadian unity. A decision in a high school to "get tough on absenteeism" could be regarded as a way of improving standards, or as a way of pushing difficult students into leaving the school.

Understandings of policy issues also are not fixed. Our sense of any given issue is likely to change over time as events unfold and as we learn more about a particular matter. Sometimes these shifts take place over a relatively short time. A school board wishing to close a school may begin by seeing the issue as one of saving money. By listening to others and thinking about it themselves, they may come to see that the issue for parents is one of preserving a community and of maintaining a certain quality of education. Keeping a school open may be seen as a matter of equity by some. The board might then shift its own definition of the issue away from financial matters to a broader concern with educational questions. Sometimes the shifts are much slower, as we saw in the slow but dramatic shift of ideas and policies toward support for integrating physically disabled students into the schools. Indeed, when we examine the historical record and see how sure people were about the rightness of policies we now see as completely misguided, we should be less sanguine about our current practices and keep in mind that years from now these, too, may well be seen as erroneous and unproductive. At the same time, we do not have the benefit of hindsight, and at any given moment people must act on the best information and judgement available, no matter how imperfect it might be.

The Struggle to Define Issues

Politics necessarily involves disagreement and debate. Many people are uncomfortable about conflict, especially when it involves education and our strongly held belief that we should "do what is best for the children." But there is disagreement about what is best for the children. When important public issues such as education are at stake, there are likely to be strong differences of opinion about what should be done, especially in a country as heterogeneous as Canada. Indeed, if there were no differences of opinion, there would be no issue in the first place. The danger is that when opinions vary, those who have the power will simply impose their will. Democratic practice requires something more than this, since it is based on the idea of consent of the governed. The ideal is to have political decisions made through a process of open and fair public debate. However, this is much easier said than done.

In many cases, people have neither the time nor the interest to develop an in-depth understanding of a given policy issue. There are simply too many issues to consider for one to become an expert, even if one really wanted to. To understand most issues, the majority of people rely on information that comes to them through their own experience, through their contacts with other people, and, in the case of larger-scale issues, through the media. An important question about any policy issue, then, is who is framing the agenda and shaping the way in which people think about the issue. During any political debate, the various parties are making efforts to change how people think about the issues in order to build support for their particular point of view. Political debate is largely an attempt to persuade people to see issues in a particular way.

Evidence and Argument

Two important vehicles for persuading people are **evidence** and **argument**. Although the two are distinct, they are also very much intertwined. Political decisions cannot simply be determined through an appeal to facts, but neither should they be reduced to questions of who has how much power; rather, a combination of evidence, argument, reason, and persuasion are all essential to the political process.

In part, policy decisions about education are matters of evidence. We seek to know which course of action is most likely to allow us to attain our objectives. Research may play an important role in shaping policy because it provides evidence about the results of various policies. Our experiences also provide evidence and shape our thinking about what policies are most desirable. For example, there is generally less use of punishment, and particularly physical punishment, in schools than there used to be. This is partly because both research and the experience of teachers indicated that punishment was not very effective in fostering appropriate behaviour by students. Instead, studies showed that positive reinforcement was often a much more successful technique of behaviour management. As teachers began to see that their experience corroborated the research, their behaviour gradually changed.

Research has had a checkered influence on education, in Canada and elsewhere. In general education, policies and practices appear to rest more on history and intuition than on a foundation of empirical research (Gaskell, 1988; Cousins & Leithwood, 1993). Many educators see research as largely irrelevant to their everyday work. Researchers may put little emphasis on communicating their work to those in the school system, preferring to write for academic colleagues. And the entire education research enterprise in Canada is very small, with neither the federal nor the provincial governments providing much funding for research in education. It has been quite common for provincial or school district policy documents to be issued without any reference to relevant research. Compare this with health care, where the importance of high-quality research is widely recognized and funded.

But evidence is not necessarily a neutral matter that concerns the discovery of some objective truth. Ideological predispositions may also shape what we see and accept as being relevant evidence. Normally, the parties to a political debate will try to produce various kinds of evidence supporting their views (see Box 3.1). A minister who favours provincial examinations might provide data showing that achievement levels in universities are not increasing, or data from opinion polls showing that many people favour such exams. Teachers opposing the policy would then bring forward evidence showing that greater emphasis on testing changes instruction by obliging it to focus more on the narrow set of issues to be tested.

Evidence both shapes and is shaped by our ideas and opinions. Many policy issues go beyond what can be decided by the research findings or the lessons of experience. This is because policy matters usually involve questions of **values**. They cannot normally be determined through evidence alone, although evidence can play an important role. There are matters about which there may well be disagreement and debate. To return to the example about physical punishment, over the last few decades there has been an increasing conviction that hitting children is not an acceptable practice. While this shift in attitude may have been influenced by research, it also goes beyond the findings of research to reflect changing social values regarding the treatment of children.

Box 3.1
Learning Well ... Living Well

In 1991, the Government of Canada released a document, entitled *Learning Well ... Living Well*, that expresses an ideological view of the challenges facing education in Canada. The rhetoric in the report shows how the government uses both argument and evidence to support its view of education. Other possible versions of the issue are simply ignored.

Most importantly, the report places its whole emphasis on the link between learning, jobs, and international competitiveness. "If Canada is to remain internationally competitive, we must somehow develop a new learning culture. ... More and better learning means more and better jobs. ... " In defining what it calls "sources of the learning challenge," the report lists four factors, three of which are economic. The next section is entitled "Learning: The Key to Prosperity, Competitiveness, Good Jobs and Quality of Life." Note that quality of life is fourth on the list, not first. Moreover, the emphasis on competitiveness is tied to an emphasis on external standards and measurement. In a section called "What the System Needs," the report lists the first requirements as "standards and measures of performance" for each course and institution.

To bolster its argument, the report uses a variety of devices. There are many quotations from prominent individuals and organizations that support various points made in the report. However, almost all the people or organizations quoted are from the economic sector; one hears from business leaders and labour organizations, but not

(continued)

(continued)

from soup-kitchen workers or the unemployed. The report also contains many snippets of data that have been divorced from their context in order to support its argument. For example, one table shows changes in educational requirements for anticipated new jobs from 1986 to 2000, but it fails to explain what is meant by a "new job" (a definition that is immediately problematic, if one thinks about it). The report notes that about 30 percent of Canadian students "drop out before finishing high school" without mentioning that many of these students are victims of poverty or discrimination.

The report also is careful to avoid any suggestion that the federal government should provide more financial support for education. It notes in several places that the federal contribution is already large, and that Canada is a comparatively high spender on education, implying that more effort is needed rather than more money.

Absent from the discussion are basic human considerations — the frustration and despair of students who see no future for themselves in our schools or our labour market. Also absent is more than passing reference to equity issues. There is no mention of the divisions created in a society where some have so much and others so little (Greene, 1990). There is no mention of the link between social class and educational attainment, even though this connection is firmly established in Canadian research (Radwanski, 1987). There is almost nothing to suggest that education could or should be pursued for any reason other than getting a better job and earning more money; no acknowledgement that learning can be intrinsically worthwhile and contribute to a satisfying life whether or not it contributes to international competitiveness.

Thus, whatever one's opinion of its conclusions, *Learning Well ... Living Well* is a good example of how evidence and argument are marshalled to support a position that is essentially ideological.

Argument, on the other hand, has to do with giving people reasons for believing something. Reasons may or may not rest on evidence. Arguments often rest on moral claims about what is worthwhile or important or right. For example, an argument about the importance of strengthening competitiveness in our schools is really an appeal to see the world in a particular way, and therefore to take certain kinds of actions. Given this overall view, it may be argued that rigorous monitoring of student attendance shapes the kinds of attitudes necessary to succeed in the work force. Argument, then, is more ideological in its origins, since it is based on a view of what constitutes a desirable world; but argument and evidence are closely linked in that beliefs affect our view of evidence, and evidence, in turn, may alter our beliefs.

People also use argument to clarify their own beliefs about an issue. We may learn more about what we really think as we try to advance arguments for our view that will convince others as well as ourselves. The requirement to convince others means that arguments cannot appeal only to selfish motivations, but must also be couched in terms of the public good (e.g., fairness or justice). Actions are not seen as legitimate unless they can be defended in these terms.

Emotion often plays an important role in policy debates, especially when an issue speaks to deeply held beliefs or interests, such as the welfare of our children. There may be angry meetings, protests, and even violence. Conflict can be frightening because it tests the bonds of our society and our willingness to live with one another. When carried too far, conflict can produce terrible results. But conflict can also play a creative role in society. If people feel they have a real say in the society in which they live, they may be more willing to accept that others must also have a say and that compromises must be made. Out of disputes about ideas can come better ideas. Out of disagreement can come constructive compromise. There can be no democracy without the willingness to tolerate political conflict. Indeed, Tinder (1991) suggests that "[t]olerance must extend far enough to be dangerous. Otherwise it is a mere formality, a courtesy I extend to those who think and act on the whole as I do, and not a policy that accepts important disagreements and differences" (p. 180).

In short, there is no one set of rules or rational procedures that can be applied to determine all political choices. These must simply be worked out through various political means. There are, however, criteria that can be applied to determine whether the process of political debate is fair. Judgements can be made both about the evidence being presented and the arguments being advanced. Is information about the issue widely available, or is it hidden from view? Does evidence come from reliable sources? Are all the available data being presented, rather than just those that support a particular point of view? Are divergent opinions all given a reasonable hearing, or do some parties control the debate? Do the various parties have a reasonable ability to make their views known? Is the debate cast in terms that invite reflection on the various positions, and dialogue among them, or is it cast in emotional terms that detract from thoughtful discussion? In applying these questions, we can make a decision as to whether we are promoting a political debate that meets the test of democratic values.

Who Will Be Involved?

How an issue is defined is related to who is providing the definition. Because education is important to the well-being of our entire society, everyone has some stake in what our schools do and how they do it. This means that education policy is important not only to governments, students, and teachers but also to parents and society as a whole. The politics of Canadian education involves a large number of different actors. Some, like departments of education, play roles that are quite well defined, while others, such as parent groups or business lobbies, have more diffuse roles. These various groups are often referred to as **stakeholders**, meaning that they have a stake or interest in the enterprise of schooling.

Who Participates?

Let us begin with the formal players. In Chapter Two, we examined the basic structure underlying the provision of public education in Canada. All three levels of government — federal, provincial, and local — are involved in education. Each level has particular powers and responsibilities. However, there are often conflicts between the levels of government over particular issues, as we shall see shortly. Beyond governments, an enormous variety of groups play an active role in educational politics and policy. Some of these groups are involved more or less constantly, while others may be involved only in particular issues.

One set of groups represents the key participants in the educational system, often referred to as **internal stakeholders**. In each province, there are associations of teachers, school trustees, and school administrators (usually different associations for school principals and for school district superintendents). Sometimes there may be several distinct associations for these groups, as in Ontario where elementary- and secondary-school teachers have their own associations (see Chapter Eight). These groups have had a very influential role in setting education policies. Support staff — secretaries, bus drivers, maintenance and caretaking personnel — are unionized in many parts of the country. Their unions may also play an active role, but in most provinces the associations of teachers, trustees, and administrators have been predominant.

In the past, ministries of education usually discussed important policy changes in advance with these latter groups before changes were implemented, leading to a highly consultative policy process (Manzer, 1994). In recent years, however, this has been changing. As education has attracted growing political attention, provincial governments have been making important policy decisions with much less advance consultation with internal stakeholders. Sometimes public consultation processes such as commissions or white papers have been used instead. Educational groups have been unhappy about their decreased influence, and the political process has become more conflictual.

The role of parent and community groups has also changed. Not long ago parents had a voice only when they organized themselves and demanded to be heard; school boards were seen to represent the public on most issues. However, in the last few years all provinces have institutionalized school committees that include parents, and sometimes nonparent community members. Initial evidence (Menzies, 1996) is that these bodies do not yet exercise very much influence, but their creation does mark a recognition of the political role of these players.

In recent years, as political conflict over education policy has sharpened in many areas, a number of permanent lobby groups have been formed to represent parents on key issues. For example, Canadian Parents for French, an organization committed to the strengthening of French immersion programs, has had a strong impact on these issues in many provinces. The Association for Children with Learning Disabilities has played an important role in the development of policy in special education, and is an important and powerful lobby group in many areas. Many other similar groups exist across the country.

Rarely given an explicit role in education politics or policy are the students themselves. Since students are commonly cited by all the parties as the prime beneficiaries of schools, and the reason we have schools, it seems odd that they have typically had no formal role in making decisions about various aspects of schooling. In Chapter Four, consideration is given to the legal status of student governments in schools. Considered from a political point of view, however, students have very little power. They lack organization, knowledge, wealth, and connections. As a result and despite the rhetoric, they can be — and often are — ignored when important decisions about their futures are being made. Where student involvement does exist, it is typically of a token nature, with little or no real influence on subsequent decisions.

There are many other groups whose main focus is not on the educational system, but who may have an interest in particular educational issues. Business organizations, labour unions, and various community groups are **external stakeholders** who may become involved in particular education policy issues. Business groups, such as the Conference Board, have been especially influential, and tend to stress good work habits such as punctuality, or skills such as entrepreneurship. Peace organizations may lobby for the inclusion of curriculum material on peace. Child welfare organizations may want the schools to place more stress on educating children about violence and its prevention. Taxpayer groups may organize to press school boards to spend less money and thus avoid increases in local property taxes. Because education affects everyone in the society, every organized group can potentially have an interest in educational issues. Many educators feel that such lobby groups are much more powerful than they used to be.

The media also play an important role in many debates about educational issues because they have such a powerful influence on how people see issues. The media are often criticized for focussing primarily on the negative and giving precedence to stories that are critical of schools. The coverage of education tends to be episodic, and issues are rarely given in-depth treatment. At the same time, most Canadian adults do not have children in the schools, and so may rely heavily on television and press reports as they form their opinions about education policy issues, just as people do for many other areas of public life. School systems are only beginning to think about how to adjust to the powerful role of mass media in shaping education politics.

Who Should Participate?

An ongoing question in politics is who should be allowed to participate in the decision-making process. In the case of the educational system, many people will have an interest in formulating policy decisions. For example, teachers and students are almost always affected directly by policy decisions, but so too may parents, other school staff, and all sorts of individuals and organizations. Many people tend to think that everyone affected by a decision should have a right to participate in making the decision, but that view raises important questions. For one thing, what does it mean to participate in making a decision? Have we participated if we have expressed our point of view, even if it carried no weight in the decision? Is it participation to appear before a school board and to make a presentation that is ignored in the board's decision making? Or have we participated only if we are satisfied with the outcome? One point of view, discussed in Chapter Two, is that we have all participated simply by electing a school board or provincial government. Once elected, a governing body may, but need not, consult us again about each particular decision. After all, being elected is what lends a governing body the authority and legitimacy to make decisions at all. But others would argue that democratic societies rely on consensus when deciding policies, and that consensus can be achieved only if everyone who so wishes can play an active role in the decision-making process, even though this may make the process slower and create additional conflict.

Participation has been seen as a positive value for different reasons. One argument has to do with **effectiveness**. Some believe that people will be more accepting of a decision, and more willing to abide by it, if they have had a chance to participate in making it. This view is often expressed in regard to various educational innovations, where the belief is that teachers are more likely to implement changes if they have had a say in shaping those changes. The effectiveness argument will be true in some cases, but not in others, depending on how important the issue is and how strongly people feel about it. The stronger people's views are about an issue, the less likely it is that participation alone will build commitment to the decision. So, while teachers may be willing to agree to support an attendance policy because it has been arrived at through staff discussion, they would not likely agree to have their own jobs eliminated simply because that decision had been made after discussion by all.

The second main argument for participation is a **moral** one. People have a right to participate in important decisions affecting them, regardless of whether their participation makes the process more effective, or leads to a better decision, or results in consensus. This belief is the foundation of the idea of democratic government. In regard to schools, however, it is not clear who has this right to participate. Much of the literature stresses teachers' participation in decisions. But what about students? After all, they are deeply affected by almost every educational policy, yet often have no voice at all (Levin, 1994a). What about parents, who rarely play an active role in shaping school policies? And what about the community generally? If schools are important to everyone, then perhaps everyone should participate in formulating educational policy. But is such an idea at all practical? Moreover, not everyone wants to participate in every decision. Teachers, for instance, may be content to leave many decisions to school administrators, reserving their own time and energy for the decisions they feel are truly important.

How Does Participation Occur?

Much of our political process is oriented toward groups. Voting, of course, is done by individuals. And individuals can make a difference in the political process through their courage and leadership. But political decisions are made and influenced by groups of people and organized around particular interests, whether broad (a group wishing to improve the public image of education) or narrow (a group wanting a different principal in the local school). It is school boards or provincial Cabinets as collective bodies that struggle with budget and policy issues; it is groups of people who organize to lobby for or against particular policy proposals. Indeed, when people are motivated to act politically, they look for group support almost instinctively. The parent who is unhappy with the school and the teacher who feels aggrieved by an administrative decision will both look for support from others, whether neighbours, colleagues, a parents' assocation, or the teachers' organization.

Despite the development of more open political processes over the last 100 years, the ability to participate politically, like so much else in our society, is not distributed equally. People with more money and more connections will have more political influence. Well-financed groups, which can afford to hire skilled staff and mail out professional-looking newsletters, will often be more influential than neighbourhood groups that rely on volunteers working in the evenings. Groups that understand the political process, have easy access to decision-makers, and know the jargon may exercise influence disproportionate to their numbers. This influence extends to defining the issues, as discussed earlier, as well as to affecting a particular policy choice.

In the case of education, the policy process is often dominated by the established groups — governments and stakeholder organizations. They are already organized, and tend to have staff and money. The people know and are used to dealing with one another. They are already present in many of the decision-making forums. This fact tends to push the policy process in particular directions. Each group normally acts to protect the welfare of its own members. If the key decisions are being made by people who are already part of the system and benefiting from it, there might well be less likelihood of significant change. Those most in need of the political process to advance their interests — children, poor people, recent immigrants — are often least able to mobilize themselves to take advantage of it. Aboriginal people have often been excluded from political participation. So were women: being denied the vote, being unable to own property in their own name, and being economically dependent on men made it very difficult for women to establish a voice in educational governance.

The lack of participation of some groups, however, does not necessarily occur through such overt processes. After all, every adult citizen in Canada is now entitled to participate in political processes. But people are still excluded through factors such as process and language. For example, appearing before a school board requires some familiarity with what a school board is and does. It may require the ability to write a brief and present oneself as a fellow professional. It may require familiarity with current legislation and regulations. Being able to associate a particular grievance with an issue that is of genuine public concern is an important ability. These skills are far more likely to be found among people who are well educated and well connected to the political process.

Political processes can also be designed to be inhibiting. For example, many school boards will allow delegations to appear and ask questions, but will make no comments and will reserve their own discussion of the issue to a later, private portion of the meeting. The delegations thus appear as suppliants requesting a favour rather than as equals expressing a point of view. A delegation has no chance to learn what the board may think of its views, and why. The same is largely true of briefs submitted to various provincial commissions. When a commission receives 1000 or more submissions, how much impact will one more or one less have? How would one know? Why bother?

Language is another effective barrier to participation. Education, like other fields, has developed its own terminology, its own jargon. Those unfamiliar with "word attack skills," "powers of school boards under the *Schools Act*," "most appropriate placement in the least restrictive environment," and the many other specialized terms in education have difficulty participating in discussions. Professionals may use jargon, whether consciously or not, as a way of showing their own skill and, effectively, diminishing the contribution of others.

At the same time, it is important to realize that even relatively uninfluential groups can, with the right resources and assistance, mobilize and have an impact on educational decisions. Accordingly, one test of a participative process is to ask how much weight the least powerful carry in the process. If their voices are not heard, we have reason to wonder if the process is as democratic as we might want. We might also want to consider what measures could be taken to make our political processes more open, and to enhance the participation of the least powerful.

Box 3.2
Participation: Royal Commissions in British Columbia and Ontario

One of the vehicles governments use to help form public policy is the royal commission. Royal commissions usually include extensive processes of public consultation so as to gather as broad a range of views as possible. A look at who participates in these processes is instructive in understanding how people do or do not participate in political events.

In 1987, the Government of British Columbia set up a royal commission to provide recommendations on the basic direction the province's education system should take. Chaired by lawyer Barry Sullivan, the commission held 66 public hearings and 54 meetings with teachers, and participated in 23 student assemblies. The report of the commission, issued in 1988, listed the 2 350 groups and

(continued)

(continued)

individuals who had appeared at the hearings or submitted written briefs. An analysis of these lists shows that about 60 percent were individuals and 40 percent were organizations. The great majority of the organizations were affiliated with schools — school boards, teachers' groups, and parents' groups.

The report notes that the commission "also met, and received briefs from, representatives of government agencies and major provincial organizations with special interest and expertise in the field of education" (p. 6). The latter included groups representing superintendents, principals and vice-principals, secretary-treasurers, school trustees, teachers, independent schools, and university faculties of education.

The Ontario Royal Commission on Learning conducted an even more extensive consultation process. It held more than 40 sets of public hearings, visited 36 schools, and received 1400 oral presentations, 1500 written briefs, 350 telephone call comments, and 1500 e-mail comments. It also organized a series of outreach meetings in malls, detention centres, and social service agencies. An analysis of the lists of submissions indicates that about half were from organized groups and half from individuals. A wide variety of groups were involved, although the large majority of group submissions were from educational organizations — school boards, administrators, teachers, and parent councils.

Both commissions also commissioned research to support their work, largely from university professors.

It is no surprise to learn that even the most open consultative process will tend to be dominated by those with the strongest stake in the system, and also by those with the skills, time, and other resources to take advantage of opportunities for participation. Although both commissions made considerable efforts to hear from all interested parties, some groups had much more input than others.

Sources: Based on B. Sullivan. (1988). *A legacy for learners: Report of the royal commission on education.* Vancouver: Province of British Columbia; Ontario. (1994). *For the love of learning: Report of the royal commission on learning.* Toronto: Publications Ontario. Reproduced with permission.

What Is the Decision-Making Process?

For most political issues, there is no straightforward, predefined decision-making process. Politics is essentially related to questions of who has, and is willing to use, power. For any given issue, this is not known at the beginning. For one thing, power is itself an elusive matter. It is not something that can be stored or counted, but rather a function of relationships among people and organizations — which can change rapidly and unexpectedly. When a long-standing government, with a powerful state bureaucracy behind it, suddenly collapses in a matter of days (as has happened in many countries in recent years), it is clear that official power does not always bring real power.

The ability to exercise power depends on the particulars of an issue. Sometimes what seem to be relatively simple and straightforward decisions can become highly contentious. For example, a provincial government has the power to prescribe curricula for schools. Usually this occurs without any public furor. But in some cases, such as family life education or streaming in secondary schools, these decisions can become intensely political, and the official power of the province will be used cautiously, if at all. In other cases, issues that looked contentious may turn out to be reasonably simple to resolve.

The shape that any particular political process will take is thus unpredictable. Things have a habit of turning out quite differently than we might expect. Depending on circumstances, it is often necessary to make changes to the process, to redefine the issue, or even to start all over again part way through the process. Dror (1986) refers to this as "fuzzy gambling" — a very serious game in which not only the odds but also the rules change as the game proceeds, and where surprises often occur.

Policy decisions are made formally through governing bodies, such as legislatures or school boards that pass laws or motions, or through administrators who issue directives. Often, however, the important part of the process occurs well before the formal decision is taken. Much of the debate about a proposed piece of legislation will occur within the Cabinet and government bureaucracy before the bill ever gets to the legislature. Similarly, a school board may do much of its hard bargaining over issues outside of the formal board meeting, in discussions among trustees. A politician or an administrator may talk with many other people before finalizing a decision officially. The meeting described in the prologue to this chapter is an illustration of the difference between a formal decision — to be made, in that case, by the school board — and the real decision process. Lengthy participation processes and internal debates mean that decision processes can sometimes take a very long time — years in many instances — even though the formal decision at the end may occur in a matter of minutes or even seconds. Although it is the responsibility of the minister of education to approve new curricula, when these documents reach his or her desk a committee of teachers has probably already been at work for several years on the new curriculum, including its pilot testing in schools. Unless there are very serious concerns, formal approval is usually just that—a formality.

Of course, decisions can be controversial at different levels, meaning that there are different sorts of political processes. In addition to the politics of elections and protests, there are the bureaucratic politics that take place within an organization. There can be quite a bit of politicking within a school board or school over a decision in which the general public is not particularly interested. For example, a decision about workload distribution among a school staff can lead to a great deal of discussion, lobbying, and unhappiness among teachers without attracting much attention from parents. Similarly, decisions about which new curriculum is next to be developed by the department of education may be controversial among teachers but not the public.

Courts also play a role in shaping political decisions. Courts may require political bodies to take action by deciding that some current state of affairs is inappropriate (for example, rules governing the privacy of students' files) or by finding an existing law to be invalid and therefore in need of amendment or abolition (for example, rulings regarding the governance of official minority language schooling). The role of courts is discussed more fully in the next chapter.

Provincial Governments and School Districts

Some elements of the decision-making process in provincial governments have already been discussed in Chapter Two. In most provinces, the main responsibility for decision making lies with the Cabinet and its committees. These groups receive advice from civil servants and from political sources such as ministerial advisers, committees of the political party, backbench members of the governing party, and a wide variety of people and groups who may have access to the premier, the Cabinet, or the minister of education.

Provincial governments also use a variety of other mechanisms to deal with educational policy issues. These may include delegating particular functions to boards or commissions, creating advisory boards, sponsoring commissions of inquiry of various kinds, or undertaking studies of issues. When a government is not sure how to proceed with an issue, for example, it may create a commission to study the matter in more depth and make recommendations; in recent years, many provinces have established commissions on education. Some issues that have the potential to be contentious are delegated, either in legislation or through Cabinet order, to a separate board or agency. For instance, questions of teacher certification may be handled by a board composed of representatives of the teachers' organization, the provincial government, the school districts, and other interest groups. This group considers various issues relating to certification and makes recommendations to the minister. Similarly, appeals from property owners to have their property transferred from one school district to another are often heard by bodies created by—but with some independence from—the provincial government.

School districts are created through provincial legislation. The relationship between provincial governments and school districts can be highly political in that each party often would like the other to do something differently. There are political pressures exerted by provincial governments on school boards, and by school boards on provinces. Because it is school districts that actually deliver educational services, the provincial government must achieve most of its policy purposes through the districts. Implementation of a new program, a shift in the handling of special education, more emphasis on learning about AIDS, increased physical fitness—implementation of all of these depends on the active co-operation of schools and school districts.

Although provinces have the power to compel school districts to carry out provincial policies, they were for many years generally reluctant to use this power. School boards have been known to criticize provincial governments quite severely, causing political embarrassment, and in some cases school boards may be closer to the feelings of their constituents. More recently, provinces have been moving to change the role of school boards and school districts. In some cases, provinces have assumed functions that were previously given to school boards, including more direction on curriculum and more provincial assessment of students' progress. In 1994, the Alberta government initiated a plan to have superintendents appointed by the province instead of by school boards, but later withdrew this proposal because of intense opposition from boards.

Many provinces have acted to reduce the number of school boards, ostensibly to save money. New Brunswick has moved to having only two school districts — one English and one French — while Newfoundland, Ontario, Nova Scotia, and Alberta are among other provinces that have reduced substantially the number of school boards. Whether fewer but larger boards will have more political influence remains to be seen.

Provinces have several means — varying in their degrees of coerciveness — with which to influence what school boards do. First, a province can pass **legislation** requiring boards to implement a particular program. For example, many provinces have required school boards to implement some form of parent council, and there has been provincial legislation on reporting achievement results that has required schools to adopt new procedures and to deal with new issues. Second, a province can issue **regulations** under existing legislation. For example, the minister of education can issue a regulation limiting the number of professional-development days schools can have. Third, a province can issue a **policy statement**, which, though not binding in law, does put considerable pressure on school districts to comply. For example, a province can issue a statement outlining what it believes school districts ought to do to evaluate teachers, or the steps to be taken in reporting achievement to parents. A school district would need to mount a convincing case to support taking any other direction.

Fourth, a province can provide **direct service** in a high-priority area, by-passing the school boards by setting up its own programs. This option is not often used now by provincial departments of education, although the provision of correspondence courses is still a provincial responsibility. At one time, most schools for deaf or blind students were run directly by provinces, but many have now been turned over to school districts. Provinces do provide direct service in areas closely related to education, such as employment training.

Fifth, a province can provide **incentives** for boards to do something. For example, the ministry or department of education might provide grants to start new programs (as happened twenty years ago with special education), training to teachers in a particular area (such as computers), or materials (such as videotapes on health), free or at low cost, all as a way of inducing school districts to do something the province wishes them to do. Sixth and finally, a province can **mobilize opinion** as a way of putting pressure on school districts. A minister of education or the premier of a province can make speeches and public statements urging school boards to make their budgets public, or to have school advisory committees. If the idea catches on with the public, school boards will find themselves under pressure to respond, even though there is no official or legal requirement for them to do so.

School boards, on the other hand, also put political pressure on provinces. Their prime means for doing so is to blame various problems on the provincial government, which is, after all, the more senior government. The provincial government may provide less money than a school board wants, resulting in program changes or higher local taxes, which the board will then blame on inadequate provincial funding. The province may require school districts to implement various programs against the board's wishes; the board may then blame the resulting problems or concerns on the actions of the province. Thus, each party uses a variety of political devices to make it appear to be advancing the public interest.

Politics within School Districts

Although most of the legal authority for education rests with the provinces, much of the strongest debate occurs at the local level, within a school district. Typically in such cases there are two or more factions within the school or district that have very different policy goals. The prologue to this chapter offered one such example. Another good example is a school district caught between a group that wants to expand programs and another group that wants to reduce property taxes. The first group argues that schools face new problems and challenges that require increases in staff, training, and equipment, all of which cost money. The second group believes that schools are already too expensive and that taxes must be reduced by cutting programs or staffing. The former group may be made up mostly of parents of children in the schools, while the latter may consist primarily of people who do not currently have children in school. The school board can be caught in the middle of this debate, which may be very heated and involve stormy meetings, boycotts, threats, and highly polarized positions.

Another reason for political debate in a school district may have to do with the perceived fairness of resource allocation. People living in a particular area may feel that their local school is not being treated as well as another school in another part of the district. Boards can face conflict over which school will be renovated next, which school will get an additional teacher, or which school will be allowed to develop a new program. Conflicts within a school district are often mirrored by conflicts among the school trustees. In many school districts, school trustees are elected by ward. Each part of the district elects one or more trustees who together make up the board. Trustees may thus feel a strong allegiance to the interests of their particular ward when it comes to issues such as budget allocation or school closings. Even though the board must finally make a single, binding decision, the debate at the school board itself can then be very intense, and conflicts can be very difficult to resolve.

Such heated issues are not, however, the norm. For the most part, education proceeds with very little political debate. School board meetings tend to be uneventful, even dull to the outside observer. Conflict and debate, when it does occur, is frequently over relatively minor concerns. Major issues in schooling, such as grading, promotion practices, curricula, or equitable treatment of all students, are rarely the subject of public or political discussion. Indeed, given the importance of schooling, some commentators believe that there should be more public debate over pedagogical issues.

Advocating more public debate is one thing, but finding ways to create it is another. There are significant obstacles to doing so. The nature of the mass media, discussed earlier, is one problem. Moreover, there are many issues competing for public attention at any one time. Those whose main interest is health care, the environment, or economic policy also want more informed public debate. Do people have the time and energy to be involved in all of these?

There are, however, strategies schools could use to foster more discussion about important educational issues. Providing more information to parents and inviting their opinions is one method, while bringing information about schools to the attention of the broader public (e.g., through open houses, displays, or public forums) is another. More effort could also be made to keep print and electronic media reporters informed about educational issues.

Politics within the School

Individual schools are not exempt from political issues. Politics within the school are known as micropolitics (e.g., Blase, 1993; Ball, 1987; Malen, 1994). These issues can be internal or external. Internally, teachers may disagree with one another, or with the principal, as to which program areas are most important. Some staff may want stricter grading standards, while others may see grades as inherently unfair and educationally unsound. Staff may disagree on how best to teach reading, or on how much emphasis to give to art and music programs. Or there may simply be personality conflicts — people who do not like each other, or who feel that some colleagues are not doing their fair share of the work. A skilful administrator must be able to identify such conflicts and to work to resolve them in ways that respect everybody's interests yet also give primacy to educational goals and needs.

Pressure may also be placed on the school by a dissatisfied community. For example, school boards have been the objects of considerable lobbying by groups of parents who want special programs for gifted and talented students. Instead of reaching out to work with people to meet their needs, some schools will try to avoid responding by treating parents as ignorant, by using technical language that cloaks real meaning, or by stalling. For schools that display a genuine interest in the community's character and needs, the community can be an enormous source of strength and support, as will be seen in Chapter

Seven. But when schools lose touch with their communities, they can find themselves subject to very powerful pressures to change.

The Complexity of Political Decision Making

The term **decision-making process** is actually a rather simplistic and abstract way of describing how decisions are made. What appear to be simple decisions on the surface can have far-reaching consequences. The decision to consolidate rural schools has had major implications not just for schools, but for rural life in Canada. The decision to establish or maintain provincial examinations has reduced teachers' control over their classrooms in some important ways. The decision to move control of education on reserves to First Nations has had significant impact on those jurisdictions. More mundane decisions, such as reassigning a teacher or changing a dress code, can have major effects on individuals.

Many political issues are revisited again and again. Thus, rather than think of political decisions as final, it would be more accurate to think of them as temporary accommodations that may be changed again at a later date. We have already discussed several tensions that have been constants in Canadian education—the tension between the common public school system and the need to accommodate the diverse interests of a multicultural society; the tension between local control and centralized control of schools; and the tension between the role of professionals and the role of citizens in directing schools. Language and religion have been particularly important as major forces affecting education in Canada. These issues persist in education policy, manifesting themselves over and over again as particular decisions are made.

Some may view the unceasing debate as tiresome, wishing that the issue could be decided once and for all. It may make more sense to be glad that we live in a world in which we can learn from experience and remake our future to take advantage of what we have learned. The possibility of improvement — the chance to make things better — is always open to us. In the 1960s, hundreds of small Canadian schools were closed. Now, in most provinces, school closing decisions are made much more carefully and with a great deal of community participation. Fifty or 100 years ago, Aboriginal young people were taken away from their families and placed in residential schools, where they were forbidden to speak Native languages. Today, many more Aboriginal children go to school in their own communities, and there is a slowly increasing emphasis on teaching in Native languages.

We are not suggesting that things are getting better in every way. While some situations improve, other problems are as serious as ever and new problems are constantly arising to challenge us. But the debate about what we should do, together with the willingness to think and argue about what is best for education, is a vital part of trying to make the world a better place.

What Factors Influence Policy-Making?

The evidence is that most political decisions are influenced by many factors. We can identify four broad categories of influence on decisions: political, economic, ideological, and pragmatic.

Political influences concern who is in favour of, or opposed to, a particular position, without necessarily considering the merits of their position. Political considerations are always important and should be taken seriously. When making a decision, both elected officials and employed staff must weigh who is for or against it, and how intense the opposition may be. Provincial and federal governments may take opinion polls, or they may pay attention to letters and phone calls. A school board will assess its perception of the balance of opinion in its community. A school principal will think about how staff members feel about any given issue, and about how those with different opinions might be won over. The weighing of opinion before making a decision is a reasonable and universal political practice.

Box 3.3
Ongoing Themes: Accommodating of Immigrants and Languages

Canada has for a long time been substantially a nation of immigrants. Part of the reason for developing public schools in central Canada in the mid-nineteenth century had to do with the desire to ensure that the large numbers of German, Scottish, and Irish immigrants were socialized into the dominant values of the Canada of that day. There was no thought to accommodating or supporting the maintenance of immigrants' own cultures and languages. The same was true of the great waves of immigration around the turn of the last century, when hundreds of thousands of Ukrainians, Mennonites, Jews, Icelanders, Poles, and others came to Canada. The schools saw their task as being one of teaching these people "Canadian" ways, that is, teaching them to adjust to Canada as it existed when they arrived.

An inspector of schools in Saskatchewan wrote in 1918:

> The people of foreign countries who come to Canada after having reached maturity ... will never become "true Canadians" ... but there is an important duty to perform in seeing that the children of these newcomers are given every opportunity to receive proper training for intelligent citizenship. ... [The] public school ... is the great melting-pot into which must be placed these diverse racial groups, and from which will eventually emerge the pure gold of Canadian citizenship (Anderson, 1918, p. 8).

(continued)

(continued)

More recently, there has been an increasing, though by no means universal, tendency to allow greater diversity in the schools, to be more accepting of different ways of living that Canadians of different origins may have. Schools have begun to offer programs in the languages of immigrant communities. But these general statements disguise the controversies that persist. Heritage language programs are primarily offered outside of regular school hours. The Peel Board of Education in Ontario lost a court battle to prevent a Sikh student from wearing a *kirpan* (a ceremonial dagger) to school. There has been heated debate in many Canadian communities about the creation of French immersion schools, which has sometimes meant busing non-immersion students to schools outside their local area. Disputes about what, if any, religious exercises should be held in schools have been quite bitter in some provinces.

Some people criticize government bodies for making decisions based on their popularity. The use of public-opinion polls to shape government policy is one manifestation of this tendency. While polls can be used and policies can be endorsed cynically simply to favour what is popular, the issue is not so simple. After all, we elect governments to do what we favour; it is hardly logical, then, to dislike them for taking our views into account before making decisions! It is not evident that people would be more satisfied if decisions were made without regard to their views.

An alternative influence to the use of polls or other opinion measurements lies in the pressures brought to bear by various groups, as discussed earlier. This has its own problems, as the best-organized and loudest lobbies may be representative of quite small numbers of people. For example, polling has consistently shown that the great majority of Canadians favour the provision of sex education in schools, but lobbies against sex education have been effective enough to block programs for some years, and to alter their content in many parts of the country.

Policy decisions are also affected by **economic considerations**. Especially in the current scene of attempts to reduce the level of government spending, political choices will often be constrained by financial realities and by the possible effects of policy choices on the economy as a whole. (In Chapter Five, we will take up more fully the way in which the availability of money affects what choices are possible.) Much of the current debate in Canada about education policy, for example, is framed in terms of how education can contribute to economic growth, even though this is only one purpose of education.

Ideology plays a critical role in shaping politics and policy choices. By ideology we mean people's deep-seated beliefs about how the world is and how it ought to be—beliefs that are held at such a deep level that they are rarely called into question. Everyone has such beliefs, many of which were inculcated when we were young (partly through the schools, it might be added). Ideology is what shapes, in large part, the agenda of political parties and of individuals. If one begins with the belief that people will not work unless they are policed and compelled to do so, then one is inclined toward policies such as more testing of students or closer evaluation of teachers. If one believes that poverty is an underlying cause of educational problems, one will be inclined to support programs and activities that reduce or ameliorate some of the effects of poverty, such as school nutrition programs or preschool programs. The ideology of individuals and groups will have a critical effect on many policy decisions, chiefly by shaping the alternatives that are considered in the first place.

Ideology intersects with **pragmatic** considerations, however. What we *want* to do has to be matched with what we think *can* be done. Each of us takes for granted certain assumptions about what is possible, assumptions that also shape our political proposals. Whatever our ideological convictions, we don't propose what we believe to be impossible. An election commitment to eliminate winter storms in Canada would be popular if anyone believed it could be done, but because it isn't seen as possible it never gets on the agenda. To take a less fanciful example, a proposal to ensure that all students learn to read well in the primary grades, while widely seen as desirable, would probably also be seen as impossible, and hence would not likely command much political support. Goals have to be fitted against capacities in designing policies.

Outcomes of Policies

A policy is usually intended to achieve certain results. Each policy is guided by some underlying logic of cause and effect as to how the desired results can be obtained—if we do X then Y will follow, or if we want Y then we must first do or have X. If we require students to attend school, they are more likely to learn. If we place a curriculum unit on environmental protection in Grade 5, students will learn about this important subject. If we evaluate teachers regularly, they will be better teachers, which in turn will result in students learning more. These chains of reasoning, however, are not always explicit in the policy itself; they may have to be inferred.

If education was simply a matter of writing the right policies, it would be relatively easy. Unfortunately, the world is rarely as neat as logic would have it, and there are several slipping points between a policy statement and the anticipated results. For one thing, actions intended to have one effect may have quite another, or even several different ones, when put into practice. For example, if students are given grades as an incentive for them to learn more, the goal of getting good grades may become more important than the goal of learning. Every policy has such unanticipated consequences.

Moreover, making a policy statement is one thing—having the policy implemented is quite another. The fact that laws have penalties for breaking them shows that people do not always do what they are told. Every policy statement is violated sometimes, and some policies are hardly observed at all. In schools, we have learned that writing new curriculum documents will not by itself change what teachers teach or how they teach (see Chapter Nine). If a policy does not fit with what people believe, or how they are used to behaving, it is not likely to have the desired impact unless a major effort is made to help, cajole, or threaten people into changing their behaviour. Hence, policy statements, though important, do not by themselves guarantee particular results. The success of a policy depends on the people who have to put it into practice; in schools, this is most often teachers and students.

As an example, consider the case of the Ontario (1968) report *Living and Learning* (popularly called the Hall–Dennis report, after its co-chairs). The report called for massive changes in education, including moves toward team teaching, ungraded elementary schools, and more student choice. Over the years, the "progressive education" philosophy of the Hall–Dennis report has been roundly attacked as undermining the success of Canadian schools through excessive permissiveness. However, research on classrooms (discussed in Chapter Nine) suggests that most of the Hall–Dennis recommendations were never put into practice. Most schools continued to use traditional methods of grouping, teaching, and evaluating students. The rhetoric of reform was far more significant than the practice (Manzer, 1994).

How do we know what the outcomes of policies are? In a surprising number of cases, we don't. Many educational policies have continued for decades without any careful attempt to assess their consequences, whether planned or unintended. Schools continue to use certain kinds of instructional approaches (a large amount of talking by teachers and seatwork by students), organizational practices (division by age into grades or semestering secondary schools), and motivational practices (rewarding good behaviour with stickers, tokens, or prizes) without collecting very much evidence as to how well these practices work. In an enterprise such as education, which is committed officially to the pursuit of knowledge, it seems odd that there is so little reflecting on the results of our own actions. Research on education, which is one (though only one) way of learning about the impacts of policies, is a small and relatively uninfluential enterprise in Canada; very few current school practices can be justified on the basis of research findings.

Why should this be so? One reason is that policies are not simply, as was just suggested above, intended to achieve particular consequences. Most education policies have multiple purposes and try to serve multiple interests. In addition to having some impact on what happens in the schools, they may be intended as symbolic statements about what is seen as valuable, to make particular groups feel included in the process, or (as we will see with respect to laws in the next chapter) to be vague enough to allow a wide variety of responses at the local level. Of course, if a policy is primarily symbolic in intention, its purpose is achieved as soon as it is promulgated; what effects it might actually have is another matter entirely.

This may seem an unduly cynical position. It may suggest that politics is hopeless and venal, and that we should look for alternative ways of organizing ourselves. But it is much easier to criticize than to find a better alternative.

Conclusions: Politics and the Public Good

Unhappiness with politics is not hard to find. Many Canadians feel that our current processes are not serving their needs, that politicians are self-serving and interested only in their own re-election, and that somehow politics has become preoccupied with the wrong things, while the big issues facing our country are not being addressed (Plank & Boyd, 1994). Political processes can lead to conflict, bad decisions, and bad results. Any political process can be improved, and such improvements should be sought. But it is vitally important for each citizen to retain his or her faith that political processes, whatever their faults, are important and worth struggling over. Democracy rests on the belief that people by and large can and will make reasonable decisions about how a society should work. These issues are worked out through politics.

There is a common perception in education that politics is something to be avoided — that education should somehow be "above" politics. School administrators, for example, often talk about politics as interfering with their more important educational obligations. The theme of this chapter, however, is that education and politics are inextricably and necessarily bound up with each other, so that important decisions about education must by their very nature also be political decisions.

Critical statements about educational politics by educators often imply that schools would be better if educators made the important decisions themselves. Thus, one alternative to politics is to turn more decisions about education over to the professionals. In this model, teachers and administrators would make all of the policy decisions affecting education.

While such a model might appear inviting to those of us who work in education, it has serious problems. Many decisions about education do rest with professional educators, but educators themselves are by no means in agreement about matters of educational policy. Teachers disagree among themselves about grading policies, the best way to teach languages, discipline, and many other issues.

The claim to expert authority must also rest on some demonstrated knowledge, unique to the experts, that entitles them to make decisions exclusively. We might accept that professional educators have important advice to give about teaching and curriculum, but do we think that they should establish the goals of schools independent of what students, parents, and other people want?

Does the decision about whether to put more stress on science a matter in which educators have some particular expertise, or is it a judgement that involves all of us in deciding what we value? Does the decision about whether schools should be based in neighbourhoods or instead be open to all rest on expertise? In fact, most of the truly important decisions about education are matters that require judgements on the part of all of us, not educators exclusively. Moreover, education is publicly funded, and it is difficult to think that the public will provide billions of dollars for education while leaving the entire determination about the use of the money to teachers and administrators. According to Haller and Strike (1986), "If one believes that educators are entitled to an authoritative say about the goals of education, one must be against democracy" (p. 241).

This brings us to the second vehicle that is often suggested as a substitute for politics — the use of markets. In this view, education should be turned into a commodity, much like cars. People should be free to buy as much or as little as they want, wherever they want. Such a model tries to eliminate political judgements and replace them with the decisions of individual consumers. Despite current conventional wisdom, there are even more problems with simple market solutions than there are with governance by experts. For one thing, it is possible to argue that there are no truly free markets left in the world, and that all markets are affected in important ways by decisions made through public political processes. Given the highly interdependent nature of our world, it is just not possible to separate one area of economic and social activity from others. To take one example, the money available for education may be affected by changing employment levels in industry, but these in turn may be affected by the number and quality of people completing educational programs.

It is also important to note that education is something that benefits not simply the person being educated, but all of us, which makes it a *public good* (more will be said about this in Chapter Five). Suppose, under a market system, some people decided to get no formal education at all. Would we be satisfied with this? Would we even want to allow it? Compulsory attendance laws all across the world bear witness to the view that education is too important to be left entirely to individuals' choices. If so, then we cannot simply rely on market mechanisms to replace political decisions.

We have taken the position that politics, despite its meanness, messiness, and shortcomings, is a necessary and fundamental part of education. Teachers need to be aware of political processes, and they need to see themselves as political actors. There are many ways in which teachers can influence politics. Many teachers are actively involved in political parties. Teachers have been elected and have held Cabinet positions in Canadian governments. Others are active in teachers' organizations working for the reforms and changes they value. Many teachers have been elected as school trustees in the places they live because of their deep concern for education. Teachers are also active as parents and in many community organizations.

For many teachers, their most important political work occurs in the school and with students. Teachers make a political contribution when they practise democratic values in their classrooms, treat students with respect and empathy, discuss important issues with students, work to break down stereotypes, collaborate with their colleagues for the betterment of the school, and create closer ties between the school and the community. As was pointed out in Chapter One, the role of the teacher is a moral one, and the teacher's moral actions provide very clear political messages about her or his views of justice and right.

Political processes, like other human processes, are far from perfect. It is easy to see why people get frustrated with them. But for better or worse, politics is the way in which human societies make decisions about many important things. We therefore need to understand something about politics and to work for change if we are to understand and improve schools.

Exercises

1. Schooling is greatly affected by a wide variety of policy decisions, some of which are listed at the beginning of this chapter. Working first individually and then in small groups in your class, define what you mean by the term **policy**, then brainstorm as many areas of education policy as you can. Indicate whether, to your knowledge, these policy decisions are made by teachers, students, parents, school administrators, or others.

2. Taking one or more of the policy areas defined in Exercise 1, define how this area is political, using the definition of politics on pages 61–62. How does this issue shape (1) what is taught; (2) to and by whom it is taught; and (3) where, when, and how it is taught?

3. Again taking one of the policy areas you have defined, find out what the current situation is in your province. What measures or policies, if any, are in place, and how did they come to be there? Is this issue controversial? Why or why not? Good sources of information for this inquiry could be local school administrators, local school trustees, teacher organization officials, or officials of the provincial Department or Ministry of Education.

4. Select a current educational issue in your province or community (perhaps one that has recently been in the news). Think about how the issue has been defined. Whose definition of the issue appears to be uppermost? What other definitions or views of the issue might exist that are not being expressed? Why aren't they?

5. Find a position paper or brief on education that was written in your community. (It need not be recent; archives are good sources for such material,

and so are groups such as teachers' or trustees' associations, or parent groups of various kinds. If there has been a public inquiry or commission into some aspect of education, the briefs submitted to it are likely available to the public.) Comment on how the brief uses evidence and argument to advance its point of view. How fair and open-minded do you think the position in the brief is?

6. Identify a stakeholder group in education. Interview a member of this group to determine the group's position and its actions on one or two current issues. Look for the inside story, not just platitudes.

7. Attend a meeting of your local school board. Keep careful notes on what you observe. In what ways does the meeting contribute to or prevent the careful and full debate of important policy issues in education? Was the meeting, in your view, political? Why or why not?

8. Using one or two of the issues identified in one of the earlier exercises, develop a list of people (individuals or groups) who would be affected by a decision made about that issue. Should all those affected have some role to play in making the decision? Do they? How, if at all, should the decision-making process on this issue be changed in regard to participation?

9. Pages 78–79 list several possible policy levers that provincial governments can use to influence the actions of school districts. Identify an example of the use of each of these levers in your province.

10. Suppose you were an elected official facing a difficult political decision, such as whether to sell condoms in high-school washrooms. What strategies might you use to work toward a good decision based on community discussion? What if it were a K–12 school?

11. Construct your own case study of a political issue. Your case should: (1) describe the issue; (2) identify the persons or groups with a strong interest in the issue, and describe what that interest is; (3) describe what actions have been taken with respect to the issue in the last few years; and (4) speculate as to the possible future course of the issue.

12. Using one of the policy issues identified in an earlier exercise, reconstruct the logic behind the policy. What is the chain of causal reasoning underlying the policy? Do the assumptions being made seem reasonable to you? Why or why not?

13. Interview one or two teachers. Ask them their views on politics in education. How, if at all, are they involved in politics? Do they see their work in the school and classroom as political? Why or why not?

Further Reading

The general literature on the politics of education is enormous, and the Canadian literature is also substantial. In the former category, some particular noteworthy books with sometimes unconventional views include Deborah Stone, *Policy Paradox and Political Reason* (Scott, Foresman, 1988); Virginia Held, *Rights and Goods* (Free Press, 1984); and Murray Edelman, *Constructing the Political Spectacle* (University of Chicago Press, 1988). Two interesting British approaches to changing politics are Geoff Mulgan, *Politics in an Anti-Political Age* (Polity Press, 1994) and Anthony Giddens, *Beyond Left and Right* (Polity Press, 1994). Ronald Manzer's important book *Public Schools and Political Ideas* (University of Toronto Press, 1994) provides a very thorough discussion of the politics of language, religion, and secondary education in Canada, tying these into a history of Canadian liberal thought. The U.S.–based Politics of Education Association has issued a series of yearbooks that deal with important political issues, though largely from an American perspective. Examples include Catherine Marshall, *The New Politics of Race and Gender* (Falmer Press, 1993) and Jay Scribner and Donald Layton, *The Study of Educational Politics* (Falmer Press, 1994; includes a chapter by Canadians Richard Townsend and Norman Robinson).

Among many, many other Canadian works, we mention only a few examples. Essays on Canada's decentralized system can be found in P. Nagy and J. Lupart (eds.) (1994), *Is There a National Role in Education?* On the way in which research and the media interact to shape understanding of a particular issue, see John Willinsky, "The Construction of a Crisis: Literacy in Canada," *Canadian Journal of Education, 15*(1) (1990), and Henry Milner's 1986 book, *The Long Road to Reform: Restructuring Public Education in Quebec* (McGill-Queen's University Press), is a good discussion of the politics of language and religion in Quebec. An interesting discussion of the politics of language in the Ottawa area is Hanne Mawhinney, "Policy change in education," in *Policy Research and Development in Canadian Education*, edited by Robert O'Reilly and Charla Lautar (University of Calgary, 1991). The same author's "Systemic reform or new wine in an old bottle," *International Journal of Educational Research, 23*(6) (1995), is a discussion of Ontario reforms in 1995. Richard Townsend's *They Politik for Schools* (Toronto: OISE Press, 1988) is a study of the perspectives of legislators and school board members across Canada. Rod Dolmage has written about "Interest groups, the courts, and the development of educational policy in Canada" in *Journal of Education Policy, 7*(3) (1992).

CHAPTER FOUR

Law and Education

▼ PROLOGUE

Toni was the first to arrive in the seminar room at Foothills Collegiate, so she fixed herself another cup of coffee and sat back waiting for the rest of the group to join her. A final-year Bachelor of Education student, she was glad that she had signed up for a pilot field-based collaborative project at the Faculty of Education. The project was designed to enable students to spend more time working in schools, with part of their course work built around their school experiences.

There were five other Faculty of Education students in the school doing student teaching, and as part of their program they met twice a week as a group with the team co-ordinators — Cynthia Phillips, a science teacher at the school, and Ian McKenzie, a professor at the university, who not only supervised their student teaching, but also taught them a course entitled "School Organization."

On the main campus, "School Organization" was viewed by most of Toni's friends as a dry course — not irrelevant, but fairly boring. Perhaps, she thought, she was lucky to have two good teachers, but in the school this course seemed far from dry. It was a chance to study and talk about a whole range of issues that seemed to be directly related to what she was trying to get done in her classroom. Each class began with an open discussion period in which any member of the group could raise an issue or question that had arisen from their teaching.

Now that the rest of the group had joined her in the seminar room and exchanged greetings, the class began. Aaron, one of the students, initiated the discussion: "You know what has really been frustrating me this week? It's all the red tape that is involved in trying to arrange a class field trip. I talked to the principal, and by the time he'd finished telling me about all of the regulations and all of the approval forms I'd have to get filled out, I just said, 'Forget it, I'll do something else.' And in the end it's the kids who suffer."

Cynthia, the teacher, broke in: "Well, I know what you mean. There are a lot of procedures that have to be followed in this division, which is fine if you're planning weeks in advance, but it makes doing things on short notice pretty difficult. But you know, field trips are potentially dangerous situations, and as professionals we need to make sure that we are proactive in minimizing any danger to the students. In part it's simply a matter of protecting yourself from being taken to court by a parent. If something does go wrong, and if you comply with all the regulations, you're likely to be protected. But more than that, it's a matter of being professional, of doing one's job in a professional manner. And let me tell you, there is nothing worse than having something go wrong on a field trip — like a student going missing — and running around wondering what has happened and wishing you had been more careful with your instructions, supervision, or parental approvals!"

"I think it's really important," said Semareh, another student, "that we know the law so that we can stay out of trouble."

That statement got the whole class talking. Karl burst out, "Everyone seems to want to sue the teacher these days! I had a student say to me, 'Don't touch me or my parents will sue you,' and I wasn't even within reach of him. I'd just told him three times to go back to his desk."

Narina said, "I was talking about some of this stuff with Ken — you know, he's the Head of English — and he was talking about some parents who threatened to take him to court over some poetry he was using in class just because it wasn't in the provincial curriculum guidelines. The poet was, but not the particular poem he was using. And they said it was offensive! It seems to me that we need to be lawyers as well as teachers!"

Ian, their professor, spoke up: "We're going to be taking up many of these questions later in this course, but I think there are some important points to be made. First, Aaron and the rest of you mention the importance of being able to be creative and educative without being tied up in red tape. Second, Cynthia has noted the need to be proactive, to anticipate possible dangers and avoid them. Related to that is a third important issue, perhaps a bit more theoretical, that asks how we regulate school life in such a way that learning is taking place and at the same time the rights of all participants — students, parents, teachers — are being respected. I think this is where the law is particularly important, and should not be seen so much as an obstruction to the innovative teacher but rather as an attempt to balance and regulate the parameters of appropriate teaching practice. And if you look at how the courts have actually ruled in Canadian cases, you'll see that educators have been given considerable discretion by the courts, but that doesn't mean we're gods or above the law.

"So I think this discussion is important at several levels. How can I protect myself from being sued? How can I avoid potentially dangerous and inappropriate behaviour? And how can I better understand my role as a professional? Perhaps, Cynthia, we should stay with these questions for the rest of today's class?" ■

This chapter examines some key aspects of law as it affects teaching and schools. The first part of the chapter provides a basis for thinking about legal issues, including

1. why law is important to educators;
2. the processes through which laws are made and interpreted;
3. the concept of natural justice and its relevance to education;
4. the meaning of "rights;" and
5. the nature and impact of the *Charter of Rights and Freedoms.*

The second part of the chapter discusses some of the important legal aspects of schooling, including

6. the powers and duties of teachers;
7. negligence and liability;
8. child abuse;
9. attendance at school;
10. maintaining order and discipline;
11. student rights and democratic practices;
12. teaching practices such as curriculum and the school year;
13. placement of special education students; and
14. copyright.

Other important legal issues related to such matters as jurisdiction over education, minority languages, the status of teachers, and collective bargaining are discussed in the relevant chapters elsewhere in this book.

Why Does Law Matter to Educators?

As the prologue to this chapter shows, legal matters can have an important impact on the work of teachers. At the most basic level, teachers need to be concerned about the safety of their students, and teachers can be sued or prosecuted, possibly leading to loss of their ability to teach, if they neglect their responsibilities. More importantly, law is one of the primary forces that has shaped, and continues to shape, Canadian education.

We can think about law as giving a certain shape to the web of relationships affecting schools. Laws both outline and limit who can teach, what can be taught, who will be taught, and how the various parties involved in education should treat one another. Many aspects of schooling, particularly the relationship between teachers and students, are deeply affected by law. Greater concern with human rights and the advent of the *Canadian Charter of Rights and Freedoms* are important influences on the way students and teachers are treated in schools.

While this chapter is concerned with matters of law and education, it is important to recognize that law in education cannot be detached from politics or history. All of these processes affect one another, and the way they are separated in this book is an analytical convenience, not a description of the way the world actually works.

It is helpful at the outset simply to list some of the major ways in which teaching is affected by the law in Canada.

The Basic Structure of the Educational System

- provincial responsibility for education;
- existence of denominational and linguistic minority schools and school systems;
- existence and powers of provincial ministries or departments of education; and
- existence and powers of school boards.

All of these issues are outlined in Canadian law. They were discussed in Chapter Two, and will not be taken up again here, but they are important legal influences on schools.

Conditions of Teaching

- who can teach (certification);
- duties and powers of teachers;
- conditions of employment;
- grounds for dismissal;
- labour laws; and
- collective bargaining.

Many aspects of teaching are regulated directly in law, or are subject to the provisions of collective bargaining, which is itself regulated by law. Most of these matters are taken up in Chapters Six and Eight.

Physical Safety of Students

- negligence and liability of teachers;
- trespass and site safety; and
- child abuse.

The requirement to protect students from harm has an important effect on many aspects of teaching, and creates tensions between the responsibility of teachers for their students' safety and their sense of what experiences might most facilitate students' learning.

School Attendance

- compulsory attendance and exemptions from it.

The fact that education is compulsory has an enormous impact on teaching in that it means that students must attend whether or not they want to do so.

Maintaining Order

- discipline;
- suspension and expulsion; and
- corporal punishment and the use of force with students.

If the requirement for discipline is at least partly due to the compulsory nature of education, the ability of administrators and teachers to maintain order, and the way in which they do so, is shaped by legal decisions governing disciplinary practice.

Student Rights and Democratic Practice in Schools

Freedom of speech, assembly, belief, and participation in governance by teachers and students are hallmarks of democratic society but have a particular meaning in schools.

Teaching Practices

Many aspects of teaching, such as the subjects to be taught, the content within each subject (the curriculum), the length of the school year, the treatment of exceptional children, and copyright control over teaching materials are controlled by statute or regulation.

Law and Politics

Why do schools become enmeshed in legal matters at all? Why can't they simply be left to do what is educationally sound? To answer these questions, it is important to understand that legal issues arise through disagreement and conflict. If there were complete agreement on what people ought to do, law would not be necessary. People have very different ideas as to what kinds of actions might be acceptable. To provide a greater degree of compliance than would otherwise occur, laws are used to make some actions compulsory, prohibited, or regulated in some fashion. It is important to remember that law is intended to compel people to behave in certain ways, based on the assumption that without law they might not do so. Law necessarily involves imposing some view of the world on people who do not necessarily share that view. Thus, law usually is rooted in some conception of morality, of what is good. For the same reason, conflict is part of every aspect of law, and education is no exception since it too is an area in which people have very different ideas about what is necessary or desirable.

These conflicts are not always overt. Many aspects of school law are so taken for granted that they seem inevitable, as if there were no other way things could be done. The fact that students begin schooling around the age of 6, that the school year runs from September to June, that teachers have the right to bargain collectively, and that school boards are locally elected—these are all practices that are not usually questioned today. However, many laws that are now taken for granted were the subject of vehement debate at the time they were enacted. Chapter Two referred to the heated debate over the consolidation of schools in rural areas in the middle part of this century. Historical study shows that other aspects of schooling, such as making it compulsory, were also controversial at the time (Henley & Pampallis, 1982). Particularly in Canada, legislation regarding the linguistic and religious aspects of education has been very controversial (e.g., the extension of funding to Catholic schools in Ontario in 1984, or the changes in language requirements in Quebec schools in the 1970s and 1980s). The discussion in Chapter Three of how political decisions are made indicated that, although we tend to think of laws as embodying some sort of public good, they have in fact been substantially determined by people or groups with political power. When any law is enacted, some people gain and others lose. For example, when we pass laws that create school boards and bestow certain powers upon them, we are also limiting the influence on schools of others, such as teachers or parents, who, under a different system, might play a greater role. The changing arrangements for education across the provinces and over time show that there are always options about how best to conduct public education. Changing social conditions and beliefs also generate demands for changes in law.

Legislation and Judicial Interpretation

Once a law is passed, the surrounding debate and conflict may be gradually forgotten, and people may come to regard the law as being more than the outcome of a political disagreement. In some cases, however, the conflicts continue even after a law has been created. Legal issues arise when someone feels that some current policy or practice is undesirable or unfair, and challenges that policy or practice. There are two ways such a challenge can be made. A **political** effort can be made to have the law changed, or to have a new and different law enacted. Or a **judicial** challenge can be made whereby the courts are asked to rule that a policy or practice does not meet the requirements of existing law.

Chapter Two discussed the controversy in the nineteenth century over the role of local school boards. As a result of this controversy, several different pieces of legislation were enacted to try to give legal shape to a view of how education ought to be governed. A more recent example concerns legislative provision for the education of special-needs students. Many people worked very hard for many years to have provincial legislatures provide legislation that would require school districts to pay more attention to the needs of students who are physically challenged or mentally handicapped. Most provinces now have a legislative provision requiring schools to provide education for all students. Political efforts to change laws are not always effective, but they can be when given the right conditions.

A judicial challenge may assume that existing laws are adequate but are not being understood or applied correctly, or it may question the very legitimacy of a law. The courts will then be asked to require that the law be enforced in a different way, or even to indicate that the law is inappropriate and must be modified or scrapped. Such court challenges have played a major role in education historically in regard to issues of language and religion such as the rights of linguistic minorities discussed in Chapter Two. They are becoming increasingly important in other areas, partly due to the existence of the *Charter of Rights and Freedoms*. For example, a number of recent court cases in Canada have helped to define the educational rights of exceptional or special-needs students and their parents. Many court cases over the years have also dealt with such matters as the appropriate grounds for dismissal of teachers, and with school discipline practices.

These two routes to changing law parallel the two aspects of the legal system. Laws are created by the Parliament of Canada or by provincial legislatures. The creation of any law is thus a political process that is carried out by elected officials. However, once enacted, the responsibility to enforce and interpret laws belongs to the courts, which are made up of appointed experts—lawyers and judges. Each of these aspects of law will be considered in turn.

Legislation, Regulation, and By-Laws

Parliament and provincial legislatures make a wide variety of laws. Some provincial laws, such as public school or education acts, deal directly with education. But many other pieces of legislation also have important implications for schools. Labour laws affect the working conditions and status of teachers. Criminal law, including the *Young Offenders Act*, affects the way schools handle certain kinds of offences and disciplinary issues. Child welfare legislation places certain requirements on schools in regard to child abuse, among other things. Copyright legislation affects the availability of teaching materials.

Many provincial and federal laws include sections that authorize the particular minister to make regulations. Regulations typically involve the details of carrying out some intention or action contained in the legislation (see Box 4.1). For example, provincial education laws authorize ministers of education to provide funds to school boards. The precise way in which such funds are allocated is usually determined in the regulations. Whereas laws are passed by legislatures, regulations are made by the Cabinet (either federal or provincial). They are then made public by the government, and have the force of the law under which they are enacted. Regulations are much easier to alter than are laws, since the changes can be made in private by the government. In any particular case, the government will decide, when it brings forward legislation, which matters should be spelled out in the law itself, and which should be reserved for Cabinet decision and amendment through the regulation process. In education, in addition to finance formulas, such matters as the organization of the school year, the qualifications for teacher certification, and various matters of curriculum are usually subject to regulation. In some provinces ministers may also issue policies that have legal force.

Box 4.1
Examples of Regulations under Provincial Statutes

Alberta Regulation 36/89 (Feb., 1989)

This regulation governs French immersion schools. It provides that "A board may, by resolution, authorize the commencement of a French immersion program in a school and on passing the resolution shall inform the Minister in writing." The board is also authorized to determine, in Grades 1 and 2, how much time will be given to French and English instruction in the program. However, after Grade 3, the regulation requires at least "(a) 300 minutes each week [of English language arts] for each student in Grades 3 to 6; (b) 150 hours each year for each student in Grades 7 to 9." The regulation also provides that at least 50 percent of the time in Grades 1 to 6, and 40 percent in Grades 7 to 9 shall involve French as the language of instruction.

Quebec Basic School Regulation (1988)

This regulation lays out the basic services and the organizational framework for Quebec secondary schools.
1. Educational services include instructional services, student services and special services. The purpose of those services is to promote the students' overall development and integration into society. ...
6. Services to educate students about their rights and responsibilities are designed to increase students' awareness of basic rights and the attendant responsibilities. The purpose of these services is, in particular, to promote student participation in the various student associations. ...
38. A student who shows that he has achieved the objectives of a program by passing a test administered by the school board is not required to take that program. ...
39. The student's parents or the student himself, if he is of full age, must receive, at the beginning of the school year, the school's rules and regulations and the calendar of its activities, a summary of the student's programs of studies, a list of his textbooks, the names of all his teachers, and the name of his homeroom teacher. ...
43. The school board must ensure that the parents of each student or the student himself, if he is of full age, receive, at least five times per school year, a written evaluation report on the student's academic performance, behaviour, and attendance.

In addition to laws passed by Parliament or provincial legislatures, and regulations made under those laws, there are other important documents that have legal status. Many organizations are given legal status through federal or provincial legislation. School boards are legally authorized and given particular powers through provincial laws, as are municipalities. These organizations cannot make laws, but they can make by-laws, which are also legally enforceable within the statutory powers granted to the particular organization through its legislation. For example, school boards pass by-laws to determine their own structure and operations. School boards also make formal policy decisions about school sites, school boundaries, budgets, and staffing, and others carry out these decisions because they are made by a duly constituted authority. To take another example, teacher organizations, which are themselves legally authorized through provincial legislation, may make rules of conduct that are binding on their members.

The Courts

Courts play a vital role in the legal system in that the application of law hinges on judgements about particular cases, and these judgements are made by courts and judges. As a matter of course, every law requires interpretation as to how it applies to a particular circumstance. However, because human situations are so varied, there is no law, no matter how carefully written, that can take every possibility into account. In some cases, laws are deliberately vague because there is such political disagreement over what they should say that the matter is partly left to the courts to decide. The *Charter of Rights and Freedoms* is one example of a law with language requiring the courts to decide what specific clauses meant. As some of the issues discussed later in this chapter demonstrate, the work of interpreting law is a continuous process.

Over time, laws may also need to be reinterpreted to meet newly emerging needs or changing circumstances. Legislation that is not revised can become outdated. It is then left to the courts to apply existing laws to new circumstances. For instance, Canadian copyright law was only recently revised; important issues of copyright relating to computer software, photocopying machines, videocassettes, and other media were not covered under the 1924 law, which had remained in force up until the revision in 1988. In education meanwhile, emerging issues such as the teaching of special-needs students, access to student records, or parental rights in determining school programs are not always defined in the education statutes. Clearly, judges have a very important role in shaping the practical applications of a particular piece of legislation.

The Canadian legal system generally recognizes the supremacy of the legislature, which means that our courts tend to be reluctant to give instructions to elected bodies as to what they must do. On the other hand, courts are not concerned just with interpreting laws. They also have the authority to declare that a particular law is invalid. This may occur when the requirements of one law are seen to conflict with the requirements of another. In such a case, a court may then rule that one of the laws is invalid and must be changed. In this way, judicial decisions can lead to legislative change. The *Charter* has often been used as the basis for arguing that a particular law is invalid (see Box 4.2). Thus, the courts also have the potential to play an important role in making laws as well as interpreting them.

Box 4.2
Areas of Impact of the *Charter of Rights and Freedoms*

Collective Rights

- Minority language rights: Anglophones in Quebec and francophones in other provinces have been guaranteed the right to have and to manage their own schools.
- Students with disabilities: Parents have been given an increased role, though certainly not complete control, in determining appropriate programs (see also Box 4.3).
- Funding of Catholic and other religious schools: Ontario's decision in 1984 to fund Catholic schools through Grade 13 was upheld, but the courts have ruled that other religious groups do not have a right to public funding.

Individual Rights

- Religion: The secular nature of public schools has generally been upheld, but reasonable religious expression by minorities has also been upheld (e.g., wearing of turbans by Sikhs).
- Freedom of association claims by parents and teachers have not been very successful.
- Mandatory retirement provisions have been upheld.
- Natural justice rights of students and teachers have received limited protection.

Source: Derived from A.W. MacKay. (1995). The rights paradigm in the age of the Charter. In R. Ghosh and D. Ray (Eds.), *Social change and education in Canada.* (3rd ed) Toronto: Harcourt Brace 224–39. Copyright © 1995 Harcourt Brace & Company Canada, Ltd. All rights reserved. Reprinted with permission.

There are several different kinds and levels of courts in Canada, each of which has particular authority and responsibility. The nature and role of courts are determined through both federal and provincial legislation, with the exception of the Supreme Court of Canada, whose structure and role is defined in the Constitution. The Supreme Court plays the most significant role for several reasons. First, its rulings are binding on all other courts in Canada. Second, controversial cases in all areas of law may be taken to the Supreme Court for a ruling that will provide clear direction to the lower courts, and thus a common interpretation of the law across Canada. Third, the Supreme Court is responsible for determining how the various clauses in the Constitution will be interpreted.

In making decisions, courts take into account not only the arguments of the lawyers who represent the various parties involved, but also any applicable legislation and previous court decisions (precedents). Often more than one piece of legislation will apply to a particular case; when the various laws conflict, the judge must sort out the conflicts before rendering a decision. Precedents are important in influencing judges' decisions. Indeed, over time a body of precedents (often called "case law" or "common law") emerges to guide legal decision making. Precedents, though important, are rarely completely binding, since the circumstances of each case are somewhat different. Moreover, as people's views change, the meaning of the circumstances of a particular case also changes until an earlier judgement is no longer seen as appropriate. In this sense, law is never a fixed and final matter, but is constantly changing and evolving.

Court decisions are also guided by certain basic legal concepts. One of these, often found in judicial decisions, is the concept of **reasonableness**. Many court judgements make reference to the matter of what a "reasonable" person might have been expected to do under a certain set of circumstances. The fact that reasonable people can often disagree over what is reasonable makes a concept such as this one particularly hard to define precisely, as we will see later in the chapter.

Natural Justice and Fairness

One of the most important legal concepts is **natural justice**, or, more accurately, fairness in legal procedure. Natural justice has to do with whether the law has been applied fairly, regardless of the actual content of the law. An unfair law could still be applied in a way that respects principles of natural justice.

There are two basic aspects of natural justice. First, the person judging any particular situation should not be biased. This is usually taken to mean that the decision-maker should not have a direct interest in the case. Thus, if a teacher has accused a student of cheating, the teacher should not act as judge in the case also. The second requirement is that the person accused has the right to a fair hearing — that is, to understand the charge being made, and to give his or her side of the story. As with the concept of reasonableness, the meaning of natural justice often requires interpretation in any given set of circumstances. We will see later in this chapter the difficult challenges that the concept of natural justice may pose for many current school practices, especially in areas such as student discipline.

The *Charter of Rights and Freedoms* has focussed much more attention on the concept of natural justice as it relates to legal matters involving education. Section 7 of the *Charter* guarantees the right to fundamental justice. Although the meaning of fundamental justice will only gradually be determined through court decisions, it appears to have a broader application than does natural justice. Natural justice deals with procedural fairness rather than with the substance of a law. In applying the *Charter*, however, the Supreme Court has generally considered both aspects — whether a law was applied fairly, and whether the law was itself substantially fair or just. This broader application will give courts a much wider scope in reviewing the actions and decisions of educators.

Is the Legal System Fair?

Although we like to believe that our courts are impartial arbiters of justice, courts, like other human institutions, are far from perfect. For one thing, ability to gain a hearing in court may depend on having enough money to hire good legal counsel. In a case that might reach the Supreme Court, lawyers' fees can be many thousands of dollars, which makes this avenue unavailable to many people, regardless of how strong their case might be. For example, a student wishing to challenge a school board will have a much harder time finding the money for lawyers than will the school board. Cases may also be decided on legal technicalities that have little to do with their substantive merits. Judges, like other people, are subject to biases and stereotypes. Some groups of people are more likely than others to be sent to jail for the same offence, and some judges tend to give harsher sentences than others for the same transgressions (Manitoba, 1991). Thus, in the justice system, as in politics, there are significant inequalities.

In the past, political decisions made through legislatures and school boards have been far more significant for the schools than have been those made in the courts, with some exceptions in areas such as language and religion. This situation is changing under the *Charter*, which provides more grounds for judicial challenge to school practices (MacKay, 1995; Sussel, 1995). Before examining the *Charter* and its implications, it will be helpful to have a more general discussion of the nature of rights.

The Meaning of "Rights"

Many educational issues are framed as questions of rights. We say that teachers have (or do not have, depending on our opinion) a right to voice their opinion about school policies. Parents have (or do not have) a right to see their child's school records. Children have a right to be protected from harm. But what are rights? Where do they come from? These questions have been of interest to people for thousands of years. There is no agreement on the answers, but over that time some useful ways of thinking about rights have arisen. Rights can be classified as

- normative and legal;
- procedural and substantive;
- negative and positive;
- individual and collective; and
- personal and property.

Normative rights are those rights that people believe every individual should have, while **legal rights** are those that are officially recognized in a particular society. Considered logically, normative rights come first. A normative right is something we possess by virtue of being human. We don't have to do anything to earn this right; it is ours automatically. When we criticize a foreign government for being dictatorial, we are doing so using a conception of normative rights. Examples of normative rights would be the right to a fair trial, the right to free speech, and the right to be free from arbitrary discrimination. Many common normative rights are set out in international documents such as the *United Nations Universal Declaration of Human Rights* and the more recent *United Nations Convention on the Rights of the Child.*

Having a normative right does not necessarily mean that one is able to exercise it. Exercising a right requires three conditions: (1) that the right has been officially recognized through a law or rule; (2) that there is a process for settling disagreements over rights; and (3) that there is a way for people to enforce the particular right. To take the example of free speech for students, there must be some law, rule, or policy that specifies this right. There must be a forum for determining when a particular case is one of free speech or not. Finally, there must be a way for students to have that right enforced when it is violated.

Legal rights arise out of normative rights. When enough people begin to believe that some right ought to belong to them, and are prepared to work vigorously to have it established in law, legal recognition of the right may follow. Note that it is people's sense that things are not right as they stand, and their willingness to work for change, that may bring changes in law and subsequent changes in recognized rights.

Consider rights for physically disabled people. For many years, the ability of disabled people to enter buildings, to hold jobs, and to be part of normal life were simply not seen as rights. Gradually the climate of opinion began to shift. Advocacy groups worked hard to make the point that physical disability ought not to deprive people of their ability to live normally. A great deal of effort over many years went into persuading governments and the public that current practices were unfair and should be changed. As this belief became more widespread, legal recognition slowly followed. Laws were passed prohibiting discrimination in jobs or housing on the basis of physical disability. Schools began to integrate physically disabled children into their classes. People were able to bring about changes in law and policy that reflected and influenced changing social attitudes.

The legal recognition of normative rights is by no means automatic. Everyone can recognize that there are many situations, in Canada and elsewhere, where something widely regarded as a normative right is not yet a legal right. In many parts of the world, even the most basic human rights are not respected. And even the formal recognition of a right in law does not mean that the right will always be protected in practice. Various laws that protect rights are regularly violated, either deliberately or unintentionally — hence the need for courts to resolve disputes about issues of rights.

Rights, like other legal issues, involve conflict. The claimed rights of one person or group often conflict with the claimed rights of some other person or group. With respect to schools, it is clear that provincial governments, school boards, school administrators, teachers, parents, and students all have some rights. It is easy to see that these parties will disagree about many issues. For example, if teachers have the right to inflict corporal punishment, then students clearly do not have a right to be free from physical coercion in schools. If school boards have the right to dismiss teachers in order to reduce their budgets, then teachers' right to job security is substantially limited. If provinces can prescribe curricula that teachers must teach, then teachers do not have a right to academic freedom, parents do not have a right to determine what their children learn, and students do not have a right to pursue their academic interests. Magsino (1995) notes that there are conflicts among the rights claimed by parents, by schools, and, increasingly, by children.

Another important way of thinking about rights exists in the distinction that can be made between **procedural rights** and **substantive rights**. To put it simply, a procedural right is concerned with *how* things are to be done, while a substantive right concerns *what* is to be done. Take a situation in which a student was suspended from school for challenging something a teacher did. The student might have been given the opportunity to attend a hearing and to make a statement in his or her own defence, thus honouring the student's procedural right to "a fair trial." On the other hand, the substantive right to be free from punishment simply for expressing an opinion may have been violated. The most important procedural right is what is usually called natural justice, which was discussed more fully on page 102. Procedural rights are important, but without substantive rights they are insufficient.

A third distinction is between **negative rights** and **positive rights**, or, as they are sometimes termed, option rights and welfare rights. A negative right is the right to do something free from restraint; hence, it involves a choice or option. The rights to free speech and free assembly are examples of negative rights; you can exercise them if you wish to do so. Positive or welfare rights, on the other hand, involve the right to have or receive something. The right to education, for instance, can exist only if educational services or programs are available. Thus, positive rights imply an obligation on the part of somebody other than the holder of the right — often the government — to do or provide something to enable people to exercise their rights. Western societies such as Canada have tended to give more weight to option rights than to welfare rights.

A fourth way of thinking about rights has to do with **individual rights** and **collective rights**. Respecting the rights of an individual may impose costs of some kind on the collectivity, whether it be a class, community, or country. Providing education to multihandicapped children can be very expensive, a cost that is borne by the community to meet the child's right to be educated. The collective rights of minority language and religious groups are protected sometimes at the cost of the majority.

Finally, one can distinguish between **personal rights** and **property rights**. Personal rights (e.g., freedom of speech and religion, the right to vote) belong to all individuals who are members of the society. Nobody has more or less of these rights than anybody else. Property rights, on the other hand, belong only to those who have property. They accrue not because of who you are, but because of what you have. Those who have more possessions will also have more rights. Historically, property rights have often taken precedence over personal rights. The right to vote, for example, was for many years restricted to those who held property. Property rights have also been used in the past to limit the rights of workers to form unions, to bargain collectively, and to strike. Indeed, the rights of property owners have often been used to restrict the ability of governments to take action on behalf of the collectivity.

The *Charter of Rights and Freedoms*

In 1982, as part of the new Constitution, Canada adopted the *Charter of Rights and Freedoms.* (See Appendix for the complete text of the *Charter.*) It did so only after a great deal of debate over whether a constitutional statement of rights was desirable.

Canada has a mixture of legal and political practices and institutions drawn from many sources — British, French, American — which were themselves drawn from earlier Roman, Greek, and Aboriginal practices and ideas. The British legal tradition has no formal constitution, and no set of rights that are defined by a single legal document like the *Charter.* Instead, rights in Britain have emerged gradually, primarily through political and legal processes; that is, the British Parliament has made laws that have either given or extended legal rights. The American system, on the other hand, began with a set of legal rights enshrined in the Constitution, and has since relied on the courts for interpretation and enforcement. Some people feel that the American approach provides stronger protection of rights because legislatures may be swayed by short-term political considerations to act in ways that limit people's rights (especially the rights of minorities, who may have little political power). Others feel that it is a mistake to give lawyers and judges so much authority to shape our society. They argue that elected officials rather than appointed judges (who are not accountable to the public for their decisions) ought to be responsible for the important task of determining rights. After considering both systems, Canada opted in 1982 for a written charter, closer to the U.S. model.

The *Charter* outlines a number of rights that all Canadians have. Before discussing these rights, it is important to note some limitations that apply to them all, the most significant of which is the fact that the *Charter* applies only to the acts of government or governmental agencies; individual citizens and corporations are not required to abide by its provisions. Thus, a private company cannot be sued under the *Charter* for discriminating on the basis of sex, but a school or school district, because it is a government agency, can be sued on those grounds.

All rights in the *Charter* are potentially limited by Section 1, which allows "such reasonable limits prescribed by law as can be demonstrably justified in a free and democratic society." In interpreting the *Charter*, as is the case in many other legal issues, courts give weight to the concept of reasonableness. They have to decide if particular actions or decisions made by people or organizations can be considered reasonable. An interpretation always involves judgements about such measures as the state of society and public attitudes. The Supreme Court has begun to hand down decisions that show how Section 1 will be interpreted—decisions that emphasize the requirement that limits be shown to be both necessary and reasonable in relation to the good to be achieved (MacKay, 1995).

Several sections of the *Charter* have particular relevance to education.

Section 2 guarantees to all Canadians freedom of religion, belief, assembly, and association. These rights are, however, quite restricted in schools. Students are clearly not free in schools to say whatever they believe, to associate with whomever they wish, or to be in whatever places they choose. Students are often subject to dress or conduct codes that limit their freedom of expression and assembly. Criticism of school practices and personnel may be considered a punishable offence. School newspapers are often censored by staff members.

A second area of the *Charter* that may have important consequences for schools concerns the provisions in Sections 7 and 11 regarding natural justice. School discipline practices frequently appear to violate principles of natural justice. For example, teachers often accuse students of misdemeanours and impose punishments on them without explaining precisely what the transgression is and without providing an opportunity for the students' position to be heard. In effect, students may be compelled to give evidence against themselves (prohibited under Section 11c). Students are not always presumed innocent until proven guilty by a public and impartial tribunal (Section 11d). Appeal processes may not exist, and so on.

Section 15 of the *Charter* is particularly important for educators in that many practices in schools could be considered to be discriminatory in some respect. Consider a few examples. Public school legislation in most provinces specifies the ages at which students must attend school—typically from ages 6 to 16. Many provincial laws and school acts also end the right of attendance at age 21. Section 15 prohibits discrimination on the basis of age. Is it, then, discriminatory for provinces to require compulsory attendance at certain ages? Is it discriminatory for provinces to deny a right to attend school after age 21? Is it discriminatory to deny students entry to Grade 1 unless they turn 6 before a particular date? Or can such limitations be justified as "reasonable"?

Section 15 may raise more questions than it answers. What is meant by discrimination? Is any distinction based on any of the criteria in the section discriminatory? If not, what makes a distinction qualify as discrimination in the negative sense? Moreover, Section 15—which allows discrimination if its goal is the "amelioration of conditions of disadvantaged individuals or groups" — invites questions of what is meant by ameliorating, and how we would judge whether a particular measure is ameliorative.

Section 15 also prohibits discrimination on grounds of mental or physical disability. Is it, then, discriminatory to create separate classes for learning disabled or mentally handicapped students? One might argue that these provisions are not a violation of the *Charter* as they are intended to improve the condition of these students, thus falling under the exception in Section 15(2). But do separate classes improve the situation of students? Most separate classes for specific kinds of students, such as blind children, have recently been eliminated on the grounds that they did not provide the most effective education. The Supreme Court has ruled that such separate classes are not necessarily discriminatory (see Box 4.3.)

Impact of the *Charter*

Various issues raised under the *Charter* can arouse strong feelings in people. Some educators feel that the *Charter* will limit their professional autonomy and judgement, will make discipline in the schools too lax, and will give too many rights to minorities, with the cost being borne by the majority.

What the *Charter* will mean in practice is being determined gradually by decisions made by Canadian courts, and especially the Supreme Court. So far, the courts have been relatively conservative in interpreting the *Charter*. They have supported many restrictions on freedoms as being required by other, equally important social needs, and therefore as falling within the "reasonable limits" clause of Section 1. The courts have tended to give considerable weight to the opinions and knowledge of professional educators (MacKay, 1995). Courts that have overturned current laws or practices have often stated what is inappropriate, and they have suggested that the appropriate legislative body frame a new law that would not be inappropriate. For example, in the matter of minority language rights in education, courts in Ontario, Alberta, and Manitoba have all said that then-existing provisions did not meet the requirements of the *Charter*. But not one of these courts has told the province in question just what it should do to meet those requirements; that responsibility has been left to governments and to the political process.

The *Charter* has clearly had some impact on education, and will continue to do so (see Box 4.2). It has made people more aware of the extent to which issues of rights are important in thinking about the way schools are organized and operated. There is more thought given now to how students, parents, and teachers might feel about a particular policy or provision. Increasing legitimacy is being given to the right of parents to have some input into school policies, and principles of natural justice are playing a more prominent role in school policies. We can expect this trend to continue for the foreseeable future, with the *Charter* acting to change schools gradually rather than quickly. The end result may be schools that are significantly different in their treatment of rights (Sussel, 1995).

Box 4.3
Some Legal Cases Related to Special Education Placement

1. In the case of *Eaton v. Brant,* parents of a child with cerebral palsy attempted to overturn the school board's decision that their daughter could not be cared for properly in a regular classroom. The Supreme Court ruled in 1996 that excluding a disabled child from a regular class even when the parents disagree is an acceptable form of discrimination provided that it is based on a careful assessment of the best interests of the individual child (Supreme Court of Canada [1996, S.C.J. No. 98]).

2. The parents of an autistic child in Quebec took issue with the school board's placement of the boy in a special class for severe developmental disorders. They wanted him integrated into a regular school program. The Quebec Court of Appeal ruled that integration is not a right under Quebec law, and that the *Quebec Charter of Rights and Freedoms* does not guarantee a right to be integrated into regular classes. However, the court did suggest that school boards should integrate disabled students wherever possible (cited in Anderson, 1995b).

3. In a New Brunswick case, the court sanctioned a legal agreement to end a dispute between a family and a school district. The agreement committed the district to providing an integrated or mainstreamed program for a Grade 9 girl, but also provided that she need not be integrated with other students at all times (cited in Goguen & Poirier, 1995).

Laws Affecting Teachers and Schools

The way laws are applied to schools differs, in some important respects, from the way they are applied to other settings. The fact that schools are charged with the education of young people has affected the way courts have applied the laws. So far, Canadian courts have been willing to permit schools to act in ways that would not necessarily be permitted in a workplace or similar setting because of the schools' educational responsibilities. But beyond this, the nature of education also requires teachers to ask about how they should deal with legal matters.

First, schools are unlike other organizations because they create "offences" that would not be considered wrong or that would not be subject to punishment in other social settings. For example, going to the bathroom at the wrong time can be an offence in a school, whereas it would rarely be considered so in other places. The same is true of being discovered in the hallway during classes, talking out of turn, or copying someone else's work. In a setting where large numbers of young people are required to attend, and are supervised by relatively small numbers of adults, some rules will be necessary to keep order. The question facing educators is one of the appropriate balance between the requirements of order and the degree of freedom necessary for effective education.

The educational task of schools also imposes obligations on educators that might not be found in another environment. In an educational setting, everyone should be concerned with the development of students as persons—with their intellectual and moral growth, not simply their behaviour. We don't want students merely to comply with our instructions; we want them to understand why these instructions are necessary, and why it may be in their best interest to do as they are asked. This means that educators have a constant obligation to try to teach students.

Any event in the school, even a transgression by a student, can be seen as an opportunity to educate the student. For example, if a student is suspected of plagiarizing, a teacher might want to use the opportunity to discuss with a class what plagiarism means, why it is wrong, and what the conventions are in citing other people's work. It may well be more important to have all students learn from a situation than to punish one student for doing something inappropriate. Thus, what is required for educational purposes may not be the same as what a strict view of the law might demand. Because schools are institutions that are supposed to care about students, many teachers would want to think very carefully about the best course of action when a student is suspected of a crime. Do teachers simply call the police, or do they try to work with the student to help him or her cope with the problem? Teachers' moral obligation to help students may at times conflict with the narrower legal aspects of a situation; those may push teachers to act as agents of the state rather than with the care implied in being a parent (Dickinson, 1989). Some theorists have termed this the tension between an ethic of justice and an ethic of caring (Noddings, 1984).

As well, if the school is to fulfil its mandate to prepare students for citizenship, it must surely have a role in educating them about their rights and responsibilities. It is difficult to see how students can become responsible adults if, while in school, they are not informed about issues of rights, or if their opportunity to learn to exercise rights and responsibilities, and to participate in political processes, is highly restricted.

Closely related to all of these points is the changing legal status of children. At one time, children were seen primarily as the property of their parents, and very few controls were placed on what parents could do to and with them. Children are now accorded far more significance as persons, both legally and morally, than was the case 100 years ago. Increasingly, children are seen to have legal rights even though they are not legally adults. The legal system has responded to changes in social values by acknowledging children's status as persons whose legal interests may be separate from those of parents or schools. The state, meaning government, has gradually assumed increasing authority to intervene in the affairs of families to protect the rights of children. The enacting of child abuse legislation is only one example of this long-term and important trend, a fuller description of which can be found in Magsino (1995).

The Legal Status of Teachers

Teachers act as **educational state agents** (MacKay & Sutherland, 1992, pp. 32–76) who are recognized in law as having a certain degree of authority over the students in their charge. This authority comes from statute law (where provincial school legislation, as well as a variety of other pieces of related legislation, recognize teachers' powers and duties) and also from case law precedents. The enterprise of education is recognized by the law and the courts as requiring that adults have the ability to supervise, control, and discipline young people. Traditionally, teachers have been said to stand *in loco parentis* — that is, to have within the area of their responsibility the same authority over students as would a reasonable and careful parent, and to be expected to act, at minimum, in such a manner. Today, the idea that the authority of the teacher stems from the doctrine of *in loco parentis* has been substantially supplemented, and perhaps even supplanted, by the legal duties and requirements of teachers acting as agents of the state. The role of parents has also changed, and governments have come to play a more important part in family–school relations (Magsino, 1995). However, in certain areas, such as that of teacher negligence and liability, the comparison of the teacher to the reasonable and careful parent remains a critical legal judgement.

Physical Safety

Negligence and Liability

Teachers are expected not only to educate students but, like parents, to take responsibility for their safety and well-being. Parents send their children to school believing that the school will take reasonable precautions to safeguard their children from physical or mental harm. However, as might be expected when large numbers of people are involved, accidents and tragedies do occur. Over time, a body of law has grown that helps determine what the responsibilities of schools are for keeping students safe. The law governing these matters is not found in statutes, but in the common law of court decisions and precedents created over many years (Dickinson, 1995).

When a student is injured while under the care of the school, an attempt is made to assess responsibility for the mishap. If the school or one of its employees can be found to be negligent, then the family may be able to claim financial compensation for its loss. The amounts of compensation can be quite substantial. For example, if a student is paralyzed, he or she will need lifelong care and support, which comes only at a high price. If the school is at fault, it may be required by the courts to provide these funds.

Vicarious Liability

Although negligence is normally the result of some individual's action or lack of action, in the case of teachers and schools the school district usually assumes the legal liability. Therefore, even though a student may have been injured while under a teacher's care, it is the school board that will be sued (if there is a lawsuit) and the school board's insurance coverage that will pay for any damages. This is known as **vicarious liability** (the employer assumes the liability for the actions of employees).

If, however, the teacher acted negligently, the school board can in turn sue the teacher to recover its costs. For example, if a teacher drove students on a field trip and was involved in an accident in which students were injured, the school board would normally assume the liability. But if the teacher had consumed alcohol above legal limits at the time, the board might be able to sue the teacher personally to recover the damages it may have had to pay to students' families. Vicarious liability is thus an important but not a total protection to teachers.

The Meaning of Negligence

The concept of **negligence** implies three things. First, there must be a legal duty to care, which means a duty to act in a way that avoids causing harm to others when such harm might reasonably have been foreseen. Teachers would normally have such a duty toward their students during school hours or school activities. Second, negligence can occur only when there is a breach of the duty to care. That is, the person's actions must be inconsistent with what we would ordinarily expect from a reasonable, caring individual. Finally, some harm — actual damage — must result from the breach. There can be no legal finding of negligence if there is no harm, or if the harm did not result from the breach of duty. To take our earlier example, the drunken teacher would not be legally guilty of negligence if no accident — and thus no student injuries — had occurred. Nor would the teacher be liable if the injury occurred through some cause other than that teacher's drunkenness. (That such conduct is unprofessional and might well be punished by the school district is a separate issue.) Harm, however, is not necessarily confined to physical injury. A psychological trauma suffered by a student might well be considered to be as important a harm as a physical injury.

These principles seem clear, yet their application in particular cases can be very difficult. Just how far does the duty to care extend, for example, and what kind of behaviour constitutes a breach of it? If children are playing on the school playground, how closely must they be watched? What about children on their way to or from school? What about students working with tools in a school shop?

In the courts, situations such as these tend to be decided on questions of what is reasonable. The courts have generally held that teachers should act toward their students as would a "careful parent," although it has also been recognized that teachers are responsible for many more children at any given time than are most parents. In making a determination of appropriate care, among the factors that may be considered are the number of students being supervised; the nature of the activity; the age, skill, and training of the students; and the nature and condition of any equipment. Taking all of these into account means that it is very difficult to generalize as to what conduct may or may not be considered negligent; however, Box 4.4 summarizes four important indicators of sufficient supervision identified by Giles and Proudfoot (1990) and derived from Canadian judicial decisions.

Thus, teachers of younger students would be expected to exercise more careful supervision of, say, students crossing a street than would teachers of older students. While the courts have held that schools should provide adult supervision of playgrounds, they also acknowledge that the school district cannot be expected to maintain careful watch over every student at every moment. In a school workshop equipped with power tools, careful attention to the inherent dangers associated with such equipment is necessary. Teachers would be expected to provide clear instructions to students regarding safety procedures in operating equipment and would be obligated to provide adequate supervision while such tools were being used (Anderson, 1986). A key point in this regard is that legal precedents have indicated that teachers must expect children to behave foolishly or recklessly, and so extra precautions must normally be taken to guard against injury. In the case generally cited as the origin of the concept of the "careful parent" (*Williams v. Eady* [1894]), the judge ruled, in the language of the time, that a teacher was required to

> take such care of his boys as a careful father would take of his boys, and there could be no better definition of the duty of a schoolmaster. Then he was bound to take notice of the ordinary nature of young boys, their tendency to do mischievous acts, their propensity to meddle with anything that came in their way.

Box 4.4
Indicators of Sufficient Supervision

- The school or classroom activities are being carried out in an orderly fashion, and discipline is good.
- The person responsible for supervision is competent.
- The person responsible for supervision is present. While the absence of the supervisor is not an automatic determinant of liability, such an absence would be examined very carefully to determine whether the presence of a supervisor would have made a difference.
- There are clearly stated student-oriented rules through which students are informed of the inherent dangers and provided with instruction regarding safety.

Source: Adapted from T. Giles and A. Proudfoot. (1990). *Educational administration in Canada* (4th ed.). Calgary: Detselig, pp. 150–51. Adapted with permission.

For example, potentially dangerous chemicals would need to be locked carefully away when not in use, even if students had been warned that they were dangerous and should not be handled or ingested. The warning itself would be an insufficient safeguard, given that students might act contrary to it.

Field trips are another area where risks of negligence have occurred. Although securing parental permission forms prior to departure may well be advisable, such forms in no way diminish a school's responsibility for student care; nor do they prevent a parent from suing if the school is seen to have been negligent. The courts have held that people cannot sign away their basic legal rights; therefore, a permission slip does not absolve the school from its obligation to safeguard students' welfare.

Teachers' liability for the safety of their students in school is also related to their status as **occupiers** and students' status as **invitees**. Occupier's liability relates to the law that covers the liability of an owner or occupier of buildings and grounds for injuries suffered by people while in the buildings or on the grounds. Depending on the reasons for a person's presence on a property, the courts recognize three hierarchical categories of persons: invitees, licensees, and trespassers. Students in schools fall into the category of invitee, which requires the highest standard of care from teachers as occupiers and school boards as owners. As such, teachers and school boards have a duty to take reasonable steps to ensure that the school premises are safe. They have a proactive responsibility on their part to inspect the premises regularly for hazards that might endanger students. Children who visit school grounds on weekends — and not for the purpose of school-organized activities — would more likely be classified as licensees, in which case the duty of care is reduced. Children breaking into a school would be categorized as trespassers. Here the duty of the occupier is minimal, limited essentially to not deliberately creating hidden dangers or traps to injure the trespasser.

More extensive discussions of various aspects of liability can be found in MacKay, *Education Law in Canada* (1984). In cases of liability, as in so many other areas of law, the facts of a particular case (and their interpretation by a court) are as important as any principles. Teachers need to take issues of care and liability seriously, but not become so worried about negligence that they forget their primary duty to provide education to students.

Child Abuse

All provinces have enacted legislation that requires any adult to report to police or to child welfare authorities a suspicion that a child is being abused physically, sexually, or emotionally. This legislation is not part of legislation on schools, and is usually the responsibility of agencies other than schools, most often child welfare agencies. Because teachers have so much contact with students, they are often the first—or the only—adults to suspect that a child is being mistreated (Tite, 1994).

Box 4.5
Liability Cases

1. In a British Columbia case, a student was enrolled in a metalwork class, but missed the initial classes when much of the safety instruction was done. One day, when a less qualified substitute teacher was with the class, the student lost an eye while working on a lathe. His suit against the school board was dismissed because the student had been given safety instructions, but did not follow them. The judge did find that the school district was negligent for having an unqualified substitute teacher in charge of the class, but this negligence did not itself contribute to the injuries, and so no damages were payable (Anderson, 1991a).

2. In an Ontario case, a group of students were playing on a high jump mat outside the school during recess. Students had been told several times not to play on the mat. However, they continued to do so, and a boy fell off and broke his arm. There was no teacher supervising that area of the yard at the time, although there were two other teachers elsewhere in the yard. The court found the school 80 percent liable for the accident because it should have foreseen that the mat was a source of danger. Simply telling students not to use it was insufficient; something should have been done to prevent students from continuing to play on the mat. The student was awarded $36 000 (Anderson, 1992).

3. Another Ontario case concerned a 14-year-old girl who was practising volleyball under the supervision of a teacher. While trying to volley the ball near a wall, she stumbled and struck her head, and a few minutes later collapsed, feeling ill. She went to her next class, but then went home as she still felt ill. Subsequent medical examination showed no sign of a fracture or other head injury. The court dismissed the lawsuit, saying that the teacher was qualified to coach, and that the students had not been instructed to perform activities that were foreseeably dangerous ("No liability ... " 1991).

The increasing attention that is being given to child abuse is also part of the gradual but important change in our attitudes toward children, which was discussed earlier in this chapter. When dealing with suspected cases of child abuse, there are several legal points for teachers to remember:

1. You are required by law to report your suspicion of abuse, even if you do not have any concrete evidence to support your belief.
2. You must make a report to the legally stipulated authority, usually the police, or to the child welfare authorities; reporting only to your principal is not sufficient.
3. You can be found guilty of a crime if you have knowledge or suspicion of abuse and do not report it to the proper authorities.
4. Your identity will not be disclosed to the person who is suspected of committing the abuse.
5. You cannot be punished or prosecuted for making a report that proves to be incorrect, as long as you did so in good faith.

A discussion of the legal aspects of child abuse, however, hardly begins to raise all of the other important elements of the matter (Beck, Ogloff, & Corbishley, 1994). For instance, what constitutes a strong enough suspicion to justify reporting a suspected case of abuse? After all, many of the possible symptoms of abuse, especially in regard to emotional abuse or neglect, might be found in most children at one time or another. What if a child does not want to have the abuse reported for fear that the family will be torn apart by an accusation? What if the report is made, but there is not enough evidence to warrant criminal charges? (This is a real concern with child abuse since the sole evidence for the allegation may be the unsubstantiated word of a child, which does not have the same force in a court of law as does the testimony of an adult.) What if no charges are laid, but the abusing adult is provoked into greater abuse by the fact that an investigation is being conducted? These are some of the concerns that a teacher must consider in regard to a suspected case of abuse.

Particularly troublesome for teachers is the matter of suspected abuse committed by teachers. These accusations usually involve alleged sexual abuse, which can mean anything from inappropriate touching of the student to sexual intercourse between a teacher and a nonconsenting student. Though the number of teachers accused of abusing students is very small, because teachers are in a position of trust the accusation is particularly serious. Teachers convicted of abuse will normally have their teaching certificates revoked, prohibiting them from being teachers.

However, in many allegations of abuse, it is not easy to know where the truth lies. The difficulties in such cases are well described by Dolmage (1995a). When a teacher is accused, his or her (though almost all accusations are made against males) career as a teacher is placed in jeopardy, even if no charges are ever laid by police. The employing school board must decide whether an accused teacher can continue to teach in a classroom. Even though Canadian law requires the presumption of innocence until one is proven guilty, school boards face a real dilemma in handling teachers suspected of abuse. Are the teacher's rights to take precedence over the possible safety of students? Frequent practice in such cases is to suspend the teacher from duty, or to reassign the teacher to duties that do not involve teaching, until the allegation is resolved.

Police and Crown attorneys usually do not lay criminal charges of abuse unless they feel they have enough evidence to make a conviction a realistic possibility. Difficult questions arise, such as whether to believe teacher or student when there is no other evidence. A criminal conviction requires the judge or jury to be convinced "beyond a reasonable doubt." But the responsibility of the school board goes beyond this standard. The standard of proof for a civil case, such as wrongful dismissal, is less strict than it is in criminal cases. Thus, a school board could fire a teacher accused of abuse but not convicted of the offence if the board felt that it had reasonable grounds for believing the teacher guilty. Many parents would probably want the board to take such action.

Growing attention to child abuse has also affected some aspects of teachers' behaviour in the classroom, and sparked fears among teachers that they may be unjustly accused. Some teachers may feel that they should avoid touching any child under any circumstances. While the fear is understandable, at this point the evidence suggests that teachers may be overreacting. Very few teachers have been either convicted or fired for abuse of students. As in cases of negligence, a teacher who acts with reasonable care and prudence is unlikely to find himself or herself in difficulty. Hugging or holding primary-age children, for instance, is a common and justifiable practice, recognized as such by the courts. For example, charges against a Grade 4 teacher in Newfoundland were dismissed by the Court of Appeal with the recognition that some reasonable degree of physical contact between a teacher and students was appropriate (Anderson, 1991b). On the other hand, for a male teacher to hug a high-school-age female student is probably not wise, except under unusual circumstances.

As in other matters raised in this chapter, the legal requirements vis-à-vis child abuse, while valuable, do not solve the most troubling problems. No set of rules can substitute for professional judgement.

School Attendance: The Right to an Education

There is some debate among educators and lawyers as to whether people have a right to education, or whether education is something the state provides at its discretion. The *United Nations Universal Declaration of Human Rights* and the *United Nations Convention on the Rights of the Child* both treat education as a right, but provincial legislation in Canada is inconsistent, with some provinces using the term "right" and other provinces simply talking about education being provided. Nonetheless, most people tend to think of schooling as something to which we have a right.

Education statutes talk about the right to attend schools, not the right to receive an education. This distinction is an important one for two reasons. First, it implies that schools do not have a legal obligation to ensure that students benefit from attending. Schooling must be made available, but whether the student learns is apparently not a matter of law. Secondly, the statutes imply that students do not have a right to forms of education other than those the schools provide. If, for example, a student contended that he or she learned best in an informal, on-the-job setting, or at home, or through working in a library, legislation does not suggest that the schools have any legal obligation to provide education in these types of alternative settings. The issue of appropriate placement for special education students, discussed later in this chapter, is a particularly interesting instance of what schools are required to do to meet the needs of students.

Box 4.6
Legislative Provisions Governing the Right to Schooling

Alberta *School Act*, 1991, 3(1): Every individual (a) who at September 1 in a year is 6 years of age or older and younger than 19 years of age, and [who is a citizen or lawful resident of Canada] is entitled to have access in that school year to an education program in accordance with this Act.
3(2): A [school] board may permit an individual [who is younger than 6 or older than 18] to have access in that year to an education program. ...

Quebec *Education Act*, 1990, 1: Every person is entitled to the preschool developmental and cognitive learning services and to the elementary and secondary instructional services provided for by this Act ... from the first day of the school calendar in the school year in which he attains the age of admission to the last day ... in the school year in which he attains 18 years of age, or 21 years of age in the case of a handicapped person. ...
The age of admission to preschool education is 5 years on or before the date prescribed ...; the age of admission to primary instruction is 6 years. ...

Smith (1994) reviewed the status of procedural rights related to school attendance, such as the right of parents to be involved in shaping students' programs, and found that these were not well defined in provincial legislation.

A further interesting feature of the right to education is that this right is, in fact, compulsory. Most rights are available to people who wish to exercise them, but school attendance is different because it is legally required. It is worth thinking about why our society would want to force people to exercise a particular right. Compulsory attendance does clearly imply that the benefit of education extends beyond the individual to society itself, and that this larger benefit is sufficiently important to require universal attendance. Furthermore, understanding of the compulsory-attendance provisions in schools must take into account the history of schooling in Canada, and the view commonly held by the governing class in the nineteenth century that children must attend school to be taught the behaviour and values that would enable them to fit into society. It was not necessarily the school's function to teach children the values of their parents and families.

According to MacKay (1984), making school attendance compulsory means that the education provided should be valuable, otherwise it would be "an abuse of state power" (p. 72). Whether compulsory attendance can be justified legally under the *Charter* is an interesting but, as yet, unexplored question.

Home Schooling

Closely related to the issue of compulsory education is the matter of home schooling.

A small number of parents—perhaps 10 000 students, or 1 in 500, are involved (Smith, 1996)—choose to educate their children at home rather than send them to school. This is usually because the parents have strong objections to the schools. Such objections can be religious in nature (parents may want their children educated in a particular religious tradition, such as Judaism, that the schools do not follow) or philosophical (parents may not like the way in which schools provide education).

Most provincial legislation in Canada gives parents the option of educating their children at home, as long as the education provided is approximately equivalent to the standard found in the public schools. Provinces have been easing restrictions on home schooling, and some now require schools to support parents who are home schooling (Smith, 1996) (see Box 4.7). Many school authorities have been strongly sceptical about home schooling, arguing that children must attend public schools to be educated properly. Others have taken the opposite view and asserted that parents should have the right to choose what kind of education their children receive.

Maintaining Order in the Schools

We noted earlier that in an attempt to maintain order, schools create various rules and place restrictions on students that are not ordinarily found in other social settings. Examples include rules governing movement (where students can be), privacy (lockers, personal possessions), appearance and dress, and conduct (smoking, fighting, taking turns). Canadian courts have consistently upheld the rights of schools to restrict students' behaviour for purposes of maintaining an orderly atmosphere in the school. These restrictions can extend "not only to ... studies, attendance, homework and behavior, but to hair styles, clothing, manners and morals, social activities, speech and association" (Hurlbert & Hurlbert, 1992, p. 39).

However, the courts have also begun to insist that such rules have some clear justification, and that their application must respect students as persons. School authorities will need to show that the limitations placed on students are indeed necessary for the orderly conduct of schools. Tolerance for rules that are set and enforced in an arbitrary fashion does appear to be diminishing, and greater attention is being paid to

---

Box 4.7
Legislative Provisions Governing Home Schooling

Ontario *Education Act*, 1990, 2: A child is excused from attendance at school if (a) he is receiving satisfactory instruction at home or elsewhere. ...

Saskatchewan *Schools Act*, 1995, 3–0.1.1566: A pupil may be exempted from attendance at a school, and no parent, guardian or other person shall be liable to any penalty imposed by this act, where: ... (A.2) the pupil is receiving instruction in a registered home-based education program.

principles of natural justice. This may mean that rules will need to be clear and specific rather than vague and general, that students will have to be informed of the rules in advance, and that some procedure for review or appeal of decisions may be required (Harte & McDonald, 1996). Examples of these developments as they relate to issues of order and discipline can be seen most clearly in the handling of some of the more extreme situations in schools, which are discussed in the following sections.

Search and Seizure

Canadian students, like all other Canadians, have the right to be free from illegal and unreasonable search of themselves or their possessions. Usually courts must balance this right against the public's right to be protected from crime and wrongdoing. Court decisions in Canada have supported the right of school administrators to search students or their property when there are reasonable grounds for suspecting some wrongdoing. For example, the right of a principal to search the clothing of a student who had been observed with illegal drugs was upheld by a court (Hurlbert & Hurlbert, 1992, p. 115). However, schools do not have the authority to search students or their lockers arbitrarily, that is, without some grounds for suspicion (Dickinson & MacKay, 1989, p. 390). As in other instances, much would likely depend on the facts of the case, and the extent to which the teacher or principal had good grounds for believing that the student was engaged in some significant wrongdoing. The greater the invasion of the student's privacy, the more serious the cause must be. The same would be true for searches of students' lockers. Random searches might well be held to be wrong, while searches of particular lockers where there is a suspicion of, say, stolen goods, might well be upheld by the courts. However, due process provisions, such as informing the student of the reasons for the search and allowing her or him to be present with a witness, would also be advisable.

Disciplining Students

The ability of schools to discipline students comes from two sources, one being the *in loco parentis* status of teachers and administrators in schools. As well, education legislation in most provinces provides specifically for the right of the school and school board to make rules and enforce discipline on students. These statutes are typically silent on what this provision might mean, and few higher-court cases have applied the *Charter* guarantees to students. On the whole, Canadian courts have, as has already been noted, accepted that schools can make and enforce rules that can reasonably be considered necessary to maintaining order. But in this area, too, reasonable provisions consistent with the *Charter* and with natural justice are gradually becoming standard in schools.

Corporal Punishment, Violence, and the Use of Force with Students

One of the most controversial forms of discipline in schools is the practice of corporal punishment. Canada's *Criminal Code* (Section 43) allows teachers to use physical force against students: "Every school teacher, parent, or person standing in the place of a parent is justified in using force by way of correction toward a pupil or child, as the case may be, who is under his care, if the force does not exceed what is reasonable under the circumstances." Over the years, the courts have limited the use of corporal punishment in various ways: the punishment must be for purposes of correction; it must be reasonable given the offence; it cannot leave a permanent mark or injury; it must be suited to the pupil's age; and so on. Hitting a student on the head, or with a metal bar, would not be seen by the courts as justified, while a slap on the hand with a rubber strap would be (Hurlbert & Hurlbert, 1992, p. 202).

More important than the *Criminal Code* in this area, however, are changing social values about the use of physical punishment. There is less and less public support for hitting children, for almost any reason. The Law Reform Commission of Canada has advocated the abolition of corporal punishment (Hurlbert & Hurlbert, 1992, p. 194), as have many teachers' associations and other groups of educators. Many school districts in Canada have prohibited the use of the strap, and use has declined even where not prohibited. Some feel that corporal punishment would be overruled by the Supreme Court as a violation of the *Charter* prohibition on "cruel and unusual punishment" (Section 12), but this assertion has not yet been tested. On the other hand, a New Brunswick Court decision suggested that school board or provincial policies prohibiting corporal punishment could not overrule teachers' rights under the Criminal Code to use corporal punishment (Anderson, 1995a).

While there is considerable consensus concerning the educational inappropriateness of corporal punishment in schools, teachers' associations have recently expressed growing concern about student violence in schools, and about violence directed at teachers. This has focussed greater attention on issues of workplace safety and school security, and to the need for teachers to be protected by Section 43 of the *Criminal Code* when using force against a student for reasons other than punishment. Examples of such a situation might be to restrain a student from harming other people, breaking up a fight, or, as in the case of *Regina v. Sweet* (1986), preventing a student suspected of a breach of discipline from escaping investigation.

In *Regina v. Sweet*, a student suspected of smoking marijuana in the school was apprehended and told by a teacher to wait while the vice-principal was called to deal with the incident. The student refused and attempted to push his way past the teacher, who tried to prevent him from leaving. In the scuffle that followed, the teacher was elbowed in the stomach and had his hand bitten. The student was charged with assault, and in court maintained in his defence that he was justified in using force because his detention was unlawful under the *Charter*. The judge rejected this defence, citing Section 43 of the *Criminal Code*, which empowers teachers to use force in such situations.

The available evidence does not necessarily support the view that violence in schools has increased (Dolmage, 1995). Nonetheless, schools have responded to the concern by taking two sorts of steps to try to curtail violence—using what might be called educative and disciplinary strategies. Many schools have implemented programs that are aimed at preventing violence by helping students learn to solve disputes through peaceful means. Examples include the Second Step Program and a variety of mediation, peer-counselling, and other conflict-resolution programs. At the same time, many schools and school systems have introduced so-called "zero tolerance" programs, in which violent actions lead automatically to severe consequences such as suspension or expulsion. Zero tolerance policies do send a clear message to students and parents about the school's attitude toward violent behaviour, but they do not solve problems: some provision still has to be made for students who may have been expelled, the causes of the problems are not dealt with, and cases inevitably arise in which the consequences simply do not fit the supposed offence—for example, bringing a paring knife to school to cut one's lunch.

A balance is clearly needed that protects both students and teachers and allows the school to be orderly without undue coercion. MacKay and Sutherland (1992), in reviewing recent court cases, conclude that

> teachers have, for better or worse, been well protected by the courts. ... The commonly held view by teachers that the law does not allow one to use force to discipline a student is not supported in the case law. It is school policies, responding to public opinion, that have limited the use of force by teachers (p. 21).

Suspension and Expulsion

Legislation in each province provides for the suspension and expulsion of students from schools. **Suspension** is a temporary ban on attending school, while **expulsion** is a permanent ban. Legislation generally gives the school board the authority to make suspension decisions, and boards delegate that authority by resolution to the school; however, the decision to expel a student permanently can be made only by a school board. School board policies normally spell out suspension procedures, including what provisions of natural justice must be observed (e.g., whether or not the student has the right to a hearing before suspension). Provisions for hearings and appeals before expulsion are found in most provincial legislation.

Schools have had almost total latitude from the courts to suspend students for any reason the school or school board deems sufficient, ranging from violating rules to committing a crime. One likely impact of the *Charter* may be to require school boards to be clearer about the kinds of grounds on which a suspension can be justified, and to show how these are required to maintain order in a school. Schools will continue to be able to suspend students who endanger others or who refuse to accept the basic rules of the school. But whether a school could legally defend itself for suspending a student who had spoken publicly against a school policy or criticized a teacher is not nearly as certain.

Democratic Practice in Schools

The *Charter* guarantees Canadians the right to elect governments. Whether students in schools have such a right has not been argued before the courts. One might think that learning in practical terms about political processes would be an important part of what secondary schools teach. Yet student councils in most Canadian secondary schools are heavily restricted and monitored by school administrators. The Toronto Board of Education's *Student Rights Policy* is an instance where the right to student government has been institutionalized (see Box 4.8).

Canadian schools have had wide latitude in the past to limit students' rights to express themselves freely and to assemble freely. For example, schools have frequently limited students' right to publish their opinions in school newspapers, to organize political activities in the school, and to circulate or read certain kinds of materials. Some experts believe that the application of the *Charter* will eventually force schools to be more careful about how and when they limit students' ability to speak and write what they think; however, there have been few cases to provide a sense of how the courts will rule on these matters.

Box 4.8
Excerpts from the Toronto Board of Education
Student Rights Policy

- The student body in every Toronto secondary school has the right to elect a student council and every student has both the right and the responsibility to participate in this process.
- Every council has a right to develop a written constitution. ...
- Every student has a right to hold office in student government, subject only to such regulations as are established by the council itself in its constitution.
- From time to time the student government may wish to meet in a private session. The principal should be notified in advance and given the reasons. ...
- The council may select delegates to attend school staff meetings in a speaking, but non-voting capacity. ...

Source: Toronto Board of Education. (1993). *Student rights policy.* Toronto: Board of Education, pp. 17, 18.

Issues of order illustrate most clearly the dilemma posed by the schools' educational mission. It is hard to see how an institution can inculcate in young people respect for the law and for the rights of others, as well as an understanding of democratic processes, when these same principles are not embodied in the actual operation of the school. If students are treated arbitrarily, subjected to rules they neither support nor understand, and denied avenues for the peaceful expression of their opinions, then surely there is something educationally wrong. There is, of course, a need to keep order in schools, but one must surely wonder if the educational rationale cited here does not justify some greater tolerance for diverse behaviour and diverse points of view than is found in many schools. Are students' dress, hair length, or written opinions (provided they are not libellous) so prejudicial to the effective conduct of education that they justify restricting students in ways that would not occur outside the school?

Teaching Practices

The School Year

Various aspects of the school year, including precise dates, number of professional-development days, and holiday breaks, are usually controlled by provincial regulation. School districts may be given some options regarding the organization of the school year, but the most important aspects are provincially regulated. School years differ from province to province in regard to number of days, starting dates, holidays, and professional-development arrangements.

Curriculum

In all provinces, the authority to set curriculum is given by statute to the minister of education, meaning, in practice, the ministry or department of education. While some provinces provide much more specific direction than do others in this area, provincial regulations or policies usually specify the courses or subjects to be taught at each level and the amount of time to be given to each course or subject. They may also prescribe certain forms of student evaluation, such as provincial tests or examinations. Provinces generally prescribe sets of authorized textbooks as well, although schools or teachers may have some choice within the overall list. Most provinces provide some curriculum flexibility, allowing schools or school districts to offer some courses (usually following provincial approval) that are felt locally to be of particular importance or benefit. (See Chapter Nine for a fuller discussion of curriculum.)

Educational Malpractice

Although schools and teachers can and have been sued for failing to safeguard a child's safety, there has not yet been a successful case against a Canadian school for failing to educate a student—what might be called the pedagogic equivalent of medical malpractice (Dickinson, 1995). In Canada, such matters as incorrectly identifying a student as handicapped, allowing a student who cannot read to graduate, or simply failing to provide reasonable instruction, though we might condemn each as an example of professional misconduct, have not yet been considered reasonable grounds for lawsuits.

Special Education Students

The rapid growth of special education in Canadian schools has raised a number of legal issues. Do the schools have the right to classify students whom they feel require some sort of special program? Do parents have that right? Must the schools provide programs for different kinds of exceptional students? Few of these issues are currently covered in Canadian legislation, and there are many contentious cases in which there is a disagreement between the school and the parents as to the appropriate program for a child. In some cases, parents are resistant to the school's desire to change their child's program, while in other cases parents are pressing the school to provide some program that the school is reluctant to offer.

The provision of appropriate education to meet the needs of each student is increasingly accepted as a right in Canadian education. Most provincial legislation now reflects this requirement (Goguen & Poirier, 1995). For example, Section 144(1) of the Saskatchewan *Education Act* states that "every person ... shall have the right ... to receive instruction appropriate to his age or level of educational achievement." In some provinces, however, this right is still qualified. The question of what is meant by an appropriate education is also far from evident. Does it mean special separate classes or does it mean that all students, regardless of particular needs, should be in the same classrooms? The issue is complicated because educators and parents may have different opinions. Some have fought to have exceptional students, such as those with physical disabilities, placed into regular classrooms (an issue discussed more fully in Chapter Nine), while others have fought to have particular needs, such as learning disabilities or giftedness, met in separate programs or classes.

A review of provincial provisions (Smith, 1994) came to the conclusion that parents have little legal standing when it comes to influencing the delivery of special education services for their children. There does appear to be an increasing trend toward applying principles of natural justice to special education, which would require that students and parents be kept informed of the school's proposals for students, and that they be given the right to a hearing. The school must be cautious about acting in a manner that contradicts students' and parents' views unless it can present good reasons for doing so. At the same time, as they have in other areas of law, courts have recognized that schools have a degree of expertise in these matters that should not lightly be set aside to accommodate parents' wishes. The area of student classification is not, as a rule, dealt with in provincial education statutes, and it is currently an area of much controversy and court action.

The cases outlined in Box 4.3 suggest that courts will give schools latitude to make special education placements that are reasonable under the circumstances, but that the schools must show good faith in trying to meet the educational needs of students. Parental wishes may be less important than a reasonable educational justification.

Copyright

Copyright law is an interesting example of the division between personal and property rights, as noted on pages 105–106. Written material, music, art, videos, and computer software are considered property, just like a house or a car. Copyright law, which comes under the jurisdiction of the federal government, restricts a person from using someone else's work without the originator's permission. Often this law means that one must pay to reproduce by any mechanical or electronic means a book, article, or other material. In other words, the right of the community to benefit from ideas is subordinated to the right of the individual to profit from them.

Until recently, Canada's copyright law dated from 1924 and did not deal adequately with newer forms of communication such as computer software, VCRs, and mass photocopying. The copyright law has been revised to strengthen the protections to copyright holders. Teachers cannot make multiple copies of an article or play for an entire class. Nor is it permissible to rewrite something in slightly different language and then copy it. Libraries have placed warnings over photocopying machines to discourage people from making illegal copies. Teachers cannot legally videotape a television program for classroom use unless formal permission has been given by the copyright holder. There have been prosecutions of individuals and organizations (Walker, 1996) for violating copyright laws.

In response to the significant problems that these restrictions threatened to create for schools, colleges, and universities, provincial governments, acting on behalf of schools, have entered into agreements with an organization called CANCOPY in order to allow schools to make limited numbers and kinds of copies for nonprofit educational purposes. The provinces pay CANCOPY a fee for these rights, and CANCOPY in turn distributes these monies to authors, artists, and any other creators of the work. Most public schools are now covered by such agreements. They allow some (but by no means unlimited) photocopying of stories, plays, articles, poems, books, and artistic works. Typically, CAN-COPY agreements allow unbound class sets of up to 10 percent of a publication. There are restrictions on what can be copied, so teachers should obtain full details from their school library or administration to ensure that they are complying with the copyright law.

CANCOPY agreements do not include nonprint materials such as videos or computer software. These are also subject to copyright protection, so teachers need to be sure that permission has been obtained before making copies of any such materials. Computer software is sometimes covered by a **site licence** that allows an organization to use software in all parts of its operation without having to buy multiple copies. Some provincial governments have also negotiated copyright agreements that allow schools to use videos or computer software under certain conditions.

Conclusion

Legal issues are playing an increasing role in schools. Many of the issues and conflicts that have been endemic to schooling are now being addressed in part through court action. It is important that teachers be aware of the impact of law on schools, and of the implications of such major documents as the *Charter of Rights and Freedoms*. At the same time, teachers should not see themselves as lawyers, not be so struck by legal issues as to forget that their first obligation is an educational one. Teachers and schools can benefit from a careful consideration of legal issues, both old ones and those newly emerging, but it is best if this consideration takes place within a framework of educational purposes and values.

Exercises

1. Find in the library an index to the provincial statutes in your province. Through a scan of the list of statutes, identify those that could have a significant impact on education, and mention briefly the kind of impact they might have.

2. Find a recent piece of legislation in your province that relates to education. This could be an amendment to a schools or education act, or some other legislation that affected schools in a significant way. Think about which groups or interests might have favoured or opposed this legislation. Who gained or lost from its passage? Why? Using *Hansard* (the record of debates in the legislature), review the debate over this legislation. What arguments were advanced for and against the proposals? Why? Whose interests appear to have prevailed in the debate?

3. Find a copy of a provincial regulation made under the *Schools Act*. What provisions are in the regulation? Why are these provisions not in the legislation itself? How often has the particular regulation been altered in the last five or ten years?

4. Find and read a copy of a court decision (any level of court) on a recent case involving education. What arguments did the judges use to support their particular decision? Was their decision consistent with previous decisions on the same sort of case? Why or why not?

5. Write a brief essay indicating whether or not you think the courts should play a greater role in Canadian schools. Give specific examples to support your point of view.

6. In what ways is the *Charter* affecting Canadian schools? Is its impact, in your view, positive? Why or why not?

7. Choose one of the pairs of rights listed on page 103. Illustrate how this distinction might apply to a specific instance of a legal issue involving schools.

8. "Schools are not sufficiently respectful of the rights of their students." Agree or disagree, supporting your answer with specific examples.

9. Imagine you are a senior civil servant in the Department or Ministry of Education. You have been asked to give the minister advice on legal aspects on home schooling, together with a brief (two-page) justification for the stance you have taken.

10. Arrange a class discussion of how schools can best deal with issues of violence. What should be the relative balance between educative measures, such as mediation programs, and disciplinary measures, such as zero tolerance or suspension policies?

11. Most student councils in high schools are primarily concerned with social activities. Should student councils assume a more active role in the governance of the school? Why or why not? If yes, how could such a change be fostered?

12. Go to a nearby high school. Find out as many of the school's rules as you can on the matters discussed in this chapter. Write a letter to the school principal explaining why you think these rules are (or are not) consistent with principles of justice and education.

13. Review one or more of the regulations in your province that govern the work of teachers in the areas of curriculum, student evaluation, allocation of time to subjects, and textbooks. Write a brief paper outlining the impact on teachers' instructional activities of these regulations.

Further Reading

A fuller discussion of many of the issues in this chapter can be found in several chapters in Ratna Ghosh and Douglas Ray (Eds.), *Social Change and Education in Canada* (1995). The relevant chapters include those by MacKay on rights; by Dickinson on teachers' duties and authority; by Esbensen on students' rights; by Magsino on parents, children, and the state; and by Goguen and Poirier on the educational rights of exceptional students.

Some of the major books with extensive discussions of legal issues in education are now getting somewhat dated due to more recent court decisions. Examples are MacKay (1984); Dickinson and MacKay (1989); and Hurlbert and Hurlbert (1992). Several new books on the subject are available. Sussel (1995) uses examples such as AIDS, status of women, and exceptional children to argue that the *Charter of Rights and Freedoms* is changing the nature of education and law in Canada. The second edition of Larry Bezeau's *Educational Administration for Canadian Teachers* (1995) also discusses many legal issues in education.

Journals devoted to law and education include *Education and Law Journal, School Law Commentary,* and *The Journal of Law and Education.* All contain articles and case reports on legal issues in education. *Canadian School Executive,* published monthly, has regular articles on legal issues, including brief reviews of important current court decisions.

CHAPTER FIVE

Resources for Education

▼ PROLOGUE

This should be interesting, thought Linda Chartrand as she entered the conference room at the board office. She had hesitated only briefly before agreeing to the request from the assistant superintendent to serve on the district's new strategic planning committee. Partly she had agreed because the meetings would be held during the daytime, and substitute coverage for her class would be provided. Between school committees, the district teachers' association, professional-development activities, and marking and class preparation, Linda already had so many after-school commitments that she was rarely home before 6:00 P.M. But mostly she'd been fascinated by being part of the process of thinking about where their organization was going to be going in the years ahead.

The first meeting had been gentle and noncommittal. Everyone was introduced, and all had a turn mentioning long-term issues they felt were particularly important to the district. Today they were to try to priorize a small number of critical issues the district would have to face. There were a dozen people on the committee, including teachers, principals, the assistant superintendent, the superintendent, two school trustees, and two parents. As each person had said her or his piece, Linda had been struck by the diversity of views around the table. Most people seemed to feel that the main problem was the inadequate resources provided by the provincial government, although some also seemed to think that the schools would be fine if only parents did their job properly.

Within a few minutes, the conversation turned to the question of funding. "I've been teaching for twenty years," said Alice Kubota, a teacher at one of the elementary schools, "and it's getting harder each year. First of all, we have to try to keep in touch with new developments in teaching, such as co-operative education and student assessment portfolios. Then the province keeps adding things to our program, such as family life education, drug prevention, and computer education. Parents are more demanding about teachers being able to justify what we're doing and why. On top of that, there are more children with severe problems in our classes than ever before. Some of these kids need pretty well full-time attention all by themselves, and if they don't get it they can disrupt the entire class. At the same time, we're hearing that there is no more money, and we'll have fewer staff, less professional development, and smaller budgets for supplies and materials. Teachers are committed and hardworking, but there is a limit, and we've reached it. If we're going to cope with the pressures, there will have to be more money."

Grace Volcy, one of the trustees, then spoke: "I understand the pressures that teachers are feeling. You may sometimes think that the school board isn't sympathetic to the problems, but we are. But we have problems too. Our local taxes are already among the highest in the province. The provincial government has threatened to pass legislation limiting our ability to set local taxes above a certain level. And we can't really look to the province for more money. They've got a big budget deficit, and they don't want to increase taxes either. In fact, every indication is that next year we will have bigger budget problems than ever. It would be nice for the trustees if teachers agreed to forego any salary increases next year; that would allow us to maintain programs."

"Why should teachers pay the cost of problems they didn't create?" asked Azim Khan, the president of the local teachers' association. "It's typical of our society for business to make mistakes, throw people out of work, causing all kinds of social problems, and then to suggest that teachers should pay for it by accepting contracts with no wage increases. Our salaries have been falling steadily behind inflation the last few years. We've accepted it because teachers are committed people who care about kids. But it can't go on any longer. The school board needs to explain clearly to the public that good education costs money, but poor education is a hell of a lot more expensive in the long run."

"Maybe it's not just a matter of how much money," chimed in Lori Pambrun, one of the parents. "People in this community care about education, and we're prepared to pay for good schools. But do people see the link between the amount of money we spend and the quality of education? Schooling costs much more than it did twenty years ago, yet we seem to have more problems than ever before. Now I know that these aren't necessarily the schools' fault. We've already said that as society changes, so do the problems facing schools. And heaven knows there are plenty of problems outside the schools. But doesn't that suggest that maybe we need to do things differently? For example, Tamara over there is a community liaison worker. She's done a great job of getting things going in that school, things regular teachers don't have time to do. One of them is bringing many more volunteers into the school, which frees teachers' time to work with students. Isn't there a way we could think again about how we use our resources, and whether we couldn't do it better?"

As the discussion went on around her, Linda found herself thinking about Lori Pambrun's comments. They made sense to her. She knew that money would continue to be important, and a source of controversy, but already she could see ways in which her school might rearrange staffing duties to meet some needs. ... ■

This chapter addresses the following questions about money and education:

1. What do we mean by resources for education?
2. How is education presently funded, and how has this system of funding come about?
3. How do governments at various levels raise resources for education and allocate them?
4. How are resources used within schools and school systems?
5. Does the education system get enough money to adequately perform its functions?
6. How much impact do resources (or the lack of them) have on schools and on students?

These questions are especially pertinent today when issues of spending, taxation, and the role of government are very much in the public eye. The desire to cut government spending, deficits, and taxes puts enormous pressure on education and other public services. It is especially important for teachers to understand the basic economics of the education system.

The chapter will show that there are many kinds of resources available for education, and that these resources are not necessarily used as effectively as they might be. Societies, through governments, make decisions about how important education is, and these decisions are political ones. There is no simple and right answer as to how much money to provide for education, how best to raise that money, how best to provide it, or how best to use it in schools. These are questions that require and deserve public attention and debate.

The Concept of Resources

When people think about resources for education, they are most often talking about money. People tend to measure the quality of our schools in terms of how much money is spent on them. Thus, educators may argue for additional funds to meet new needs and critics of schools may talk about the perceived lack of value given the increasing amounts spent on education. School boards may talk about the programs they can or cannot deliver because of public resistance to tax increases. Teachers are particularly aware of the ways in which their work is constrained by lack of money or other resources.

All this is not surprising; money plays an important role in education, and in our society generally. It is often seen as the common denominator of value for many things. In education, however, it is misleading to use money as the only, or even the most important, indicator of value or quality.

An educational system contains many kinds of resources. Many of these are purchased goods, such as buildings, equipment, books, and supplies of various kinds. Here it might be reasonable to assume a link between spending more and getting more: more money buys more library books, or more computers, or a bigger or better-equipped building. But goods are not the critical part of education. Far more important are the people who work in a school, the students who attend a school, and the people who live in the school's community, along with their skills, interests, motives, and effort. These resources cannot easily be counted but are nonetheless critical to the process of education. Two teachers may command the same salary yet be quite different in their ability to work with students. The students themselves will need or want quite different kinds of teaching or support services from the school. A community that sees schooling as an essential route to success is quite different from a community that sees schools as irrelevant to their needs and lives, or even as oppressive institutions. There are very important resources whose nature and impact cannot be translated into monetary terms. The data on spending levels tell us very little about them.

Thus, the conventional view of resources as involving only money is too narrow. Before returning to the question of how resources are used, however, it is important to understand the basic framework through which education in Canada is currently financed — where the money comes from, and how it is allocated and spent.

How Is Education Financed in Canada?

The great bulk of funds spent on education in Canada are raised and distributed by governments. There are two main sources for these funds — those raised by provincial governments and those raised by school districts. In Canada as a whole, about 58 percent of total school spending currently comes from provincial governments and the rest from local taxes, with a very small proportion coming from tuition fees (Canadian Education Statistics Council, 1996). The exception to this picture is education on Indian reserves, which is funded by the federal government, either directly or through grants to bands. The sources of school district funding vary significantly from one province to another.

Although many people see the current system as somehow natural, financing arrangements have changed considerably over the past century. When Canadian schools were first established, most of the funds were provided locally through fees, property taxes, or, in the case of religious schools, support from the church. During the twentieth century, provincial governments have taken an increasingly important role in governing and financing education, so that today there are no tuition fees in public schools and local revenue in most of Canada is far less significant than provincial revenue. Moreover, the federal government plays an important role in providing revenue to many provinces, which influences how much provinces may feel able to spend on education.

The change in the relative roles of the various providers indicates a change in our national beliefs about education. At one time, students and their families

were regarded as the prime beneficiaries of education and therefore as the appropriate sources (through fees) of revenue for education. We now accept, as a country, that we should provide elementary and secondary education free of charge to
all students.

This policy change is not self-evident. Rather, it reflects the view that education is not simply a benefit to the student who receives it. Instead, we think of
education as a **public good** from which every member of society benefits. It is an
integral part of our understanding that all of us should pay for education
through our taxes because we believe that a more educated population will be
better for all of us.

Yet clearly there is a private benefit to be derived from education. For example, we know that those who receive more education generally tend to earn
more. In 1994, the average income of persons with a university degree was
about $37 000, while the average income of those with eight or fewer years of
education was about $13 000, a difference of almost 300 percent (Statistics
Canada, 1995). One possible implication of these differences in average income
for future funding practices is that those with more education might pay part of
the cost directly, since their potential earning power is much greater. The retention of tuition fees in colleges and universities is a partial reflection of this view.
In public schools, however, the absence of fees reflects several other
beliefs — that no student should be prevented from obtaining an education
 because of poverty, and that our tax system will, in any case, result in those who
earn more paying more. As we shall see, the evidence does not provide a high
level of confidence that either of these assumptions is correct.

Students are not the only beneficiaries of education. What about employers,
 who are provided through public funds with an educated labour force that they
employ to earn profits? In Canada, companies do not pay for the school system
directly, and pay only a small proportion of the total taxes governments use to
support education. Moreover, the total share of taxation raised through corporate
taxes has been declining in Canada for many years. An equity argument might
also justify more financial support for education from private industry. Thus,
there is nothing magical about our current division of the financial burden of
education, even though we tend to take it for granted as the natural way of
organizing things.

In recent years, there has been much argument in some countries, though
less so in Canada, about the virtues of market systems and the desirability of having education conducted through market mechanisms. Advocates of this
approach believe that education would be improved if people had more choice
about the schools their children attended.

Chapter Three discussed some aspects of markets as social policy devices.
The argument for applying market approaches to the financing of education has
a certain appeal, but it has also been subject to much criticism (Kerchner &
Boyd, 1988). Given the important public benefits of education, inevitably there
will be a significant degree of public regulation of schools, a position acknowledged by even the staunchest advocates of market systems. There is no country

in the world in which the state does not play the major role in providing and financing primary and secondary education. Thus, the issue that is usually debated in education concerns the degree of choice people should have in selecting schools rather than the imposition of a market system.

Since governments are, and will likely remain, the predominant funders of education, it is important to understand something about how they obtain and allocate their money. We will begin with some general comments about taxation, and then consider in turn each of the three levels of government in Canada: federal, provincial, and municipal. Because of the political and constitutional make-up of Canada, each level is intimately connected with the others.

Taxation

While a thorough consideration of principles of taxation is beyond the scope of this book, it is important for those in education to have some basic understanding of taxation, since this is how public schools (and, to a considerable extent, private schools) are financed. It is impossible to discuss educational expenditures without a sense of where the money comes from. There is no agreement on an ideal tax system, any more than there is agreement on the ideal education system. People disagree quite strenuously about such matters as the role of taxation, the kinds of taxes that should be levied, and who should pay how much. Decisions about how many—and what kinds of—taxes to levy are political decisions made by governments.

As Table 5.1 shows, the different levels of government in Canada rely on different kinds of taxes to generate revenue. For the country as a whole, income tax is by far the most important, although for school districts in some provinces, property taxes are far more important.

In considering taxation, it is important to think not just about a single tax, but to keep in mind the entire flow of revenues from people to governments, and vice versa. In Canada, as in other industrialized countries, government is inextricably bound up with the entire operation of the economy. There can hardly be a person in Canada who does not receive some substantial portion of his or her income from public funds, either directly or indirectly. Hundreds of thousands of Canadians work for one of the levels of government, or work in services (e.g., health care or education) that are almost entirely funded by governments. Teachers are, of course, among this group; their salaries are paid from tax revenues. Millions of people receive payments from government through such programs as family allowance, pensions, or employment insurance. Others receive benefits through taxation incentives such as deductions for retirement savings, investments of various kinds, political contributions, and tuition fees. Many private companies derive much of their revenue from supplying goods or services to government, whether these take the form of consulting, supplies, equipment, office space, construction, or the many other items that governments purchase. And all of us benefit from at

Table 5.1

Main Revenue Sources of Canadian Governments

Federal (1995/96) total $145 billion	Provincial (1994/95) total $170 billion	Municipal (1994) total $70 billion	Overall (1994) total $303 billion
Income tax 55% personal 45% corporate 10%	Income tax 29% personal 25% corporate 4%	Transfers 45%	Income tax 40% personal 34% corporate 6%
Consumption tax 23%	Transfers 19%	Property tax 38%	Consumption tax 20%
Premiums 13%	Consumption tax 18%	Sale of services 12%	Property tax 11%
Other 9%	Other 34%	Other 5%	Premiums 10%
		Other 19%	

Notes:
• Municipal includes school districts.
• Transfers are from one level of government to another — e.g., federal to provincial; provincial to municipal.
• Premiums include such things as Employment Insurance and payroll levies.
• Consumption taxes include the GST, provincial sales taxes, cigarette and gasoline taxes, etc.
• Other includes fees, service charges, natural resource royalties, etc.

Source: Statistics Canada, Public Sector Finance, 1995–96. Reproduced with permission.

least some of the services that government supplies (education, health care, transportation, law and order, environmental protection, and so on).

Thus, people not only pay taxes but benefit from them as well, a point that is often ignored when concerns are raised about taxation levels in Canada. The question is not simply one of who pays taxes — although this is very important—but of how much one pays in relation to how much one benefits. It may be reasonable to believe that a given distribution of taxation is wrong, that the money raised is not spent as well as it could be, that the wrong people are paying, or that the wrong people are benefiting, but these questions should involve consideration of the total picture rather than just a small part of it.

Approaches to Taxation

Governments are generally seen to have three approaches to taxation available to them. They can tax **income** (how much we take in), **wealth** (how much we have), or **consumption** (how much we spend). Income tax is, of course, an example of the first of these. Taxes on inheritances, property, and capital gains are examples of the second, and provincial sales taxes or the Goods and Services Tax (GST) are examples of consumption taxes. Governments typically use some combination of the three approaches.

In Canada, there is a general belief that taxation should be based on ability to pay. We have accepted (though not always put into practice) the principle that those who have more should contribute proportionately more. This concept is termed **progressive taxation**. Thus, the rate of income tax goes up as income rises, meaning that higher-income earners should pay a larger proportion of their income in taxes. Most Canadians believe that our tax system should shift money from those with more to those with less, although there is disagreement on the extent to which this should be done. However, the application of the principle of progressive taxation depends a great deal on the particular form of taxation. This is because wealth, income, and consumption are distributed quite differently among people.

Income tax is still the single biggest source of government revenue. In Canada in 1993, the top 20 percent of families took in 43 percent of market income (that is, earnings before taxes and transfers from government), while the bottom 20 percent of families got just 2.2 percent (Ross, Scott, & Kelly, 1996a). This distribution has been getting more unequal over time. Governments have attempted to compensate for inequalities in income by raising tax rates for those with higher incomes, and by offering tax deductions or credits for those with lower incomes. Tax money is also distributed directly to those with lower incomes through various social programs. This redistribution does make a difference—once taxes and transfers are taken into account, the bottom 20 percent of families have 7.5 percent of all income, while the top 20 percent see their share drop to about 36 percent (Ross, Scott, & Kelly, 1996a). However, income remains highly unequal, even with taxes and government transfers.

The distribution of wealth is far more unequal than the distribution of income. In 1984, the small number of Canadians whose individual wealth was more than $200 000 held 37 percent of the bank deposits, 43 percent of Canada Savings Bonds (CSBs), 72 percent of all stocks, and almost 48 percent of all financial assets. On the other hand, the much larger number of Canadians with net wealth of less than $15 000 had 4 percent of bank deposits, 3 percent of CSBs, 1 percent of all stocks, and 3 percent of total financial assets. And, whereas those with wealth above $200 000 had 14 percent of all debt (including mortgages), those with wealth under $15 000 had 16 percent of all debt (Statistics Canada, 1986). Thus, while income is unequal by a ratio of 6:1, wealth is unequal by a much higher ratio. Osberg (1981) estimated that the wealthiest 5 percent of Canadians held more than 40 percent of all the wealth in the country (most of which was inherited rather than earned), whereas the bottom 10 percent had no net wealth at all (i.e., their debts were greater than their assets). Because most wealth is not in the form of annual income, a change in patterns of wealth would require much higher taxation of assets, not income. For example, Canada currently has few taxes on inheritances, even though inherited money has been the most common way in which people become rich (Osberg, 1981).

Property tax, which is a form of tax on wealth, is particularly relevant because in many provinces it is an important source of funds for education, either through a provincial or a local property tax. There has been a general feeling that property tax is unfair, especially to farmers, senior citizens, and others on fixed incomes. Farmland may produce very little annual revenue but have a high value if sold and thus be taxed at a rate that stretches the farmer's income. Moreover, because farms occupy large amounts of land, even a relatively low tax per hectare may mean a high total tax bill. Most people would see this as unreasonable taxation, even though the land does represent wealth. On the other hand, an individual or business may generate substantial revenue yet pay little tax because of various deductions and reinvestment provisions. Property tax can thus be a way of taxing wealth that would otherwise avoid taxation. Some provinces have attempted to deal with this quandary by providing programs of tax rebates that reduce or refund property taxes to target groups such as farmers, seniors, or others with low incomes.

Property tax is also a good example of the intermeshing of various taxes, since property owners who rent out their property for income can deduct the cost of property taxes from their taxable income, and thus pay less income tax than those who live in their own homes. On the other hand, profit from the sale of one's own home is not taxed, whereas profit from the sale of a revenue property is subject to capital gains tax. What, then, is the real impact of a particular level of property tax? The answer is that it depends very much on individual circumstances.

Consumption taxes are yet another matter. One might assume that the less money one has, the greater the share one would spend on goods and services, and therefore the harder hit one would be by consumption taxes such as sales tax. This is the belief behind the program of federal tax credits and rebates for the GST. On the other hand, proponents of the GST argue that it actually brings in more revenue from the wealthy because it taxes spending on previously untaxed services such as travel, eating out, and even the services of tax accountants.

As we have seen, each form of taxation has its own advantages and disadvantages, and each is based on a certain view of what constitutes fairness. Most economists believe that some combination of all three forms of taxation is needed to achieve the best balance and greatest degree of fairness.

The Financial Role of the Federal Government

The federal government has been an important provider of revenue for many provinces, with some provinces receiving as much as 40 percent of their total revenue in the form of transfers from the federal government. For the last 60 years, our national fiscal arrangements have reflected the belief that all Canadians are entitled to a basic standard of services. If provinces had to rely on their own resources to finance services such as health or education, poor provinces would be hard-pressed to provide services at nearly the same level as the richer provinces, so the federal government, which has greater taxing power, has used some of its funds to provide extra assistance to those provinces. The money came through a number of different avenues, some related to specific services such as health care or social assistance, and others giving provincial governments the ability to spend the funds on whatever their priorities were.

In the last few years, as part of its effort to reduce spending, the federal government has been limiting or reducing its financial support to provinces. Federal cost-sharing in the area of social assistance has been limited, and cash transfers for health and postsecondary education have almost disappeared. Federal equalization payments, however, remain a very important source of funds for some provinces.

In making these changes, the federal government has been creating budget problems for the provinces, which now have to decide whether to cut their own spending, levy higher taxes to make up the shortfall, or transfer the problem to hospitals, school systems, and municipalities by in turn reducing provincial grants to those bodies.

Reductions in federal funding also reduce the ability of the federal government to influence programs and services in Canada. In education the federal role has always been quite limited, but provinces will be even less inclined to look at federal proposals or national programs given cuts in the financial support they are receiving from Ottawa.

The Provincial Role

Provinces provide financial support for education just as they do for other services such as health care or highways. These funds are usually drawn from the general revenue of the province, which includes all federal government transfers and the revenue that the province collects through such means as income taxes, sales taxes, property taxes, fees of various kinds, taxes on products such as gasoline, tobacco, or alcohol, and so on.

Each provincial government determines as part of its annual budget how much money it will spend on education in that year, just as it does for any other service. The budget process generally involves the provincial Cabinet deciding how much money is available and how much of what is available should go to each of the various areas of expenditure. There is no simple or easy way of making these decisions, which have to do with the conflict between the desire to keep taxation levels as low as possible and the desire to have services that are of as high a quality as possible. Both are important political objectives that a government must balance in some way.

In determining how much revenue is available, a government must not only estimate the revenue from existing sources but also determine whether it wishes to change any tax rates, which will further alter revenue. In Canada, the prevailing climate of opinion (which we have tried to show is not necessarily well justified) is that taxes are too high, which puts pressure on governments to reduce taxes and therefore limit expenditures. Many provinces have recently passed legislation that requires a balanced budget.

At the same time, governments must balance many competing demands for expenditure. In making spending decisions, ministers have to consider various public priorities for services, the built-in increases in costs (such as inflation), changes in the demand for a service (e.g., an increase in the number of elderly people who require hospital beds), and the government's own beliefs and commitments as expressed in election promises. For at least the last ten years, governments across Canada have faced serious problems of trying to reconcile the demand for services with the desire to avoid tax increases. In the last few years, most provinces have chosen to cut spending quite sharply.

Table 5.2 shows the main sources of revenue and expenditure for several provinces and for all the provinces together. The table illustrates several issues in provincial finances. Some provinces are highly dependent on federal transfers. Newfoundland has very high income tax rates but still doesn't raise much revenue because average incomes are low. Alberta benefits greatly from oil revenues and has no provincial sales tax. Each province has a different revenue situation. Variations in expenditure are less significant; provinces tend to have roughly similar sorts of services and so have roughly similar patterns of expenditure.

Table 5.2

Main Sources of Revenue and Expenditure for Several Provinces

Sources of provincial revenues, 1992–93	Newfoundland ($3.3 billion)	Ontario ($46 billion)	Alberta ($13.6 billion)	All provinces ($145 billion)
Income tax	16%	34%	25%	29%
Property tax	less than 1%	3%	2%	4%
Consumption tax	21%	23%	6%	19%
Federal transfers	45%	9%	16%	21%
Natural resource royalties	less than 1%	less than 1%	20%	3%
Provincial expenditures, 1992–93	**$3.7 billion**	**$58 billion**	**$17.4 billion**	**$172 billion**
Health care	21%	20%	24%	26%
K–12 education	16%	9%	9%	12%
Postsecondary education	6%	6%	6%	6%
Debt service	15%	11%	12%	13%
Social services	14%	22%	15%	19%

Source: Statistics Canada, Public Sector Finance, 1995–96. Reproduced with permission.

Provincial Granting Systems

Determining the total provincial amount to be spent on education is only part of the process. Most of the money spent by the provinces is actually given to school boards. This occurs through a funding formula, whose purpose is to provide a basis for determining how much money will be given to each school district. While each province has a different formula, almost all have the same basic components.

Components of Formula Funding

There are three basic formula elements through which most provinces provide funding to school districts. In most cases, the first and largest amount of money takes the form of a **block grant** based on the number of students. Sometimes the student count is weighted, such that students in more expensive programs (e.g., special or vocational education) or those who are taught in more expensive to maintain settings (e.g., small or remote schools) are given a higher value in the count than other students in recognition of the extra costs of educating them.

targeted funding

useful

The second component is **categorical funding**, in which a province provides additional funds for particular programs or services. There are two reasons for categorical grants. First, they may be based on the assumption that school boards would not spend enough on such activities of their own accord — hence the province ties its money to the activities it wishes to support. Examples of categorical grants include those for special education, language education, and computer purchases. Second, a province may provide categorical funding as a way of recognizing that the costs of certain services, and therefore the provincial contribution to those costs, will vary a great deal from one district to another. An example would be the cost of transporting students by school bus. An urban district may have quite low transportation costs, while those of a rural district might be much higher. If each received the same funding per pupil, the rural division would have less available for instruction after it paid necessary transportation costs. Thus, most provinces tie transportation funding to actual costs through a categorical grant.

The final major component is **equalization funding**, which is important in provinces where school boards raise a significant share of their revenue through taxes levied on local property (discussed more fully in the next section). Just as provinces vary in wealth, school districts vary in the revenue they can raise from a given level of property tax. A district with many large homes or a considerable amount of industry is able to raise much more revenue than is a district with fewer and poorer people. Moreover, the ability to raise money from property taxes is not related to the number of students in schools. A district with many large homes and small numbers of children is doubly advantaged over a district with lower-value property and more children, in that it raises a large amount of money but has fewer students to pay for.

Provinces recognize this disparity and may provide additional funds to poorer districts as a way of equalizing their access to revenue. Equalization payments can be determined in many different ways, but the central idea is that a district's spending level should depend on the political choices it makes, not on whether it happens to contain highly valued property. This process is analogous to the federal government's equalization payments to poorer provinces. Of course, when the province pays all or nearly all the costs of education, there are no equalization grants of this kind.

Vertical and Horizontal Equity

The importance of the various components within the total provincial funding scheme varies from province to province. Some provinces put more weight on block grants, while others emphasize categorical grants or equalization. It is important to realize that there is no perfect funding formula.

Two different notions of fairness are recognized in the literature on education finance. One is **horizontal equity**, the idea that everyone should be treated the same. The principle of horizontal equity suggests that per-pupil spending should be roughly the same in all schools and all school districts. Equalization grants attempt to achieve horizontal equity in a province by providing each district with about the same amount of money per pupil.

The concept of **vertical equity** means that fairness lies in recognizing that different people have different needs, and that to treat everyone the same is patently unfair. For example, because rural schools may spend much more money on transporting students, to give them the same amount per student as urban schools is not equitable. Nor does it seem reasonable to assume that students who grow up in wealthy families, with access to good housing, plenty of food, and a steady family income, should have the same amount spent on their education as students who grow up poorly housed and poorly fed. Some students will clearly require more time and attention if they are to be successful learners. If schools are to promote a more equal society, the principle of vertical equity suggests that they will need to pay attention to and support some students more than others. Equalization grants attempt to create both horizontal and vertical equity by providing for equal spending per pupil in the same category (e.g., elementary, secondary) and differential spending per pupil across categories (e.g., special or vocational education).

Provinces contain many kinds of school districts—urban and rural, richer and poorer, with smaller or larger schools—and people disagree about which aspects of education are most important. These factors make it impossible for any funding formula to take all the differences into account in a way that all parties will perceive as fair. Such decisions, like so many others considered in this book, are political choices that are informed by people's goals and values. Most provinces make at least some changes in their grant structure almost every year, and may introduce entirely new formulas every five to ten years to try to meet changing conditions.

Independent Schools

All provinces have at least a few independent (also called private) schools. An independent school can be defined as a school that is not governed by a public school board, and that is selective about whom it admits as students, whether the selection process is based on grounds of ability, religion, or some other criterion. Students are usually charged tuition fees. Most private schools in Canada are religious in orientation.

Provincial policies on the funding of private schools vary a great deal. Provinces such as Ontario, Nova Scotia, and New Brunswick provide almost no support for private schools, whereas Quebec and the western provinces do provide some public funding for private schools under certain conditions. As discussed in Chapter Two, many provinces have publicly funded dissentient schools; the difference is that these schools are not considered private under the terms of the definition given here.

In no province do private school enrollments make up more than a small fraction of the total enrollment. The highest proportion is found in Quebec, with about 10 percent of students educated in private schools. Despite the relatively low enrollment figures, however, public funding of private schools is still a matter of controversy since it raises many fundamental questions about what it means to have a public school system.

Capital Funding

Capital generally refers to durable items such as buildings or major pieces of equipment. Most provinces fund school buildings (either new or renovated) through a separate funding process. Typically, school districts must submit proposals justifying their requests to build new schools or to renovate existing ones. Provincial governments then approve or reject such projects on a case-by-case basis. Once approval is given, the province pays most or all of the cost, depending on the policy in each province, up to a specified level. Provinces usually have a set of standards for determining what can be included in a building, and how much the province will contribute. However, the actual responsibility for construction, including hiring architects and contractors, usually lies with the school board.

A new school can cost anywhere from $1 million to $15 million to build depending on its size, facilities, and location. Of course, schools in remote northern areas are much more expensive, as are schools that contain vocational facilities, labs, or swimming pools. A smaller province, such as Manitoba or New Brunswick, has around 800 schools. If a school lasts approximately 80 years, then such a province needs to replace some 10 schools a year, at a total cost of $20 to $50 million. At the same time, other schools could require extensive renovations or additions. If most of the school buildings are old, pressures for capital spending will naturally be higher.

Provinces may spread out the cost of building through **amortization**, which is essentially what a family does when it buys a house and repays the cost plus interest over a number of years through a mortgage. In 1992–93, the provinces spent approximately $2.5 billion on capital and debt-servicing costs (Canadian Education Statistics Council, 1996, p. 34), compared with some $30 billion on the operating costs of schools.

The Role of the School District

The financial role of school districts depends greatly on the provincial arrangements regarding local taxation. In 1988 these arrangements varied enormously, with some provinces paying 99 percent of the total cost of education and others paying around 50 percent. In the latter group of provinces, local school boards provided the remainder of the revenue through property taxation. However, in the last few years a number of provinces have changed funding arrangements so that the great bulk of school funds are raised and allocated provincially. If Ontario makes the financing changes that were announced in early 1997 as this book was being written, only Saskatchewan and Manitoba will be left with significant amounts of funding for schools coming from local property tax.

Where provinces provide almost all the money, the role of the local school board is changed dramatically. With no ability to raise additional revenue, the school board is left with the task of managing whatever resources the province provides.

In jurisdictions that do have local taxation, school districts typically compare the amount they will get from the province with the amount they would like to spend. In recent years, school districts have faced flat or declining provincial support but increasing costs for such items as salary increments in collective agreements, special education, supplies, and utility costs. In other words, school boards face trying budget pressures very similar to those at the provincial and federal level to balance revenue and expenditure. Exercise 18 at the end of this chapter, in which readers are asked to role-play a school board budget meeting, indicates how difficult these choices can be.

Property Tax and Mill Rates

In contrast to the federal and provincial governments, which have a wide variety of tax sources, school boards raise funds almost entirely from taxes on property. Each property in a province has what is called an **assessed value**. In some cases, assessment of property is done by local governments, while in other cases it is province-wide. Assessment is an attempt to give a fair relative value to all property so that property taxes will be fair. As has been noted already, some school districts have much more valuable property than do others and can raise more money with the same tax rate.

It can be very difficult to determine the relative value of properties, especially if they are of different kinds. How does one equate the value of a farm with the value of a city house or a factory? What about the fact that two similar houses may have very different values depending on property prices in a given community? It is not surprising, then, that there are constant debates about property assessment schemes, and that under almost any scheme there will be appeals from property owners who feel that their assessment is unfair.

The total value of all property in a given school district or province is the basis on which property taxes are levied. A school district or municipality will charge taxes at so many **mills**, with a mill meaning $1 in tax for every $1000 of assessed value. The school board can obtain the same amount of revenue regardless of the actual assessment of a property simply by changing the mill rate; to the property owner, a higher mill rate on a lower assessment is the same thing as a lower mill rate on a higher assessment. This is why the actual assessed value of any single property does not matter, but fairness in assessment across properties does.

Does Education Get Enough Money?

Debates about changes or improvements in education invariably turn to questions of money. Many people working in education feel that not enough money has been spent on public education in recent years, and that, as a result, the quality of education provided is falling.

The question is, how does one determine how much money is enough? One of the first possible steps to take is to look at the total amount spent. We pointed out in Chapter Two that public education is a large enterprise. In 1995–96, some $35 billion was spent on elementary and secondary schools in Canada. An additional $15 or $16 billion is spent by the country's colleges and universities, while the amount spent on education and training by private and public companies, nonprofit organizations, and individuals, though it has not been estimated with any accuracy, may well be as large as the spending on schools (Canadian Education Statistics Council, 1996). However, it is hard to judge what these numbers mean: is $35 billion an appropriate amount to spend on education or not?

One standard sometimes invoked is that of comparisons with other countries. Because countries use quite different methods of accounting for their spending on education, however, international comparisons of this kind are very difficult to make with confidence. Moreover, differences in geographic conditions, such as population density or climate, can create significant variations in transportation, construction, and heating costs, to name a few. Nonetheless, international comparisons are frequently made. Canada is often said to be among the highest-spending countries in the world on education. However, this comparison includes postsecondary education, where Canada has a high participation rate and primarily public funding. If the comparison is limited to public schools, Canada ranks more in the middle of the industrialized countries. The

Economic Council of Canada (1992, p. 32) found that Canada was seventh among sixteen industrialized countries in terms of public spending per student when related to the size of each country's economy. Most comparisons put the Scandinavian countries at the top in spending, with countries such as Japan and Germany nearer the bottom.

A more frequent standard is to compare past and present spending levels. This can be done in many different ways, and the results one gets depend in part on the indicator chosen. Table 5.3 gives six different spending comparisons utilizing 1971 and 1991 data. Using some of these indicators, spending appears to have increased substantially, while by using other indicators, spending appears to have decreased. How can this be?

Indicators such as those in Table 5.3 always involve more than one factor. Consider expenditure per pupil. Changes in per-pupil expenditure levels may be due to changes in funding levels, but they may also be due to changes in the number of students. Thus, if the number of students decreases, costs will not necessarily decrease proportionately, in which case per-pupil spending would rise even though no deliberate change has been made in the level of service to students. Similarly, if enrollment rises, per-pupil spending may fall with no change in the level of service. If a school has, say, 10 teachers, 200 students, and a total budget of $1 000 000, the per-pupil cost would be $5 000. If the following year there were only 190 students, the per-pupil cost would rise to $5 263 per pupil, even though nothing had changed in the school's operations. Similarly, if the enrollment rose to 220 and all the new students were accommodated in existing classes by making each class slightly larger, the per-pupil cost would fall to about $4 545, again with no real change in the school's program. Thus, per-pupil costs are a reasonable measure of relative spending only when enrollment is stable. Economists would say that unit costs in education (with each pupil considered a unit) are inelastic with regard to enrollment, meaning that they do not change in either direction as rapidly as enrollment can change. In Canada, per-pupil expenditures in real dollars rose rapidly after 1970, but a large proportion of the increase was due to the substantial decrease in school enrollment from 1970 to 1980, which occurred without a corresponding reduction in numbers of teachers.

Similarly, changes in the number of students can affect other indicators. The pupil–teacher ratio fell quite sharply in the 1970s because enrollment fell (in total by about 25 percent), but instead of reducing the number of teachers in proportion, school systems kept their staff and launched new programs and services requiring more staff, such as librarians, guidance counsellors, and increased special education. However, the slower growth in education spending related to declining enrollments did lead to education dropping in terms of its share of total provincial spending.

Governments have been facing significant pressures to spend more in other areas. Health care is one field that has taken an increasing share of provincial expenditures in recent years. Spending has also grown in relatively new areas of government activity, including the environment and workplace safety. Another factor to consider is that such comparisons depend a great deal on the year with

Table 5.3 Indicators of Education Spending over Time

	1971	1991
Gross pupil–teacher ratio (the total number of uncertified teachers, including administrators, divided by the total number of students)	20.8:1	15.8:1
Explanation: When student enrollment fell rapidly in the 1970s, the number of educators stayed the same or increased, allowing schools to mount new programs and provide additional specialist and support services.		
Total spending on elementary/secondary education	$5.3 billion	$33.3 billion
Explanation: Over this time, the consumer price index (CPI) grew by 295%. Teachers' salaries (see below) also grew rapidly as a young teaching force became more qualified and more experienced.		
Spending on elementary/secondary education as a percentage of total provincial government spending	30%	20%
Explanation: School enrollments have decreased since 1971 while governments face mounting demands in other areas, such as health care, and debt costs have risen sharply.		
Total spending on elementary/secondary education as a proportion of the total economy (GDP)	5.6%	5.0%
Explanation: As the number of students declined, education took up a smaller share of the total economy. However, had spending remained at 1971 per-pupil levels, education would have been 3.9% of GDP in 1991 rather than 5%.		
Expenditure per pupil as a proportion of economic capacity (GDP per capita)	22%	28%
Explanation: Most of this increase occurred as a result of the recession of 1991–93, in which the economy shrank while education expenditures stayed even or rose slightly.		
Average salary per educator	$10 029	$55 979
Explanation: Salary scales for teachers grew by 7.3% per year, but actual average salaries increased by 9% per year because educators gained additional qualifications and experience and thus moved higher on the pay scale. Over the same period, the consumer price index grew by 7.1% per year and the economy as a whole (GDP per capita) grew by 8.8% per year.		

Source: Adapted from François Gendron. (1994). Does Canada invest enough in education? Reproduced by authority of the Minister of Industry, 1997, Statistics Canada, *Education Quarterly Review, Cat no. 81–003, 1994, Volume 1, Number 4,* pp. 10–25.

which one starts. In this case, 1970 marked a high-water point for education expenditures in Canada: the baby boom was at its height, educational facilities were expanding rapidly, and teachers' training, experience, and salaries were growing rapidly. One would expect that, as the system matured, the rate of increase in spending would level off somewhat.

In looking at the data in Table 5.3, it is also important to understand the impact of changes in the economy. For example, a large part of the increase in overall spending on education is accounted for by inflation; that is, it costs more to do exactly the same things. To eliminate the impact of inflation, analysts use the concept of **real dollars**: converting the amounts from different years to reflect the same amount of actual purchasing power.

Another set of indicators compares spending on education to the size of the economy as a whole. This is typically measured in relation to **gross domestic product**, or **GDP**, which is essentially the total value of all the goods and services produced in the economy. Here problems arise when the economy shrinks, as it did in the recession of the early 1990s. When this happens, spending on education accounts for a larger share of the total economy even if education spending remains constant.

The indicator on teachers' pay shows some other complexities of measuring change over time. Teachers' salary scales—the amounts paid to teachers depending on their qualifications and experience—rose from 1971 to 1991 by an average of 7.3 percent. However, the actual pay of teachers rose by about 9 percent per year because teachers gained additional qualifications and experience that moved them up on the scales. Which is the "true" measure of teachers' pay? In fact, there is no single true measure; each has to be considered in its overall context. Had the teaching force maintained the same qualifications in 1991 that it had in 1971, average salaries would have been significantly lower. However, the 1971 teaching force was relatively young and relatively poorly qualified. For example, many teachers in 1971 did not have university degrees, while this qualification is practically universal now.

Finally, it should be noted that using a twenty-year comparison with 1991 as the final year is potentially misleading for several reasons. Real spending on education rose most rapidly in the 1970s and more slowly in the 1980s, and appears to have peaked in 1992–93 and to have declined in the three following years. Pupil–teacher ratios appear to be increasing for the first time in 30 years. If declines in spending continue, real spending in 1997–98 may be at about the same level as it was ten years earlier. As well, fluctuations in spending vary quite dramatically by province from year to year, so that considering national averages can hide quite dramatic changes in particular years in specific provinces. For example, real spending rose in Ontario by 5.8 percent in 1991–92 but declined by 2.5 percent in the following year (Canadian Teachers' Federation, 1996, p. 13).

The comparative standard for government expenditure on education also depends on what is being compared. In one sense, $35 billion is a great deal of money. It is about $7000 per student per year (or more than $1000 per year for every person in Canada). It is equal to about 5 percent of Canada's gross domestic product (Gendron, 1994), which is the measure of the total size of the Canadian economy. In other words, we spend 5 percent of our national wealth on elementary and secondary education.

In another sense, $35 billion is not all that much. It amounts to about $35 per student per school day, or about $7 per hour based on a five-hour day. This isn't that much more than one would pay a baby-sitter. To take another perspective, in 1993 Canadians spent about $55 billion on new automotive vehicles, and General Motors of Canada alone took in revenues of more than $21 billion (Canadian World Almanac, 1995).

Another common approach to judging the adequacy of education funding is to invoke standards of service. We might argue that education needs more money in order to provide better special education services, to hire more counsellors in elementary schools, or to buy more computers. Of course, this argument assumes that such services must be added on top of all the existing services and programs, and that nothing now in place can be changed or replaced. Similarly, one might say that more spending is needed in order to achieve such goals as reducing the number of drop-outs or improving reading levels. This assumes that there is a direct correlation between the amount of money spent and educational outcomes.

Finally, there is an economic approach to calculating whether we are spending enough on education. We can think of spending money on education as an investment that yields a return in the form of more educated people, higher earnings, more economic activity, and so on. In theory, one can calculate the return on this investment just as one knows that a bank deposit pays 3 percent or a CSB pays 5 percent. Economists have made just such calculations, with the most recent Canadian evidence indicating a return of approximately 10 percent as being a reasonable estimate (Vaillancourt, 1992). Once the return on education is estimated, it can be compared with the return on spending in other areas, such as health care or highways; then, if education is a better investment, we should spend more on it—if it is less rewarding, we should transfer spending to other areas.

This seems like a straightforward and eminently sensible approach. The difficulty is that return on investment requires the translation of all the outcomes of schools—and the outcomes of whatever other service is used for comparison—into monetary equivalents. The calculations involved require not only arbitrary assumptions but also information that is not readily available. Given that many of the goals of education are intangible and long term, how are the results to be calculated? How do we measure whether people have come to love to learn as a result of their education? And even if this could be measured, how much weight should be assigned to it in calculations of return on investment?

In short, the debate about whether we spend enough money on education cannot be resolved through information alone. People's beliefs about the value of education relative to other spending priorities will have a major share in determining how they view the issue—whether they see the glass as half full or half empty.

How Are Resources Used in Schools?

Another way to consider the adequacy of funding is to ask what we buy with the money spent on elementary and secondary education. There are two usual ways of thinking about expenditure patterns. One is to organize them by functions. In Canada in 1992–93, as Table 5.4 shows, about 60 percent of funds were spent on instruction, capital, superannuation (pensions), and other. Considering only operating budgets (i.e., excluding capital spending for construction and renovation of buildings) raises the proportion of funds in each of the other categories.

A second way to think about spending has to do with the distinction between **purchased** and **hired** resources. Purchased resources are the things one buys — buildings, equipment, supplies, and so on. Hired resources are essentially people. Education expenditures are heavily focussed on people, which is what is meant by calling education a **labour-intensive** activity. In schools, things are far less important than people. By far the most important single item of expenditure in schools is teachers' and administrators' salaries, which make up more than 60 percent of total operating costs. All salaries — including those of secretaries, caretakers, bus drivers, and others — total 80 percent or more of education spending. Most of the spending on nonsalary items occurs at the provincial or school district level, as shown by the school budget (based on an elementary school in Manitoba) in Table 5.5.

In this respect, education is like other services (e.g., health care), but unlike those economic activities that have switched resources from labour to capital in the form of equipment. A good example of the latter is agriculture, which has vastly reduced its work force by using more machinery. Most industries, too, have steadily reduced the number of workers required for a given level of production by using more machinery.

Table 5.4

Distribution of Public School Expenditures, 1992–1993

Instruction (includes educators' salaries, supplies, equipment)	58%
Plant operation (heat, maintenance, repairs)	10%
Capital (new buildings and major renovations or equipment)	9%
Superannuation (pensions)	5%
Transportation of students	5%
Other services (administration of schools and districts, provincial departments of education, libraries, audio-visual)	13%

Source: Canadian Education Statistics Council. (1996). *A statistical portrait of elementary and secondary education in Canada.* A joint publication of Statistics Canada and the Council of Ministers of Education, Canada, Cat. no. 81–528, p. 34.

Table 5.5

A Sample School Budget for an Elementary School (Enrollment: 550)

1 principal, 0.3 vice-principal	$ 95 000
25 classroom teachers	1 400 000
2 kindergarten teachers	100 000
1 ESL teacher	50 000
1 resource teacher	50 000
1 librarian	50 000
1 special education teacher	50 000
Total instructional staff	$1 795 000
3.5 special education support staff	$ 65 000
4.2 teacher aides	70 000
2 clerical support staff	50 000
5.5 caretakers	180 000
Total support staff	$ 365 000
Supplies and equipment	$ 51 000
Textbook purchases	20 000
GRAND TOTAL	$2 130 000

Note: These figures do not include expenses incurred by the school district, such as transportation costs, larger maintenance projects, professional development, and other items. School budgets account for about 80% of total spending on education.

What Is the Impact of Resources on Education?

Closely tied to the question of whether we spend enough on education is the question of how much difference money makes. Obviously money is important; without it we would not be able to build schools, hire teachers, purchase textbooks, and so on. Just as obviously, as was pointed out at the beginning of this chapter, money is not everything. A wonderfully constructed building is not a school without good teachers to work in it; and teachers who do not know their subject, or who do not care about their students, will not be effective no matter how much they earn. Nonetheless, it is important to ask how well we use the money that is available for schools.

One problem we face in studying the impact of resources on education is that learning is not a production process, despite the frequent use of factory metaphors such as "producing capable students" (Levin, 1994c). Rather, education is a process of development. Cars or houses are produced by people doing things to raw materials such as metal or wood. But becoming educated is something students must do for themselves, although many other people may help them along in the process. Thus, while there are agreed-upon ways of making products, ways of becoming educated are likely to vary as much as people vary. We can't say that if we just did a, b, and c, every student would become educated; indeed, such a claim is antithetical to the meaning of education. The impact of resources on educational outcomes, then, is likely to be a difficult subject on which to produce firm evidence.

Another problem we encounter in studying the effectiveness of education resources is that there is little variation in school spending and organizational patterns across Canada, which makes it difficult to judge what might happen under other arrangements. Just about all schools have a principal, a number of teachers assigned to grades or subjects, some specialist or support teachers (such as resource teachers), one or more secretaries, and one or more caretakers. Almost all schools organize students in grades in elementary school and by subjects in secondary school. The organization of time tends to be quite similar across the country. Even class sizes do not vary greatly across school districts or provinces. If schools varied more in their use of resources we might be able to get a better sense of which combinations of resources were most effective.

Given the diversity in students, in communities, and in the subject matter of education, this standardized approach seems rather puzzling. One might well think that it would make sense to organize schools quite differently depending on the students, the setting, and the subject matter. Yet we do not do so. As a result, we simply do not know very much about how resources affect the work of schools. There has been great debate in the educational research literature about whether the funds devoted to education have been spent to the greatest benefit (see Baker, 1991; Hanushek, 1994b; Odden & Clune, 1995). Twenty years ago, the conventional wisdom was that more money meant better education (i.e., by providing better facilities, more equipment, smaller classes, and better-qualified teachers). However, research evidence suggests that per-pupil spending levels are not strongly related to student outcomes in the form of test scores (Hanushek, 1989). Nor has the research linked spending levels to other outcomes of education, such as employment, career success, or life satisfaction (Walberg, 1991). The research does not show that money is unimportant, but it does indicate that current spending patterns may not be optimal.

More than 80 percent of the money in education is spent on people, particularly teachers and other instructional staff. The overall ratio of students to teachers has been declining in Canada for more than 20 years, from 21:1 in 1971 to 15:1 in 1991 (Gendron, 1994), though recent spending cuts are changing this pattern. Research has not shown a strong link between these changes in staffing and improved achievement. The best available evidence suggests that classes would need to be substantially smaller than they are at present — fewer than twelve or fifteen students on average — and that teaching methods in those classes would need to change in order for reduced class size to have important impacts on achievement (Odden, 1990).

Changes of this order are both difficult and expensive to make. To give an indication of the financial impact of changes in the pupil–teacher ratio, at current staffing levels and salaries, a further drop of 1 in the ratio of students to educators in Canada—from 16:1 to 15:1—would cost another $1 billion per year, or about 3 percent of total current operating expenditures. Class size matters a great deal to teachers, who find teaching less stressful when classes are smaller. Teachers' views and preferences are important, but from another point of view, it would be surprising to find that class size was linked firmly to educational outcomes. After all, would we not expect the impact of class size to depend on the teaching methods used, the students in the class, the subject being taught, the quality of the curriculum and resource materials, and other such factors?

No single educational practice is likely to be effective all the time. Thus, it is probably not the best policy for us to focus all our resources on a single approach to schooling, whether it be smaller classes, more computers, or new curricula. But there are two related ways in which to consider improvements in the use of educational resources. The first is to employ a broader conception of the resources that are available to us. The second is to use our resources in more diverse ways to meet the diversity of educational needs and settings.

We noted at the outset of this chapter that schools have tended to employ a narrow definition of resources, focussing on money and on paid staff. Yet there is good reason to believe that other factors are at least as important in affecting the success of our schools (Levin, 1994b). If one were to try to list those things that will have an important impact on the kind of education students obtain, one would probably begin with aspects of the students themselves — motivation, background, self-concept, and so on. Also very important would be the students' families and living situations (Levin, 1995a).

We do not ordinarily think of students or their families as resources that we might use for educational purposes. Yet an increasing body of research points to ways in which, by altering our view of students and families, education might be strengthened — for instance, by working more closely with parents schools can help them to develop their children's skills and knowledge. Chapter Seven discusses these issues in more detail.

It is also the case that schools currently organize their resources around teaching, though, as we have said, education is better viewed as a process of development and learning by students. If schools were to take seriously the idea of students as active learners, they might be far more receptive to making more use of other organizational practices. Among those practices that appear to have support from the research are peer tutoring, student work groups, co-operative learning, and independent study. Approaches that emphasize the role of students as learners also have the advantage of stressing self-direction and intrinsic rewards for learning, which are universally cited as important educational goals.

Some commentators have advocated much more use of computers as another vehicle for encouraging independent student learning. A considerable body of literature on computer-assisted instruction (CAI) indicates that it is reasonably effective, but although computers are increasingly available in schools, they have not yet had a major impact on the overall instructional program (Snider, 1992). (The potential role of technology is discussed more fully in Chapter Ten.)

Even within the usual focus on teaching, there may be ways of bringing new resources into play by modifying organizational and instructional practices. For example, the way in which time is used in schools could be reconsidered. Time allocations to subjects are relatively standard across classes and grades. In other cases, time allocations are based on our view of which subjects are most important. But evidence indicates that students simply require more time for some subjects, particularly those, such as second languages or mathematics, that are primarily learned in schools. Time requirements depend not on the priority of the subject, but on the background, interests, and needs of students (Holmes & Wynne, 1989). To use another example, the idea that every secondary-school course should consist of an equal number of hours of instruction seems quite out of step with what is known about learning. If some subjects are harder to learn, presumably they should have more time devoted to them.

There are many other possibilities. Research shows that such common practices as retention in grade and ability grouping do not appear to be helpful and may actually waste resources. The assignment of students to particular teachers is often made on bases other than the learning styles and preferences of the students or teachers. Classes tend to be of similar size in most subjects, even though different subjects may well lend themselves to teaching styles that work better in smaller or larger classes. And so on.

Experiments with a variety of practices such as those mentioned, with careful assessment of the results in comparison with more standard practices, would be an appropriate way of learning more about the relative merits of alternative uses of resources. Later chapters examine some of these questions from the standpoint of teachers and administrators in schools.

Conclusion

Questions of taxation, federal and provincial budgets, formula funding, and mill rates seem far removed from the world of the classroom teacher. Yet teachers are only too aware of the impact of resources on their work. The extra couple of students in the class, the absence of a teacher's aide, the lack of a music teacher in the school, the lack of course options resulting from fewer teachers, inadequate science equipment or library collections — all of these have direct effects on everyday teaching. Yet without knowing how the overall financing system works, teachers remain in the dark about how and why decisions are made, and how they might be influenced or altered.

Teachers see the need for more money and resources for schools because they see how these things could make their work more effective. It is important for teachers to explain to parents (and the public) why spending on education matters to students. But Canadian schools are facing real budget pressures, so in addition to pressing for more funds, educators also have to give careful thought to how resources can be used most effectively. Every teacher has the potential to change the use of resources in ways that are not only efficient but also educationally sound.

Exercises

1. Public education in Canada is funded almost entirely by governments, chiefly provincial ones. Are the current arrangements optimal? What other funding sources are there? What arguments could be made either for or against a change in the relative shares of education costs paid by the various sources identified?

2. Central to the funding of education are the concepts of public and private goods that result from education. What do these concepts mean? Give examples of public and private goods resulting from education. Which of these do you see as being more important? Why?

3. Do you think Canadians currently pay too much tax? Why or why not? Is this true for all Canadians or only for some?

4. Construct an argument for changing the balance of taxation in Canada so as to tax wealth, income, or consumption more than at the present rate.

5. Should property taxes be a significant source of revenue for education? Why or why not?

6. Provinces have been providing an increasingly large share of education funds. Is this appropriate, or should local school boards be responsible for a significant share of revenue? Defend your answer.

7. What balance between block, categorical, and equalization grants do you think is most appropriate in a provincial granting system? Why?

8. Analyze your province's current funding system. To what extent does it embody concepts of horizontal or vertical equity? Illustrate with specific examples. (Your class may want to consider inviting someone from the provincial ministry or department of education to respond to these questions.)

9. How much education property tax does a typical home-owner in your community pay? A typical farmer? How does this compare with other communities in your province?

10. Is public education in your province adequately funded? Why or why not? Support your answer.

11. Conduct a class poll of spending priorities. Given a number of areas (e.g., health, highways, environment, child welfare, agriculture, economic development, tax incentives for business, and others), where would those in the class rank education? Where would people outside the university rank education? Why?

12. What outcomes of education might we want to use in attempting to determine the value of education spending as an investment? How might we measure these outcomes?

13. Interview a school official or school trustee to determine the authority over budgets, both revenue and expenditure, that school districts have in your province.

14. Attend a school board budget meeting. Report on the ways in which the board made budget decisions. What criteria were used? Which issues seemed to be of greatest importance? Was the process used an effective one?

15. Why do you think research has not been able to demonstrate a strong link between education spending levels and outcomes?

16. Obtain the staffing and budget data for a local school. Consider alternative ways in which the same amount of money might be used. What are the reasons for the existing distribution?

17. Suggest some ways in which we might reallocate education resources in order to be more effective. What sorts of organizational changes in schools would be required for such reallocation to be workable?

18. In groups of about five to ten people, work through the following budget exercise. One person in each group is to act as a neutral observer who does not take part in the discussion but watches how it proceeds. One person is to play the role of superintendent. The others should play the role of school trustees.

School Board Budgeting Exercise

Note: This exercise assumes that a local school board has significant revenue-generating ability through property taxation. As noted earlier in the chapter, this is no longer true in most provinces. However, maintaining the taxation element gives the exercise added sharpness because it requires the school board to face the choice between reduced services and increased taxes. Hence we believe the exercise is still meaningful, even if in a particular province an actual school board would no longer face the choice in quite the same terms.

Task: You are to constitute yourselves as a school board. You are faced with final budget decisions for the school division. The budget must be submitted to the provincial government within a week.

Background: You are elected school board members in a school district with a mix of suburban and rural schools. Your current local property tax rate is relatively high. You have an extensive range of programs, including French immersion, special education, band and music, vocational programs in your high schools, and so on. Your division has 20 schools, including three high schools. Schools range in size and include a number of very small schools in the rural part of the district (each with fewer than 200 students) that are being kept open at the request of the local parents. Salaries of your teachers are above average, and your pupil–teacher ratio is about average. You have a strong teachers' association and are entering the second year of your current collective agreement, which calls for the total payroll to increase by about 3 percent, primarily to pay the cost of increments and to fund improvements in working conditions. Enrollment has been declining somewhat in recent years, which has worsened the financial situation of the district. The current distribution of your budget follows.

Provincial financial support this year is likely to be slightly less (a reduction of between 1 and 2 percent) than it was last year. Your superintendent, whom you hired a year ago, has proposed a budget that calls for the preservation of most existing programs. He has recommended some reductions in maintenance staff, in transportation (by extending the distance at which busing would be provided), and an overall increase in the pupil–teacher ratio that would increase average class sizes by about two students. He is also proposing an "excellence fund" of just under 1 percent of total expenditure, or $400 000, to support school improvement through additional expenditures primarily in the area of teacher professional development, technology, and program development. The total package for next year calls for a budget increase of less than 1 percent, but given provincial restraint, your local tax levy would increase by about 11 percent. Your tax rate currently is a little above average; this increase would put you close to the highest.

School board elections are to take place in your district next fall. Your electorate includes vigorous lobby groups for program enhancements, such as more computers or more special education, and a strong citizens' group pushing for lower spending and taxes. The board has had strong opposition in the past both when it has tried to increase property taxes and when it has tried to cut programs.

Decision: Your school board must make the following decisions:

• What is the total budget that you will submit to the province?
• What specific expenditure increases, if any, will you approve? What cuts in spending, if any, will you make?

- What increase in local taxes, if any, will you propose?
- How will you justify your decisions to parents, taxpayers, and voters?

You may also want to consider the educational rationale for your decisions.

Budget Information — Average School District

Current-year data
Total enrollment—6 000 students
Pupil–teacher ratio—16.5:1 (Staff: 365 professionals)
Expenditure per pupil—$7 000 (Total budget: $42 million)
Salaries and benefits—80% of budget ($33.6 million)

Expenditure by category
Regular instruction—61% (includes immersion 8%)
Exceptional (special education)—10%
Vocational—3%
Administration—4%
Support services—7%
Transportation—4%
Operations and maintenance—11%

Revenue by source

	This year	Next year (proposed)
Province	$29.4 M—70%	$29.0 M—68%
Municipal taxes	$11.3 M—27%	$12.1 M—29%
Other	$1.3 M—3%	$1.3 M—3%

Proposed budget for next year: $42.4 million, an increase of $400 000 or just under 1 percent.

Increase is made up of
- Salaries—3% ($1 000 000, chiefly increments required by the collective agreement)
- Other ongoing programs and expenses—3% ($300 000)
- "Excellence fund"—1% ($400 000)

Balanced by proposed reductions
- Reduction of maintenance staff in all schools—$125 000
- Increase of 1 in pupil–teacher ratio (elimination of 22 teaching positions)—$1.1 million
- Elimination of transportation for students living less than 2 km from school—$75 000

This budget would require an increase in local taxes of 7 percent to raise the additional $800 000 (half needed for additional expenditure and half to compensate for reduced provincial support). Average school tax on a home is currently $1 000; a 7 percent increase would make the average $1 070.

Each 1 percent additional local property tax raises $110 000.

Further Reading

The best overview of education finance in Canada is Stephen Lawton's *Financing Canadian Education* (Canadian Education Association, 1996). The most sophisticated current book on education finance is David Monk, *Educational Finance: An Economic Approach* (1990), which has an especially thorough treatment of resource allocation issues in schools and classrooms but is quite focussed on the United States. A shorter introduction to the literature in this area appears in Henry Levin, "Mapping the economics of education," *Educational Researcher*, (May 1989). The 1992 report of the now-defunct Economic Council of Canada, *A Lot to Learn: Education and Training in Canada*, also has a worthwhile discussion of many aspects of education finance.

Many issues around finance and economics are the subject of considerable controversy, some of which have been noted and referenced in the text (such as class size). Discussion of alternative uses of resources in schools can be found in Holmes and Wynne, *Making the School an Effective Community* (1989), and in Levin, Fowler, and Walberg, *Organizational Influences on Educational Productivity* (1995). Other important works include Eric Hanushek, *Making Schools Work* and Benjamin Levin (1994b), "Rethinking resources in education." An interesting perspective on allocation of resources within the school can be found in Karen Hawley Miles' 1996 article, "Freeing resources for improving schools: A case study of teacher allocation in Boston public schools." Other works by the writers cited in this chapter will also be relevant.

CHAPTER SIX

Teachers, Administrators, and the School System

▼ PROLOGUE

"**H**ey, it's great to see you again." Toni grinned broadly at Aaron, her former classmate in the Faculty of Education. "How's the job? Are you going crazy the same as me?"

"It's tough," Aaron replied. "I'm working harder than I ever have before. But I'm enjoying it too. There are really good people on the staff at my school, and they've helped me a lot. So has my principal. I've been given some extra prep time. So I feel as if I'm making progress, even if I don't always feel that the kids are making as much as I want them to!"

"You mean you actually know what other teachers in your school are doing? I don't even know all their names yet, and I haven't had time to speak to most of them."

"What about at your orientation?" Aaron asked. "Didn't you meet everyone there? Didn't you get a chance to talk about school programming? And what about your team meetings?"

"What orientation?" Toni replied. "I arrived, was shown my classroom, given my class list, told where the textbooks were, and that was that. The teachers next door to me have said hello, and invited me to let them know if I need anything, but they're busy too, and I hate to bother them. Some of the teachers haven't even introduced themselves yet. Teachers don't have meetings except for staff meetings, and those are usually full of administrative details like handling lunch money; I don't know what you mean by 'team meetings.' I'm the only new teacher on staff, and I'm spending every evening and most of the weekend just trying to keep up. In addition to the regular teaching, I've been given a bunch of supervision tasks that nobody else wants to do. I'm already dead tired, and it's only October."

"That sounds tough," Aaron commiserated. "Our staff works in grade-level teams, so we meet every week during a common prep period to talk about programs, particular kids, and teaching ideas. I'm working really hard too, but I also feel I'm learning an incredible amount and the other teachers are really helpful. But what about your principal? Isn't he helpful?"

"I wouldn't exactly describe Mr. Plett that way," said Toni. "He talks mostly to the two other men on the staff; he doesn't seem to have much respect for or interest in the women. He certainly hasn't been helpful to me. I never see him. The norm in the school just seems to be that you do things on your own. Aside from getting the paperwork done, or whatever the latest board policy is, everyone, including the teachers, seems to prefer to be left alone to teach in their own way. Even when there are discipline problems, I definitely get the feeling that Mr. Plett expects me to solve them on my own, and I'm not sure he thinks I can do it."

"I can't believe how different my school is," Aaron responded. "My principal has been in my class at least a half dozen times already. He just drops in for a few minutes, chats with some of the kids, and gets a sense of what we're doing. The next time I see him he's always got some positive remark to make about something he saw in the class. And he spent an hour with me after the first week, talking about how I was doing, offering suggestions, and most of all letting me know that he was there to support me. Even our staff meetings are pretty good. We spend most of the time talking about educational issues — language development, new program ideas, grading practices, and so on. We've got a school discipline policy, and I talk with other teachers quite a bit about what they're doing with particular kids."

"You know," Toni mused, "I thought that teaching was teaching, wherever you were. But talking to you makes me realize how much difference the kind of school you're in can make to your attitude. When I listen to your enthusiasm I realize how important the principal and other teachers are." ■

Prospective teachers are generally motivated by their desire to help children and to foster learning. At the same time, it is important to remember that teaching is also a job for which people are well paid, and one that occurs in a defined setting, with particular rules, procedures, and conventions.

When a new teacher begins a first job, or when an experienced teacher changes schools, she or he moves into a setting that is already formed. The school has a history, a set of practices, a culture ("the way things are done around here"), and a group of people who may have been there for some time. The new person must learn about these practices and habits and, for the most part, adjust to them. Although new teachers often begin their careers with a great deal of idealism about how they can change *things*, they may soon encounter aspects of their work that instead change *them*.

Some of these conditions are inherent in the history and development of schools as institutions and of teaching as an occupation. Other conditions are created by the administrators who run the schools. Teachers need to understand how their work is shaped by these conditions. To that end, this chapter reviews the school as a workplace and teaching as an occupation, including the roles of teachers and administrators. Features such as hiring, pay, and evaluation are reviewed, and some of the tensions inherent in these activities are identified.

Who Are Canadian Teachers?

There are approximately 260 000 full-time teachers in Canadian schools, a figure that has remained more or less stable over the past twenty years. Because of a relatively low turnover in teaching, the average age of teachers has been increasing from under 35 years in 1972–73 to more than 40 years in 1992–93. The proportion of the Canadian teaching force under the age of 35 years has been falling steadily from more than 60 percent in 1972–73 to less than 25 percent today, while at the other end of the career ladder the proportion of teachers 45 or older has doubled from 20 percent at the beginning of the 1970s to 40 percent today (Canadian Education Statistics Council, 1996, pp. 68–69).

Traditionally, teaching in Canada has been done mainly by women, especially at the elementary level. In the early part of the century, more than 75 percent of teachers were women (Lockhart, 1991, p. 29). Not coincidently, teaching at the time was also a low-paying, low-status job that offered little in the way of career prospects. Despite these disadvantages, teaching was for many years one of the few careers open to women. An increase in pay, status, and working conditions during this century went along with a rapid increase in the number of male teachers, particularly in secondary schools. However, women still constitute a substantial majority of Canadian teachers — slightly more than 60 percent in 1992–93 (Canadian Education Statistics Council, 1996, p. 68). The limited available evidence appears to indicate that relatively few teachers are drawn from the ranks of Canada's recent immigrant, visible minority, and Aboriginal communities, even though these groups provide an increasing proportion of Canada's student population (Thiessen, Bascia, & Goodson, 1996).

Although it may seem obvious to say so, teachers are also a well-educated group. Almost all teachers now have at least one university degree, compared with about 15 percent of the Canadian adult population (Canadian Teachers' Federation, 1992). Taken in combination, these attributes also suggest that the social class composition of the teaching force has changed. At one time, teachers came predominantly from blue-collar or working-class backgrounds, and teaching provided a path for social mobility. Today, many teachers come from middle-class backgrounds (Lockhart, 1991, p. 55).

Supply and Demand for Teachers

The ability to obtain a teaching job depends first on whether job openings are available. This, in turn, depends on the total number of teaching positions (what is often called the **stock** of jobs), and the number of vacancies that occur over time (often called the **flow** of people). Even in provinces with a very large teaching force, if only a few people actually leave their jobs, there will be few vacancies for new teachers. Similarly, if the total number of teaching jobs drops, which may occur when provinces and school districts face very tight budgets, turnover in the teaching staff will not result in many vacancies because the empty positions will be eliminated.

Job availability also differs across provinces and across regions within provinces. Those provinces with rapid population growth normally require more teachers. Some rural and northern parts of Canada have traditionally had difficulty recruiting enough qualified teachers, although these areas have often offered the most opportunities for new teachers. In general, urban areas tend to have more applicants and fewer vacancies, although high living costs in some cities have discouraged applicants and made it harder for urban districts to complete their staffs. Even when urban boards do have vacancies, they may be able to hire experienced teachers who wish to move from more isolated teaching locations, further exacerbating the staffing problems in rural and northern Canada. A pattern has developed in many parts of Canada in which new teachers begin their careers in rural or northern districts, sometimes moving to urban districts after a few years of experience.

As the Canadian teaching force ages, some analysts expect there to be a large-scale turnover sometime in the next decade. A large number of teachers will reach retirement age at approximately the same time, beginning late in the 1990s. One cannot, however, be confident that simple age projections provide a good basis for conclusions about vacancies in teaching. Too many other variables influence the rate of turnover. A significant number of teachers have tended to leave teaching for other occupations; if this pattern continues, it will reduce the numbers reaching retirement age. Compulsory retirement has been struck down by courts in some provinces as a violation of the *Charter of Rights and Freedoms*, which means that some teachers may choose to continue working after age 60 or 65. On the other hand, school boards in some provinces have early retirement programs that encourage teachers to retire beginning at age 55, which would have the effect of spreading out the turnover of teachers over a longer period. Whether individuals choose to retire early or late may also depend on such matters as the adequacy of pensions, the general economic climate, feelings about teaching as a job, changes in patterns of health, and so on.

The School as a Workplace

What sort of workplace is the school? One way to address this question is to ask what schools are like or what metaphors or models come to mind when we think about schools. The metaphors we use to describe something are far more powerful than comparisons; metaphors actually shape the way we think about things, and therefore the way we behave (Morgan, 1986).

Two metaphors are commonly used in relation to schools (Firestone & Herriott, 1982). One compares schools to factories, as discussed in Chapter Five. In most versions of this metaphor, students are seen as products, teachers are seen as the workers who produce the products, and administrators are the supervisors and managers who tell the workers what to do. The overall image is of a highly controlled system in which authority rests squarely at the top and obedience to orders is important. Decisions about goals and strategies are made by administration; activities and behaviour of staff are controlled by standard rules and procedures that tell people what to do and when to do it. The metaphor of the school as factory has been very influential in shaping the organization of schools and the work of the teachers and students within them.

Schools have also been compared to professional organizations like hospitals. In this metaphor, students are the patients and teachers are the doctors; administrators play a limited role in providing facilities and funds, but do not control professional practice. This model accords much more authority to the staff, and considerably less to administrators. The workers are highly knowledgeable and responsible for deciding what needs to be done and how it will be done. The rules governing good practice are developed by staff, not promulgated by management. Decisions are made and standards are set collegially, with research playing a major role in shaping practice. However, there is still little authority for the clients/patients/students in this model.

Each metaphor contains some elements of truth, but neither is a completely accurate description of schools. By considering or combining elements of both the hierarchical model and the professional model, it is possible to understand some of the dynamics of schooling and thus the work of teachers. The tensions between the two models can be seen in many aspects of the work of teachers.

A critical element in thinking about any workplace is the locus of control over the work. Who determines what work is done, when, where, and how? Authority over schools officially rests with provincial governments and school boards. These bodies may (though they are not required to) delegate authority to administrators and teachers. As employees of school boards, teachers are required to comply with instructions given by school boards and school administrators. Teachers have very limited influence over their teaching assignment. They must teach at certain times in certain classrooms, and they do not choose their own students. In all these respects, the work of teachers is highly constrained and controlled.

In these ways, the school is a **bureaucratic, hierarchical** organization. The term "bureaucratic" derives from the work of sociologist Max Weber, and refers to a hierarchical organization that is governed by rules, staffed by people with expertise, and operated on the basis of standard procedures and practices. Although the term is often used pejoratively now to mean organizations that are overly rigid and wedded to strict rules, the development of bureaucracies was a major improvement over previous organizations that operated on the basis of favouritism, patronage, and the whims of those in positions of power. We are now so used to the concept of equal treatment for all that we have forgotten how unusual this practice used to be in the operation of governments. Moreover, a certain amount of organization and standardization seems both necessary and desirable in operating a school system that involves large numbers of students and staff, and a varied and complex body of knowledge.

Box 6.1
Working Conditions: Class Size and Preparation Time

Class Size

For most teachers, the number of students in the classes they teach is a critical factor in shaping their work. The 1992 report on teaching by the Canadian Teachers' Federation provides evidence on how important class size is to teachers, and on how much it can vary across the country.
- In British Columbia, elementary-school class sizes averaged almost 23 students, but some school districts averaged as few as 15, and others as many as 24. About 70 percent of high-school classes had fewer than 26 students.
- In Ontario, average class sizes in primary grades ranged from 18 to 29.
- The provincial contract between the Government of Quebec and the Protestant teachers provided for a maximum of 25 students in Grade 1; 27 in Grades 2 and 3; 29 in Grades 4 to 6; and up to 32 in secondary schools.

Preparation Time

Another important working condition for teachers is the amount of time they have each day when they are not actually teaching a class. This is commonly called preparation (or prep) time. CTF data show that "the common pattern ... is 30 to 40 minutes per day for elementary teachers, one period a day in semestered secondary schools and two of eight periods in non-semestered schools" (p. 65).

There are, however, considerable variations here. In British Columbia, elementary teachers have 60 to 90 minutes per week, while in Winnipeg they have 180 minutes per cycle (six days). Secondary teachers in Nova Scotia have six 40-minute periods per six-day cycle, while in Ontario arrangements can include a period each day, 100 minutes per week, or 20 percent of scheduled class time.

Source: Canadian Teachers' Federation. (1992). *Teachers in Canada: Their work and quality of life.* Ottawa: CTF, pp. 60–61, 65. Reproduced with permission.

In other respects, the school is a **professional** organization like a hospital. Teachers normally have a considerable amount of autonomy within their own classes as to how they teach. While teachers must follow a prescribed curriculum, many curriculum guides give teachers considerable choice in how they approach the subject. Matters of teaching methods and style, approach to discipline, treatment of students, and overall classroom atmosphere remain, in most cases, subject to the discretion of teachers. Even when there are official policies, teachers often modify or ignore them. For example, a teacher may enforce the school attendance policy or the school discipline policy selectively, if at all. Teachers thus have more autonomy than exists in many other jobs in which workers are not only told what to do, but also how to do it.

Chapter Eight examines the concept of what it means to be a professional teacher. At this point, we need only note that the two major aspects of schooling—its hierarchical and bureaucratic organization on the one hand, and its professional character on the other—create tensions and dilemmas for teachers and for administrators. Some of these are explored in the pages that follow.

Characteristics of Teaching as an Occupation

Teaching has been the subject of a number of important studies over the years. One of the first of these, *The Sociology of Teaching*, was written in the 1930s by U.S. sociologist Willard Waller. In 1975, Dan Lortie published his book, *Schoolteacher*, though the book was based on data collected years earlier in the 1960s. A powerful study of Australian teachers by R.W. Connell, *Teachers' Work*, was done in the mid-1980s. In the last decade, there have been many further studies about the nature of teaching as an occupation, including Rod Dolmage's recent Canadian book, *So You Want to Be a Teacher* (1996). All of these studies have come to quite similar conclusions about some of the basic characteristics of teaching. Although considerable efforts are now being made to change some of these characteristics, the best available evidence still suggests that they are typical of Canadian teaching (Canadian Teachers' Federation, 1992).

Teaching still remains largely an *isolated* job. Teachers work most of the time with students, and tend to have little interaction with other adults. This is true not only of new teachers, who may feel that they are left to "sink or swim" on their own, but also of experienced teachers. Many researchers have pointed out that teachers not only work separately from one another, they tend not to talk with one another about that work.

Isolation is related to the *lack of a common technical culture of teaching* (Fullan & Stiegelbauer, 1991, p. 119) that guides practice. There is a heavy focus on what might be called "the tricks of the trade" — specific activities that have proven successful in the classroom. Each teacher learns to teach individually, and each has a unique style. Unlike some other occupations in which there are generally agreed-upon standards of practice, teachers tend to reject the idea that there is a best way to teach. Staff-room conversation often focuses on topics unrelated to teaching, or perhaps on individual students. But few schools provide conditions under which there is sustained and serious discussion among teachers about what teaching is and how best to do it.

Teaching involves *conflicting roles*. Teachers want all children to succeed and to develop a love of learning, yet much of their time and energy goes into controlling students' behaviour and evaluating students according to external standards. The more one tries to reach students individually, the more one may feel conflict with other aspects of schooling, such as the need to sort students by ability or the pressure to have students conform to rules and standards.

Teaching is also highly *uncertain*, and it is very difficult for a teacher to know when he or she is successful. While short-term measures such as grades and test scores are important, most teachers are far more concerned about the long-term development of their students. Teachers tend to rely much more on their own judgements about students than on any other measure. Overwhelmingly, teachers report that hearing from or about former students who have been successful is a very important form of reward.

Many teachers feel that they have a *limited ability to have an impact*. Influences such as the students' families and friends, or social phenomena such as television, are thought to have more impact on students than do the schools.

All of these characteristics are important in shaping the way people think about teaching. For the most part, these characteristics tend to make teaching a difficult and uncertain enterprise. The hierarchical, bureaucratic model is less suited to an environment where there is no common technical culture and where outcomes are uncertain. Yet a professional model is difficult to implement in a setting where people work in isolation and face conflicting demands. In neither case is it likely that simply giving orders to people will prove a very successful strategy.

The Role of School Administrators

These characteristics of teaching create difficulties in defining the role of school administrators. In hierarchical organizations such as factories, workers take directions from — and are supervised by — bosses. Schools often use essentially the same model, with teachers being directed and supervised by principals and superintendents. This is such a common feature of schooling that we take it for granted. Yet the factory model, even a factory model modified by the ideas of Total Quality Management (Morgan & Mugatroyd, 1994) does not seem to fit schools very well.

Is it necessary to have school administrators who exercise this kind of control? What would happen if schools operated more like hospitals, in which doctors individually and collectively make most of the treatment decisions, and in which administrators are primarily involved with keeping the organization cohesive and functioning? What would happen if school principals and superintendents were elected by teachers, or by teachers, students, and parents? What would happen if teachers took turns being responsible for administrative duties in the school? It seems likely that patterns of authority would change considerably. One might glean some tentative ideas by comparing schools to organizations that have different methods of determining leadership. For example, in universities, administrators are often hired for a limited term through open and participative processes; in collectives, leadership is shared and rotated; and, in political systems, leaders are elected. In principle, any of these practices could also be used in schools.

Regardless of these possibilities, Canadian school and school district administrators — principals and superintendents — are charged by their superiors
(school boards) with supervising the operation of the schools. It is their job to
ensure that the organization's goals are being met, and that its policies and procedures are being followed. However, these are difficult tasks for the administrator
to accomplish. For one thing, as was discussed in Chapter One, there is much
uncertainty about what the goals of schooling are or should be. Furthermore,
education is not an activity that can be specified. Teachers can't simply be told to
do X and be assured that the result will be children who can read and write.

But even when teachers are given directions, the administrator cannot be
sure they will be followed. Schools are characterized by strong norms of teacher
autonomy. Once the classroom door closes, teachers are often substantially free
to teach what and how they like, so long as they observe certain limits. In many
schools, if there are not too many complaints by students or parents and if there
is not much disorder or noise, teachers are left alone to do as they wish. This
means that administrators cannot be sure that all teachers are either teaching the
same things or teaching them in the same ways.

In short, the professional aspects of teaching and the norm of teacher autonomy mean that administrators have limited ability to exercise influence through
the giving of orders or commands. Rather, administrative influence rests on other
kinds of mechanisms. In a classic formulation of the nature of authority, sociologist Max Weber talked about three types of authority: traditional, legal, and
charismatic. Each of these can be seen in the operation of schools.

Traditional authority used to be the most common type of authority. People
were obeyed because they held positions that required obedience. Thus, mon-
archs, the nobility, or religious leaders were obeyed because it was normal to do
so in a given social order. While traditional authority is less important in our
society today than it has been historically, it still plays an important role. The traditional authority of administrators rests on their positions, which give their
wishes and instructions a legitimacy that those of other people may lack. A suggestion made by a principal may often carry more weight with staff than a suggestion made by a teacher, simply because principals occupy positions of authority and are assumed by and large to know what they are doing.

Legal authority operates through the structural or organizational features of
the school. Administrators hire and evaluate teachers. They assign teachers'
workloads and have an important role in determining how difficult a teacher's
work will be. They can issue instructions that teachers are legally obligated to
obey (although, as we have pointed out, this strategy is not always effective).
Administrators often have control over resources teachers want, such as budgets
for supplies and books or access to professional-development opportunities. They
can determine whose ideas get support and whose do not. Administrators also
play a critical role in teachers' career prospects. A good reference from an administrator is usually vital to a promotion. Principals can and do use these mechanisms to influence or control teachers' behaviour.

Charismatic authority rests on the personal characteristics of the leader. Some people are able to command obedience by the force of their personality; they are impressive enough for others to want, or at least to agree, to do what they suggest. Indeed, when we use the word "leadership," we are often talking about charismatic authority, which rests on certain intangible qualities of the leader.

Leadership

Recently, there has been a marked revival of interest in the idea of leadership in schools. Research over the last ten years or so has emphasized the important role of the principal in creating and sustaining improved schools. This research has led to calls for school principals to become much more oriented toward providing active leadership. Graduate programs and in-service training for school administrators are giving increasing emphasis to what is called "educational leadership" as opposed to the relatively routine and administrative style described earlier in the chapter.

Many studies, in education and other fields, have examined the nature of leadership and the characteristics that make people effective leaders. This research shows that the idea of leadership is far from simple. On the one hand, it does appear that some individuals in leadership positions can make a considerable difference to their school or school district. There is much anecdotal evidence, and a growing body of research about school administrators who were able to strengthen school programs, improve morale, create conditions under which students learned more, and inspire teachers to be better at their work. Effective principals have a strong interest in instructional issues. They tend to be highly visible in the school. They both initiate and support improvement efforts by teachers and students. They work hard at creating a positive school climate, a sense of purpose and efficacy, strong working relationships among teachers, and shared power and responsibility.

On the other hand, as the excerpt from Greenfield (1979) in Box 6.2 shows, leadership is not always and necessarily a positive thing. No recipe exists for being an effective leader. What works in one school with a certain staff, student body, and community will not necessarily work in another school — an idea that is sometimes called the **contingency theory of leadership**. Some of the education literature on effective leadership portrays good leaders as knights in armour who rescue failing schools almost single-handedly, triumphing over all kinds of obstacles. A number of Hollywood movies have reinforced this image of the good principal. But the reality is much more complex. Some teachers may want a strong, interventionist principal, while others may want a much quieter form of support from their administrator. The requirements of leadership may also vary depending on the staff, the students, the program, and other aspects of the school.

Box 6.2
Two Views of Leadership

An evocative image of leadership for restructuring schools needs to focus the attention of school administrators on the use of facilitative power and second-order changes in their schools. ... The incentive for people to attempt significant improvements in their practices is stimulated through experiencing transformational leadership practices.

Transformational leaders assist staff in developing and maintaining a collaborative, professional school culture. They create conditions which support teacher development. And they enhance the collective and individual problem-solving capacities of staff.

Source: Ken Leithwood. (1992). The move towards transformational leadership. *Educational Leadership, 49*(5), 8.

Lacking their own independent visions of what to do or what to be, most individuals become what others now, or before them, have created for them. Administration thus involves an act of creation and compulsion. From all that might be, the administrator seeks to cause certain actions and events to prevail over others. The administrative act has force when people become and fulfill an ideological vision of what should be in the world. ... there is a profound sense in which to be a teacher or principal is to become a force as violent as ... being a pilot of an aircraft in a fire-bombing raid.

Source: Thomas Greenfield. (1979). Organization theory as ideology. *Curriculum Inquiry, 9*(2), 107. Reproduced with permission.

There are also important barriers to effective leadership in both schools and other organizations. Promoting change may bring increased conflict and a sense of uneasiness as people try to work out new practices. It may not be sufficiently recognized that changing our old and familiar patterns of behaviour is very difficult to do, even when there is a willingness to do so. A principal who presses for change may encounter resistance from staff, students, or the community. Even when people recognize that improvement is needed, they may naturally not be anxious to engage in the hard work required to bring about improvement, especially when, as is true for many teachers, their jobs are already demanding and the rewards of change are quite uncertain.

Any leader's capacity to be effective is also partly dependent on external circumstances beyond his or her control, such as the level of resources, support from higher levels of authority, or crises that may occur. The need to cope with a sudden budget decline can distract everyone from a long-term educational agenda. A new curriculum requirement from the provincial government may mean that professional-development time has to be reallocated. Just as a cautious principal can block teachers' ideas, so a superintendent or school board can stifle a principal's initiative if they wish to do so. A large number of circumstances could make it difficult for even the most talented leader to be effective.

Some administrators prefer not to play a leadership role, even if it were possible. Perhaps their personal inclination is simply not to rock the boat, or perhaps school systems, again like other kinds of organizations, tend to promote people who are cautious and favour the status quo rather than those who are bold and independent in their ideas. Some research evidence supports the idea that principals tend to underestimate the amount of scope they have to bring about change. It is no surprise therefore (though it may perhaps be a disappointment) to find that few principals seem to play a strong leadership role in their schools. Canadian research found that only about 10 percent of school principals fit the characterization of "systematic problem solvers" (Leithwood and Montgomery, 1982).

The dialogue that began this chapter illustrated how different schools can be in their operation, and the importance leadership can have in creating these differences. The next section discusses typical and exemplary practices in relation to many of the aspects of life in schools for teachers.

Hiring

Hiring has at least two requirements. The first is to define the qualities needed to fill a position; the second is to use some process to select a particular person who, presumably, best embodies those qualities. In practice, however, neither requirement may get explicit attention.

While the hiring process for teachers has common elements, it varies widely across schools and districts. In some settings, time may be taken to gather staff opinion or community views, and to think about the kind of person who is wanted for a position. For most teaching positions, however, selection begins with a review of the paper qualifications (résumé, experience, type of certificate) of various candidates, and the creation of a short list of persons to be interviewed.

School boards have the formal, legal responsibility for hiring teachers. In some cases, most of the authority for hiring teachers is given to school principals, who review applications, determine who will be interviewed, conduct the interviews, and recommend a candidate to the superintendent and the school board. In some districts, most of these tasks are the responsibility of superintendents, who then assign teachers to particular schools. The principal may have little or no role in choosing his or her staff. In other districts, especially small, rural ones, school trustees are directly involved in interviewing prospective teachers and making decisions about hiring.

There has been little Canadian research on the process of hiring teachers, but some evidence suggests that this varies just as the authority for hiring varies. Some schools or districts rely heavily on interviews. In some cases, though it may occur infrequently, other teachers or parents may be involved in interviewing. However, research on personnel selection indicates that performance in an interview cannot accurately predict performance on the job (for a review of the research, see Gorton & Schneider, 1991). Many districts or schools may rely heavily on an applicant's references, and particularly on comments from teachers or administrators who have seen the applicant in a teaching situation. For new teachers, the student teaching experience is very important in that it provides some evidence of competence that an administrator may use in making a hiring decision. Working as a substitute teacher can also be a way of becoming known and hireable in a school, although substitute teaching can be more difficult and less satisfying than regular teaching.

Subject-matter expertise is naturally an important consideration in hiring. The growth in French immersion in Canada made it relatively easy in the last decade for new teachers with good French-language skills to find employment. Those with skills in specialist areas such as computer applications, special education, or music have also been at an advantage in the job market. As new priority areas emerge, such as science in elementary schools, administrators will look for applicants who have these skills. However, there is anecdotal evidence to suggest that hiring may also depend on entirely extraneous factors, such as whether the applicant is willing to undertake extra-curricular activities or whether the applicant grew up in that particular jurisdiction. Many school systems like to hire teachers who graduated from their own schools. Employment equity, discussed later in this chapter, may be a hiring consideration. Another criterion is whether the candidate will "fit in" with a particular staff. The goal of hiring may be to minimize the risk of problems rather than to find the most dynamic and effective person. The evidence suggests that university grades are often given little importance in hiring decisions.

The uncertainty in hiring processes reflects the elusiveness of the concept of the "good teacher." A more detailed discussion of teaching occurs in Chapter Nine; at this point, it is sufficient to note that there is no consensus on what good teaching is, or on how to decide if a particular person is a good teacher. This of course makes hiring much more difficult. One alternative that is being used in some settings is to use hiring as an opportunity to initiate a debate or discussion within a school regarding what qualities and skills are most important in a teacher. The very discussion of these matters can itself contribute to building consensus on issues of teaching and learning.

Contracts

Teachers are formally the employees of school districts. When hired, a teacher normally signs a contract with a school district. However, the contract typically lays out only some of the most basic aspects of the job, such as the notice required for resignation or dismissal. There may be different kinds of contracts for different teachers. A standard contract applies to people who are taking on permanent, full-time positions. However, teachers who are going to be employed temporarily, part-time, or as substitutes may have a different form of contract with fewer protections and benefits. A number of provinces, for example, now allow school districts to hire teachers on temporary contracts that expire automatically at the end of the school year. These contracts give school districts more flexibility in their staffing from year to year, but at the price of eliminating job security for teachers in this category, who must wait to find out each spring if they will have a job the following year.

It is also important for prospective teachers to understand that an undertaking made either by them or the school district through a letter or even a conversation or phone call is also a form of contract. Any agreement entered into by two parties may be recognized by the courts as a binding contract, even if it is not a formal document.

Induction

Induction refers to the process with which new teachers begin their careers. For many years, concern has been expressed about the way in which first-year teachers are treated. In some cases, new teachers may be given teaching assignments other teachers do not want. These could involve teaching several different subjects or different grades. Whatever the teaching assignment, new teachers may simply begin on the first day, with no orientation, no support system, and little help in dealing with problems that inevitably arise. The folklore that sees the first year of teaching as a sink-or-swim experience rests on a long history (Fullan & Stiegelbauer, 1991, pp. 301-9).

Fortunately, many school districts are now taking measures to improve the experience of first-year teachers. Administrators are realizing that it is to the school's and students' benefit to make the first year as satisfying as possible for new teachers. It is increasingly common to find districts providing measures such as orientation sessions, mentoring arrangements with more experienced teachers, lighter teaching loads, extra support from the principal, group meetings of beginning teachers, or special professional-development opportunities to support new teachers. Improving the first year of new teachers is a relatively easy, yet potentially powerful, way of improving schooling.

Fullan and Stiegelbauer (1991) sum up the induction process as follows:

> Whether [new] teachers experience the sink-or-swim individualism characteristic of traditional school cultures or the inbuilt support of collaborative work cultures makes a huge difference in whether they stay in the profession and how good they will become if they do ... there are few things as deterministic of the entire career of a teacher as getting off to a disastrous or a strong start" (p. 304).

Salaries

Teachers are generally paid annual salaries. Salaries are determined through collective bargaining between teachers' associations and either school boards or provincial governments (an issue discussed more fully in Chapter Eight). Pay rates for teachers in Canada are normally tied closely to the teacher's experience and education. The more years of postsecondary education, the higher the starting salary. Most collective agreements also provide that teachers will get an increase in salary, called an increment, for each year of teaching experience up to a specified maximum number of years. Teachers working in remote or isolated communities may also be paid extra, whether through a higher salary scale or some form of isolation payment (Dolmage, 1996).

Table 6.1 shows a sample teacher salary scale. Pay levels vary from province to province, and in provinces where collective bargaining of salaries is carried on locally (see Chapter Eight), salaries vary across school boards.

Teachers' pay, like that of other public-sector workers, increased significantly over the past 30 or 40 years up until the early 1990s. Early in the 1900s, teachers were badly paid. During the Depression years, many teachers had their salaries reduced every year, or worked only for room and board (Shack, 1993). But this situation began to change in the 1950s with the establishment of unions as a major force. By 1989, the average salary for Canadian teachers was about $48 000 (Sale, 1992), while in comparison the average weekly industrial wage in Ontario (among the highest in the country) in 1991 was $560, or about $29 000 per year (Statistics Canada, 1992). Using a somewhat different analysis, Lockhart (1991, p. 127) shows that teachers' salaries gained steadily against the average individual wage for the 30 years after 1955. Recent years have been characterized by pay freezes, unilateral salary roll-backs, days off without pay, and reductions in professional-development days for teachers in many provinces. Nevertheless, these figures show that Canadian teachers remain, on the whole, quite well paid compared with most other Canadian workers (keeping in mind the problems of comparison raised in Chapter Five with respect to education funding).

Note that teachers' pay provisions are generally based on the bureaucratic organizational model and are thus related only to paper qualifications and to years in the organization. Other aspects of teaching, such as skill or commitment, or the voluntary assumption of additional duties and responsibilities, are not recognized in the pay scale. For many years there have been calls, especially in the United States, to implement some form of merit pay in which teachers who are judged better by some standard are paid more. Given the characteristics of teaching mentioned earlier—its uncertain, nontechnical, and isolated nature—determining merit is extremely difficult. Moreover, teachers do not control most of their conditions of work, which means that their ability to work is at least partly determined by someone else. Merit pay is a troublesome concept under these circumstances, but one that continues to generate interest in educational policy debates (Cohen & Murnane, 1986).

Table 6.1

Sample Salary Scale for Teachers

Years of teaching experience	Years of postsecondary education			
	4	**5**	**6**	**7**
0	$32 605	$34 631	$36 662	$38 708
1	33 949	36 322	38 359	40 390
2	35 702	38 049	40 041	42 407
3	37 567	39 991	42 061	44 449
4	39 433	41 925	44 097	46 808
5	41 305	43 868	46 458	49 170
6	43 167	45 800	48 822	51 870
7	45 106	48 140	51 519	54 570
8	47 804	50 856	54 222	57 286
9	50 697	53 588	56 935	59 981

Working Conditions

Working conditions refer to the multitude of factors that affect the everyday working situation of teachers. Examples of working conditions include class sizes, number of courses taught, preparation time during the school day, expectations for extra-curricular activities and supervision of students, placement of difficult students, expectations for marking and for reporting to parents, and so on. The entire set of working conditions is important in shaping teachers' work. For example, it usually takes more effort to teach several different courses than to teach the same course to several different groups of students, but this also depends on the size of the classes and the kinds of students. Many teachers prefer to teach students whom they believe are more capable and more motivated to do well in school. Some teachers have found their work made significantly more difficult by the placement in their classes of students with severe behavioural or other problems, an issue discussed more fully in Chapter Nine.

Teachers' duties are assigned by school boards and administrators, and teachers are required to take on the assigned duties unless their collective agreement specifies otherwise. A teacher can be assigned to teach any grade or subject, regardless of his or her training, except in the few instances where provincial regulations require a specific qualification. For example, in some provinces teachers must have a special certificate, acquired through additional training, to work as special education teachers. A teacher's workload can be changed at the end of, or during, the school year. Aspects of working conditions, such as maximum class size (whether or not there are split-grade classes) or the amount of nonteaching (preparation) time teachers must receive, may be regulated either by the collective agreement or at the discretion of the school district or school administration (see Box 6.1). However, for the most part, teachers have relatively little control over their working conditions, which puts schools closer to the bureaucratic than to the professional model.

Teachers' working conditions are affected significantly by developments outside of the school. For example, if unemployment increases, more children may have to cope with declines in family income and living standards, and with the increased frustration of an unemployed parent. Poverty has, for many reasons, a very strong negative impact on children's ability to benefit from school. Increasing violence in society may be coupled with more violence in the school. Children subjected to an unending barrage of TV commercials urging them to buy and own things may have difficulty seeing the value of school activities.

Professional Development

All schools and school systems recognize the need for teachers and administrators to continue to learn about their work. Professional development or in-service training are the names given to the various formal and informal opportunities given to teachers to improve themselves. Professional development can include everything from informal after-school teachers' meetings to university degree programs.

Most Canadian school systems provide structured professional-development activities. Provinces normally set aside a certain number of days in each school year (from five to twelve days is typical) when schools can be closed to students to allow teachers to meet. In addition to these, schools may organize a wide range of other professional-development activities either outside of school hours or during school time (using substitute teachers to cover classes). Many teachers devote considerable amounts of their own time and money to study and improvement activities of various kinds.

Despite the amount of effort that goes into their preparation, studies typically report that teachers are not very satisfied with their professional-development experiences, which are seen as having little impact on subsequent activity in the classroom (Riffel, 1991). The ideas raised may be unrealistic, may require substantial skill (which teachers are not able to develop in one or two days), may not fit with the rules and procedures of a school, or may be popular one year but forgotten the next. All of these problems reduce the potential value of professional development. Fullan and Stiegelbauer (1991, p. 319) point out that effective staff development must involve both specific instructional changes and related changes in the ways in which teachers work, so that the instructional changes can be both implemented and well supported.

The development of a professional model of teaching has generated much more interest in making professional development a valuable process. Much of the change in professional development has been influenced by educational research that has supported practices such as peer coaching (in which teachers work with one another to improve particular aspects of their teaching) and reflective practice (in which teachers gather information about their own teaching and use it as the basis for planning changes). Increasing efforts are also being made to integrate professional development with other school activities such as evaluation practice or curriculum development, to provide ongoing support for teachers who are trying to make changes in their practice, and to create collaborative relationships among teachers to support change. These developments have the potential to make schools places of learning for teachers as well as for students.

Supervision

The degree to which teachers are supervised in their work also varies enormously from school to school. In some schools, teachers rarely see another adult in their classroom during the course of the year. Outside intervention occurs only when there is a problem, such as excessive noise or a complaint from a parent. In other schools, principals and staff members are frequently, if briefly, in one another's classes for various reasons.

The very fact of supervision as a normal feature of schools is an indication of the influence of the bureaucratic model. In professional settings, however, supervision by superiors is typically replaced by a peer-governed process of quality control in which members of the profession set up systems to examine one another's practice.

Teachers have mixed opinions on the matter of supervision. On the one hand, most teachers value the autonomy they have in the classroom, and their ability to organize teaching in a way that they feel suits them and their students. This is consistent with the lack of a common approach to teaching, noted earlier in this chapter. Teachers may worry that too many visits by an administrator will result in more external control over their work and more instructions to them to change what they are doing. On the other hand, most teachers have a real interest in improving their teaching, and they recognize that feedback from others can be very helpful in doing so.

Recent thinking in education, as indicated earlier, emphasizes the role of the principal as an educational leader. This orientation urges principals to shift their priorities from administrative duties to improving their schools' instructional programs, and to achieve this goal by working closely with teachers (Pajak, 1993). Under the instructional leadership approach, principals spend much more time in classrooms, learn about what teachers are doing, and discuss educational issues with them. This approach seeks to move schools closer to a professional model of organization. There is not enough evidence yet to show that large numbers of principals are in fact changing their practice, but it is reasonable to expect that teachers will have more visits to their classrooms than used to be the case.

Evaluation

Almost all educational jurisdictions have policies requiring the formal evaluation of teachers on a regular basis. First-year teachers can expect to be evaluated more frequently (and more carefully) than more experienced teachers.

Evaluation has two purposes. One of these is to help teachers improve their teaching; this is commonly referred to as *formative evaluation*. The second function of evaluation is to find and deal with teachers whose performance is not acceptable; this is called *summative evaluation*.

Most teacher evaluation policies attempt to combine both these functions in a single set of practices. The evaluation most commonly in use involves a *conference model*. The person doing the evaluation (usually, but not always, the school principal) meets with the teacher being evaluated to discuss and agree on how the evaluation will be conducted. This may involve matters such as how many classroom visits will be made, when they will be made, what specific aspects of teaching will be looked at most closely, and any other matters that either the teacher or the principal may wish to have considered. Following whatever classroom visits and other measures have been agreed to, the evaluator and the teacher will meet again to discuss the results of the evaluation. The evaluator will provide a written report on the evaluation, and the teacher will have an opportunity to comment on the report. The evaluator may then revise the report in light of the teacher's views. A final version of the evaluation report, together with any written comments the teacher wishes to make, are normally placed in the teacher's personnel file, which is held by the school district. These procedures have been developed and adopted to protect teachers from unfair and arbitrary evaluation that could lead to dismissal.

At the heart of the debate about teacher evaluation is the distinction between hierarchical and professional models of schools. In a hierarchical model, it is clearly the job of managers to evaluate workers and determine whether they are competent. In a professional organization, however, managers may not be knowledgeable enough to make judgements about competence. Hospital administrators do not judge the quality of medical practice, for example. Instead, evaluation in professional settings relies primarily on peer assessment and on standards of practice.

Teacher evaluation efforts have been troubled by several problems. First, it is difficult to combine formative and summative evaluation in a single policy. Many commentators on the issue feel that as long as teachers are concerned that the evaluation may be used against them, they are unlikely to be open in raising concerns about improvements in their own teaching. Making decisions about whether to retain teachers on staff is not consistent with creating an open climate for discussing teaching and its improvement.

There are also serious technical problems with teacher evaluation. The point has already been made that there is no single style of good teaching. Indeed, people will disagree in many cases on what good teaching is. When agreement on good practice is hard to obtain, there is an obvious problem in evaluating when good practice is occurring. For example, a teacher may favour a more open and student-centred teaching style, while the evaluator favours a more controlled and disciplined approach. It is not evident that one of them is right and the other wrong, but their different views would certainly affect the evaluation.

Most teacher evaluation occurs through classroom visits by evaluators. But there are questions about the validity of this technique. Are evaluators' judgements, based as they are on only a relatively brief time in a classroom, the best measure of good teaching? What about cases where the evaluator knows little about the particular subject or age group? What happens if the evaluator and the teacher happen to dislike each other? There are many potential sources of bias in evaluations done through observations. Some writers have suggested alternative means of evaluating teachers, such as using students' ratings, students' test scores, or evaluations by other teachers. Each approach may have some value, but each also has significant weaknesses. There is no agreement in the research on any particular evaluation practice that can be demonstrated to have a high level of validity.

The empirical evidence on teacher evaluation also shows that much of the evaluation work being done has little or no impact on what teachers do (Lawton et al., 1986). From the summative side, only a very small number of teachers are found to be so deficient in their teaching that formal action of some kind is taken; a British Columbia study estimated this at less than 2 percent (Housego, 1989). In the overwhelming majority of cases, evaluation reports are quite positive. However, many teachers find these reports to be of little use to them. While it is always nice to be told one is doing a good job, teachers often express the desire to be given feedback that will help them continue to improve; formal evaluations rarely provide such feedback.

In the last few years, some school districts have begun to move toward a form of evaluation policy called the **two-track model**. Under this scheme, most teachers do not have formal evaluations. Instead, they work with their administrator to define areas in which they would like to review their teaching practice and make changes. The plan they develop for doing so might include professional-development activities, work with fellow teachers, directed reading, classroom observations by administrators, or other steps. This work is carried out strictly for purposes of self-improvement. No formal reports are prepared, and no evaluative comments are placed in the personnel file. The teacher may develop a **portfolio** of lesson plans, student work, and other material that can be used to discuss her or his teaching with colleagues and administrators. The focus is entirely on improving one's teaching.

A smaller number of teachers will be in a formal evaluation track. Teachers might choose to be evaluated formally, perhaps because they want something on their record about their teaching performance. Alternatively, administrators may identify teachers whom they wish to evaluate formally. These could be new teachers, teachers moving into a different subject area, or teachers about whose competence the administrator may have concerns. For teachers in the formal mode, the procedure would be similar to that described for the conference model. The two-track model is intended to increase the emphasis on the improvement of teaching, while reserving more formal evaluations for the relatively small number of cases where they are wanted or needed.

Academic Freedom

As employees of a school district, which is governed by provincial regulations and curriculum requirements, teachers are not free to teach whatever content they want. In universities, professors are recognized as having academic freedom, which means that they are able to teach in their classes the knowledge they consider to be most important and worthwhile, even if these ideas are controversial or unpopular.

No such right appears to exist for teachers in the schools. Teachers are required by law to teach the curriculum as established by the province or other legitimate authorities, and to obey the legitimate instructions given to them by administrators and school boards. A teacher can be dismissed for refusing to do so. In the well-known Alberta case, Jim Keegstra taught for years an anti-Semitic version of history in which he held Jews to be responsible for most wars, economic depressions, and other human tragedies. Keegstra was eventually dismissed by the local board of education, not because of his anti-Semitic teachings, but because he had refused to obey an instruction from the superintendent to teach only the Alberta history curriculum (Schwartz, 1986).

Keegstra was not involved in a case of academic freedom; there can be no academic freedom to teach what is false (Hurlbert & Hurlbert, 1992, pp. 221–33). It is true, however, that teachers in schools are not free to determine what subject matter they will teach. Nor in most schools is it easy for teachers to raise in their classes controversial issues such as politics, sexual behaviour, religious values, or abortion. Teachers must exercise caution to ensure that their approach to controversial issues fits with the required curriculum, is as fair and objective as possible, and is appropriate to the needs and abilities of students. Many school districts have policies on teaching controversial issues, and require teachers to obtain permission from school administrators before raising these issues in class.

Dismissal and Tenure

At one time, school boards had the right to dismiss teachers more or less as they pleased. They did not need to provide reasons for their decision. The history of Canadian education has many examples of teachers being fired because they did something controversial, or because they disagreed with or challenged a decision of the school board, regardless of their competence as teachers. For many years in Canada, getting married was grounds for automatic dismissal for any female teacher.

Over time, teachers have been able to protect themselves from arbitrary firing. Most of the improvement occurred through collective bargaining, as teachers' organizations and school districts made agreements that were intended to protect teachers from unjustified dismissal. The increasing acceptance in Canadian law and practice of the concept of natural justice has also had a role in protecting teachers; natural justice requires that reasons be given for a dismissal, and that the person being fired have some sort of right to a hearing.

At present in Canada, teachers can be dismissed for several reasons. First of all, school districts, as employers, have the right to eliminate teaching jobs for budgetary or programmatic reasons. A school board may decide to reduce its teaching staff because it has fewer students, or because it wants to avoid a tax increase. Depending on the provisions in collective agreements, layoffs of this kind may be based on seniority or other criteria, or may be at the discretion of the school board.

New teachers normally hold what are called probationary appointments for one or two years, depending on the province. This means they can be dismissed by a school board during this time without having a right to a third-party appeal through arbitration. School administrators may decide to end teachers' employment before the probationary period is over because it is much easier to do so at that point in time.

Once teachers have been in a particular school district for more than the probationary period, they acquire tenure or, in more formal terms, the **right to due process**. This means that a teacher cannot be dismissed without being given reasons for the dismissal, and without having the right to challenge the dismissal through a process of arbitration. Though the precise arrangements vary from province to province, to dismiss a tenured teacher the employer must be able to convince an impartial arbitration board that it had valid reasons for its decision.

What are valid reasons for dismissing a teacher? The most common reasons have to do with evident inability to do the job properly, such as alcoholism, being convicted of a serious crime, extensive absenteeism without justification, or other such actions. Teachers can also be dismissed for failing to obey a legitimate instruction of the school board. Teachers, as employees, are required to obey the reasonable instructions of their employer. Thus, if a school board instructed teachers to follow a particular curriculum, a teacher who refused to do so could be dismissed. Finally, a teacher can be dismissed for incompetence, that is, for failing to carry out his or her teaching duties effectively.

None of these grounds for dismissal can be applied in a simple way, however. Through a series of laws and court decisions, an understanding has gradually developed of what would constitute reasonable grounds for dismissal. In almost any attempt to fire a teacher, the school board would have to show that it had given the teacher notice that there was a significant problem, and that the board had made real efforts to help the teacher eliminate the problem. A school board that had a concern about a teacher's competence would need to show that the teacher had been informed (usually in writing) of the concern, and that efforts had been made to help the teacher improve his or her skills. Only when such efforts had been made, and had clearly failed, would a move for dismissal have very much likelihood of being successful.

Teachers' organizations continue to play an important role in safeguarding teachers' rights to continued employment. A teacher who fears dismissal will usually contact his or her association to seek advice and assistance. When dismissals end up in arbitration, the teacher's costs are usually borne by the teachers' association.

The demonstration of incompetence as a teacher is particularly difficult to establish to the satisfaction of an arbitration board, for many of the reasons already mentioned in regard to teacher evaluation. The significant difference of opinion as to what good teaching is makes it very difficult to show that a particular teacher — especially one who has taught for a number of years — is incompetent. While the protection of teachers from arbitrary or unfair dismissal is important, it is possible that this protection sometimes comes at the expense of students who do not have unions to lobby for their rights or legal provisions to protect them. As was noted in Chapter Four, the ability to take advantage of legal protections is not equally distributed, and often those who are most vulnerable also have the least ability to act to improve their situation.

The problem of dealing with performance problems of teachers takes on another dimension when one considers it in the context of teaching as a career. As teachers age and acquire more years of experience, their attitude toward their work may well change. What should be done with a teacher who, after twenty years of dedicated and effective teaching, has lost enthusiasm for the job? What happens with a teacher whose work is significantly affected by other aspects of her or his life, such as the death of a spouse or an aging parent who requires constant care? Dismissal is a very blunt and powerful instrument, and one that is probably inappropriate in most situations. Instead, schools need to have ways of working with teachers to ensure continued effective performance. The aging of Canada's teaching force, and the problems associated with this change, has only recently begun to attract a large amount of research and policy interest.

An alternative mechanism for disciplining teachers is rooted in the professional model of doctors or engineers, in which the professional group is responsible for disciplining its own members. Teachers' organizations in Canada have pressed for such authority, as discussed in Chapter Eight.

Affirmative Action/Employment Equity

Affirmative action is primarily a U.S. term. Ontario judge Rosalie Abella (1984), who completed a major study on the issue for the Government of Canada, preferred the term **employment equity**, by which she meant efforts to create a more balanced representation of various groups in a given work force. Employment equity has broad application in Canada in many sectors of the labour force and in many different industries. The federal government, for example, requires all companies with which it contracts to develop and implement an employment equity strategy.

Employment equity is regarded as necessary because work forces may become highly segregated in terms of gender, race, or ethnicity, and because certain groups have had enormous difficulty in finding employment. With respect to teachers, two areas of employment equity have been predominant in Canada.

Women and Administration

Although slightly more than 60 percent of Canadian teachers are women, the overwhelming majority of school administrators in Canada (including principals and superintendents) are men. Tables 6.2 and 6.3 provide recent data on these proportions. The women who are in administrative positions are primarily in elementary schools. Generally, the further up the administrative hierarchy one goes, the smaller the proportion of women. The information in Table 6.3 shows that in recent years there has been some overall increase in both the number and the proportion of female principals and vice-principals in Canadian schools, but in neither case do these figures come close to constituting a balanced or representative situation.

Why should anyone (female or male) care what the proportions of men and women are in school administration? There are several important reasons. Most simply, it would be inefficient, as well as wrong, to systematically exclude a whole group of people whose skills and talents would thereby be lost to us. It is preferable to try to draw on the widest possible range of abilities in dealing with the many issues facing schools. Some feminist authors have gone further, contending that women often have a different approach to school administration—one that is valuable and should be encouraged. They argue that female administrators are more likely to emphasize instructional issues in the school, and to stress teamwork and participative decision-making (Shakeshaft, 1989; Fullan & Stiegelbauer, 1991). These predispositions are highly consistent with the recent research on effective leadership and effective schools discussed earlier in this chapter. If women are more likely to display these attributes, as the research suggests, there should be more efforts made to appoint female administrators. Overall, changing attitudes in this area reflect the general change in society regarding the role of women; here, as in so many areas, school policy and practice tend to reflect larger social issues.

Table 6.2

Percentages of Male vs. Female Teachers and Administrators

Position	Percent male (Range among provinces)	Percent female (Range among provinces)
Chief superintendents/ Directors	94–100	0–6
Secondary-school principals	88–100	0–12
Secondary-school teachers	50–72	28–50
Elementary-school principals	62–85	15–38
Elementary-school teachers	14–31	69–86

Source: R. Rees. (1990). *Women and men in education.* Toronto: Canadian Education Association, p. 88. Reproduced with permission.

Table 6.3

Canadian School Principals and Vice-Principals by Gender

	1981–82	1992–93
Principals		
Female	1 362 (13.2%)	2 545 (24.1%)
Male	8 940 (86.8%)	8 007 (75.9%)
Total	10 302 (100%)	10 552 (100%)
Vice-Principals		
Female	974 (16.8%)	2 527 (34.8%)
Male	4 825 (83.2%)	4 743 (65.2%)
Total	5 799 (100%)	7 270 (100%)

Source: Canadian Education Statistics Council, Statistics Canada, No. 81-528-XPB (1996), p. 70.

Research regarding the subject of women in administration has largely focussed on why there are so few women in administrative roles, and on what steps might be taken to increase their numbers. The research indicates that the barriers to women entering school administration are many and complex. Women appointed to administrative positions are, on average, more qualified and more experienced than are men, but are more likely to wait to be encouraged before applying for administrative positions (Tabin & Coleman, 1993).

Women also face significant external obstacles. As those who still bear the prime responsibility for child care, women must often choose between their desire to have an active career and their desire to be an active parent. Parenting for women—but not for men—often results in career interruptions. Sharpening women's dilemma is the fact that administrative jobs often require additional work during evenings and weekends. Women who are single parents with administrative aspirations experience even more tensions between work and parenting. Finally, women who wish to work may also face difficulties in finding good-quality child care. All of these obstacles led Lockhart (1991) to conclude that "the evidence over the last quarter-century has not supported the assumption that the low proportion of women teachers in [administrative] positions ... is explainable in terms of their lower career commitment" (p. 32).

But beyond the barriers noted above, there are also barriers to the promotion of women that have to do with our concept of merit. We usually think of merit as hiring the best person for a given job. In practice, however, merit may not be the principal consideration in hiring. More stress may be placed on hiring someone who is known to us, with whom we get along well, or who will "fit in." Moreover, the criteria we have in mind when we think of the "best person" are not necessarily justifiable or fair. If we think that to be a successful high-school principal a person must be large and have a powerful voice, then we automatically exclude most women (and many men) from consideration. Earlier in the chapter, reference was made to the differences some researchers found between the administrative styles of men and women. If it is the typical male style that is valued by those doing the hiring, then women are less likely to be promoted, despite their experience and academic qualifications.

All of this suggests that women face barriers to promotion that are not of their own making, and that concerted effort will be needed to produce a greater degree of equality among educational administrators.

A Representative Teaching Force

Many of the same issues surround the role of minority groups in our schools. In many Canadian cities, large numbers of students come from various ethnic minorities, yet few teachers and administrators originate from these same groups (Lockhart, 1991, p. 34). In some cities, and in much of northern Canada, large numbers of students are Aboriginal, yet there are relatively few Aboriginal teachers and administrators in the schools. Without suggesting that effective teaching requires that student and teacher share a common cultural background, at least three quite different justifications can be made for a representative teaching force. The importance of teachers as role models for minority students is one such justification, but equally important is their presence to challenge the development of stereotypes and prejudices among majority students. Second, if schools do indeed value a multicultural curriculum, then such teachers are likely to bring to the system a range of knowledge, skills, experiences, and sensitivities that would be enriching. Third, from an employment perspective, school systems might justifiably be asked to examine why, as major employers, they do not draw equally from the population of their communities, and to take steps to remove unreasonable barriers in their hiring and personnel practices.

As in the case of women, the causes of this situation are multiple and complex, and they are also different for different minority groups. In the case of Aboriginal people, high-school graduation levels have until recently been so low that few qualified for admission to university preparation programs. Some immigrants, on the other hand, have emigrated with credentials in teaching from their home countries, but these have not been accepted in Canada. Similar to the equality issues that face women, there appear to be definite barriers that most minorities encounter in their efforts to become teachers and administrators.

Canada has a number of innovative programs that train Aboriginal and other underrepresented groups as teachers. Many Canadian universities, including British Columbia, Brandon, Saskatchewan, Manitoba, Lakehead, and McGill, operate programs that specifically recruit Aboriginal people into teaching, and provide them with recognized university credentials. Usually these programs pay particular attention to Aboriginal cultural issues, Aboriginal languages, and the requirements of both northern and urban schools, where most Aboriginal children go to school. These programs have brought about a substantial increase in Aboriginal teachers in First Nations schools. However, in provincial schools, with or without large Aboriginal or minority student populations, the small number of Aboriginal and minority teachers remains a challenge. Some school districts have begun the process of reviewing hiring procedures in order to eliminate culturally biased practices, and to recruit actively teachers from underrepresented groups. Few school jurisdictions in Canada, however, have employment equity policies comparable to those required of many federal and provincial government agencies. Nor have university faculties of education, though they constitute the entry to teaching, paid much attention to these issues, except through the special programs already mentioned.

Employment Equity Measures

What steps can be taken to increase the numbers of women, Aboriginal people, and other underrepresented groups among teachers and administrators? A wide range of employment equity programs has already been established in organizations. Although much of the debate over employment equity focuses on the idea of quotas (in which some portion of a set of jobs is reserved for members of target groups), the use of quotas is in fact relatively rare, and is only one of many ways to strengthen the presence of affirmative-action target groups. Some of these include

- specific efforts to find qualified applicants from target groups, and to encourage them to apply;
- providing training to target group members to increase their qualifications and chance of being selected;
- providing training to those on selection committees in order to guard against unwarranted biases in hiring;
- providing guidelines for job criteria that are not systematically exclusive of certain groups (e.g., qualifications such as height or coaching experience); and
- changing workplace conditions to make jobs more attractive to target group members (e.g., providing day care or allowing staff flexibility with respect to religious holidays).

Some people see employment equity as controversial because they believe it constitutes a form of reverse discrimination that works against people who are not members of an affirmative-action group. However, the *Charter of Rights and Freedoms* clearly allows such provisions in Section 15. Furthermore, until we are successful in having a distribution of teachers and administrators that is more consistent with the overall population, employment equity measures appear to be warranted, and are likely to continue.

Conclusion

Canadian schools tend to embody very similar policies and procedures for organizing the work of teachers, from hiring through workload determination and supervision. There is nothing inevitable about these arrangements, and arguments have been made for significant changes to them. As long as current processes are largely taken for granted, however, the necessary debate and discussion about better alternatives will not occur. Teachers need to be aware of the reasons for current practice, and to think about ways in which the organization of their work might be improved.

Exercises

1. Obtain an age profile for teachers in your province and, if possible, data on attrition rates from teaching. What estimates might you make of the numbers of teachers who might be leaving teaching in the next five to ten years? What factors might change teachers' plans to retire or leave teaching?

2. Think of a metaphor for the schools and try to describe what characteristics schools might have based on the metaphor you have chosen. For example, if you think of the school as a garden, you might consider what elements would play the role of seeds, fertilizer, sunlight, water, and so on. Alternatively, if you think of the school as a living creature, you might consider what elements constitute the heart, lungs, eyes, and so on.

3. Interview one or two teachers. Ask them to identify the best and worst aspects of teaching. Ask about differences in the various schools in which they may have taught. What conclusions can you draw from their comments?

4. Observe the work of the principal in the school in which you are student teaching or observing. How often is the principal in classrooms? What does he or she do while there? What sort of communication does the principal have with teachers? What is the primary content of these communications? As you see it, what is the principal trying to accomplish in the school?

5. Find out how teachers are hired in a local school district. Are all jobs advertised? How many people are interviewed? Who does the interviewing? Who makes final decisions about hiring? Who else is involved in hiring decisions?

6. Find out what provisions, if any, are made to induct new teachers into a local school or district.

7. Do a brief write-up of professional-development activities, either in the school as a whole or as practised by one or two teachers. What activities do people participate in? How useful do they seem to be?

8. Obtain a copy of the teacher evaluation policy in a local school or district. To what extent does it embody the traditional model described in this chapter? What other features does it have?

9. Try to obtain the written judgement of an arbitration proceeding over teacher dismissal. What arguments and evidence were advanced for and against dismissal? Which arguments appear to have been most successful? What grounds did the arbitrator use in arriving at a decision?

10. Conduct a class role-play of a teacher talking with her or his principal about a policy with which the teacher disagrees. Ask various students to take each part, and see what different strategies people use.

11. Obtain the list of school administrators from a local school district. Compare the numbers of men and women at each level. How have these proportions changed over the last ten years?

12. Ask the provincial teachers' association or society whether any school districts in your province have employment equity or affirmative-action plans. Obtain a copy of such a plan if you can. What are its central features? What impact do you think such a plan will have? Why?

Further Reading

There is relatively little literature available on many aspects of the situation of teachers in Canada. The Canadian Teachers' Federation (1992) is one good source, and Statistics Canada publications are another. Dan Lortie's *Schoolteacher* (University of Chicago Press: 1975) on U.S. teachers and Connell's (1985) study on Australian teachers, *Teachers' Work*, are excellent portrayals of the ways in which teachers experience their work. Dolmage's (1996) book, *So You Want to Be a Teacher* provides an up-to-date and thorough review of the characteristics of the Canadian teaching profession, as does Alexander Lockhart's (1991) book, *School Teaching in Canada*.

On the topic of women and administration, Reynolds and Young's (1995) book *Women and Leadership in Canadian Education* provides a valuable Canadian source on gender, educational administration, and leadership.

CHAPTER SEVEN

Parents and Families, Communities and Schools

▼ PROLOGUE

Jan and Gordon left the staff meeting together and walked down the corridor to the general office. Picking up a cup of stale coffee, they went into Jan's crowded office, cleared off a couple of chairs, and sat down. At the staff meeting, Gordon, the principal of Fernwood Elementary School, had presented the board's budget projections for the next year; they were going to require some cutbacks in staff positions. On top of these general cutbacks, the board had informed him that the funding for Jan's position of community liaison worker would no longer be provided separately by the board, but instead would have to come out of the school's general staffing budget.

Gordon had told everyone at the meeting that he would be initiating a series of discussions over the next few days with all of the staff before any decisions were made about the plans for next year. However, from the discussions that followed his announcement there emerged many different opinions among the group over staffing priorities. Furthermore, while Jan was a well-respected staff member at the school, it was clear that her position was, once again, in jeopardy. While Rina and Wayne, the early childhood teachers, had stated that they simply couldn't run their program without her, other teachers had made their own claims for support positions, including instructional assistants for their classes, guidance teachers, and librarians.

"Well," said Gordon, "this is going to be a tough few weeks. So what else is new! One of these years maybe we'll get a budget that actually lets us do our job. You know, it's ironic, we have built a program of parent and community involvement here that *really works*, and yet every year we've had to fight to keep the funding for your position. And without you, or at least without your position, it would be really difficult to do half of what we're doing now. Even our own teachers, who *know* how important you are, still seem to see what you do as different from the heart of our job as educators. It says something about what we think schools are, and how children learn."

"Yeah, we really do need the position," replied Jan now. "You know, there are days when I really don't think that I've achieved anything, but when you look back over what we've been able to put in place over the last five years, we do have something to be proud of here. The early childhood centre, the volunteer program, the preschool and before-and-after-school day cares, the job training programs, the parents' association, and all the other stuff. You know we had over 100 parent volunteers in our school last year —

that's nearly a quarter of all students' families. And it makes a big difference: the teachers appreciate the help, and they notice the positive effects it has on the kids when they see mums and dads working together with the teachers. But if individual teachers have to do all the recruiting, organizing, and co-ordinating on their own, it won't work as well; they just don't have the time to do it all, especially when there are problems to be resolved. And if the parents don't feel that they are both welcomed and put to good use, they're not going to keep volunteering. By the way, I need your signature on the funding application to the Phillips Foundation for our summer school program. That's looking quite promising."

At that moment, Rina and Wayne knocked on the open door and walked into the office. "OK," Rina said abruptly, "we've got to get organized here. We can't lose Jan, period. Our early childhood centre is absolutely essential to everything else that happens in this school, and we need Jan's help to make it work."

The centre, a large multipurpose room in the school, was funded by a special grant from the province and specialized in providing learning activities for children from birth to age 8. Its two full-time staff were also responsible for maintaining a drop-in centre for parents with infants, organizing play groups for preschool children and their parents, and co-ordinating the "book mates" home-reading program at the school. They also organized parent workshops and worked collaboratively with the primary-grade teachers to provide supplementary learning activities.

"And," Rina continued, "if the Grades 5 and 6 teachers don't see how vital these activities are, then we've got some consciousness-raising to do in the next little while."

Gordon got up to leave. "OK, look, we'll get back to this and keep talking. You know where I stand on the importance of parent and community involvement. You know, I think we really need to rethink the way in which most teachers and parents view each other. It's so out of touch with the needs of schooling in the 1990s. Perhaps it all has to begin with the faculties of education and the ways we train and socialize our new teachers." ■

It is largely taken for granted that families and schools are both primary institutions involved in the socialization and education of society's youth; it is also well documented that home influences have a substantial impact on school success. But in spite of this intertwining of objectives, and the interactive effects of each institution on the other, the relationships between parents and teachers are most often characterized by distance and suspicion rather than close collaboration. Lightfoot (1978) has noted the irony in the fact that "families and schools are engaged in a complementary sociocultural task and yet they find themselves in great conflict with one another" (p. 20). Beginning teachers at all grade levels have ranked relations with parents as one of the most difficult aspects of their work, along with classroom management, student motivation, and responding to individual differences (Veenman, 1984).

Recently in Canada and internationally, there have been calls for a much greater degree of school-initiated co-operation and collaboration between parents and teachers. A growing body of research is being cited to support the assumption that teachers and parents share common objectives for children that are best achieved when they can work together. The first part of this chapter examines those issues with respect to the following questions:

1. How do families affect school experiences and school success?
2. How do families and schools normally interact?
3. What models exist for restructuring parent–teacher relationships, and what claims are made to support them?

While parent/family and teacher linkages are important aspects of school life, and critical to the role of the teacher, there is a broader context to be considered. Families do not exist in isolation; they live with other families in groups that might loosely be referred to as communities. Several authors (e.g., Coleman, 1987) have drawn attention to the significance of community expectations and community "social capital" in the production of effective schools. Accordingly, in the second part of this chapter, we examine the relationship between schools and families in their capacity as communities.

Families and Schools

We have suggested throughout this book that schools and classrooms/teachers are inextricably linked to the wider social settings within which they are embedded, and that the influences of these external realities invade the classroom in both obvious and subtle ways. The relationship between families and schools represents a critical element of that linkage, only a small part of which constitutes the formal and concrete interactions between parents and teachers.

Regardless of whether teachers commute considerable distances to school, arriving just before the start of the school day and leaving immediately after it is finished, or whether parents ever physically set foot in their children's school, teachers and parents meet vicariously every day in the lives of students. The consequences of these invisible meetings have been shown to have profound influences on the type and range of experiences provided to students in school and ultimately contribute to their success in school. Lightfoot (1978) captures something of this pervasive but often invisible presence:

> As children enter the classroom, their families also come with them. In the child's head he brings his familial experiences (his half eaten breakfast, his fight with his

bully brother, his mama's warm hug). In the teacher's perception he comes as his parents' child (with the bright arrogance of his doctor father, with the embarrassed reticence of his shy, withdrawn mother). And in the mother's heart a piece of her relives her own school history as she tries not to communicate her own tortured memories of school by offering words of fond encouragement (p. 10).

Parents do many things that influence their children's experiences of schooling: they feed and clothe them and deliver them to school (or to the school bus); they teach them many things before they enter school, and continue teaching them over the course of their school life. Parents also provide their children with educational resources — toys, books, computers, work space — and educational experiences that complement school experiences. They monitor and support students' work in school by taking an interest in their children's work, by requiring them to complete their homework, by regulating the time spent viewing TV, and by reinforcing the importance of school success. And they advocate on their children's behalf in their dealings with the school—asking for help, requesting particular placements and teachers, and, in extreme cases, transferring their child from one school to another, or from the public system into the private system.

But "families" and "parents" cannot be treated as a monolithic mass with a common set of characteristics. In fact, the *only* characteristic they share is that they are responsible for children. Among many other things, families vary markedly in terms of material circumstances, internal structure, and cultural location. As shown in Chapter Five, family income in Canada is distributed quite unequally; single-parent families headed by a female are particularly likely to have low incomes (more is said about these issues in Chapter Ten). *These family circumstances do not define "good families" and "bad families." Nor do they make children more or less intelligent or more or less educable.* Nevertheless, they have been consistently shown to have powerful effects on students' treatment and experience in school and on school outcomes.

A great deal has been written on how families affect educational outcomes. Much of this literature has attempted to link school success with particular family characteristics, and to explain school failure in terms of families that lack these desired qualities. This approach has become known as the **deficit theory**. It is inadequate because, among other things, it leaves unquestioned the organization of schools, their curriculum, and the practices of teachers; and it is particularly dangerous because it offers teachers a stereotype of students that encourages them to expect success from certain children and failure from others based on factors that have nothing to do with the abilities of the child.

A more useful strand of the literature on school success emphasizes the *relationship* between families and schools. **Reproduction theorists** suggest that school success is closely related to the degree to which the culture of the home corresponds with the culture of the school. Each child brings to school knowledge, values, skills, and dispositions that are acquired outside of school, primarily through her or his family interactions. This cultural capital, they suggest, is differentially valued and rewarded by the school system, with schools possessing a systemic preference for dominant white, middle-class male values, language, and views of the world. The consequence of this world view is that children's school experiences vary greatly — children are labelled differently, exposed to different learning experiences, and subject to different relationships with their teachers (McLaren, 1989).

Sociologist Basil Bernstein's (1971, 1975) research on language use within middle-class and working-class families in Britain led him to argue that while these families varied in their forms of language (stemming from differences in patterns of child rearing and family interaction) they used *equivalent* speech forms. In other words, what was at issue was not correct and incorrect language use but rather different cultural forms. That schools sanction one speech form and seek to correct the other distances certain students and families from their schools.

In their earliest expressions, these theories have been criticized for their overly mechanistic interpretation of the processes of schooling, and for failing to show in detail how this reproduction of the status quo could occur even when parents and teachers were committed to the success and well-being of all students. More recent work has given increasing attention to the details of life in schools, and to the recognition of schools as contested sites of cultural production. These analyses continue to illuminate the processes by which schools reproduce inequalities within the wider society. However, they go further in recognizing the very complex and often contradictory nature of students' relationships, both with their teachers and their families; these analyses also argue that schools need to be recognized as potential sites of social transformation as well as sites of social reproduction.

Manicom (1981) illustrates in some detail the ways in which schools often make very explicit assumptions about the work that the family (usually the mother at home) has already done. She points out, for example, that when children initially learn to paint, they tend to mix paints indiscriminately. Red paint brushes are dabbed into a variety of other colours; the result of this cross mixing is that the paint is soon a uniform grey that is undesirable to both student and teacher. If a parent has done some prior work at home, such as instructing the child to "place paint brushes only in similarly coloured paint jars," then one can proceed to other, more complex levels. If no one has given such instructions at home, the teacher must help develop the child's skills until they reach this level. This, Manicom suggests, is where the trouble starts for children whose socio-economic circumstances make it difficult for them to meet the teacher's expectations. Generally, the practices of middle-class parents tend to complement the work expectations of teachers, while the demands of child care, employment, and meeting basic needs with which poorer families must struggle often conflict with the demands of teachers (see also Griffith, 1995). It is a crucial impediment to learning that when observing differences in "who can draw" the teacher is really seeing differences in experience with drawing and not innate talent or ability. Because of their work demands, it is easy for teachers to see these differences in terms not of experience (needing a few extra lessons), but of ability. What is insidious about such a judgement, Manicom continues, is that it quickly leads to formal and informal forms of tracking and stratification based on explicit and tacit labelling procedures (cited in Olson, 1991, pp. 167–68).

The research on schools and families concludes that families are powerful institutions whose influence over children affects all aspects of their lives, including their experiences of schooling. This impact occurs irrespective of any formal interaction between parents and teachers, and can work to seriously disadvantage, as well as assist, students in their schooling. In examining the formal ways in which schools and families interact, and the ways in which such interactions might be expanded and improved, the theoretical perspectives introduced above provide a prerequisite conceptual framework for raising important questions of power and participation: which parents are being involved, on whose terms and in what areas of school life, and with what intended and actual outcomes for which students?

Separate Worlds: Traditional Patterns of Parent–Teacher Relations

Despite the role that families play in promoting educational success, schools have generally made only limited attempts to develop structured links with parents, and home–school relations are often still characterized by a considerable degree of unease. There are several explanations for this. Traditionally, social scientists have pointed to the inherent incompatibility of families and schools as social institutions in terms of their goals, roles, and relationships. Within the family, children and adults form small and enduring social units that are characterized by highly personal and emotional bonds of dependency and support. These cohesive social units operate in marked contrast to the ways in which large numbers of students are required to relate to a relatively few teachers in schools and classrooms that are, more or less, bureaucratically organized, and where relationships are typically task-specific and sometimes impersonal. Given this incompatibility, it was argued that homes' and schools' separate purposes are best achieved independently, when "teachers maintain their professional, general standards and judgements about children in their classrooms, and when parents maintain their personal, particularistic standards and judgements about their children at home" (Epstein, 1986, p. 277).

A further barrier to parent–teacher collaboration is created by teachers' long-standing ambition to be afforded the status and prestige of true professionals. Inasmuch as such aspirations are seen as requiring teachers to be the possessors of a unique and specialized body of knowledge that is unavailable to others, the pursuit of such recognition has the dual effect of both devaluing, in the eyes of the school, the knowledge that parents possess about their children and discouraging teachers from sharing their knowledge with "non-professional" parents, even though these are essential elements of meaningful collaboration. When this drive for professional status is placed within the context of the deficit view of "dysfunctional" families noted earlier (particularly the view that portrayed working-class, ethnic minority, and single-parent families as deficient, and that cast the school system as the remedial or compensatory mechanism designed to overcome these limitations), it is hardly surprising that little effort has been made to develop broad-based initiatives that could transcend the structural differences that characterize families and schools, and work collaboratively toward commonly held educational objectives.

As a consequence, parent–teacher relations often remain poorly developed — left up to the efforts of the individual teacher, reaching and involving only some parents, and directed away from central issues of instruction and governance. The fact that any parent approaching his or her child's school in Canada is still more likely to encounter a sign saying "All Visitors Must Report to the Office" than one that says, in several different languages, "Visitors Are Welcome" reflects both a continued sense of separation and the responsibility assigned to administrators to act as gatekeepers of access into the life of the school.

While parents may receive, usually via "pupil post," a steady flow of communication from schools, this is generally a one-way flow of information that is far more likely to address basic administrative matters (field-trip permission slips, head lice, notification of an upcoming professional-development day on which students do not attend school) or public relations (publicizing carefully selected events and achievements in the school) than it is to invite/initiate a dialogue with parents on instructional issues. Report cards and parent–teacher conferences, while offering the possibility of actual information sharing and two-way communication vis-à-vis central issues of individual student learning, often fail to live up to this promise. These occasional and brief encounters are often ritualized and trivialized to the satisfaction of no one: teachers lament the fact that "the parents we need to see never come," and those supposedly hard-to-reach parents feel that they are neither listened to nor heard.

A survey of some 1300 parents conducted in the United States in 1981 is illustrative of a more general pattern of interaction. The survey reported that, despite the typical profusion of school notices, 16 percent of parents received no memos from their children's teacher; over 35 percent did not attend a parent–teacher conference; some 60 percent never spoke to the teacher on the phone; about 70 percent never helped the teacher in the classroom or on field trips; nearly 60 percent rarely or never received requests from the teacher to become involved in learning activities at home; and fewer than 30 percent received advice from teachers on how to help their children in reading and mathematics (Epstein, 1986, pp. 280–81).

Justifications for Collaboration

Arguments in favour of greater parental involvement in schools, as noted in Chapter Two, include philosophical and political beliefs that participation in such a key social institution is essential to the pursuit of democracy; that public education is too important to be left to educators; and that without participation the interests of those currently less well served by public schools will not be improved. A second, more pragmatic/political argument suggests that broad-based participation is essential as a way of mobilizing and maintaining public support for schooling in an era of fiscal restraint and shifting demographics.

While we believe firmly in the importance of the first of these arguments and acknowledge the logic of the second, it is a third set of arguments — one that tends to be focussed more narrowly on school outcomes — that is of primary concern in this chapter. The essence of these arguments is stated boldly by Berla (1991):

> The research is overwhelmingly clear: when parents play a positive role in their chil-
> dren's education their children do better in school. This is true whether parents are
> college educated or grade school graduates and regardless of family income, race, or
> ethnic background. What counts is that parents have positive attitudes about the
> importance of good education and that they express confidence that their children
> will succeed. Major benefits of parent involvement include higher grades and test
> scores, positive attitudes and behavior, more successful academic programs, and
> more effective schools (p. 16).

Many such claims are made in the literature. Ziegler (1987), in a research report for the Toronto Board of Education, states with similar enthusiasm, "The evidence suggests that no single focus has the potential to be as productive for students as the closer linking of home and school, of parents and teachers" (p. 4). Given what we currently know of the complexities of schools, and the failure of trends in education to deliver radical improvement, we should treat such claims with caution.

A Typology of Parental and Family Involvement

Collaboration among parents, families, and schools can take many forms; in fact, effectiveness is likely to be predicated on families being able to assume a variety of roles based on their specific needs and the particular conditions of each school. Over the last two decades, some of the most comprehensive research and writing in this area has been done by Joyce Epstein with The Centre on Families, Communities, Schools, and Children's Learning in the United States. Epstein

---

Box 7.1
Parents Are a School's Best Friends

Based upon a U.S. review carried out by the National Committee for Citizens in Education of more than 50 research studies that examined the connections between parental involvement and student achievement, Henderson (1988) concluded: "If school improvement efforts are judged successful when they raise student achievement, the research strongly suggests that involving parents can make a crucial difference" (p. 149). Furthermore,

- Studies show that programs designed with a strong component of parental involvement produce students who perform better than those who have taken part in otherwise identical programs.
- Students in schools that maintain frequent contact with their communities outperform those in other schools.
- Children whose parents are in touch with the school score higher than children who have similar aptitude and family background, but whose parents are not involved.
- Parents who help their children learn at home nurture attitudes that are crucial to achievement.
- Children who are failing in school improve dramatically when parents are called in to help.

Source: Anne Henderson. (1988, October). Parents are a school's best friends. *Phi Delta Kappan,* 149. Reproduced with permission.

(1995) suggests six main types of partnerships among parents, families, communities, and schools relating to

1. parenting;
2. communicating;
3. volunteering;
4. learning at home;
5. decision making; and
6. collaborating with the community.

Each of these approaches is summarized in Box 7.2, and with the exception of issues related to Epstein's category of decision making, which have already been discussed in Chapter Two, and issues of collaborating with the community, which are given special attention in the second half of this chapter, each is discussed briefly below.

Parenting

It is not the task of teachers or schools to dictate to parents how to raise their children. Nevertheless, schools can play an important supporting role in helping families provide for their children's health and safety, and the development of parenting skills that complement children's growth and experiences in school. Examples of such activities might include the early childhood centre described in the prologue to this chapter; invitations to parents to join teachers for workshops on issues such as conflict resolution, adolescent relationships, learning styles, or peer tutoring; the operating of food banks or clothing exchanges through the school; or the use of community liaison workers to assist with the reception and settlement of new families into a school's neighbourhood.

School–Home Communication

Expressed in simple terms, school–home and home–school communication refers to the need for schools to transmit messages and share meanings with parents about school programs and children's progress. Such endeavours are rarely simple. In a few — primarily rural settings — large amounts of such communication still occur with relative ease and informality. Parents and teachers who share many common experiences and expectations of the school meet frequently and comfortably in their everyday lives in the community. Yet these circumstances are increasingly the exception. In an urban community, large schools draw students from geographically, economically, and culturally diverse neighbourhoods that are often quite distinct from those of their teachers. In such contexts, interactions do not occur frequently; nor can common experiences and expectations of schools be taken for granted. Effective communication between home and school is unlikely to occur unless it is formally initiated, promoted, and nurtured by the school. Today the phrase "hard-to-reach parents" is often used, but we also need to understand the parental perspective that defines the issue differently as "hard-to-reach schools."

D'Angelo and Adler (1991) refer to effective communication as "a magnet that draws together the spheres of influence that affect children's lives: school, home, community and the peer group" (p. 350). They categorize such communication into written communication (memos, newsletters, report cards); face-to-face communication (conferences, home visits); and technological communication (recorded telephone messages, computerized attendance callbacks, homework hotlines, and videos). Some schools have now begun to develop comprehensive strategies for home–school communication, making creative use of multiple forms of communication from each of these categories. In this process, the importance of carefully planned, ongoing, face-to-face interactions that begin early in a child's school career (or even prior to the start of his or her formal schooling) is generally acknowledged. Such interactions have the most potential for establishing and nurturing personal relationships of confidence and trust, which can then be reinforced with other written and technological forms of communication.

Box 7.2
Epstein's Framework of Six Types of Involvement and Sample Practices

Type 1 Parenting

Help all families establish home environments to support children as students.

SAMPLE PRACTICES
- Suggestions for home conditions that support learning at each grade level.
- Workshops, videotapes, computerized phone messages on parenting and child rearing at each age and grade level.
- Parent education and other courses or training for parents (e.g., GED, college credit, family literacy).
- Family support programs to assist families with health, nutrition, and other services.

Type 2 Communicating

Design effective forms of school-to-home and home-to-school communications about school programs and children's progress.

SAMPLE PRACTICES
- Conferences with every parent at least once a year, with follow-ups as needed.
- Language translators to assist families as needed.
- Weekly or monthly folders of student work sent home for review and comments.
- Parent–student pickup of report card, with conferences on improving grades.
- Regular schedule of useful notices, memos, phone calls, newsletters, and other communications.
- Clear information on choosing schools or courses, programs, and activities within schools.
- Clear information on all school policies, programs, reforms, and transitions.

Type 3 Volunteering

Recruit and organize parent help and support.

SAMPLE PRACTICES
- School and classroom volunteer program to help teachers, administrators, students, and other parents.
- Parent room or family centre for volunteer work, meetings, and resources for families.
- Annual postcard survey to identify all available talents, times, and locations of volunteers.
- Class parent, telephone tree, or other structures to provide all families with needed information.
- Parent patrols or other activities to aid safety and operation of school programs.

(continued)

(continued)

Type 4 Learning at Home

Provide information and ideas to families about how to help students at home with homework and other curriculum-related activities, decisions, and planning.

SAMPLE PRACTICES

- Information for families on skills required for students in all subjects at each grade.
- Information on homework policies and how to monitor and discuss schoolwork at home.
- Information on how to assist students to improve skills on various class and school assessments.
- Regular schedule of homework that requires students to discuss and interact with families on what they are learning in class.
- Calendars with activities for parents and students at home.
- Family math, science, and reading activities at school.
- Summer learning packets or activities.
- Family participation in setting student goals each year and in planning for college or work.

Type 5 Decision Making

Include parents in school decisions, developing parent leaders and representatives.

SAMPLE PRACTICES

- Active PTA/PTO or other parent organizations, advisory councils, or committees (e.g., curriculum, safety, personnel) for parent leadership and participation.
- Independent advocacy groups to lobby and work for school reform and improvements.
- District-level councils and committees for family and community involvement.
- Information on school or local elections for school representatives.
- Networks to link all families with parent representatives.

Type 6 Collaborating with Community

Identify and integrate resources and services from the community to strengthen school programs, family practices, and student learning and development.

SAMPLE PRACTICES

- Information for students and families on community health, cultural, recreational, social support, and other programs or services.
- Information on community activities that link to learning skills and talents, including summer programs for students.
- Service integration through partnerships involving school; civic, counselling, cultural, health, recreation, and other agencies and organizations; and businesses.
- Service to the community by students, families, and schools (e.g., recycling, art, music, drama, and other activities for seniors or others).
- Participation of alumni in school programs for students.

Source: Joyce L. Epstein (1995). School/family/community partnerships: Caring for the children we share. *Phi Delta Kappan, 76*(5), 701–12. Reproduced with permission.

Robinson (1994) expands the topic of home–school communication by reminding us that educators need to communicate effectively with all members of the public regardless of whether or not they currently have children attending public schools. To this end he suggests that we should think of at least six "sub-publics": parents with children in the public school system; parents with only preschool children; nonparents under the age of 40; parents with children who have finished school; parents with children in private schools; and, nonparents over the age of 40. Based on his research in British Columbia, Robinson argues that each of these subgroups has quite different attitudes toward schooling and different interests in communicating with schools, which call for quite different communication strategies.

Involving Parents in Schools

Most schools, especially elementary schools, make some use of parents as volunteers, although these activities are often left to the initiative of the individual teacher and remain largely unstructured at the school level. A parent volunteer may work in specific classrooms as an aide to the teacher; in the library, cafeteria, or on the playground; or at special events such as field trips or fundraisers.

Working one-on-one with students as a teacher aide, in addition to enhancing the educational productivity of the classroom, has the potential to provide parents with teaching skills that may be directly transferable to their home situation and their own children. Furthermore, while it may be impossible for many parents to be in school during the day, the normal presence of parents in the school may have other substantial benefits. As Ziegler (1987) notes, "the presence of parents in the school not only provides more adults to teach reading or offer help and support to children but also transforms the *culture* of the school" (p. 34).

A key element in many efforts to develop parental involvement in the daily life of schools has been the setting aside of space in the building for a parents' centre, which serves as a place for parents to meet and work, allows for face-to-face contact between parents and teachers, provides materials for parents to take home, and facilitates a substantial and co-ordinated parental presence in the school.

Distinct in several ways from the early childhood centre described at the beginning of this chapter is the parents' centre at Ellis School in Boston (Davies, 1991). In developing the centre, a small classroom was set aside and furnished with adult-sized chairs and tables, a sofa, coffee pot, and hot plate; a telephone was another essential piece of equipment. The centre was staffed by two paid, part-time parent co-ordinators from the community. It acted as a focus for school, family, and community communication through a variety of means, including recruiting parent volunteers requested by teachers, organizing a small library of books and toys for children, providing English as a Second Language (ESL) classes requested by parents, and acting as a referral service for parents who needed help in dealing with social service and other agencies (Davies, 1991, p. 379).

Involving Parents in Learning Activities at Home

Aside from the initiatives to promote work with parents in schools, there are the school-initiated strategies, involving all or most parents, that attempt to increase the "educational effectiveness" of the time that children spend with their parents. Such strategies may include activities designed to reinforce general skills and behaviours such as study habits, problem-solving abilities, and conversation skills, as well as specific learning strategies that are closely linked to the work that students do in their classrooms.

Becker and Epstein (1982) identify a large number of such strategies, and classify them as follows:

1. techniques that involve reading and books;
2. techniques that involve discussions between parents and children;
3. techniques based on informal activities and games;
4. tutoring and teaching techniques; and
5. formal contracts between parents and children.

Probably the most common and frequently evaluated forms of home-based learning activities involve parents, or other family members, reading to or being read to by their children in the early grades of their school careers. This is an approach that Ziegler (1987), after reviewing the research, concludes "involves little training for parents and is very effective in promoting children's interest in reading and ability to read" (p. 18).

An example of such an initiative was the Parents-as-Partners project developed by the York Board of Education in Toronto (Shuttleworth, 1986). The project was intended to improve the reading of those children having difficulty by having parents provide informed help at home, and by establishing support procedures that increased school–home collaboration. Parents were expected to listen to their children read for at least twenty minutes a day, and were assisted by a resource teacher in developing nonjudgemental listening skills. The project, which included the use of reading record cards and home visits, produced substantial improvements in student reading, greater enjoyment of books, improved school–home relationships, and an increase in library circulation in both school and community libraries (Shuttleworth, 1986, p. 43).

Unfortunately, initiatives such as these, though relatively common in the early grades of school, become increasingly rare as grade level increases. One reason for the decline is that parents tend to become less confident of their ability to help their children; as well, without direction and support from the school, such forms of parental collaboration tend to taper off and disappear (even though the research suggests that it can remain important to student learning).

In Britain, a large-scale project designed to promote parental involvement in their children's learning is called IMPACT (Merttens, Newland, & Webb, 1996). A part of this project involves specially structured home learning activities that foster interaction among students, family members, and teachers. In the United States, the TIPS (Teachers Involve Parents in Schoolwork) process developed by Joyce Epstein and Karen Salinas (1991) of Johns Hopkins University in concert with classroom teachers offers similar initiative. While these approaches do not ask parents to act as teachers, and expect students to be responsible for their homework, they do challenge the widely held expectation that homework should be done on one's own.

The Potential of Parental Involvement

Despite some of the claims of its proponents, parental involvement is not a simple remedy for all the criticisms that continue to be laid at the classroom door. In their review of parents and schooling, Flaxman and Inger (1991) remind us that efforts to achieve parental involvement may not always reach the parents who most need to be involved, may stress skills that parents may not want to learn, and may risk implying that school success is only for those children whose parents are willing to conform to the norms of the school (p. 4). Yet recent research, summarized in Box 7.3, suggests that strategies that increase parents' involvement in their children's schooling can have a significant role in improving student achievement. This is particularly likely when strategies are a comprehensive, well planned, long term part of an overall school plan rather than a remedial strategy, and when they continue beyond the elementary grades of schooling. Comprehensive initiatives require school and school system support. Teachers can do a certain amount on their own to foster close relationships with parents, but substantial developments require additional resources for the community—liaison workers (to provide in-service support and to facilitate collaboration), parent centres, and additional time for teachers to develop materials for parents. These special resources, though not substantial, are likely to be essential to any significant and sustained improvement in schooling. Flaxman and Inger (1991) offer something of a counterbalance to the parental involvement crusade when they conclude that

> [it] is not an educational panacea. For children to be better educated and for schools to reform, many things also have to happen. We need to find the right ways to educate children for a changing economic and social world. We need to reassert the place of education in developing values and civil behaviour. And parents, or their substitutes, have to raise their children, who are, more than ever, on their own. To achieve better school systems, we have to re-create families and communities that are now seriously disorganized, in new forms that the changing times demand and for all social classes. Schools, in turn, have to become flexible enough to restructure and innovate and change old models and practices long proved ineffective—even if this means radical change in governance, curriculum, and professional training. Parent involvement is a tool for these changes because it is a mechanism that links society, schools, and homes (pp. 5–6).

Box 7.3
Paths to Partnership: What We Know and Don't Know

Joyce Epstein, co-director of the Center on Families, Communities, Schools and Children's Learning, and Professor of Sociology at Johns Hopkins University in Baltimore, suggests the following key themes from recent research on improving parent–school collaboration:

- Programs at all levels reveal similarities between parents and educators where differences were once assumed. Parents and teachers are finding that they share common goals and need to share more information if they are to reach those goals.
- Programs must continue across the years of childhood and adolescence. Educators ... now recognize the importance of school–family connections through the high-school grades.
- Programs must include all families, including those traditionally considered to be "hard to reach."
- Programs make teachers' jobs easier and make them more successful with students.
- Program development is not quick. Long-term and sensitive work is needed for real progress in partnerships.
- Special grants have been an important catalyst in the United States for innovations in parent involvement.
- Family–school co-ordinators (under whatever title) may be crucial to the success of programs to link schools, parents, and communities. Co-ordinators guide school staffs, provide in-service training for educators, offer services to parents, and perform other tasks that promote partnerships.
- Parent centres in the school or in the community are important ways of making parents feel welcome.
- Even with rooms for parents, practices need to emphasize reaching and involving families without requiring them to come frequently to the school.
- In the 1990s, technology can help improve many types of involvement.
- There are still vast gaps in our knowledge that can be filled only by rigorous research and evaluation of particular types of school–family connections in support of children's learning.

Source: Joyce Epstein. (1991, January). Paths to partnership. *Phi Delta Kappan,*
        p. 349. Reproduced with permission.

Communities and Schools

The focus in this chapter thus far has been on the relationship between families and schools, and its importance in producing school outcomes. We now broaden our discussion to include a more extensive set of interactions that involve parents' *collective* activities, as well as those of people who do not have children or whose children are not of school age. These people, living and working close to schools, are often referred to as the "community," although, as will be noted shortly, a strong sense of community in most public school neighbourhoods is a relatively rare occurrence today.

Coleman and Hoffer (1987), in their study of public and private schools in the United States, found that the community surrounding Catholic private schools constituted a very significant educational resource. These communities, with their social networks and common norms of behaviour, supported individual parents both in their interactions with schools and with the supervision of their children's behaviour. Referring to this as **social capital**, Coleman and Hoffer note, "The feedback that a parent receives from friends and associates, either unsolicited or in response to questions, provides extensive additional resources that aid parents in monitoring the school and the child, and the norms that parents, as part of their everyday activity, are able to establish act as important aids in socializing children" (p. 7).

Similar situations exist within the Canadian public school system, although they tend to be relatively uncommon. Symons (1992), for example, describes in rich detail the ways in which the taken-for-granted educational expectations of a small, western Canadian, largely Mennonite farming community powerfully supported the work of the school, contributing to the culture of academic excellence that characterized the local high school. Furthermore, this support occurred with only traditional and very limited forms of parental involvement in the daily life of the school.

In most public schools, however, students are drawn from a geographically defined catchment area rather than from a true community in the sense described above. Rather than being supported by a closely knit social group that holds a common set of values and expectations, the public school has become a meeting place for a plurality of interests and loosely structured communities. Within such settings, students develop a peer culture that may work either in harmony or in opposition to the educational goals of the professional staff. In some schools, virtually all of a student's relationships outside of the family are with other students in the school, while in other schools students may have a much wider set of relationships. Likewise, the norms of the student culture may be in harmony with those of the school or may serve to undermine them. Several authors (e.g., Connell et al., 1982; Willis, 1977) have described peer cultures, in both public and private schools, that are viciously sexist—to the extent of invalidating even the most antisexist school practices — and that inadvertently make the case for single-sex schools (Shakeshaft, 1989).

Community Schools

Calls for community schools that are more responsive to their communities come from many quarters, and are driven by many different visions and expectations for schools, their clientele, curriculum, and governance. Despite their differences, most share a desire to reduce the separation between school and community and between "school knowledge" and "real knowledge."

To this end, the school's clientele may be expanded from the traditional school-aged cohort to include all ages, from prenatal and early childhood to adults, with the traditional school year replaced by a year-round program. In some jurisdictions (see Box 7.4), the community school has been able to provide, by means of collaboration between social services — social workers, guidance counsellors, health-care workers, teachers, and so on — multiple services that are essential in meeting the individual needs of all students in the school. An extension of this approach to community schooling is the recognition that in some — perhaps many — situations, schools may not be the best places for students to learn; the community itself may be the best classroom of all. Alternative schools within the public school system have a relatively long history of breaking down divisions between school and community in cities such as Toronto and Vancouver.

School–Business Partnerships

The connections between the world of school and the world of work have been an ever-present dimension of Canadian public schooling: schools are charged with the task of preparing society's youth for adult life, and work—in its broadest sense —is an essential part of that life. At certain times in Canadian history, these relationships have been characterized by relative separateness, stability, and an absence of controversy. At other times, usually associated with economic upheaval, they have become highly charged and controversial and subject to redefinition.

In the last decade or so, many Canadian business leaders, in step with their international counterparts, have come to see their interests closely associated with the ways in which schools contribute to the preparation of a skilled and competitive labour force and have sought a stronger role in influencing school programs. At the same time, Canadian public schools have seen their funding levels shrink, forcing educators to look for new resources to support their programs. As a result of these sorts of forces, some school systems have begun to radically rethink their relationships with businesses and have established a wide range of school–business partnerships (Cressy, 1994; Etobicoke Board of Education, 1996).

Efforts to create so-called partnerships cannot be viewed uncritically. Indeed, they have at times raised moral and ethical questions that go to the heart of the purposes of public education (Barlow & Robertson, 1994). The educative roles of schools are not always compatible with the corporate agendas of the business world. Implicit in the term "partnership" is that benefits will accrue to all partners, and this makes it important that those involved in establishing such initiatives focus on the common ground where the benefits to student learning are clear and uncompromised.

Box 7.4
The York Board of Education Community School Guidelines

To become a community school within the York Board of Education, the school and the community organization must make a joint application indicating that the following guidelines are in the process of being implemented:
- *A community related curriculum.* Education in the school should be enhanced by the use of a variety of community resources (people, organizations, and facilities) to enrich its curriculum and program — through students going out into the local community to learn, as well as through the use of community resource persons (i.e., volunteers) in the programs of the school.
- *A focus for community involvement.* Parents and other citizens should be encouraged to participate with the principal and staff in the planning process as it concerns the program of the school and the educational needs of students.
- *A resource for community development.* The school and its staff and students should be actively involved with citizens and community groups in identifying needs and mobilizing resources to improve the quality of life in the community.
- *Community use of facilities.* School facilities, when not in use for regular educational purposes, should be available for persons of all ages to pursue community education, recreation, and cultural, social service, and child-care needs both during the day and in the evening.
- *A sense of community partnership.* The school should participate with other community service agencies in the planning and delivery of community services according to local needs.

Source: D. Shuttleworth. (1984, September). School community relations in the '80s. *Canadian School Executive,* 20.

The Etobicoke Board of Education in Toronto offers the following definition of a school–business partnership:

A partnership is a mutually supportive arrangement between a school or school board and a large or small business, post secondary institution, government department or community agency. Its main purpose for establishment is to benefit learners, though it is a given that both participating organizations can and should benefit from the association (Etobicoke Board of Education, 1996, p. 2).

This definition is accompanied by a set of guidelines that include the following (p. 9):

- the arrangement must benefit learners;
- the association should benefit both partners;
- the partnership should be cost-effective;
- the activities must be consistent with the Vision, Values and Goals of the Etobicoke Board of Education;

- the partnership should not contravene the policies and/or procedures of the Etobicoke Board of Education;
- any school entering into partnerships must do so with companies, organizations, and institutions that demonstrate good corporate citizenship.

In Nova Scotia, the provincial government has begun entering into partnerships with business consortiums for building and equipping public schools, whereby new schools are built and operated by private businesses and leased by the province. The provincial government's case for the advantages of such a partnership is summarized in Box 7.5.

Conclusion

Educational research has provided compelling evidence to demonstrate the powerful effects that families and communities can have in promoting student success in school. In the light of this research, many schools have sought to find ways to build collaborative relationships with parents, individually and collectively, and to work toward realizing a true educational partnership between home and school. Such efforts have often involved a painful struggle to overcome deeply ingrained suspicions on both sides. Grant (1988) describes the dominant attitude of families toward school as "benign skepticism combined

---

Box 7.5
School–Business Partnerships: A New Way to Build Schools in Nova Scotia

The way schools are being built is changing in Nova Scotia. In the past the province would simply pay to have a school designed and built for the local board.

The people the school was designed to serve — students, teachers and parents — weren't consulted nearly enough. These days are gone. Nova Scotia is the first province in Canada to be committed to building schools in partnership with private business and the communities involved.

Everyone benefits.

The business partners own and operate the school and they make use of it after hours under the supervision of the School Board and the Department. Builders do the best and quickest job possible because the school belongs to them.

The community gets a better school because its members help design it and because the owner will always be on site to make sure everything works.

Through leasing arrangements, the government can build more schools more quickly.

Other schools in the area will benefit by being able to share the resources of the new high school through the use of advanced technology.

with intelligent consumerism" (p. 132). Yet despite the fact that co-operation has often proven to be a fragile state of affairs, working effectively with families and the community in the 1990s remains one of the critical elements of the teaching profession.

Exercises

1. Reread the prologue at the beginning of this chapter. Based on the information provided there and the material in the rest of this chapter, prepare a presentation by Gordon, the principal, on the importance of school–community relations to successful schools. Address it to his staff, the school board, and the Faculty of Education.

2. Parents who rarely attend parent–teacher conferences, or who do not interact comfortably with the school, are often referred to as hard-to-reach parents. We do not generally talk of hard-to-reach schools. List some of the ways in which schools might purposefully (or accidentally) discourage parental participation in student learning. How could these barriers be eliminated?

3. Interview several parents of students in either an elementary or a secondary school. What kind of contact do they have with the school? Who initiates contact? How do they feel about their relationship with the school?

4. Interview one or more teachers about working with parents. What do the teachers do to involve parents? What are their views about the value or potential of greater parent involvement?

5. Study a local school to see what policies and practices it has in place with respect to parent and community involvement. How do these practices compare with some of those suggested in this chapter?

6. Review one reading by a reproduction theorist. Do you find her or his argument about the schools as instruments of the status quo to be compelling? Why or why not?

7. Should a school attempt to recruit teachers whose economic or ethnic backgrounds are similar to those of students in the school? Why or why not?

8. You are part of a small committee of teachers and parents that was established by your school principal to improve home–school collaboration. Currently, there is little interaction in your school between parents and

teachers, apart from one parent–teacher conference each year to discuss student progress, a steady flow of memos from the school to parents, and the very occasional parent conference to deal with the problems of individual students, usually related to discipline. Develop a proposal that outlines a rationale for increased collaboration (why you think it is important) and a one-year strategy for initiating a new collaborative relationship. What difficulties might you anticipate from parents or teachers?

9. In the chapter, it was suggested that effective communication is easiest between people who share similar knowledge, experiences, and expectations of schools. How might class and cultural differences between teachers and families create barriers to effective school–home communication? How might these barriers be overcome?

10. In Box 7.5, a case for school–business partnerships in building and equipping public schools is made. What arguments might be offered against this position?

Further Reading

A substantial body of sociological literature examines the role of schools in society and the relationships between families and schools in creating school outcomes. Connell et al. (1982) is an especially insightful study. McLaren (1989) is another important source; although it is American in much of its orientation, it includes a substantial segment based on the author's experiences with teaching in Toronto.

In the area of school and family partnerships, the work of Joyce Epstein at Johns Hopkins University and The Centre for Families, Communities, Schools and Children's Learning in Baltimore is of great importance. Much of this work is reported on in the endnotes of Epstein (1995). The work of Merttens, Newland, and Webb (1996) summarizes some of the research and practices of teacher–parent collaboration in Britain. Fullan and Steigelbauer provide a Canadian context for the subject in *The New Meaning of Educational Change* (1991).

In the area of schools and community values, Coleman (1987) and Coleman and Hoffer (1987) offer insights into both family roles in a historical context and the influences of communities on school culture and school outcomes.

CHAPTER EIGHT

Teachers and the Teaching Profession

▼ PROLOGUE

A small group of teachers stopped for a moment in the board office parking lot on their way out of that evening's professional-development symposium, which had been sponsored jointly by their school board and the local chapter of the teachers' federation. "OK, Sue, you're not far from my place. I'll drop you off," said Larry, a chemistry and physics teacher at Foothills Collegiate. "See the rest of you tomorrow." As the two of them headed for Larry's station wagon, the rest of the group — André, Lisa, and Anya — climbed into Garret's van and fastened their seat belts as they joined the line of cars filing out of the parking lot.

"Well," Garret asked, "What did you think? I thought he was pretty good." Garret was the half-time vice-principal at Foothills Collegiate, where Larry, André, and Anya taught, and where Sue and Lisa were currently completing their student teaching placement. The evening's speaker had been a superintendent visiting from out of the province. In his talk, entitled "The Extended Professional Teacher," he had described the way in which his district had attempted systematically to stimulate and support professional growth among its teachers.

"Yeah, I really appreciated what he had to say," added Carol. "I wrote down his definition of the extended professional: 'a capacity for autonomous professional development through systematic self-study, through the study of the work of other teachers, and through the testing of ideas by classroom research procedures.' But to hear how they were actually doing it — with teacher research teams conducting their own action research on key issues like student retention or violence in school, and with teachers actually sitting in on each other's classes and sharing their experience and expertise with each other — I mean, most of us talk about doing that kind of stuff, but to have a superintendent who not only encourages it but actually provides resources to make it happen, that's really exciting."

"I think what he said about making critical links to the existing research was important too," added André, "so we're not just throwing around our own opinions but also testing them against the research, and also testing the research against our own experience. I think his district would be a neat place to work — a place where they give you the time and opportunity to sit down and talk about important educational issues. What did he call it? 'Critical professional discourse,' I think. We need that sort of opportunity here if we're going to keep growing as teachers over the length of our careers."

"Well," said Garret, "you know we've tried to do that with the student teacher project. I know it's only a beginning, but we do meet on a regular basis about that, and it does link us to the university as partners in designing and supervising students' practice teaching experiences. But I agree it is pretty much a one-of-a-kind activity. In our district, it's really up to teachers to take care of their own professional development. Perhaps we should develop some school-based initiatives of our own. I think the principal might go for it, and I'm sure the staff would."

Meanwhile, as they drove away from the board office, Larry and Sue were having a quite different conversation. "He should have called his presentation 'The Over-Extended Professional,'" Larry commented. "I don't know why I came in the first place. I should be home dealing with the pile of marking I have to get back to my chemistry class tomorrow. I'll be up half the night now. I mean, it sounds all right in theory maybe, but if we're going to be seen as professionals I say what we need to do is to get serious about what it is that we do: teach kids in classrooms. If we pay attention to that, keep up on our own subject and on our teaching and make sure that the kids in our classes are learning what we're supposed to be teaching them, then I don't see how you can have time for 'action research' or whatever. I get quite angry at the number of days that some teachers spend away from their classes on curriculum committees or doing workshops and the like. Sometimes that's what I call *un*professional. I don't think we all have to be philosophers and researchers to be professional — we just have to be given the supports to do our job and then left alone to get on with it. I work damned hard, and my kids always get among the best science results in the province. That's how I'm professional, and I think that's how we should judge the profession." ∎

The professional status of public school teachers in Canada has long been a topic of debate, and some sensitivity, among teachers and teacher organizations. Nor are they alone in this concern. Soder (1990) notes that American teachers "as a group ... have been striving in the race longer than most, and they have been among the least successful in legitimating their claims to professional status" (p. 36). Among Canadian teachers, the legitimacy of their claim to be regarded as professionals is usually vigorously asserted, and the desirability of enhanced professionalism is often taken for granted. However, occupational groups do not attain professional status simply by self-proclamation; in the academic literature on professions, the discipline of teaching, along with activities such as nursing and social work, is more likely to be classified as a "semi-profession."

In the first part of this chapter, we examine the concept of professionalism and its utility in understanding and describing the work of teachers. From this examination, we will develop a position, already foreshadowed in earlier chapters of this book, for thinking about teaching as a unique kind of profession. The second half of the chapter considers the implications of this professional identity for the practice of public school teachers and the structuring of relations in public school, and also discusses the roles of teachers' professional associations in Canada.

What Is a Profession?

In everyday life, the terms "profession" and "professional" have a very broad range of meanings; in the academic literature usage, however, they have traditionally been more narrowly defined. Despite this, there is still some variation in the ways in which these terms are derived and used. Their meanings are most often developed through an examination of the characteristics of so-called true professions (e.g., medicine and law). From this examination emerges an ideal type or model consisting of a series of characteristics that serve to separate professions from other occupations. Three examples of the more widely accepted definitions of profession are included in Table 8.1. While each has its own unique emphasis and language, these definitions share the following broad characteristics:

1. A profession possesses a unique body of knowledge that is obtained by its members over a long period of formal training. Professionals are continually adding to this knowledge throughout their careers.
2. A profession is an essential service that is held in high regard by society at large; as such, its members are usually afforded high status in the society.
3. A profession is afforded a high degree of personal autonomy and is self-regulating. Professional bodies possess a code of ethics and regulate both entry into the profession and the behaviour of their members. Individual members exercise independent judgement in carrying out their work, and depend on their peers rather than their superiors for advice and direction.

Such lists of characteristics have the conceptual status of an **ideal type**: no occupation fully embodies each of these characteristics, and different occupations vary over time and from place to place in the extent to which they meet each of the defining characteristics. Given this perspective, the ideal type does more than enable us to determine whether teaching (or any other occupation) makes it into the elite ranks of the professions; as an analytical tool, it allows us to examine the ways in which teaching approximates each of these attributes so that we can better understand the nature of public schools and the organization of teaching. Accordingly, the next section examines how the above characteristics of professions have been viewed in relation to teaching.

Table 8.1

Definitions of "Profession"

Hall	Rich	Hoy and Miskel
A. STRUCTURAL/ OCCUPATIONAL CHARACTERISTICS • a full-time occupation; • substantial, university-based training; • professional associations; and • a code of ethics. B. ATTITUDINAL/ INDIVIDUAL CHARACTERISTICS • belief in service to the public; • belief in self-regulation and colleague control; • a sense of calling to the field; and • a belief in individual, professional autonomy.	• a high degree of general and systematized knowledge; • a long period of specialized, intellectual training; • intellectual practice; • a unique social service; • controls standards of entry and exclusion; • enforces a professional code of ethics; and • grants a broad range of autonomy to members.	• technical competence gained through long training; • a set of professional ideals, including a service ideal, impersonality, and impartiality; • autonomy in professional decision-making; and • self-imposed control based on knowledge standards and peer review.

Sources: R. Hall. (1986). Professionalization and bureaucratization. *American Sociological Review, 33*(1), 92–93; J. Rich (1984). *Professional ethics in education.* Springfield, IL: C. Thomas; W. Hoy & C. Miskel. (1987). *Educational administration,* 3rd ed. (pp. 148–50). New York: Random House.

Is Teaching a Profession?

The drive for recognition as a profession by Canadian teachers has often involved attempts to demonstrate a close approximation to the ideal type discussed on page 222, and more specifically to try to replicate those characteristics seen to be exhibited by high-status professions. This argument for professional status is referred to by Soder (1990) as a **similitude argument**.

A Unique Body of Knowledge

Whether or not teaching possesses a clearly defined, highly developed, unique body of specialized knowledge that is demonstrably linked to professional proficiency has been a subject of some debate. In recent years, a substantial amount of educational research has been developed to inform professional practice. There have also been efforts to systematize this knowledge into a coherent body that could be defined as teachers' professional knowledge, and that could then serve as a basis for the preparation and certification of teachers (Shulman, 1987; Travers, 1986). It would be difficult to argue that this process has achieved the status of some other professions. Osborne (1992) notes that most teachers still say that they learned most of what they needed on the job, and that most hold a relatively low opinion of their professional training. On the other hand, some researchers believe that there is a formal knowledge base to guide educational practice. The debate is illustrated in Box 8.1.

Box 8.1
The Debate over the Knowledge Base for Teaching

It is quite clear that there is no body of agreed knowledge about teaching. The number of things that are both clearly known to be true and clearly relevant to educational practice is, it seems, small. Moreover, it is not even obvious that such knowledge as we have or could have about good teaching is very important for teachers to know. A science of pedagogy might turn out to have the same connection to teaching as physics does to riding a bicycle. Physics can explain how it is possible to ride a bike and why certain techniques work and others do not. A knowledge of physics, however, is not merely unnecessary in learning to ride a bicycle, it is not even very helpful. Perhaps something like this is what is meant by saying that teaching is an art. Such a view need not require that no science of pedagogy is possible. It may simply indicate that knowing it is not very important to teaching.

Source: E. Haller and K. Strike. (1986). *Introduction to educational administration* (p. 245). New York: Longman.

In recent years, our understanding of successful teaching has increased considerably. There have been numerous successful experimental studies in which teachers have been trained to increase the academic achievement of their students. ... In the successful studies, the teachers implemented the training and their students had higher achievement and/or higher academic engaged time than did students in the classrooms of the untrained teachers. ...

The results of these studies are consistently positive and indicate that there are specific instructional procedures which teachers can be trained to follow and which can lead to increased achievement and student engagement in their classrooms.

Source: B. Rosenshine and R. Stevens. (1986). Teaching functions. In M. Wittrock (Ed.), *Handbook of research on teaching* (3rd ed.) (p. 376). New York: Macmillan.

An Essential Service

Given the long-standing compulsory nature of schooling, it is not difficult to make the argument that public schools constitute an essential service. In Canada, public opinion has generally placed a high value on schooling and the work of teachers, and although schooling has come under increased public and media scrutiny in the 1990s, public confidence remains high.

Longitudinal surveys of Canadian public attitudes toward education have been carried out by the Canadian Education Association (CEA) and by David Livingstone at the Ontario Institute for Studies in Education. In a 1990 national survey conducted by the CEA (Williams & Millinoff, 1990) people were asked to assign a grade to their community school: 80 percent gave an A, B, or C grade, and only 3.8 percent assigned an F grade. In the same survey, 85 percent of respondents awarded teachers an A, B, or C grade for their effectiveness as teachers, and similar grades were awarded to teachers in terms of their responsiveness to parents' concerns. Writing in 1995, Livingstone and Hart report that "there is no evidence of a downturn of grades in recent years" (p. 23).

Nevertheless, this recognition may not compare to the status afforded to doctors, who deal with matters of life and death, or to lawyers, whose clients are generally adults and whose services are used for matters of fundamental and immediate importance.

Self-Regulation

Until quite recently, Canadian teachers have not had responsibility for regulating the profession and have not been able to exercise control over the standards of entry into teaching or the professional conduct of teachers. Rather, it was the minister of education who retained sole authority for issuing teaching certificates and who alone could revoke them for incompetence or misconduct.

Whether or not teachers should be given this sort of self-regulating authority has long been an important source of debate, as illustrated in the different views expressed in Box 8.2.

In 1987, British Columbia became the first Canadian province to make its teachers self-regulating when the *Teacher Profession Act* (1987) established the British Columbia College of Teachers. This Act in essence assigned to the British Columbia College of Teachers sole responsibility for governing the profession's standards of entry, discipline, and professional development, and in doing so distinguished these from other interests pursued by the traditional teachers' association, such as collective bargaining and the welfare of teachers.* Since then other provinces have shown an interest in this model, and in 1996 Ontario moved to create a similar self-regulating body with the passage of the *College of Teachers Act*

* Under a subsequent amendment to the Act, professional development has reverted to the British Columbia Teachers' Federation.

(1996). The Ontario College is governed by a Governing Council of 31 people, the majority (17) of whom are elected by members of the College and must be qualified teachers, with the remainder (14) appointed by the Minister of Education to represent the broader public interest. The College is charged by the Act to set standards for teacher education and teacher practice, and to concern itself with issues of professional self-regulation as well as public accountability (Ontario College of Teachers, 1996). As with the British Columbia model, these functions shown in Box 8.3 are intended to be clearly separated from the collective bargaining and welfare activities of the Teachers' Federations in Ontario.

Box 8.2
Should Teaching Be Self-Regulating?

A Professional Bill — Now! *by Judy Bradley*

Why should Manitoba teachers get a professional bill now? Evolution — that's why. What does evolution have to do with a professional bill? A great deal. Education, more specifically teaching, in Canada has been evolving for well over 100 years. One of the most significant changes occurred in the education of teachers when it was transferred from the normal school to the university. Coupled with this transfer were the rise and development of teacher organizations focusing on economic welfare and professional development.

Teachers are now better qualified than ever before. ... They possess the knowledge, theory and methodology essential for a quality education system. The evolution of teacher education has produced teachers who are more than just givers of knowledge. But teachers have not been fully liberated and do not have the freedom to make professional decisions in their classrooms.

Schools are evolving and have reached the early stages of systems management. This kind of management allows for individuals affected by decisions within a system — in this case, teachers in the education system — to be part of the decision-making. The move towards this type of management has not yet reached Manitoba teachers, however. They still have no say in deciding who shall be granted a teaching certificate and whose certificate will be revoked in Manitoba; such decisions ultimately are made at the political will of the minister of education.

It is time for teachers to evolve into a full-fledged profession. Teachers, not politicians, must control certification, discipline and professional development of teachers. Teachers must be granted the same status as other professionals.

(Judy Bradley was the 1991–92 Manitoba Teachers' Society President.)

(continued)

(continued)

Give Up the Chase *by Ken Osborne*

Professional autonomy is not likely to win for teachers the professional status enjoyed by doctors and lawyers. The question is much more complex and demands action on many fronts, not least in terms of teacher preparation and training, both in- and pre-service.

Nor is it obvious that education as a whole will automatically benefit from teachers' achieving self-government. A happy and contented teaching force can make for happy and contented classrooms, and, therefore, education can benefit. However, happiness and contentment will not necessarily flow from self-government. They depend much more on ... mundane considerations, mostly deriving from working conditions determined by class size, administrative policies, preparation time and other factors.

Here the [Manitoba Teachers'] Society could usefully concentrate its energies. It should give up the chase for professional status and move in the opposite direction. Become not a profession but a union. Regain the right to strike. University professors belong to a full-fledged union. Why not teachers?

Moving away from the pursuit of professional status would also accomplish another objective. It would acknowledge that education is and must be a public institution. It should not be exclusively controlled by teachers. Teacher training and eligibility for entry into teaching, for example, are legitimate questions of public policy. They should not be controlled by any one group. What is good for teachers is not automatically good for education, and vice versa. The same is true for the medical and legal professions. For example, a rational health policy — advocating more community clinics, paraprofessionals, preventive medicine and the like — has been difficult to attain because of the self-interest of doctors.

Education must be open to much greater community involvement than it now is. Teachers must be willing to share power, not monopolize it. They will be better able to protect their legitimate interests by becoming not a profession but a union.

(Ken Osborne is a professor emeritus in the Faculty of Education at the University of Manitoba.)

Source: An extended version of both of these positions appeared in *The Manitoba Teacher* (1992, March), *70*(3). 16–17. Reprinted with permission.

This sort of analysis of teaching on the grounds of expert knowledge, essential service, and self-regulation serves to illustrate the ideal and subjective nature of the concept of professionalism discussed earlier. There are no objective scales for these dimensions, nor is there any real way of aggregating degrees of professionalism across the different dimensions. Measuring these characteristics remains largely subjective—the ways in which different occupations are generally viewed by the public —and it is this sort of perspective, one that employs the similitude argument, that is used to assign teaching the status of semi-professional.

Box 8.3
The Ontario College of Teachers: Roles and Responsibilities

The Ontario College of Teachers will be a professional college with authority to license and regulate the practice of teaching. The College's primary function will be to set out clear standards of practice, ensure solid professional learning goals and co-ordinate and monitor career-long, accredited professional learning for teachers.

Standards of Practice

A key challenge for the College will be to work with its members to develop flexible and appropriate standards of practice for teachers. The College will:
• Set standards to define what teachers should know and be able to do at each stage of their professional careers;
• Set standards for graduation from accredited pre-service and in-service teacher education programs;
• Monitor teacher education programs to ensure compliance with the standards;
• Develop a process to improve preparation and support for associate teachers working with beginning teachers.

Professional Learning

The College will play a major role in developing a provincial framework for professional learning. The objective is to help teachers obtain the training they need to support them in their jobs and to implement new government policies and programs. Specifically, the College will:
• Develop a professional learning framework that includes individual learning, shared learning, learning in the local community, externally initiated learning and required learning;
• Establish time frames for members to achieve their goals;
• Ensure that members are responsible for reporting their professional learning experiences to the College;
• Accredit all professional learning programs and educational institutions or agencies that deliver them;
• Ensure that learning opportunities are provided in locations and styles that meet the needs of members and of the system.

The College will also have authority to:
• Regulate teaching qualifications;
• Set membership criteria, enrol members and create a registry of teachers;
• Investigate complaints involving members, conduct hearings into allegations of professional misconduct and take appropriate disciplinary action.

Source: Adapted from Ontario College of Teachers, *Factsheets*, Sept 16, 1996. Reproduced with the permission of the Ontario College of Teachers. See also URL: http://www.oct.on.ca

An Alternative View of Teaching as a Profession

For several authors, the differences between the practice of occupations such as medicine and law and those of teaching (particularly public school teaching) suggest the inappropriateness of efforts to define and pursue teacher professionalism according to the standards established for other occupations. Fenstermacher (1990) notes three critical differences between the practice of teaching and that of medicine: "the mystification of knowledge," "social distance," and "reciprocity of effort." According to Fenstermacher, teaching requires that teachers impart their knowledge not only to their students but also, as was discussed in Chapter Seven, to parents. This requirement stands in marked contrast to the traditional efforts of most professions to lock away their specialized knowledge even when it is of the most elementary nature. Impersonality, another characteristic of professional practice, similarly makes little sense with teaching. Students are not "cases" with very specific needs to diagnose and meet, and to treat them in such a fashion contradicts what we know about good teaching. In order to learn, students must *engage* in the learning process — they must expend *effort*. This sustained "reciprocity of effort" is another factor that distinguishes teaching from other professions.

One could go on elaborating differences, but the point is that these differences do not constitute grounds for downplaying the professional status of public school teaching. What they do require is that we recast the concept of the profession as it is applied to the nature of public schools and the organization of teaching. As Goodlad (1990) suggests, any attempts to reconstruct the concept of teaching must be built on an appreciation of the moral considerations that stem from the school's enculturation (socialization) responsibilities: of the need to provide all students with access to knowledge; of the special nature of teacher–student relationships within a compulsory institution; and of the role of teachers in school renewal and educational change. In his words,

> the conditions necessary to legitimate self-proclamation of professional status include a thorough understanding of the role of education and schooling in a democratic society, an understanding of knowledge and ways of knowing that serve to interpret human experience, high-level competence in special knowledge and skills required to educate the young in these ways of knowing, and substantial awareness of the standards of excellence and equity that must characterize schools and classrooms. But full recognition of teaching in schools as a profession depends on teachers, individually and collectively, demonstrating their awareness of and commitment to the burdens of judgment that go with a moral enterprise (pp. 29–30).

An important aspect of this individual and collective commitment is contained in the codes of ethics that guide teacher practices.

Codes of Ethics

There is an obvious relationship between what it means to be a member of a profession and what it means to act professionally. As in other professions, the latter is addressed in teaching by a code of professional practice that is laid out by most, but not all, provincial teachers' associations in Canada. While each provincial association has its own code, there is a considerable degree of similarity among provinces (see Box 8.4 for an example of a code of professional conduct). Just as the characteristics of a profession cannot capture the complexities of what it means to be a profession, so too a code of ethics represents only a skeletal outline of what it means to be a professional.

Box 8.4
The Alberta Teachers' Association Code of Professional Conduct

---

The Code of Professional Conduct stipulates minimum standards of professional conduct of teachers but is not an exhaustive list of such standards. Unless exempted by legislation, any member of The Alberta Teachers' Association who is alleged to have violated the standards of the profession, including the provisions of the Code, may be subject to a charge of unprofessional conduct under the Discipline Bylaws of the Association.

In Relation to Pupils

1. The teacher teaches in a manner that respects the dignity and rights of all persons without prejudice as to race, religious beliefs, colour, sex, physical characteristics, age, ancestry or place of origin.
2. (1) The teacher is responsible for diagnosing educational needs, prescribing and implementing instructional programs and evaluating progress of pupils.
(2) The teacher may not delegate these responsibilities to any person who is not a teacher.
3. The teacher may delegate specific and limited aspects of instructional activity to noncertificated personnel, provided that the teacher supervises and directs such activity.
4. The teacher treats pupils with dignity and respect and is considerate of their circumstances.
5. The teacher may not divulge information about a pupil received in confidence or in the course of professional duties except as required by law or where, in the judgment of the teacher, to do so is in the best interest of the pupil.
6. The teacher may not accept pay for tutoring a pupil in any subjects in which the teacher is responsible for giving classroom instruction to that pupil.
7. The teacher may not take advantage of a professional position to profit from the sale of goods or services to or for pupils in the teacher's charge.

(continued)

(continued)

In Relation to School Authorities

8. The teacher protests the assignment of duties for which the teacher is not qualified or conditions which make it difficult to render professional service.
9. The teacher fulfills contractual obligations to the employer until released by mutual consent or according to law.
10. The teacher provides as much notice as possible of a decision to terminate employment.
11. The teacher adheres to agreements negotiated on the teacher's behalf by the Association.

In Relation to Colleagues

12. The teacher does not undermine the confidence of pupils in other teachers.
13. The teacher criticizes the professional competence or professional reputation of another teacher only in confidence to proper officials and after the other teacher has been informed of the criticism.
14. The teacher, when making a report on the professional performance of another teacher, does so in good faith and, prior to submitting the report, provides the teacher with a copy of the report.
15. The teacher does not take, because of animosity or for personal advantage, any steps to secure the dismissal of another teacher.
16. The teacher recognizes the duty to protest through proper channels administrative policies and practices which the teacher cannot in conscience accept; and further recognizes that if administration by consent fails, the administrator must adopt a position of authority.
17. The teacher as an administrator provides opportunities for staff members to express their opinions and to bring forth suggestions regarding the administration of the school.

In Relation to the Profession

18. The teacher acts in a manner which maintains the honour and dignity of the profession.
19. The teacher does not engage in activities which adversely affect the quality of the teacher's professional service.
20. The teacher submits to the Association disputes arising from professional relationships with other teachers which cannot be resolved by personal discussion.
21. The teacher makes representations on behalf of the Association or members thereof only when authorized to do so.
22. The teacher accepts that service to the Association is a professional responsibility.

Source: The Alberta Teachers' Association. Reproduced with permission.

The Purposes and Functions of Codes of Ethics

As a guide to professional conduct, an enforced code of ethics serves several functions. First, it provides some assurance to its clients that they can expect to be treated in accordance with established standards of practice and acceptable moral conduct. Second, it offers the general public some confidence that the profession is serving a public interest worthy of trust and support. Third, it offers a set of uniform rules and standards that define for its members acceptable professional behaviour, and that provide a basis for properly regulating their conduct (Rich, 1984, pp. 6–7).

Codes of ethics tend to combine general statements of overriding *ideals* and *principles* (e.g., "a teacher's first responsibility is to the pupils in his or her charge") and quite specific *procedures* and *rules* of professional conduct (e.g., reporting suspected child abuse). Provincial teachers' organizations are responsible for enforcing their codes, and for dealing with cases of unprofessional conduct (as noted in Box 8.3, this will become a function of the Ontario College of Teachers). While they do not have the authority to withdraw a member's teaching certificate or to remove teachers from their teaching positions, they may reprimand their members, expel them from the organization, and, in the most serious of infractions, recommend to the minister of education that their certification be revoked.

The organization of the Alberta Teachers' Association code into categories that outline the responsibilities of teachers to pupils, school authorities, colleagues, and to the profession is similar to that found in most codes.

Teachers and Pupils

The prime responsibility of teachers is the educational well-being of their students. To accomplish this task, the professional teacher creates, along with other educators, an appropriate learning environment for each student that takes into account individual interests, needs, and abilities. This commitment to each student is spelled out in the Alberta Teachers' Association code: "The teacher teaches in a manner that respects the dignity and rights of all persons without prejudice as to race, religious beliefs, color, sex, physical characteristics, age, ancestry or place of origin."

Professional competence is often recognized by the expectation (1) that teachers will participate in a career-long process of professional development; and (2), in the words of the Alberta Teachers' Association code, that "[t]he teacher protests the assignment of duties for which the teacher is not qualified or conditions which make it difficult to render professional service." Some codes, such as that of the Manitoba Teachers' Society, include the teacher's responsibility to report suspected cases of child abuse to the appropriate authorities.

Teachers and Colleagues

Professional status requires teachers to respect the expertise of their colleagues, to refrain from acting in ways that undermine professional authority, and to deal with collegial disputes in a professional manner. This means that teachers are expected to follow clearly defined procedures if they wish to criticize the professional activity of a colleague, or if they oppose decisions duly agreed upon by other teachers. Failure to do so could lead to disciplinary action by the appropriate teachers' association.

Whether such regulation of a teacher's criticism of a colleague could be deemed a violation of the teacher's freedom of expression as guaranteed under the *Charter* was a question addressed in a British Columbia court case (*Cromer v. British Columbia Teachers' Federation*). Cromer, a teacher and parent with a child attending a school in the school district in which she worked, attended a parent advisory committee at which concerns were expressed about the sex-education program in which her child was enrolled. At the meeting, she became involved in a heated exchange with her child's teacher in which she made a number of derogatory personal criticisms of the teacher. The teacher complained to the British Columbia Teachers' Federation that this violated its code of ethics, and the BCTF initiated disciplinary proceedings. Cromer maintained that the charge violated her freedom of expression as guaranteed under the *Charter*. However, at trial and on appeal the code of ethics was upheld. The Court of Appeal judge commented:

> The code of ethics is designed to avoid disharmony among teaching colleagues, and to promote professional standards, all in the interests of creating an environment where the children being taught will receive the best educational opportunity possible. The code of ethics does not preclude criticism by one teacher of another; it sets out a procedure for making criticism that is intended to increase the beneficial effects of the criticism and minimize the harmful effects.

Because the criticisms were addressed personally to the teacher and not at the specific subject matter under consideration, the judge concluded:

> In my opinion, the "freedom of expression" guaranteed by the *Canadian Charter of Rights and Freedoms* is capable of overriding cl. 5 of the code of ethics of the British Columbia Teachers' Federation. To determine whether it does so in any particular case depends on a weighing and balancing of the interests involved, as has always been the case with "freedom of expression" questions. In this case, I do not consider that Mrs. Cromer's interests in saying what she is alleged to have said were sufficient to override the interests underlying cl. 5 of the code of ethics.

The Teacher and Authority

As employees in a bureaucratic organization who also see themselves as professionals, teachers often face conflicts between what the organization wishes them to do and what they regard as being the best decision. For example, a teacher may disagree with a particular school policy, may feel that a student has been treated unfairly, or may feel that a curriculum change is not in the best interests of students. Teachers in these situations face difficult dilemmas. To what extent should they publicly express their views? A teacher who voices an opinion that is unpopular, either with colleagues or with the school administrator, runs the risk of being penalized in a variety of ways. He or she may receive a less positive evaluation, may be given a less desirable teaching assignment, or may have a harder time getting resources and support for a favourite course or project. Administrators are in a position to impose such sanctions without ever making it evident that a teacher is being penalized.

On the other hand, it is surely part of one's responsibility as a professional to voice one's views and concerns in an open and constructive manner. The Alberta Teachers' Association code deals explicitly with this by stating: "The teacher as an administrator provides opportunities for staff members to express their opinions and to bring forth suggestions regarding the administration of the school." Teachers may overestimate the likelihood of their being penalized for expressing their ideas. And surely administrators would want to know if people had serious concerns about their proposals. It cannot be desirable for people to keep quiet in public and grumble in private about decisions. Being a professional carries with it the responsibility to act in the best interests of one's profession, even when there may be a personal cost involved. All of these points suggest that teachers should take a stand on important issues.

It might also be appropriate to reflect on the parallels between teachers and students. If teachers are reluctant, despite the protections of their adult status and their membership in a professional organization, to speak out about their concerns, then much more so are students, who have none of these protections and who are much more vulnerable to coercion and retribution for expressing unpopular opinions. (Chapter Four raised the issue of the school as a democratic community in which it would be desirable to provide vehicles for everyone to express opinions in an open but constructive way.)

As in so many areas, no clear and unambiguous answer to this dilemma is possible. Teachers have to decide what steps seem warranted. Depending on the situation, discretion may or may not be the better part of valour. On occasion, a teacher might consider collective rather than individual action, since acting with colleagues provides both a stronger statement and a measure of protection from reprisal. Such decisions are essentially matters of conscience, which is another way of saying there is no formula for resolving them.

The Private Lives of Teachers

The expectations of teachers as professionals do not stop at the entrance to the school. What teachers do in their lives out of school cannot necessarily be deemed irrelevant to their work in the classroom, as clearly illustrated in the case of New Brunswick teacher Malcolm Ross. In 1996, the Supreme Court of Canada ruled that his publication of anti-Semitic books and pamphlets during his off-duty time contributed to a discriminatory and "poisoned" school environment and required that the school board remove him from any teaching position (*Ross v. New Brunswick S D*, 1996).

There has long been a public expectation in Canada that teachers lead morally exemplary lives. Some codes of ethics have chosen to avoid statements about teachers' private lives. Others articulate a requirement that teachers uphold the professional reputation of their work. For example, the Alberta Teachers' Association code requires that "[t]he teacher acts in a manner which maintains the honour and dignity of the profession" and "does not engage in activities which adversely affect the quality of [his or her] professional service."

Not so long ago, teachers could be (and frequently were) dismissed for entering a bar or a pool hall, presumably for fear that they would set a bad example for the students in their care. Although standards have changed today, teachers' private lives are still sometimes relevant to their employment. Issues of teachers' out-of-school conduct can and do arise in many different contexts. The general standard accepted in law is that private behaviour "not impair one's fitness to teach" (Hurlbert & Hurlbert, 1992, p. 186), but this does not necessarily resolve all the problems. Canadians vary widely in the standard of behaviour that they find proper or acceptable, which can create problems for teachers. Even the case of crime is not clear-cut. A teacher convicted of a crime could be dismissed from his or her job on the grounds that a criminal cannot be a suitable teacher. So could a teacher convicted of possessing illegal drugs (Zucker, 1988). But people might well differ over what sorts of crimes merit such punishment. Physical or sexual assault might seem to indicate unsuitability for teaching (though here, too, the particular circumstances might be relevant), but would a conviction for shoplifting also merit dismissal? What about driving offences?

Criminal cases, though not simple, are less difficult than other morality issues. Teachers do have some right to pursue a lifestyle of their choice, provided that their behaviour does not have serious detrimental effects on students or the school. This position was clearly stated by the courts in the case of *Shewan & Shewan v. Abbotsford*:

> Teachers must not only be competent, but they are expected to lead by example. Any loss of confidence or respect will impair the system, and have an adverse effect upon those who participate in or rely upon it. That is why a teacher must maintain a standard of behaviour which most other citizens need not observe because they do not have such public responsibilities to fulfil (1987).

Issues of sexual behaviour are particularly sensitive. One can no longer be dismissed from teaching in Canada on the basis of sexual orientation. On the other hand, Catholic school boards in Canada have dismissed teachers who were divorced, or who otherwise violated Catholic religious teaching, and these dismissals have been upheld by the courts. A married couple in British Columbia were suspended without pay for four weeks—a decision upheld by the Court of

Appeal—for submitting to a magazine a semi-nude photograph of the wife that was subsequently published.

Also delicate are issues of relationships between teachers and students. Is it wrong for a teacher to have a personal relationship with a student she or he is teaching? What about a sexual relationship? What if the student attends another school? Many people would frown on teachers dating students in their school, yet once students are 18, they are adults responsible for their own behaviour. A Canadian court upheld the continued employment of a teacher who was living with her former elementary student because they were then no longer in a teacher–student relationship (Hurlbert & Hurlbert, 1992, p. 190).

The conflict between the public's expectations of teachers and teachers' right to lead private lives of their own choosing makes it likely that other such cases will end up before the courts.

Teachers' Associations

Provincial teachers' associations exist in all of Canada's provinces and territories. In most cases, a single association represents the public school teachers of the province or territory; only New Brunswick, Quebec, and Ontario have more than one association. (See Table 8.2 for a list of associations.)

These associations perform a wide range of activities related to the well-being of their membership in particular, and to the provision and improvement of public schooling in general. Among the functions of teachers' associations are: (1) professional-development activities for their membership, in the form of seminars, conferences, and workshops; (2) member welfare supports, such as counselling on personal health issues; (3) legal and professional advice to members on such matters as contractual rights and employee relationships; and (4) lobbying and consultation activities with governments and other educational stakeholders to promote both the interests of their members and the health of the public school system. Collective bargaining on behalf of their membership has also become a major function of teachers' associations.

Most principals and vice-principals in Canada belong to teachers' organizations. Although they may have their own subgroup within these organizations (e.g., the Manitoba Association of Principals), they have traditionally seen themselves primarily as teachers who share common professional interests with their colleagues. However, this relationship is not without its ambiguities, since principals are also expected to be management representatives in their schools.

In Quebec and British Columbia, principals are prevented by law from being members of teachers' organizations. In both provinces, school administrators have their own provincial organizations. In Quebec, this organization has been long established, while in British Columbia the split from the teachers' federation occurred in 1987 as part of the legislation that established the British Columbia College of Teachers (Robinson & Wallin, 1989).

Table 8.2

Provincial Teachers' Associations in Canada

YUKON
  Yukon Teachers' Association
NORTHWEST TERRITORIES
  Northwest Territories Teachers' Association
BRITISH COLUMBIA
  British Columbia Teachers' Federation
ALBERTA
  Alberta Teachers' Association
SASKATCHEWAN
  Saskatchewan Teachers' Federation
MANITOBA
  Manitoba Teachers' Society
ONTARIO
  Ontario Teachers' Federation
    Ontario Public School Teachers' Federation
    Federation of Women Teachers' Associations of Ontario
    Ontario Secondary School Teachers' Federation
    Ontario English Catholic Teachers' Association
    L'Association des enseignantes et des enseignants franco-Ontariens
QUEBEC
  Provincial Association of Protestant Teachers
  Provincial Association of Catholic Teachers
  Centrale de l'enseignement du Québec
NEW BRUNSWICK
  New Brunswick Teachers' Federation
  New Brunswick Teachers' Association
  L'Association des enseignants francophone du Nouveau-Brunswick
PRINCE EDWARD ISLAND
  Prince Edward Island Teachers' Federation
NOVA SCOTIA
  Nova Scotia Teachers' Union
NEWFOUNDLAND AND LABRADOR
  Newfoundland Teachers' Association

Provincial Colleges of Teachers

BRITISH COLUMBIA
  The British Columbia College of Teachers
ONTARIO
  The Ontario College of Teachers

Collective Bargaining

A major function of teachers' associations has been the negotiation of collective agreements with the employer that outline the conditions of employment for their members. A collective agreement is a legal agreement between a group of workers or employees, who have organized themselves into a union or bargaining unit, and their employer. The bargaining unit must be formally organized according to relevant provincial laws. It then elects or otherwise chooses a team or committee to represent its members in negotiating a contract with the employer.

Although collective bargaining by teachers takes place in all the provinces, the procedure assumes various forms and is covered by different legislative provisions. All but three provinces have enacted collective bargaining legislation that is specific to teachers. Bargaining in New Brunswick is regulated by general public-sector bargaining legislation; in Alberta and British Columbia, it is regulated by general labour legislation.

As Table 8.3 shows, collective bargaining also varies across provinces in terms of the level at which bargaining actually occurs. In some cases, all negotiations occur centrally, and agreements affect all teachers in the province; in others, bargaining is a purely local activity between school boards and the local bargaining unit. A third version sees some items addressed locally and others centrally.

Saskatchewan's *Education Act* (1995) (Sections 234–69) illustrates the structure of bargaining in a mixed-agreement province. Section 237 states:

(1) The [provincial] bargaining committees ...
  (a) shall bargain collectively with respect to:
    i) the salaries of teachers
    ii) allowances for principals and vice-principals
    iii) superannuation for teachers
    iv) group life insurance for teachers
    v) criteria respecting the designation of persons as not being teachers within the meaning of any provision of this act pertaining to collective bargaining
    vi) the duration of a provincial agreement
    vii) sick leave for teachers
    viii) any other matters that ... may be necessary ...
  (b) may bargain collectively with respect to matters other than those mentioned in clause (2)(a).
(2) Each board of education and each [local] bargaining committee ...
  (a) shall bargain collectively with respect to:
    i) sabbatical leave for teachers
    ii) educational leave for teachers
    iii) salaries for substitute teachers
    iv) the duration of a local agreement
    v) pay periods for teachers
    vi) special allowances for teachers
  (b) may bargain collectively with respect to matters other than those mentioned in clause (1)(a).

Table 8.3

Collective Bargaining Arrangements

Local agreement	Mixed agreements	Central agreements
British Columbia	Saskatchewan	New Brunswick
Alberta	Quebec	Prince Edward Island
Manitoba	Nova Scotia	Newfoundland
Ontario	British Columbia	Northwest Territories
		Yukon Territory

Salaries and benefits represent a major component of all collective agreements, although by no means the only one. Benefit items include such matters as pensions, life insurance, disability benefits, supplementary health insurance, and dental care. Sick leave is an important element in many agreements, as are other forms of leave, such as maternity and paternity leaves, leave for religious holidays, or compassionate leave for a family death. Some collective agreements may also provide for further-education leaves (including payment of tuition or other costs by school districts) or paid sabbatical leaves. Collective agreements also contain salary and other provisions for administrators, if they are part of the bargaining unit.

Procedures for laying off teachers are also included in collective agreements. Teacher layoffs have occurred, particularly in districts with significant declines in enrollment. In such cases, contracts usually provide that laid-off teachers have the first rights to any vacancies that may arise. Collective agreements may have very complicated provisions regarding the basis for layoffs and recalls, particularly concerning the extent to which seniority will apply in determining who will lose jobs, and the procedures to be followed. There may also be some modifications of seniority arrangements to accommodate specialists in particular subjects.

Working conditions provide a third area of concern in collective agreements. A wide range of matters may be specified, including maximum limits on a teacher's teaching time, maximum class sizes, and minimum amounts of preparation time during the day or week. Some collective agreements also contain clauses that spell out teachers' supervisory responsibilities.

Finally, collective agreements may contain clauses having to do with the union, the employer, and the bargaining process. Most agreements, for example, recognize the particular teachers' association as the sole bargaining agent for teachers, and require teachers either to belong to the association or to pay fees to it if they do not belong. Agreements also have provisions for settling disputes that may arise while the agreement is in force. If a member of the bargaining unit feels that the agreement has been violated, the association may file a grievance. The collective agreement lays out the steps that must be followed to resolve the grievance, with the final step usually being binding arbitration by a third party. The arbitration process can be very expensive, however, because of the cost of lawyers for each side, so there is an incentive for both the union and the employers to settle grievances without arbitration.

Collective Bargaining Procedures

Different provinces have legislated different processes for collective bargaining between teachers and employers. Collective agreements are negotiated to be valid for a specified period of time (typically one to three years), at the end of which they must be renegotiated. While many items may stay the same from one contract to the next, others are subject to negotiation and change. Teachers' associations normally try to improve salaries and benefits in each round of bargaining, while school boards and provincial governments try to limit salary increases and maintain control of working condition issues outside the collective agreement, so as to have more freedom to arrange things as they see fit in light of public pressures and interests. The 1990s have seen several provinces introduce legislation restricting the range of issues that may be bargained collectively. In Manitoba, for example, a 1996 amendment to the *Public Schools Act* explicitly excluded the following items from being referred for arbitration: the selection, appointment, assignment, and transfer of teachers and principals; the method of evaluating teachers' and principals' performance; class size; and the scheduling of recesses and lunch times (Section 126(2)).

When the two sides in the bargaining process appear unable to come to an agreement in contract talks, collective bargaining legislation usually provides for a number of outside interventions to facilitate an agreement. These may include fact-finding, mediation or conciliation, arbitration, binding arbitration, and final offer selection. The first two of these are voluntary. Fact-finding is a process in which a neutral third party studies each side's position and issues a report outlining his or her view of the issues involved. This report is for information only. Mediation (sometimes called conciliation) involves having a third party meet with the two sides, either separately or together, to try to help them work out a solution. The parties do not have to listen to the mediator, but sometimes an outside person can cut through the bad feelings and suspicions separating the two sides.

In contrast, arbitration involves a process whereby the two sides select a third person (or persons) to settle the dispute for them. The arbitrator listens to both sides and then makes a decision as to what should be in the contract. Both sides, if they agree to arbitration in the first place, must accept the arbitrator's decision, no matter what it is. Final offer selection is a form of arbitration in which the arbitrator must pick the position of one side or the other in its entirety. The idea behind final offer selection, which remains a controversial practice, is that each side must put forward as reasonable a package as it can; if it is unreasonable, the arbitrator will select the other side's proposals entirely.

Collective bargaining can also involve the use of sanctions by either side. Teachers can engage in what is called **work to rule**, which means that teachers will withdraw all those services, such as coaching or other extra-curricular activities, that are not required in the collective agreement. Employers are entitled to **lock out** teachers or other bargaining groups, which simply means that they close the schools and stop paying salaries until the dispute is settled. Finally, employees can withdraw their services (**strike**) in an attempt to force their employer to come to an acceptable agreement with them. In spelling out the ways in which a contract is to be arrived at, Prince Edward Island and Manitoba have laid out procedures that specifically exclude the right of teachers to strike. In Nova Scotia and Quebec, strikes can only occur at the provincial level of bargaining. In Saskatchewan, bargaining provides two routes — one that involves binding arbitration, and one that involves the possibility of a strike. In the other provinces, strike or work-to-rule action and lockouts are retained as legitimate collective bargaining possibilities.

Even though most provinces do allow teachers to strike as part of the collective bargaining process, strike action by teachers remains a controversial issue that tends to generate fierce discussion within the profession. For some teachers, strike action and its impact on children's education remains incompatible with their vision of teaching as a profession committed first and foremost to the well-being of their students. Conversely, others argue that it is precisely because they are committed to the well-being of their students that they must use all options available to them to ensure effective working conditions and salaries that will attract and retain the most talented graduates. Despite the controversy, as long as teachers constitute an employee group whose wages and working conditions are set through collective bargaining, strikes are likely to continue as part of the bargaining process.

Conclusion

The purpose of discussing the professional status of teaching in Canada is not to establish a prescribed list of professional characteristics against which teaching must be ranked or to which it must aspire. Nor is it to make a self-interested case for teachers to be accorded greater status as professionals by society. Public school teaching shares certain characteristics with other professions and differs markedly in other ways. An examination of these similarities and differences can offer insights into the unique characteristics of teaching as an essential and basically moral public service (professional or otherwise), and into the expectations and demands those characteristics make of teachers.

Codes of conduct adopted by teachers' organizations provide a framework for defining appropriate behaviour for teachers, but as the prologue to this chapter suggested, there may be quite different ways for a teacher to act as a professional. And no matter what steps teachers themselves take, their status is in large

Table 8.4

Stages in Dispute Resolution

Prov.	Conciliation institution(s) involved	Mediation institution(s) involved	Arbitration institution(s) involved	Arbitration (voluntary or compulsory)	Strikes (legal or illegal)
NFLD.	1. Conciliation officer 2. Conciliation board		Arbitration board	Voluntary	Legal
P.E.I.	Conciliation officer		Arbitration board	Compulsory	Illegal
N.S.	1. Conciliation officer 2. Conciliation board	Mediation officer	Arbitration board	Voluntary at provincial level Compulsory at local level	Legal at provincial level Illegal at local level
N.B.	1. Conciliation officer or a commissioner 2. Conciliation board[1]		Arbitration tribunal	Voluntary	Legal
QUE.	Conciliation officer re clauses negotiated at the local or regional level	Mediator or board of mediation or public interest group re clauses negotiated at provincial level, except salaries and salary scales	Mediator-arbitrator re clauses negotiated at the local or regional level	Compulsory at the local/regional level (mediator-arbitrator)	Legal at provincial level except re salaries/salary scales for second and third years of three-year collective agreement Illegal at local and regional level
ONT.	Fact-finder	Mediator	1. Single arbitrator 2. Arbitration board 3. Final offer selector	Voluntary	Legal

(continued)

(continued)

	Conciliation	Mediation	Arbitration		Strike
MAN.	Conciliation officer		Single arbitration	Compulsory	Illegal
SASK.	Conciliation board	1. Mediator 2. Mediation team	Arbitration board	Compulsory if mediation-arbitration option selected* Voluntary if conciliation-strike option selected	Legal at provincial and local levels if conciliation-strike option selected but illegal if mediation-arbitration option selected*
ALTA.	Disputes inquiry board	Mediator	Single arbitrator or arbitration board	Voluntary	Legal
B.C.	1. Fact-finder 2. Public interest inquiry board	Mediation officer	1. Single arbitrator 2. Arbitration board 3. Mediator-arbitrator 4. Final offer selector 5. Special mediator**	Voluntary	Legal

* By September 21 for collective agreements expiring on December 31 (i.e., 101 days prior to the expiry date), the parties must select whether mediation-arbitration or conciliation-strike option will be invoked to resolve an impasse.

** Where the commissioner of the Industrial Relations Council is directed to resolve a dispute by the Legislative Assembly or the lieutenant-governor-in-council, one of the options available to him/her is the appointment of a special mediator. Note that the pertinent sections of Bill 19 (i.e., 137.97, 137.98, and 137.99) have not, as yet, been proclaimed into law.

[1] If a commissioner has not been appointed, a conciliation board may be appointed.

Source: Adapted from Canadian Teachers' Federation. (1992, February). Economic Service Bulletin. Reproduced with permission.

measure shaped by others, especially provincial governments, whose actions they cannot control. In defining and pursuing avenues of professionalism, teachers' organizations, whether they are regarded as professional associations or as unions, provide across Canada a strong and important structure for representing teachers' interests and for promoting public education in Canada.

Exercises

1. Consider the three definitions of a profession given in Table 8.1. Which definition do you prefer? Why? How well does teaching fit your chosen definition?

2. "Teachers will be better able to protect their legitimate interests by becoming not a profession but a union." Discuss.

3. Write a brief paper arguing either for or against the position that teaching has a knowledge base. Make use of appropriate research to support your position.

4. Write a paper arguing either for or against the Ontario model of governing teaching.

5. Review the code of ethics for teachers in your province. Do you see any problems or inconsistencies in the code? If so, what are they and how might they be resolved?

6. Interview one or two teachers about important ethical conflicts they have faced. (You will need to ensure that these discussions occur in a way that protects the confidentiality of all those involved.) How did the teachers resolve the conflicts they faced? Can you think of other ways they might have acted?

7. A fellow teacher is using teaching practices you consider inappropriate, even unethical. What might you do? Assuming that you refer the matter to your principal, what if he or she refuses to take any action?

8. School principals and vice-principals usually strive to develop strong collegial ties with the teachers on their staff. Yet school boards expect them to represent the board's management interests within their schools. Given these competing pressures, should principals and vice-principals be allowed to be members of provincial teachers' organizations, or should they have their own autonomous professional organizations?

9. In the teaching profession, salaries are determined primarily by years of postsecondary education and experience, while layoffs are determined by who has least seniority. How else might these decisions be made? What are the merits or drawbacks of these alternatives?

10. Discuss the conditions under which it may or may not be appropriate for a teacher to develop a personal friendship with a student. How do these constraints affect the practice of teaching?

11. Write or telephone your provincial teachers' association and ask for information on the range of activities and services it sponsors. How many staff are employed by the association? What is its annual budget?

12. Write a description of the collective bargaining process in your province. Who is involved? What steps occur? What mechanisms exist to resolve disputes?

13. Obtain a collective agreement for teachers in your province. What are the main provisions in the agreement? Are there any provisions you find surprising?

14. Compare a teachers' collective agreement with a collective agreement from another workplace (e.g., a factory). In what respects — and why — do the agreements differ?

15. Interview two or three teachers about the collective agreement. How important is it to them? Why? Try to interview at least one person who is directly involved with the work of the teachers' association.

16. School boards typically try to exclude many working condition items from collective agreements, while teachers' groups wish to include them. What are the arguments used by each group to justify its position? Which position do you favour? Why?

Further Reading

Goodlad, Soder, and Sirotnik (1990) and Robert Connell (1985) offer very useful examinations of teachers' work and the question of assigning them professional status. The Canadian Teachers' Federation is an important source of material on the activities of teachers' organizations across Canada. Within each province and territory, teachers' organizations also provide reports and other materials, while information on bargaining procedures is usually found in provincial legislation. A very thorough review of public attitudes toward education in Canada is contained in David Livingstone and Doug Hart's chapter "Popular Beliefs about Canada's Schools" in *Social Change and Education in Canada* by Ratna Ghosh and Douglas Ray (1995).

CHAPTER NINE

Teachers, Students, and Teaching

▼ PROLOGUE

"Linda, do you have a few minutes to spare?" Linda Chartrand looked up from her pile of marking. Toni Nord, the new teacher on staff, was standing in the doorway of Linda's classroom looking rather nervous.

"Sure," Linda said. "Come in and sit down. Please shut the door behind you so we won't be interrupted. Now, what can I do for you?"

"I wanted to ask you about the debate at the last staff meeting about students' needs and how we meet them. You seemed to feel that we need to change quite a few of our teaching practices. I know you mentioned moving away from ability grouping and changing our evaluation policies. I hadn't thought much about that, but what you said made sense in terms of my class. Can you tell me some more?"

"Well," Linda began, "my basic feeling is that sometimes we do things in schools in ways that don't help students very much. It has more to do with the way schools were 50 or 100 years ago, and with sorting students instead of helping them learn. Take the issue of ability grouping in the elementary grades. My understanding of the research is that ability grouping isn't a good strategy. Kids in the lower-ability groups actually do less reading, and the instruction they receive is quite different from that given to the kids in the higher groups. Instead of catching up, they fall further and further behind."

"But how do we teach such different kids if we don't group?" Toni interjected.

"Precisely the problem," Linda responded. "Because we have classes of 25, we need a way of managing the work for ourselves. We may talk about individualizing the program for each student, but it's pretty unrealistic given 1 teacher, 25 kids, and 6 or 8 different areas of curriculum. So the organization forces us to do something that doesn't work very well, and alternatives aren't easy to come up with. I personally like the idea of co-operative learning, but I also see that it would mean some pretty big changes, and I'm not sure I feel confident about making them without support from the principal, the staff, and the school district.

"Another problem that really concerns me is marks and grades. Of course, we need to give kids and parents feedback about how well they are doing. But I can see every year how discouraged some kids get early on when their papers come back covered with corrections. Some of them stop trying pretty quickly. Another problem with marks is that I have to give a mark or comment in each subject area. But I'd like to integrate them more, so that math was part of our work in science, and writing was part of our work in social studies, and so on. Yet the district has a standard report card we all have to use, and many parents want to know how their kid has done in each subject."

"Those are problems in my class too," Toni said. "But what do we do about them?"

"I don't think there are any easy answers," Linda replied. "We've got a system that's set up to handle big bunches of kids in a standard way, teaching them the same things, when we know very well that each kid is different in many ways. Every few years, someone comes around with the latest cure-all; we have two days of in-service on it, then we're left alone to try to implement it until the next magic strategy comes along. I think we've got to start asking ourselves tough questions about how we teach and organize for teaching, and stop expecting someone to give us a magic answer. We have to identify the problems and try out different ways of resolving them.

"You know, Toni, I'm really glad you came in. You've given me the impetus to do something. Why don't you and I try to get a few others together to meet after school one day to talk about some of these problems? There are a couple of people at the university who might want to join us. Maybe all of us can help each other try out some different strategies." ■

Part of the purpose of this book is to show how various historical, legal, political, economic, and sociological characteristics of schools affect the way we have come to think about and carry on teaching and learning. We have noted more than once in these pages that schools are the invention and ongoing creation of people. The beliefs and actions of people create and maintain the schools as they are, although, as we have also pointed out, not everyone gets to play an equal role in this effort. The review of these various influences provides the grounds for a better understanding of how teaching and learning, and teacher–student relationships, have come to assume their current form. We are now in a better position to take up these issues.

It is not possible in a single chapter to provide a complete discussion of issues involving teaching and learning. Instead, this chapter considers several key aspects of teaching and learning, including specialization, grouping, curriculum, students' and teachers' experiences of the classroom, evaluation and grading, and special education. The focus is on the ways in which the work of teachers and students is affected by the school's organization and structures, and on what might be called normal school practices, that is, what has been typical of most schools and classrooms (although generalizations of this sort are potentially misleading). Many teachers are aware of problems with current educational practice, and in a significant number of schools and classrooms serious and important efforts to make changes are taking place.

The central tasks of education involve the development of knowledge, skills, behaviour, and attitudes in learners. There is nothing automatic about the way we choose to organize these tasks, even though most current practices are largely taken for granted. At one time, young people learned most of what they needed to know at home through regular contact with parents and other adults. The concept of school did not exist. Current adult education efforts are often organized in much less formal ways than are schools.

As schooling became universal for children, mass forms of education were devised. Again, this was a deliberate choice rather than an inevitable outcome. Even the mass schooling of young people could be conducted in quite different ways from our current practices. For example, it could be noncompulsory; it could be spread over more hours of the day, with people attending at different times; it could involve more independent study or work at home; or it could be spread over more years, allowing for periods of work or other activities in-between. The literature on adult education provides many examples of alternative ways of organizing learning (Dampier & Selman, 1991). Many schools and many teachers are involved in changes in organizational arrangements that they believe will result in better education.

Consequences of a Standardized Model of Schooling

Once the decision was made to organize schools using a factory model as the main analogue, important consequences for teaching and learning came into play. The central organizational problem for any school is what to do with a large number of children and young people who are required to be in attendance for five or six hours each school day. A typical elementary school, for example, might have 300 to 400 children arriving each day around 9:00 A.M. and staying until 3:30 P.M. (preschool students, who are there only half the day, cause further complications). The school must provide activities for those children during that time, and it must make those activities educational. Schools must organize the students, the teachers, the knowledge that will be regarded as legitimate, and the time around all these people and activities. These requirements may seem self-evident, but, as the next few pages will show, they have important implications for school organization, teaching, and learning.

A first effect of school organization has to do with physical facilities. Schooling takes place in buildings that are built for that purpose. The buildings are usually separated from other activities in the community, and from places where adults (other than teachers) are found. We noted in Chapter Seven that schools tend not to have places for adults other than teachers. Students go to school in large rooms full of desks, tables, chairs, and school equipment. In many schools, windows have been blocked up to save energy, which considerably alters the feel of a room. Few schools provide places where students can be alone or work in small groups of their own choosing. Yet learners of all ages often prefer these modes of learning when given a choice. What happens in schools, therefore, is immediately constrained by the physical setting.

Because students are legally obliged to attend school, supervision and control are also important issues. The school literally has custody of the children, and must therefore ensure their presence and safety. Some of the legal ramifications of this requirement were explored in Chapter Four. The implications of the need to supervise children go far beyond legal issues, however. Organizationally, schools must ensure that students are directly supervised by an adult member of the staff. Typically, the means used to meet this requirement is to divide students into groups, with each group having an adult, usually a teacher, in charge. Thus, two other central characteristics of the school are created: students work in groups, and teachers work individually with groups of students.

Institutionalized schooling also creates the requirement for a timetable, which means that the movements of teachers and students are regulated by the schedule and the clock. Teachers must organize instruction to fit the timetable, regardless of their own style or their students' needs. Classes must begin and end at a particular time (especially in secondary schools, but also in elementary schools that have specialists on staff), which may or may not fit the educational requirements of the material or meet the needs and preferences of students and teachers. Teachers and students experience the day as chopped into small pieces, requiring them to change their mind-sets every 40 or 80 minutes, or whatever the schedule dictates. Secondary teachers may see only limited aspects of students because their contact with them is limited to particular subjects or times. Moreover, all subjects may get roughly equal time allocations, even though it seems evident that each might benefit from different scheduling arrangements.

Further important consequences arise from trying to undertake the educational mission of the school in a mass-organization setting. Schools are supposed to teach things to students, and to make efforts to have the students learn those things. The content to be taught and learned is already dictated through provincial curricula, about which more will be said shortly. The school then faces the question of how to organize in a way that ensures that the required content is in fact learned.

The Relationship between Teaching and Learning

Fundamental to understanding the nature of teaching is appreciating the uncertain relationship between teaching and learning. Learning presumably is what schools are for. The goals and objectives of schools, which we discussed in Chapter One, have to do with what students will learn, do, think, and feel, and how they will behave. We want and expect students to develop literacy and numeracy skills. We want them to develop an appreciation of ideas, skills in finding knowledge, an interest in the variety of the world, an appreciation for the Canadian way of life, and so on. We want them to learn to be tolerant, caring, thoughtful, and sensitive people.

We also know that people learn things in different ways. Learning theory is a complex field and, despite important developments in the last few decades, we are far from anything resembling a science of learning, if indeed such a science can ever develop. It is clear that learning is related in complex ways to previous knowledge and experience, to motivation, to one's life situation at any given time, to the stimuli for learning, and so on (Claxton, 1984; Resnick, 1987). It is also evident that no single approach to learning will work for all students. While there is no such thing as a typical class of students, at any given moment within a group of students one would find some who are interested in a particular subject, others who are not; some for whom the teacher's style works, others for whom it does not; some with and some without backgrounds that facilitate the task at hand; some who find the particular presentation of material meaningful and helpful, others who do not. Some students may be preoccupied with other demands made on them, whether from home or from friends. Some may feel incompetent at the subject being studied. Some may not understand the teacher's language very well. Some may find that the material and the examples don't fit the world they know. In short, people learn different things, in different ways, at different times, and with varying speeds.

Some might see this variety as a problem to be remedied, thinking that if only people were the same, schools could be so much more effective. The argument for a standard curriculum across the country or a province is an example of such reasoning. Another way to think about variety in people, though, is to value it as one of the things that make life interesting and worthwhile. What kind of world would it be if we all thought the same, felt the same, and did the same things? Uniformity would also cost us the sudden insight from a student, the flash of understanding, the humorous remark that brightens a class, the countless unexpected ways in which other people surprise and delight us by being themselves.

The organization of schools does not always reflect our knowledge about learning or about differences among people. The organizational choices that have been made mean that schooling is organized on the basis of groups of students learning the same thing, at the same time, in the same way, and at the same speed. There are standard curricula that are supposed to apply to all students in a given grade or course. Students are divided into classes, their days are divided into subjects or courses, and they are assigned to teachers for these chunks of time, on the presumption that they will learn what the teachers teach them. Essentially, the organization of learning is determined for students; they are told what to do, and when and how to do it.

Many teachers realize that education cannot be effectively standardized, and some schools have made efforts to change the delivery model to de-emphasize these features. However, it is difficult for even the most committed staff to work against the various requirements that may be imposed by provincial regulations, school board requirements, or the habits of experience.

Elementary and Secondary Schools

The teacher responsible for any given class must be capable of teaching the required subject matter. The usual way of meeting this requirement is to have teachers specialize in some manner, and to organize the students accordingly. Schools deal with this requirement differently in elementary and secondary schools.

In elementary schools, a concern for specific content, such as learning to read, tends to be combined with a strong interest in the overall development of each student. The development of academic skills is stressed, but so are behaviour, motivation, and the all-round development of the child. In the first years of education, the school focuses on the students' need to acquire the ability to do later, more specialized studies. Young children are regarded as being more dependent on adults. Elementary schools also place considerable stress on students' self-concept — the sense students develop about their own skills and abilities. Given this emphasis on basic skills and child development, the most common arrangement is for a single teacher to teach most or all of the material; thus, each teacher usually has the same group of students for most of the school day. Specialist teachers may be used in elementary schools in some areas (e.g., languages, music, and physical education), depending on the approach of a given school district, and on the availability of the necessary funds and people.

In secondary schools, much more stress is placed on specialized subject matter. The secondary school, like the university, emphasizes content over concerns about learners as individuals. Teachers' content knowledge becomes more important, so teachers specialize in particular subjects and students encounter different teachers in each subject. It is now the student's task to co-ordinate her or his school program across the various subjects. Work in secondary schools is also influenced powerfully by the organization of teachers into subject-based departments. Science teachers tend to see issues quite differently from, say, English teachers. Some departments may also have higher status than others, so that the secondary school becomes, in Hargreaves' phrase, "balkanized" (Hargreaves, 1994).

Elementary and secondary teachers may have rather different views, then, of what their job is and how best to approach it. Elementary teachers more often describe themselves as teachers of students; secondary teachers see themselves more as teachers of subjects. These differences in viewpoint can lead to significant differences in school practices such as grouping, evaluation, and instruction. For example, Canadian elementary schools tend to use anecdotal reporting, applying words such as "satisfactory" or "excellent" to students' work, while secondary schools use letter or number grades. The idea of continuous progress is an elementary-school invention; secondary schools are much more likely to see their program in discrete packages.

Grouping

As has been noted, students vary in their interests, motivation, experience, skills, and background knowledge with respect to what the school seeks to have them learn. If all learning were individualized, such differences might not be problematic. But when instruction is organized around groups of students taught by one teacher, variability can become a fundamental problem, especially since the school wants (in principle at least) every student to learn essentially the same things. Teachers and schools have always had to grapple with the tension between common goals and diverse people. Guided by the assumption that it is easier to teach students who are similar to one another in skill and interests, schools have usually dealt with this tension by trying to limit the variability in groups of students. The most common strategies used for this purpose are creating subgroups within classes and putting students into different courses or programs.

Elementary and secondary schools have different practices for reducing diversity. The most common form of grouping entire classes in elementary schools is by age, the assumption being that students of similar ages have roughly similar skills and dispositions. Of course, as any parent or elementary-school teacher can tell you, this assumption is only partly true. Each elementary classroom contains students with a wide range of abilities, interests, and motivations. One common response in elementary schools is to create, within each class, subgroups of students based on their perceived ability, and to differentiate the work to accommodate the presumed capacity of each group. This strategy is called **within-class ability grouping**. The problem with ability grouping is that it does not appear to be a very effective practice, and is especially unhelpful to those students who are least successful (Slavin, 1987). In the last few years, more schools have begun to try alternative ways of organizing elementary-school classrooms that are based on mixed-ability groups. Co-operative education, in which students work in mixed-ability groups using a particular method of undertaking and completing work, is one popular approach, but there are others as well (Fullan & Stiegelbauer, 1991, pp. 184–86; Slavin, 1994).

In secondary schools, the problem of diversity has generally been addressed through **tracking** or, as it is sometimes called, **streaming**. Rather than group students within a class, entire courses are differentiated by presumed level of difficulty, and students choose or are assigned to courses on the basis of their perceived capacity and willingness to do the work required. Most provinces organize their high-school courses into several streams, such as general, advanced, vocational, or university entrance. Students who are regarded as having less ability, or as being less motivated, are pushed toward tracks and courses considered to be less academically demanding. The result is classes that are less diverse. Support for grouping or tracking varies between elementary- and high-school teachers, with fewer than half of elementary-school teachers indicating that they think classes grouped by ability are desirable, compared with two-thirds of high-school teachers (Canadian Teachers' Federation, 1992, p. 63).

Although the diversity within classes may be reduced through tracking, the diversity in the school population is not reduced. Instead of individual teachers having to accommodate differing students (though tracking by no means eliminates these differences, either), some teachers must now teach entire classes of students who are regarded as less able, less interested, and thus more difficult to teach. It is not uncommon to find the most advanced classes being taught by the most senior teachers, with the newest teachers being given teaching assignments in the tracks that are seen as least desirable.

The research on tracking in secondary schools also shows that the practice has negative effects on the experience of students who are not placed in the top tracks. Researchers have consistently found that students in tracks called general, basic, or vocational have less actual instructional time, are assigned less challenging tasks, have fewer chances to discuss ideas, and generally have a significantly inferior educational experience (Curtis, Livingstone, & Smaller, 1992).

Herein lies the dilemma of grouping practices. It makes great sense in principle to organize students by interest and ability so as to foster appropriate teaching. But when such organization does occur, there is a very strong tendency for the students placed at the lower end of the continuum to receive less stimulating, less challenging, and less effective instruction. As Goodlad puts it, "The decision to track is essentially one of giving up on the problem of human variability in learning. It is a retreat rather than a strategy" (1984, p. 297).

All grouping practices require judgements about students so that they can be placed accordingly. Determining students' characteristics, however, is not nearly as straightforward a matter as it might seem. Most of us probably remember the experience of a teacher whose belief in our ability brought better results than we ourselves might have expected, or a teacher with whom we didn't get along and who therefore didn't motivate us to work as hard. Research supports our experience, showing that grouping is not simply a matter of assigning students based on immutable characteristics, but a matter of judgements made by teachers and schools about students. These judgements are, in turn, powerfully affected by teachers' ideas about students (Radwanski, 1987). For many years, girls were widely thought to be less capable than boys in science and mathematics. Students for whom English is a second language may be seen as less able, even though their problem is one of language, not ability. Teachers may tend to regard students from particular kinds of backgrounds (e.g., Aboriginal students or students from single-parent families) as being more likely to have academic problems. These preconceptions, however untrue, can have powerful consequences for students (Apple, 1990). In the case of science and mathematics, for example, years of conventional wisdom are being overturned as it becomes apparent that women are just as capable and just as interested as men given appropriate teaching and learning situations (Fidkalo, 1992).

Box 9.1
Two Views on Secondary-School Tracking

At the high school level separation [of students for instruction] becomes both necessary and desirable to achieve legitimate goals. ... The division of labor is a
reality. ...

[O]nce students are destined for a particular future, as motor mechanics, college
students, university students in science or applied science and so on, there is competition within that identified group for limited places. ... Therefore, students must
be evaluated in terms of their group.

In most developed western countries, the age of specialization should be around
fifteen or sixteen, permitting two or three years of specialization.

Students are sequentially developed for the futures they themselves choose. Thus
there is no question of being in a holding tank — they are making progress, slowly
perhaps, towards a chosen end.

Source: M. Holmes and E. Wynne. (1989). *Making the school an effective community*
(pp. 182–86). London: Falmer Press.

[A] curriculum is intended for all students ... we must reject any attempt to divide
the curriculum into university-entrance, commercial, general and other such
courses. We must reject also the apparently common-sense notion that only some
students have the ability or the aptitude to study an "academic" curriculum.

At the moment we are ... excluding the majority ... preparing them instead for
subordination and non-involvement. This will always be the case while we retain
separate programmes for the academic minority and the allegedly non-academic
majority.

Source: Ken Osborne. (1990). *Educating citizens: A democratic socialist agenda for
Canadian education* (pp. 48–49). Toronto: Our Schools/Our Selves.
Reproduced with permission.

Grouping practices are also affected by the structure of the classroom. The
requirement for teachers to maintain order affects their attitudes toward individual students. For example, teachers who place more value on good behaviour
may identify more boys as having learning problems because boys tend to
exhibit more rambunctious behaviour. In a review of research, Wentzel (1991)
concluded that "teachers consistently report preferences for students who are
cooperative, conforming, cautious, and responsible rather than independent
and assertive or argumentative and disruptive." Moreover, nonpromotion in the
tracking system may result as much from poor behaviour as from poor academic
performance (p. 4).

Grouping has many other consequences. Because groups carry value rankings
—with more academic groups generally seen as better by teachers, students, and
the public — the school must be able to defend the way it has judged and

assigned each student. Various kinds of tests and other devices are put in place for this purpose. Counsellors and school administrators may devote a great deal of time to this task. Much of the paraphernalia of testing and grading students has to do with making decisions about grouping. All of this is time and energy diverted from the goal of instruction.

Educators have long been aware of some of these problems, and many attempts have been made to organize schooling somewhat differently. Such changes are not easy to make since they require teachers to organize instruction differently, which is something they may not know how to do should they even wish to (Oakes, 1992). The key point to understand here is that practices of teaching assignment, grouping, and tracking are not simply spontaneous, but arise out of the basic organizational issues facing schools.

Curricula

In addition to managing the placement and the time of students and teachers, schools are also responsible for organizing knowledge—for determining what is to be learned and how it is to be taught. The content that is to be taught in each grade or subject is termed the school's curriculum. In addition to the **formal curriculum** of the school—the subjects and courses—there also exists something called the **hidden curriculum**, which has to do with all those things taught by the school (whether consciously or not) that are not part of the formal curriculum.

Formal Curricula

Covering the curriculum has already been mentioned as a central concern of teachers. The development of curricula, exemplified in Figure 9.1, is primarily organized by the Department or Ministry of Education in each province. Usually groups of teachers and subject-area experts work to write a provincial curriculum document, which is then distributed to schools and teachers. The entire process —involving writing a curriculum, pilot testing it in some schools, and revising it — may take several years. Parents, students, and noneducators are formally involved in some provinces.

As Pratt (1989) has shown, provincial curricula vary in how prescriptive they are. A few curriculum documents are quite specific, outlining topics to be covered, giving examples of activities and assignments, and specifying the kinds of learning outcomes that are sought. In most provinces, however, the documents are more like guidelines. They may still contain a set of topics to be covered and provide ideas about classroom activities, but they leave to teachers matters such as the time and effort to be devoted to each topic and the order in which material is to be taken up.

Figure 9.1

Alberta Education Flowchart on Curriculum Development

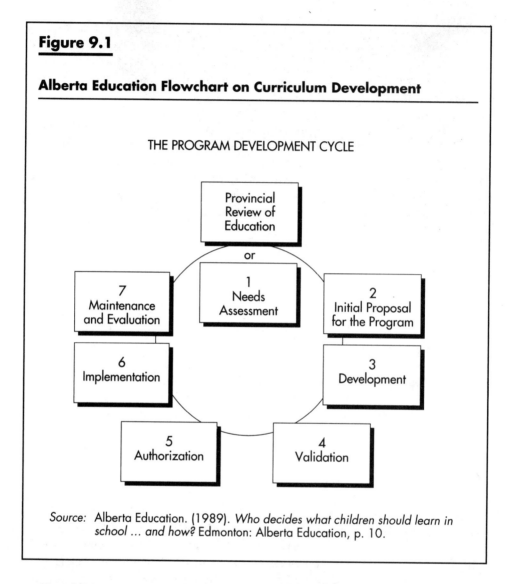

THE PROGRAM DEVELOPMENT CYCLE

Source: Alberta Education. (1989). *Who decides what children should learn in school ... and how?* Edmonton: Alberta Education, p. 10.

In addition to provincial curricula, school districts may have their own curriculum development processes in which local teams of teachers develop curriculum units in those areas a district wants to emphasize. Again, these may be more or less prescriptive. In some schools, teams of teachers may make further modifications or develop school-based curricula in a particular area.

A change in the last few years in Canada has been the move toward regional and even national curriculum development. Groups of provinces in the west and in the Maritimes have formed consortia to develop courses that will be used across each region, and a similar project is underway in sciences at the national level. Although there have long been advocates in Canada of national curricula, these projects in the 1990s are the first real effort to move in that direction.

Additional implications for curriculum development arise from changes in information technology as teachers, schools and provinces are able to learn about and exchange curriculum materials via the Internet. The availability of curriculum on the World Wide Web could be an additional step in the direction of greater curriculum uniformity across provinces.

Curriculum Implementation

Regardless of what official curriculum documents say, the critical issue is whether teachers *use* a particular curriculum document. Given the relative autonomy and isolation of most classrooms, teachers often have a great deal of latitude in using curriculum documents. Studies of curricula implementation show that the degree of use may range from leaving the packages unopened on the classroom shelf to adopting them in detail (Fullan & Stiegelbauer, 1991). Most teachers probably fall somewhere in-between, using parts, but not all, of a new curriculum given to them.

Curriculum use can be understood as emerging from two aspects of teaching. One is the teacher's thinking both about content and about teaching. Each teacher has ideas about the subject to be taught and the best way to teach it. For example, a teacher may think of literature as being primarily about the analysis of language use, and may regard carefully led class discussion of particular works as the best way to develop these skills. Another teacher may see literature as a means of reflecting on our own lives, and may want to make considerable use of small groups in teaching. A third teacher may be teaching subjects about which he or she does not feel highly knowledgeable, and thus may be inclined to use the curriculum guide almost as a textbook. These three hypothetical teachers will approach the same curriculum document in quite different ways, looking for content and ideas that are consistent with their own understandings, both of the subject and of what teaching is about. A teacher may use all three approaches at different times.

A second key aspect is the teacher's need to have a set of activities for each class of students. Ideas are not enough; both teachers and students expect that in class the teachers will tell the students what to do. Teachers face a constant need for activities to fill class time. Many teachers evaluate curriculum documents based on the extent to which these documents help them organize class time in ways that seem desirable to them. A curriculum document with interesting concepts but no description of how teachers might use it is unlikely to get very much use in classrooms.

Curricula and the Organization of Knowledge

Whatever curriculum is used, it will have built into it a set of assumptions about what knowledge is and how knowledge is structured. In any textbook, such as this one, some topics are emphasized over others. Connections are made between some ideas and not others. These decisions are not naturally present in the world, but are made by people who prepare curricula, whether these are provincial committees or individual teachers in classrooms. History books may focus on the actions of kings and prime ministers, but say little about farmers and female factory workers. Chemistry courses may talk about the composition of all sorts of compounds, but give few illustrations as to how these compounds are used or what their consequences are for the environment.

The same problems emerge in the division between subjects. Schools divide the curriculum into chunks—language, mathematics, science, and so on. These divisions are not inherent in the world, however, but are structures people have created as a way of thinking. When we look at a tree we are seeing biology, botany, chemistry, physics, geography, sociology, history, and economics at work: all are related to this tree being what it is, where it is. It is we who must choose which particular aspect is of interest to us. Moreover, in adult life, work does not proceed in the neat divisions that are used by the school to organize its curriculum. Scientists are heavily involved in the use of both mathematics and language, and may work in a setting that is highly political. Writers are writing about something, for some purpose.

Choices about how to organize the school's curriculum have to be made; we cannot teach everything. However, it is important to recognize that these are choices that reflect somebody's view of the world rather than being a necessary way of thinking. Some important areas do not appear very often in school curricula—for example, economics, business, or psychology. Education itself, an important subject of study in postsecondary education, is not part of the school curriculum. Important consequences flow from choices about which knowledge is valued in schools, and which is not. Nor are the decisions about which knowledge to value in schools made in an objective manner. The curriculum is a historical product, and thus largely reflects a white, male, middle-class view of which knowledge is valuable. Students who come to school knowing about the things that the school teaches—numbers, letters, geography, and so on—may feel valued and reinforced. Students who come to school knowing about things not valued in school—looking after a younger sibling, finding and making use of someone else's garbage, dealing with a welfare worker—do not find that same sense of reinforcement.

The Hidden Curriculum

The term **hidden curriculum** was coined by Jackson (1968), who was among the first to point out that much of what the school teaches and what students learn does not appear in any curriculum guide. For example, schools may emphasize behaviour such as punctuality, obedience, truthfulness, independence, or competitiveness. In the eyes of many, these characteristics are more important than learning to solve quadratic equations or identify elements in the periodic table. Much of what happens in schools has to do with the influencing of behaviour, rather than with the learning of prescribed content or skills. Indeed, students often get into much more serious trouble for violating the rules of the schools (e.g., fighting or being disrespectful to teachers) than they do for failing to learn whatever is in the academic program.

Another dimension of the hidden curriculum relates to the values implied by the formal curriculum. If textbooks are full of pictures of males in active roles and females in passive roles, students are more likely to absorb, however unintentionally, this view of how the world ought to be. If history courses do not talk about the ways in which government policy obliterated traditional Aboriginal cultures, or about biased policies against certain immigrant groups, or about the exclusion of women from many important spheres of life, then students do not come to understand the very different experiences some people may have of our country. If science and technology are presented as the best ways to solve social problems, students may not be able to make reasoned judgements about the appropriate role of these areas in our lives.

Reviews of Canadian textbooks and curricula have shown how many biases and opinions were built into the curriculum while being displayed as if they were the truth. In the last few years, considerable effort has been made to eliminate many of these representations. It is more than likely, though, that 20 or 30 years from now, as social values change, others will be looking at our current books and curricula and finding other kinds of bias. Indeed, the view taken in this book is that there cannot and should not be a single version of knowledge presented as if it were true for all time. As our views of the world change, our ways of explaining the world also change, and so must school curricula.

Schooling from the Teacher's Point of View

For teachers, being in a classroom with students is a highly demanding activity. At any given moment, teachers are trying to do several things at once. One concern, of course, has to do with whatever is being taught at the moment — subtracting with fractions, the geography of the Maritimes, playing the recorder, or any one of the myriad things that are part of the school curriculum. Are students understanding what is being said? Do they see the connections between one point and another? Is the material of interest to them?

These immediate curricular concerns are set in the context of long-term goals. Are students learning to learn on their own? Are students developing an appreciation of the particular subject? Are students being challenged to think for themselves? Are they learning respect for the views of others, good work habits, and persistence? Most people, including parents and most teachers, believe that these larger goals are more important than the discrete pieces of information in the curriculum, even though it is the latter that receive most of the direct attention in schools.

Teachers also need to be highly attentive to the classroom as a social setting. A prime concern of all teachers—especially new ones—is the ability to keep order in the class. If students are not focussed on the task at hand, they will not be learning what the school wants them to learn (although they may well be learning something else). Teachers have to balance their concern for an intellectually stimulating classroom with the requirement that they maintain a certain level of order. While experienced teachers rarely report maintaining discipline as a serious problem, it is much more significant for new teachers, more than half of whom reported to the CTF survey that discipline was a problem "sometimes [48%] or frequently [9%]" (Canadian Teachers' Federation, 1992, p. 87).

An awareness of the differences among students is also a constant preoccupation of teachers. Teachers quickly develop a sense of which students require more attention. At any given time, teachers are monitoring different individuals and groups in the classroom in an effort to assess how the lesson is going. Do some students have puzzled looks? Perhaps they need more explanation. Are some students gazing at nothing? Perhaps they need a reminder to help them refocus their attention. Are some students busily engaged in talking to each other or passing notes? Some action may be needed to keep the class on task.

Teachers are also aware of the need to be accountable for what they are doing. If students tell their parents about this class, what will parents think? What if the principal drops in? Will he or she support what I'm doing? Am I undermining my colleagues by doing something that is different from what they do in their classes?

The teacher is engaged in a constant act of improvisation (Clark & Peterson, 1986). While teachers begin a class with a plan of some kind (it may be carefully written out or simply carried in one's head), those with experience know that classes rarely go according to plan. As a class or lesson proceeds, a teacher is constantly monitoring what is happening and making adjustments to meet changing circumstances.

The requirement to do several things at the same time, and to adjust things as one proceeds, makes teaching very demanding. The teacher's attention is usually fully engaged all the time. While teaching, the teacher is also carrying on a silent internal dialogue. Students see only the external actions of the teacher, but much of the work of teaching occurs in the teacher's thoughts, like the 90 percent of the iceberg that is below the surface of the water. "That group doesn't seem to be following me; I'd better go over this again. ... Allan and Nadja are busy doing something else; if I just move over in their direction I may get their attention back. ... I need a better example to illustrate this point. ... Only ten more minutes left; I'd better wrap this up. ... Have they had enough time to do the problems, or do I need to assign them for homework? ... They're all so excited about the assembly this afternoon that they really aren't concentrating. ..."

Endemic Tensions in Teaching

Teaching also has several endemic tensions or dilemmas. These are problems that face teachers constantly. They are also problems that cannot be settled once and for all, but have to be addressed continuously through various sorts of adjustments and strategies.

First, as we have already noted, teachers are faced with the tension between what might make most sense educationally and what is required to keep order. In studying natural science, for example, a teacher may want to send students outside to look at plants or insects. However, this cannot be done on the spur of the moment; normally, days or weeks of advance notice are necessary for this sort of activity. Moreover, there are problems of supervision once students are no longer all under the teacher's watchful eye. How much simpler to show a film about plants, or even simply to talk about them in the classroom, perhaps with reference to a few pictures in the textbook.

Consider another example. A very common teaching technique is to ask students questions about the subject matter to see how much they've remembered. Researchers who have investigated questioning in the classroom have found that when teachers do ask questions, they allow only a very short time for students to think about answers. Typically, if nobody answers or puts up a hand almost immediately, the teacher will begin speaking again, either to give an answer or to ask another question. The time between asking a question and speaking again is called **wait or response time**. Researchers have also found, not surprisingly, that giving students more time to think before they answer results in better answers. Many teachers, however, are reluctant to have very much silence in the classroom because they fear that silence will lead to disorder. They fear that when the teacher gives up some control over the learning process, students may become inattentive or disruptive. Thus, the requirement for order may interfere with what makes most sense educationally.

A second perennial tension in teaching is that between the individual and the group. It is individuals who learn, of course, but teachers are almost always responsible for groups of students. Teachers know that within any group some students will do better at their schoolwork than others. Yet teachers cannot simply give all their attention to those who seem to need it most. Teachers constantly face the problem of how to allocate their limited time and attention. Is it better to spend the most time with the weakest students, or should one concentrate on the best students since they will gain the most? Or is the best strategy to direct one's teaching to the middle, doing the best one can with those at the extremes? There are no easy answers to these questions, even though they are faced by teachers every day.

A third tension is between adequate coverage of the curriculum and following up on students' interests. We have already discussed some curriculum issues, but it should also be noted that most curricula are designed to use all the available time during the year, and many have supplementary topics that can be taken up if additional time is available. Teachers almost always feel pressure to move ahead with the content, to make sure that all the important topics have been covered. Increased testing by provinces creates more pressure in this direction. At the same time, opportunities constantly arise in the classroom to go off in other directions. A group of students have an interest in pursuing one element of the curriculum in some depth. A topic that was supposed to be dealt with in one hour piques the class's interest and stretches into a week of discussion. Does the teacher cut this short, thereby losing the opportunity to do something that interests students and is relevant to the subject? Or does one try to scrimp somewhere else in the curriculum?

Finally, there is an important tension in schools between learning and evaluation. An important goal of schools is for students to stretch their abilities. This means taking risks and making mistakes. At one level, it is commonly accepted that we can learn a great deal from our errors. But marks and grades are a critical part of students' school life, and making mistakes confers no rewards here. A student who tries something new and doesn't do very well at it may be worse off than a student who does what she or he already knows, and learns less but doesn't make mistakes.

Teachers recognize these dilemmas. What do we do about the student who works and improves considerably, but still only gets a C? How do we encourage students to be concerned with judging their own learning if, in the end, the teacher's evaluation is what determines their fate in school (and possibly out of it, as well)? A further discussion of evaluation occurs later in this chapter.

Schooling from the Student's Point of View

Students and teachers tend to experience school life quite differently. Although the experiences of students can vary considerably depending on their teacher and their school, a consistent body of research (largely from the United States) shows that students generally find classrooms boring at all levels. Most of the time, teachers talk and students passively listen, or students work individually on tasks assigned by the teacher; students spend very little time speaking, either with one another or with teachers (see Box 9.2).

While teachers are trying to work out what to do next, students may be trying to figure out what the teacher wants, or simply trying to make the time pass. While teachers are excited about the subject matter, students have to worry about getting marks and knowing the right answers. Most significantly, students usually have little or no say about the nature of their schooling. It is something that is done to them, rather than something they do. While teachers value highly their ability to make choices about how to structure their teaching, students rarely have such choices about how to structure their learning (Cullingford, 1991).

Box 9.2
Students' Experience of School

In the early 1980s, U.S. researcher John Goodlad headed a large study of American schools, the results of which were published in a book called *A Place Called School*. The study involved visits, observations, interviews, and other data collection in 38 schools across the country, and included 900 teachers and 17 000 students. Among the results reported were the use of class time at various levels, from which the following data are abstracted:

ACTIVITY	Early elementary % OF TIME	Junior high % OF TIME	Senior high % OF TIME
Written work	28	21	15
Listening to teacher	18	22	25
Preparation for assignments	13	16	13
Reading	6	3	2
Use of AV equipment	7	4	3
Discussion	5	4	5
Taking tests	2	6	6
All other*	21	24	31

* All other includes practice/performance (in, for example, physical education, vocational, or music), watching demonstrations, being disciplined, simulations and role plays, or times with no assigned activity.

Goodlad concludes: "[T]hree categories of student activity marked by passivity ... dominate. ... We saw a contrastingly low incidence of activities invoking active modes of learning" (p. 105). "Teachers out-talked the entire class of students by a ratio of about three to one. ... Barely 5 percent of this instructional time was designed to create students' anticipation of needing to respond. Not even 1 percent required some kind of open response involving reasoning or perhaps an opinion from students" (p. 299). Moreover, students at all levels liked most the subjects in which they were most active, such as physical education, art, and vocational education (pp. 118–21).

In another study, this one done in the United Kingdom, Cullingford interviewed 110 students at the end of primary or first year of secondary schooling and concluded that:

> In some schools where classes were followed for a day, it was calculated that more than three-quarters of children's time was spent waiting for something to happen (p. 32).

(continued)

(continued)

Children do not always find time spent in a desultory way pleasurable or stimulating. They stress the fact that much of the school's routine and much of their experience of learning is boring. They find many of the tasks they are set boring, and they all find particular subjects boring. In fact they accept that school will inevitably contain boring moments. They associate many activities with boredom. And although they find ways of mitigating their boredom, they accept it as an essential attribute of school (p. 119).

Teachers express a different view. In a survey by the Canadian Teachers' Federation, teachers reported considerably more use of games, small-group activities, and class discussion than students seem to perceive, especially in elementary classes. However, the teachers also reported that seatwork (in elementary classes) and lectures (in secondary classes) were still among the most common teaching practices (CTF, p. 55).

Sources: Data from John Goodlad. (1984). *A place called school.* New York: McGraw-Hill; C. Cullingford. (1991). *The inner world of the school.* London: Cassell; and Canadian Teachers' Federation (CTF). (1992). *Teachers in Canada: Their work and quality of life.* Ottawa: CTF.

As noted earlier, the school curriculum comes divided into courses and units that are administered to students by teachers. The assumption is that students learn slowly, hierarchically, and one thing at a time. From students' point of view, these packages may have not the slightest connection with their way of seeing the world. Nor does the school delivery model correspond to current thinking about how learning occurs. Iran-Nejad (1990), in reviewing research on learning, concludes that children come to school as "spontaneously proficient learners" (p. 589) based on their self-regulated learning in a real setting, where they can learn many things at the same time and often do so unconsciously. School knowledge, in contrast, focusses on individual pieces of information that are often taken out of context.

Despite many years of effort to move toward so-called higher-level skills, the research suggests that classrooms are still heavily concentrated on getting students to produce the right answers rather than to think about important questions. The vast majority of questions that students are asked require a single, correct answer. Indeed, so pervasive is the emphasis on learning content that students come to expect it, and may be quite resistant to a teacher who tries to create open-ended debate without specifying correct answers. And, as has been noted, open-ended debates that excite students carry the risk of excessive noise and loss of classroom control.

Students' experience of schooling also depends on their backgrounds and on how the school has categorized them. Students in tracks regarded as lower ability may find that less is expected of them, that more attention is given to their behaviour than to their learning, and that their efforts to improve themselves are actively resisted. Students whose language and culture is not that of the majority may also find that they are marginalized within the schools.

Gender plays a particularly important role in shaping school experience. In most classrooms, boys speak more, are asked more questions, receive more attention from teachers, interrupt girls, and generally dominate classroom discourse (Sadker, Sadker, & Klein, 1991). Boys may be encouraged to experiment with ideas and behaviour, while girls are dissuaded (albeit subtly) from doing so. Girls' experience of schooling is often quite different from that of boys. These differences are so ingrained in our behaviour patterns that they may occur even when teachers are committed to equal treatment of both sexes.

The competitive nature of many classrooms also affects the way in which students experience school. Students are well aware that they are being rated and ranked on the basis of their ability and behaviour, at least as it is interpreted and valued by the school. What matters are marks, the teacher's praise, and being promoted into the next grade or advancing to the next level of the system. Even Grade 1 students are well aware that there are differences among them, and they recognize who is on top of the pile. Moreover, it is individual skills that count; the ability to work effectively in a group, although an important skill in the modern workplace, is only recently coming to play a substantial role in schools, chiefly elementary ones.

Classroom Control, Teacher Authority, and the Effort Bargain

Although teachers have formal authority in the classroom, the atmosphere of any class is also powerfully shaped by students. As teachers well know, a group of students who want to make a teacher's life miserable can certainly do so, and the teacher may have very little recourse. The treatment of substitute teachers by some classes of students is a case in point. Indeed, one might wonder how it is that teachers are able to command students' obedience at all. Why is it that students so often do agree to do what teachers tell them?

There are several sources of teacher authority. In Chapter Six, three ways of thinking about the authority of school administrators were described. These same categories—traditional, legal, and charismatic—can be applied to teachers and students. At a basic level, teachers have coercive legal power over students. They can punish students through poor grades, detentions, complaints to parents, and through formal disciplinary action such as suspensions. So at least some student obedience is probably motivated by a fear of these types of consequences. However, coercion is not a desirable way to manage a classroom because it is antithetical to the development of the kind of relationship between teacher and students that is conducive to learning. Effective teaching and learning require mutual trust and open communication; coercion destroys these qualities. One can help people learn, motivate people to learn, and support people in the learning process, but one cannot *make* people learn. To be effective, teachers' authority must be consented to by students because it is the students who must do the learning. Usually students consent to obey teachers, and usually they do so for several reasons other than fear of authority (Clifton & Roberts, 1992). Cullingford (1991) points out that students do accept teacher authority as necessary for effective learning, even though they may feel that the authority is not always exercised fairly.

To help explain classroom order, researchers have developed the concept of the **effort bargain** (Doyle, 1986). According to this concept, a teacher and a class of students arrive, through a complex and largely unacknowledged negotiation process, at an arrangement regarding what the learning environment in their classroom will be like. Students respond to the demands the teacher makes through their behaviour, and teachers affect students' behaviour through both their demands and their responses to students. For example, more challenging academic work creates additional tensions for students, who may seek (largely unconsciously) to reduce the teachers' expectations of them by misbehaving. As a result, teachers might come to the conclusion that students will behave only if they are given relatively simple and straightforward work to do, and if teachers do not expect too much from them. In other classes, students may accept or even welcome a high level of demand if they see it as serving their purposes in some way (e.g., their desire for the high grades that will enable them to enter university). Whatever form it takes, the effort bargain is a clear example of the way in which the need for order and control affects learning in the classroom.

Evaluation, Grading, and Testing

Students' experience in school is substantially shaped by the fact that they are evaluated and graded. Again, the primacy of evaluation is the result of deliberate choices about how to organize schooling. A school system that uses a whole series of grades in elementary school, and a wide range of separate courses in secondary school, ensures that each student will face a large number of evaluations during her or his schooling. In fact, students receive hundreds of grades or other evaluations each year for assignments, essays, tests, exams, or projects (far more than would be the case in any workplace). Most of these evaluations, and almost all of them after elementary school, are given to individual students rather than to groups of students.

The requirement that students be graded and evaluated has a whole series of consequences for teaching and learning. It can sometimes result in grades becoming more important than the knowledge they are supposed to represent. This becomes apparent when students want to know whether something will "count" before deciding how much effort to put into it. Rather than representing a measure of progress toward the goal of learning, grades instead become the goal (see the debate in *Review of Education Research*, 66(1), Spring 1996). Grades may also change the nature of the student–teacher relationship. Since the evaluations may have important consequences for students' futures, a tension necessarily arises between teacher (evaluator) and student. And, since not every student can be at the top of the class, grades also have the potential to create conflicts among students.

As mentioned above, school grades have important consequences for a student's future. They may determine whether a student enters an enrichment program or qualifies for a particular university or college program. Yet grades in school are not particularly predictive of success in adult life. Grades in university programs, for example, correlate very poorly with measures of adult occupational and personal success (Walberg, 1987). The problems with grades have been recognized for many years. In principle, it ought to be possible to provide a thoughtful and thorough analysis of students' skills and weaknesses without using any comparative measure, whether it be letters or numbers. And important changes have been made, particularly in elementary schools, in terms of assessing students' progress using other forms of evaluation (Maeroff, 1991). However, the school still plays an important role as a sorting organization, helping to determine who will have what economic and social status. Grades play a critical role in that process in that they are used by colleges and universities to determine admissions and by employers to determine hiring. Evaluation thus remains an important element of every student's experience in school.

Evaluation also presents teachers with the dilemma of deciding how to determine grades or standing. Does one reward knowledge, effort, good behaviour, or some combination thereof? It appears that test results are generally less important than behaviour in shaping grades in Canadian schools. Teachers reported that their evaluations of students assigned greater importance to effort than to any other criterion, including test performance. The only exception to this pattern was found among science and mathematics teachers in university preparation courses in secondary schools. In elementary schools, effort, social skills, behaviour, and attendance all ranked ahead of test achievement and class assignment work (Canadian Teachers' Federation, 1992, pp. 76, 81).

A further example of the impact of school evaluation practices concerns the issue of retention in grade versus social promotion (see Box 9.3). Not so long ago, it was routine for students who were having difficulty in school to be failed and required to repeat an entire year's work over again. Although failing is now less common, substantial numbers of students (at least one in six) still take more than six years to complete elementary schooling (Ziegler, 1992). This is unfortunate since a substantial body of research shows that students who are retained in grade do not improve their academic performance (Melvin & Juliebo, 1991). Nor, in various experiments, have retained students outperformed similar students who were moved into the next grade (Smith & Shepard, 1987). These data have prompted school systems to develop policies, supported by research, that make it difficult to retain or fail students. Critics have called these policies **social**

promotion on the grounds that students who lack skills should not be promoted until after they acquire them; social promotion, they argue, makes it possible for students to finish years of school without having learned very much.

The debate over retention in grade, which has gone on for more than twenty years, is a good example of the impact of school organization on teaching and learning. One might say that the existence of grades by age is an arbitrary device in the first place, since the skills and interests of children of the same age can vary greatly. If there were no grades in elementary school, there would be no problem of retention. Indeed, this is the solution that was advocated by the Sullivan Commission in British Columbia in 1988.

Box 9.3
No-Fail Policy Sparks Debate about Schools

The recent series of articles in the *Free Press* on whether to fail students or not shows how the way we define a problem has important consequences for the range of solutions we can generate. The article posed the question in the way it is typically put: Should a student who has not mastered the material in one grade be required to repeat that grade, or should the student be sent on to the next grade regardless?

This question does present a serious dilemma. Retraining students to do the work again has considerable intuitive appeal. It is an application of the old maxim, "If at first you don't succeed... ." The problem is, we know from extensive research that retaining students does not work. A large and consistent body of studies over many years shows convincingly that students who are held back a year do not usually improve their performance. Nor do they outperform students with similar difficulties who are not held back a year. Instead of catching up, they fall further and further behind. Moreover, failing a grade is associated with all sorts of later educational problems and with the likelihood of dropping out of high school. This is why so many educators argue against retaining or failing students.

But passing on students from grade to grade who do not have the required skills is also a poor strategy. After all, education is about learning something; prison is about putting in your time regardless. Social promotion raises the possibility that students can go through many years of school without learning what most of us regard as essential. And it may have the effect of absolving the school from taking responsibility for the student's lack of learning.

The resolution to the dilemma lies in posing the question differently. Suppose we asked instead: What can we do to maximize the chances that all students will learn to read and write competently? Now we have moved from a yes–no decision about failure to an inquiry into teaching and learning — surely a much more relevant way of thinking about the issue. Moreover, a different question immediately suggests some different answers. If some students are not learning using one approach, perhaps we need to try some other approaches. Education is not like

(continued)

(continued)

manufacturing, in which we can count on a particular process to produce a particular result. In education, it is the match of the student, the teacher and the situation which is essential, making it much more difficult to determine how teaching should best occur in any given situation.

Where we are not being successful, we might change the material students are asked to read and write about, and even ask students to make their own choices about what they would like to read. We might change the setting in which they learn, by moving them to a library or to a small, private room to work on reading or writing. We might change the people who try to help them, using tutors, or parents, or trusted adults, or computers, or even other students. We might change the timing, so that they worked in the afternoon (in most schools language skills are taught in the morning), or at home after supper. We might even ask students how they think they might best learn to read and write. No doubt the reader can imagine many other possibilities. The same sorts of possibilities apply to arithmetic or any other subject.

There is nothing original about any of these suggestions. Many excellent teachers in our schools already do these things. There is no guarantee that any of them will be successful, although there is evidence that there are good strategies for teaching non-readers to read. After all, this is what adult literacy programs do with considerable success.

We do not need to accept failure in schools. We can and should expect every student to learn to read and write with reasonable competence. But our attempts to do so are not assisted by sterile debates over promotion or retention in grade. Nor are we helped by attempts to blame problems on teachers, or on school policies. These debates draw attention to rewarding or punishing students (or teachers) for what they have or have not learned. Instead, we need to think hard about how to help young people learn, and organize ourselves to support them in doing so.

Source: Benjamin Levin. Letter to the editor. *Winnipeg Free Press* (July 25, 1992). Reproduced with permission.

Box 9.4
The Language of Testing and Assessment

Educational testing has become a specialized field of activity with its own set of concepts and terms, which are not always clearly understood by teachers or the public. For example, many people use the term "standardized test" to refer to any test that is set outside the school, whereas testing experts have a much more precise and limited definition of "standardized." A discussion of concepts of testing and assessment is beyond the scope of this book, but because these concepts are currently so important, all educators should become familiar with the basic terms and ideas, which can be found in many textbooks on educational measurement and in other sources.

Issues around the evaluation of students have been intensified in recent years by the growing emphasis on external testing of students. Provinces have increased substantially the amount of provincial testing, and the results are being used more publicly to evaluate the overall quality of the school system (McEwen, 1995). Canada has also participated in a number of international testing programs that compare students' achievement in many countries. The results of such large-scale testing are often reported extensively by the mass media, although international comparisons are fraught with problems (Nagy, 1996).

Many educators feel that the focus on external tests is a bad practice for at least two reasons. First, such tests may fail to measure many of the important goals and processes of schooling. It is accepted, for example, that measuring skills in areas such as problem solving through paper and pencil tests is very difficult. Efforts have been made to design large-scale tests that do a better job in this regard, but what is called **authentic assessment** — that is, assessment that is closely matched to the actual skills that are the goals of teaching—is turning out to be both difficult and very expensive.

Second, external tests are seen as driving instruction to an undesirable extent, so that teachers focus on preparing students for tests rather than on other aspects of instruction that may be more important. Insofar as tests do focus only on a limited range of skills and knowledge, the problem of diverting instruction is increased.

Proponents of testing and then publishing results, on the other hand, argue that parents and the public need better information about what students are learning and how well schools are doing in developing skills and knowledge. Some proponents explicitly support such public accountability as a way of putting pressure on educators to do a better job, on the assumption that external review is a powerful motivator — just as, one might note, schools assume that external evaluation motivates students to work harder.

Large-scale external testing of students shows every sign of continuing and quite possibly expanding in coming years, and so will continue to be an area of controversy.

Special Education

The subject of special education illustrates the interplay of educational considerations with organizational issues in schools; and although it is now a part of almost every teacher's work life, it is still a field full of debate and controversy.

The extensive development of special education in Canadian public schools goes back less than 30 years. In 1967, a report entitled *One Million Children* was published by the Canadian Enquiry into Learning Disabilities in Children (CELDIC). The report pointed out that large numbers of students were not being served appropriately by schools because insufficient efforts were being made to meet their particular needs. The CELDIC report was itself the result of organization and lobbying efforts by parents and others interested in these children. After the report's release, these groups used it to pressure schools and provincial governments to take action on its recommendations.

Over the next ten years or so, departments and ministries of education in Canada's provinces developed policies on various aspects of special education. From the outset, the development of special education has been shaped by two simultaneous but contradictory elements. On the one hand, much of special education has been heavily influenced by the concept of **normalization** (Wolfensberger, 1972), which argues that services to people with disabilities should be as similar as possible to those provided to the rest of the population. The move to normalization was not confined to schools, but developed broadly in the social services, primarily those that served mentally and physically handicapped persons. The concept of normalization implies that people with disabilities should receive specific support services to allow them to function as normally as possible, instead of being segregated in separate programs or facilities. On the other hand, a large part of special education involved identifying students as having particular problems and then programming to meet their needs, thereby setting them apart from other students. Here the dilemma of grouping, discussed earlier in this chapter, is drawn even more sharply.

Normalization played an important role in the development of special education, initiating policies such as the integration of many disabled students into regular classrooms. Previously, blind, deaf, or physically handicapped students had been taught primarily in separate schools and classes, and many mentally disabled children were not in school at all. In the 1970s, however, many such students were returned to neighbourhood schools where, it was found, they could generally cope quite well if some adaptations were made for their particular needs.

Another set of special education practices was geared toward providing educational programs for students who did not seem to fit into the educational mainstream. Concepts such as "learning disability," "hyperactivity," "emotionally disturbed," and other supposed diagnoses of student problems were developed in the 1970s, along with a whole series of testing devices that were used to assess students who fell under these categories. In many provinces, definitions of special education were broadened as well to include such services as English as a Second Language (ESL) and other learning limitations that are related to students' social background.

A delivery and support apparatus emerged alongside special education. New programs and classes were created for special needs students. New categories of teachers, such as resource teachers and behavioural class teachers, were also created, with different certification requirements in some provinces. Extensive professional-development programs were offered to teachers. Universities established special education programs and departments, journals began to publish, and research programs developed. Provinces created special education branches and provided targeted funding to support special education programs and staff. Today, running throughout the school system is a large apparatus dedicated to the area of special education, even though one supposed purpose of the activity is to eliminate the differences between disabled and nondisabled students.

The early advocates of special education wanted something much more than simply having a wider range of students included in regular classrooms. A greater degree of individualization, they argued, would be needed in all classrooms in order to meet the needs of all students without having to resort to special classes or schools. Special education would thus require major changes in the delivery of education altogether. Although the development of special education has affected schools in important ways, the basic elements of classroom organization and instruction have not altered in most schools. Critics have argued that instead of being a means of changing what schools do so as to help children, special education has served as a way of labelling children as deficient (Pellegrini & Horvat, 1995). Much of special education depends on categorizing students on the basis of tests whose validity has been called into question (Sleeter, 1986). Indeed, there is a continuing debate in the literature as to whether there is such a thing as a "learning disability," as distinct from a student who is not succeeding in school (Christensen, Gerber, & Everhart, 1986) (see also Box 9.5). Despite the debate, however, the number of students identified by schools as requiring special education has increased steadily in Canada.

Box 9.5
Learning Disabilities: The Debate

[The] claim that learning disabilities ... do not exist, and that they are merely an excuse invented by the schools to explain their instructional failures, flies in the face of an enormous amount of research and clinical evidence. The result is one of the most incredible misunderstandings of the nature, diagnosis, and remediation of learning disabilities. ...

If the methodology required to teach the learning disabled is different from that used to instruct other children, this has nothing to do with rhetoric or mysticism, but with the ethical and pedagogical necessity to adapt method to need.

Source: Ignacio Gotz. (1987). Learning disabilities: A reply to Christensen et al. *Educational Theory, 37*(3), 335–38.

A careful reading of our paper, or many of the sources we cite, will lead an objective reader to at least one conclusion: there is no professional consensus on characteristics that necessarily and sufficiently identify students as learning disabled. ...

The underlying issue is not whether there are some students with a thing called learning disabilities, but rather how well learning environments can be rearranged or changed so as to enhance the development and achievement of different learners.

Source: M. Gerber and C. Christensen. (1987). Not known, because not looked for? A response to Gotz. *Educational Theory, 37*(3), 339–41. Reprinted with permission.

Mainstreaming and Inclusion

The paradox of separation and normalization is also evident in the debate over **mainstreaming** in schools (Wilgosh, 1992). The concept of mainstreaming originally grew out of the normalization movement; many parents and educators advocated placing almost all students in regular classrooms in neighbourhood schools. The adoption of mainstreaming as a policy has meant that many students who a decade ago would have been in segregated classes have been moved into ordinary classrooms. These students can include some with significant cognitive delays and those with conditions such as cerebral palsy.

In the last few years a new term, **inclusion**, has often replaced mainstreaming. Inclusion (or inclusive schools) has a similar focus on trying to provide for all students in regular classroom settings, but whereas mainstreaming referred primarily to students with disabilities, inclusion is used to refer to students with various other differences, such as ethnicity, language, or social class.

Though many schools and teachers welcomed mainstreaming, feeling that it would benefit students, others worried about their ability to provide good education for students and about the additional demands that would be placed on classroom teachers. A survey by the Canadian Teachers' Federation (1992, pp. 64, 156) showed that less than a third of teachers, but about half of principals, felt that widespread mainstreaming was desirable. Individual cases involving this issue have been quite heated, making national news. Section 15 of the *Charter of Rights and Freedoms* has been invoked by parents and other advocates for disabled students, and a number of court cases in Canada, some of which were described in Chapter Four, have dealt with the extent to which schools can require students with disabilities to go to special classes.

Mainstreaming is by now quite well established in Canadian schools, with the vast majority of children attending either their local school or another school of their choice (a small number of students remain in separate classes or separate schools). Many teachers have serious concerns about their ability to teach severely disabled students, and about the impact of such students on the rest of the students in their classes. Some teachers may feel that they do not know enough about how to teach students who, for example, cannot speak or have little control over their movements. They may feel that one or two students end up receiving a disproportionate share of their time and attention, perhaps with little benefit to show for it. The most recent side of the debate concerns what appears to be (no solid empirical evidence is yet available) an increasing number of students with serious emotional problems, especially in elementary schools. A single student who is highly disruptive can change the entire tenor of a class and make a teacher's work much more difficult. Although the principle of mainstreaming remains important, there are also moves in Canadian schools to have more exceptions and to return to policies of separate classes for certain kinds of students. There will be continuing struggle over the extent to which all students will be placed in regular classrooms.

These debates illustrate the tensions between educational ideals and organizational practices. In principle, it ought to be possible to develop an individual program for each student and thus accommodate a very wide range of students in a classroom. In practice, teachers face all of the difficulties already discussed earlier in this chapter, without including exceptional students. The school system is organized around groups, not around individual students. Moreover, the problems associated with maintaining classroom order, covering the curriculum, and grading all students make individualization a very difficult enterprise.

Conclusion

As should be evident by now, teaching is a very difficult undertaking. Student teachers may begin their programs in education thinking that teaching is relatively straightforward: one presents information to students, and, if one treats them reasonably well and makes the classes "interesting," the students pick it up. In fact, there are many other factors at work, some conducive to learning, others not (Stahl, 1992). Teachers will inevitably encounter difficulties and dilemmas that they do not know how to handle. Although experienced teachers develop strategies for dealing with certain types of problems, even the most skilled teachers frequently encounter new situations that require them to rethink what they should do. The issues raised in this chapter, including grouping, motivation, classroom control, evaluation, and special education, are among the most important of these.

The challenge confronting every teacher is to remain open to new possibilities and to improve one's skills constantly. It may sometimes be frustrating to realize that there is no recipe for teaching, and that the teacher has to figure out anew, over and over again, what to do in a given situation. On the other hand, as we said earlier in the chapter with reference to differences among students, variety is also a powerful stimulus and source of interest in our lives and our work. As we shall see in the next chapter, many schools are making important efforts to change teaching and learning. Despite the difficulties, few teachers would want to trade their jobs for ones that are utterly predictable and therefore monotonous. As teachers, we have the requirement—and the opportunity also—to be learners all the time, discovering more about students, curricula, and education as we go. That is no small gift.

Exercises

1. Working first individually and then in groups, develop a description of the way in which you learn best (e.g., episodically vs. in intensive stretches; one subject at a time vs. several things at once, and so on). Compare your

own style with that of others in your class. Are they similar? To what extent did your schooling accommodate these characteristics? To what extent does the university do so? How might institutions do a better job of adapting to individuals' learning styles?

2. Conduct an examination of a school as a physical setting. How would you describe it? Is it comfortable? friendly? cold? Is the scale appropriate for young people? What kinds of signs, posters, or displays are there? What spaces do students use, and under what conditions? What spaces do teachers use, and under what conditions?

3. Read a book or article from the adult education literature. Write a brief paper outlining the implications, in your view, of this work for the way in which schools are conducted.

4. Study the organization of classroom groups in a class in the school where you are observing or student teaching. Do all groups do the same things? What differences can you observe in the kinds of activities given to different groups? What effect might differences in group activity have on students? You may want to ask some students how they understand the grouping process.

5. Hold a classroom debate on tracking in secondary schools: "Resolved that all high-school students should have the same basic program of studies."

6. Study the evaluation practices in the school where you are assigned. What evaluative information is communicated to students? to parents? How often? How do teachers arrive at their judgements about students?

7. Find a current curriculum guide for your province for a subject you are likely to teach. Which topics are given the most attention? given the least attention? missing entirely? How do you account for the guide's balance of topics?

8. Using any provincial curriculum guide, identify the assumptions built into the curriculum. These may be assumptions about the subject itself, about teaching and learning, or about which knowledge is valuable. Are there any assumptions with which you disagree? Why?

9. Write a brief paper on the hidden curriculum as it operates in a particular classroom. What messages other than those in the formal curriculum are being given to students? How?

10. Interview a teacher about the process of teaching. What is the teacher thinking about while teaching? How aware is the teacher of the decisions he or she is making, and the reasons for them?

11. Interview a few students in any grade. Ask them what aspects of school they find interesting, and why. Which subjects or activities do they like the least, and why? What implications can you draw from their comments about teaching and learning?

12. Observe a class discussion, either in school or at the university. Use either a frequency count or a stopwatch to measure the number of comments and length of time used by males versus females. You may want to consider reporting your findings to the class to promote discussion.

13. What is the policy of the school to which you are assigned on failure or retention in grade? How many students take more than the required number of years to complete their school program?

Further Reading

Teachers are fortunate in having an increasingly rich literature on all aspects of teaching and learning. Current and prospective teachers would benefit by reading widely, and would be able to base practice more on evidence and less on whatever happens to be the current fad.

Each area discussed in this chapter has its own, often very large, body of research. The citations in the chapter provide additional pointers, but many areas of valuable work are barely discussed here, including work on increasing students' motivation and on specific alternative methods of teaching, learning, and assessment. Good places to start are major reference works. One of the best sources is *The Encyclopedia of Educational Research*, the newest edition of which was published by Longman in 1992. The encyclopedia, in six volumes, provides an overview article and a good introduction to the literature in many of the areas considered in this chapter. A second excellent (and perhaps not quite as overwhelming) source is the *Handbook of Research on Teaching*, the third edition of which was published by Macmillan in 1986. The chapters in this volume, too, take up various issues, provide a good overview, and give many additional references. Fullan and Steigelbauer (1991) provide an excellent one-volume review of many areas. Sources on school effectiveness and school improvement are discussed in Chapter Ten of this book. The general sources cited in the Introduction are also very useful here.

CHAPTER TEN

Prospects for Education

▼ PROLOGUE

"**W**ell, I've finished my first year of teaching, and I've accomplished my two main goals. I'm still alive, and I'm not going to be fired." Toni grinned at Aaron across their coffees. The school year had just ended, and this would be the last of their meetings until the fall. She had found their get-togethers every few weeks tremendously helpful because she got a chance to talk about her own feelings and frustrations about teaching, and she also learned from listening to her friend talk about his successes and tribulations. Their support for each other had helped both of them make it through their first year of teaching.

"I'm like you," Aaron replied. "Early in the year I re-adjusted my expectations as to what I could accomplish. I realized that it would be hard enough just to do what was required, without getting fancy. But I have to say that by the spring I was feeling much more comfortable, and started to experiment with a few things. And I'm really looking forward to September. This year I just know I'll be a lot more comfortable, and much more able to do the sorts of things I want in my class — things that are good for kids."

"I agree. I do feel much better than I did in October." Toni paused. "But you know, I'm not really sure whether I'll stay in teaching for too many years."

"Why is that?" Aaron asked. "After all the work of getting through university, you want to give it up?"

"I'm a person who has high standards, Aaron," she replied. "I put a lot of effort into the things I do, and I want the results to reflect that. I worked really hard this year, and I think I did a pretty good job. But it wasn't as good a job as I wanted to do. Teaching just seems to have so many constraints, and you have to make so many compromises. There's so much trivial stuff to do that gets in the way of what's really important. Just getting permission to have a field trip can take hours of time, never mind actually organizing the trip. I'm filling in reports when I should be thinking about the next day's or week's classes. There are too many kids we don't seem able to reach. The ones who are really quiet, and even the ones who cause me so much aggravation — I really feel I could reach them if I had more time or fewer students. There are so many things happening in kids' lives that the school can't or won't affect. They're having to cope with tremendous changes all around them while we go blathering on about alliteration in poetry or photosynthesis or the causes of Confederation. Just this past week I had another kid whose parents are separating. How do I tell her just to put it aside and concentrate on her math? Sometimes I wonder if schools will ever be really educational places."

"I suppose no institution or job is perfect," Aaron said. "I can see all kinds of ways schools could be better, and all kinds of ways I could be a better teacher, too. I think that's part of our responsibility — not just to work in our own classrooms, but also to try to be part of larger-scale improvements as well. In our school, the parent organization has really been working hard this year. At first there was quite a bit of friction with the staff, and we were nervous about what they would want us to do. They had a strong desire to have a better sense of how well kids were doing, which we thought meant they wanted lots of standardized testing. Over the course of a few meetings, we began to realize that they had a legitimate interest in finding out what kids were learning, and they realized that our objection to standardized testing wasn't just self-protective. Now we've got a set of ideas about how we can give parents and the community more information about students' achievement, and they have a better idea of what some of the limits on that information are. Of course, that wasn't easy to do, but the result will be worth the effort.

"I guess that's how I feel about lots of aspects of being a teacher," he continued. "They're tons of work, but don't you feel that the challenge is an exciting one? Besides, you have so much talent at teaching that it would be a tremendous loss if you stopped."

"Well, I'm not ready to quit yet. I'm planning to give it another couple of years before I decide. For one thing, I really enjoy being around the kids; most of them are great. It's exciting to see them getting turned on by learning. And I'm excited about our new principal, who said some good things at our last staff meeting about plans for next year. It sounds as if she wants to get teachers much more involved in curriculum decisions, and work on within-grade and cross-grade cooperation in what we teach. She's asked for our ideas about possible improvements. Naturally I have a long list, although I think I'll give her a chance to catch her breath before I throw them at her, especially since I'm only finishing my first year. I don't know where I'll get the time to do these things, but it would sure be exciting if I could really be the kind of teacher I want to be and have the support of the school."

"That's the great thing about teaching," Aaron laughed. "There's always plenty of room for improvement." ■

The first nine chapters of this book have taken readers on a whirlwind tour of the organization and functioning of Canadian schools, and have attempted to review some of the main features and dynamics of the education system. We began Chapter One by saying that changes in Canadian society require not only that educators understand school organization as it exists in Canada, but also that we scrutinize it critically and ask questions about how it might be otherwise. Throughout the other chapters, we have tried to point out some of the constraints and limitations of current forms of school organization, and also to draw attention to the tensions and dilemmas inherent in schooling.

This final chapter focuses on the prospects for schooling at the end of the twentieth century. It considers the forces and pressures on schools in Canada today and in the next few years, and some of the responses schools are trying to make. Problems in changing and improving schools are also discussed. A final section re-examines the role of the teacher in creating the best possible schools.

Pressures on Canadian Schools

The ostensible work of schools — to educate children and young people — has remained unchanged for many years. However, the practical meaning of that task changes as conditions in the world change, and there can be no doubt that the world outside the schools has changed in important ways in the last few decades. By reviewing some of these changes, we may provide you with a better sense of the pressures facing schools as we move into the future.

Over the last few years, Canada has seen a great deal of debate about the quality of education and the need for improvement in schools. Critics complain of high drop-out rates, unchallenging curriculum, and poor performance by Canadian students on international tests. A number of books have been written on the subject (e.g., Lewington & Orpwood, 1993; Nikiforuk, 1993), and a variety of national organizations and provincial commissions have issued reports lamenting the failures of the education system and warning of dire results for Canada's economic and social future if improvements are not made (e.g., Economic Council of Canada, 1992; NABST, 1994).

Some commentators have argued that the complaints and fears of the critics are wrong, that schools are at least as successful as they have ever been, and that the criticism is motivated more by ideological prejudice against public services than by objective considerations of evidence. Nagy (1996) has analyzed Canadian results on various international tests and concluded that our performance has been quite good. Barlow and Robertson (1994) provide one of the best statements by Canadian defenders of schools, arguing that many of the claims made by critics — for example, about drop-out rates or the lack of skilled workers in the economy — are either exaggerated or completely false.

The debate over whether schools are better or worse than they used to be may be a fruitless one, just as is the debate over whether life today is better or worse than it was 30 or 50 years ago. It is probably more important and more useful to think about today's schools in relation to today's educational needs.

Schools, whether in Canada or in other countries, have always been subject to considerable amounts of criticism. One can find complaints about the declining quality of education going back to the ancient Greeks, and in almost every generation since then. After all, expectations for public education are very high. People expect schools to do countless things, as was seen in our discussion in

Chapter One of the goals of schools and the education system. Imparting knowledge is an important and primary purpose, but schools are also expected to teach attitudes, values, and behaviour in a whole range of areas. In a sense, schools are expected to make everyone perfect—a tall order indeed! When people see problems in society, they ask schools to try to prevent or stop them. Current examples include child abuse, drug abuse, and unemployment. When people see problems with the younger generation, they blame the schools.

In 1957, the United States National Education Association issued a pamphlet defending schools from several common criticisms that were then being voiced. Among these were:

- that progressive education had taken over the schools;
- that soft social programs were replacing intellectual work;
- that all students were being promoted regardless of achievement;
- that discipline was lax;
- that too much attention went to average students at the expense of the gifted;
- that moral values were being neglected;
- that teacher training was of low quality and value (National Education Association).

These criticisms of 1957 seem remarkably similar to those being made today, even though today's critics would often see 1957 as "the good old days."

Efforts to change and improve schools accompany such criticism. After all, the development of universal public schooling was itself a response to concerns that the population needed more schooling given changing economic and social conditions at that time. And ever since the development of public schooling more than 100 years ago, suggestions for its improvement have been made. Proposals for change have been quite diverse, however, because people's goals for schools are also quite diverse. Nor have changes been easy to make even when it has been possible to agree on what should be done. A review of past efforts to change schools illustrates some of the problems.

A Brief History of Educational Reform

A discussion of the history of educational reform could begin at almost any point in Canadian history. Let us begin, however, with the late 1950s, a time when most people finished school after eight or ten years, and the rate of high-school completion was still low (see Table 10.1). At this time, schools were criticized for not being intellectually challenging. Many critics argued that schools were too concerned with rote learning, that the curriculum was antiquated (with insufficient attention paid to the study of science), and that students did not learn to think enough. In the United States, which has often had a strong influence on Canadian education, a near panic occurred when the USSR launched the Sputnik satellite, thus becoming the first country to put such a spacecraft into orbit. As a result, the United States invested heavily in developing new curricula for schools in the sciences, most of which were also used widely in Canada in the 1960s.

In the second half of the 1960s, educational policy took another turn. There were increasing concerns that education was too restrictive and that too many children were failing. The general trend of reform in this period was toward providing more flexibility and choice in the system, with fewer restrictions on students and teachers. The initial development of special education in the 1960s was one response to these concerns.

The introduction of open-area elementary classrooms, and the concepts of team teaching and continuous progress, were other examples of educational reform. In high schools, programs were also liberalized. Students were given more choice of subjects, and efforts were made to reduce the rigid distinctions among tracks in the high school. Provincial examinations at the end of high school were either reduced in number or eliminated entirely. Curriculum processes were also altered to give schools and teachers more autonomy in defining what students would study. The first codes of rights for students were developed, and students themselves took a more politically active role, demanding a greater voice in the direction of their own education. The inspection functions of provincial departments and ministries of education, along with the requirements for provincial examinations, were reduced or abolished. These developments carried forward well into the 1970s.

By the mid-1970s, however, the mood had altered. Governments were coming under increasing pressure as the optimism about solving social problems such as poverty began to fade. Public funds for education and other purposes, plentiful in the 1960s, were less so in the 1970s. Gradually, the mood of expansion and change was replaced by a mood of contraction and conservatism. Increasing concerns—about students' lack of basic skills, and about the need for schools to return to earlier ways—eliminated the reforms of the 1960s.

Table 10.1

Educational Attainment in Canada, 1961–1986
(Percent of population 15 and over by level of education)

Year	Less than Grade 9	Grades 9–13	Some postsecondary
1961	44%	43%	13%
1971	32%	46%	22%
1991	14%	39%	47%

Source: Adapted from Statistics Canada (1989). *Educational Attainment of Canadians.* Ottawa: Minister of Supply and Services, and Statistics Canada (1995). *Statistical Profile of Canada* (Cat. No. 95–359), p. 16.

This mood continued, and indeed intensified, during the 1980s. Fiscal restraints on schools became tighter than ever before. In some provinces, funding to schools was actually cut for the first time in decades. Provincial governments, which had reduced controls over teachers, schools, and school districts, began to reinstitute central policies in a number of areas. Several provinces reintroduced or extended provincial examinations, and many provinces developed other kinds of student assessment programs to try to measure what students were learning. Curriculum choices for students were reduced. The package of changes can be thought of as an attempt to improve schools by having more controls over what was done and how it was done.

This trend continued during the 1990s (Lawton, 1992). However, it is coupled with another set of reform proposals, borrowed largely from the current literature on private-sector management, that emphasizes the decentralization of authority and provides more autonomy to local schools to manage their own affairs. Under various names, such as "empowerment" or "school-based management," these proposals seek a significant shift in authority away from provincial governments and bureaucratic systems toward local communities. Sometimes these ideas are coupled with a desire to make education more like the market system, with schools having to compete with one another for students and funds.

Whatever its inconsistencies and limitations, the spate of government policy changes and reforms shows no signs of abating, and is actually intensifying. A 1994 report by the Council of Ministers of Education (CMEC, 1994) cited dozens of provincial reform initiatives. And unlike previous periods of significant change in education, the current round of reforms is occurring in a climate of pessimism and worry, and with static or declining budgets for schools.

We have noted already that school reform is often linked to changing social conditions. Before looking in more detail at current reform agendas for schooling, then, it is useful to consider some of the main social changes that are affecting schools today.

The Impact of Social Change on Schools

While immediate changes in education policy tend to get a great deal of attention, the most important influences on schooling come from larger and longer-term shifts in Canada and the world. As noted at the beginning of this book, changes in Canada's demographics, economics, social structure, and technology have powerful implications for schools. And changes in Canada are linked more strongly than ever before to changes in the world as a whole. Schools are strongly affected by these larger social shifts (Levin & Riffel, 1997), as can be seen by looking at a few of them.

Demographics

Demographics can be defined as the study of the composition of a population, including such factors as age, sex, marital status, ethnicity, and so on. Several demographic changes in Canadian society have had and continue to have important implications for schools. Particularly important among these are the diminishing number of people with school-age children, changes in gender roles, changes in the structure of families, and changes in the ethnic composition of Canadian society.

The school-age population in Canada dropped dramatically during the 1970s, from just under 6 million in 1971 to under 5 million by 1985, a decline of about 15 percent (Canadian Education Statistics Council, 1990). The drop followed a period of rapid growth in the 1960s that was generated by what came to be known as the baby-boom generation. After this boom period, however, formerly crowded schools started to empty out. Falling enrollment was accompanied in the 1980s by tighter budgets for education and by a drop in the demand for new teachers. It is no coincidence that the 1960s, with their growing school enrollments, were a period of considerable optimism about education, while more recent times, characterized by stable or falling enrollments, have been much less optimistic. To take just one way in which numbers affect the climate of opinion, remember that for every school, the cost per student is strongly influenced by changes in enrollment. Thus, the rapid increases in per-capita spending in the 1970s were largely a result of a decline in enrollment. However, this type of data was used by some critics of education to reinforce their position that costs were skyrocketing while results were, at best, static.

But demographic change is important not simply because of the declining numbers of students in classrooms. The proportion of adults who had direct contact with schools also decreased. Fewer students mean fewer parents who are informed about what schools are doing, and about how public money is being spent. This also means that there are more people in the country paying education taxes who have no immediate stake in the schools. On top of these facts, an aging population has resulted in greater pressures being placed on governments to provide other kinds of public services, such as personal-care homes, health care, and pensions. So while education budgets were facing pressure because student numbers were falling, the political constituency most likely to support spending on schools — parents — was also declining in numbers and in relative importance.

Other demographic changes have placed increased responsibilities or pressures on the school system. A particularly important change has been the increase in the numbers of women, including those with young children, who have taken on part-time or full-time employment in the last twenty years. More than 60 percent of Canadian children now have two parents employed outside the home, although many mothers do not work full time year-round (Crégheur & Devereaux, 1991). The work of sustaining families and communities, which was traditionally performed without recognition or salary by mothers, is increasingly being done by paid staff such as child-care workers and social service agency workers (although women still carry the great share of this burden, both at work and in the home). At one time, many schools depended on mothers being at home, but this is no longer the case. The child-care function of schools is considerably more important than it was 30 years ago. The rapid increase in kindergarten enrollment in Canada, from 28 percent of 4-year-olds in 1977 to 46 percent in 1988 (Crégheur & Devereaux, 1991), is only one reflection of the increased demand for child care; the institution of day-care facilities in many schools is another.

Teachers are also very aware of the changing structure of families (Conway, 1993). One infrequently noted change is that there are now fewer children in most families, which may significantly change the ways in which parents interact with their children. Although the family of father, mother, and two children was never as typical as the textbooks suggested, it has become steadily less typical. In 1995, 16 percent of children under age 11 were living with a single parent (more than 90 percent of whom were female), and another 5.5 percent of children were living with two parents, at least one of whom was not a biological parent. In more than half of single-parent families, the parent was not employed outside the home (Ross, Scott, & Kelly, 1996b, pp. 35–36). (It might be added, however, that single-parent families were more common in the 1920s than in the 1980s due to the combined effects of deaths in World War I and the higher mortality rate of parents from disease, including women dying in childbirth.) Many teachers seem to feel that single-parent families create problems for children, but the evidence is that poverty—which will be considered further shortly—is the real villain, as well over half of such families live below the poverty line (Ross, Scott, & Kelly, 1996a). On average, women still earn much less than men in Canada, and there is very strong evidence that women end up economically worse off than men after marriage breakup. Single-parent families headed by men are much less likely to be poor. Educators need to be careful not to blame mothers for problems that are not of their making.

Another important feature of demographic change in Canada has to do with the increasing diversity of the school population in Canada. Many classrooms are much more heterogeneous today, in terms of ethnicity, prior achievement, attitude toward school, and other factors, than they were a couple of decades ago, with consequent challenges for teachers and for school organization (Riffel, Levin, & Young, 1996). Consider two aspects of this increasing diversity. Aboriginal populations in Canada are growing much more quickly than the population as a whole. The Aboriginal population is also considerably younger, on average, than the rest of the Canadian population. More than half of Canadian Aboriginals are under age 20, compared with about one-third of all Canadians. This means that an increasing proportion of students in Canadian schools, especially in western and northern Canada, will be Aboriginal, which will have important implications for curricula, teacher training and development, school governance, and a host of other aspects of schooling.

In addition, Canadian immigration patterns have changed. Two-thirds of Canadian immigrants in recent years have come from Asia, Africa, and South America rather than from Europe. Especially in large cities, classrooms are increasingly heterogeneous in their ethnic make-up, with more children from visible minorities. Teachers may have substantial numbers of students whose first language is not English, and whose culture, or whose parents' culture, is quite different from the dominant culture in Canada. Schools will face pressures to ensure that these students, like others, are receiving appropriate education from knowledgeable and concerned teachers. The challenge is more difficult because there are still relatively few Canadian teachers drawn from the ranks of ethnic minority groups (Thiessen, Bascia, & Goodson, 1996). Cultural differences also create new issues for schools in their dealings with parents and communities whose values may be quite different from those espoused by the school. Because ethnic communities tend to be concentrated in particular parts of a city, some schools and classes will need to be particularly sensitive to these issues. For example, Moslem or African-Canadian or Aboriginal parents may be interested in special programs, or religious services, or even separate schools for their children in order to support their sense of cultural identity. A number of projects of this sort are in place in various Canadian cities. The charged debate about funding of private schools is also partly related to issues of diversity as ethnic or religious groups look for schooling opportunities for their children.

Economic and Labour Force Changes

Criticism of schools and proposals for reform tend to follow broader economic cycles. When economic times are good, people tend to criticize the schools for being too conservative and restrictive. In the 1960s, at a time of prosperity, the call was for schools to become more open, liberal, and relevant. In the 1980s, with a less optimistic economic outlook, the demands on schools were largely reversed. The last few years in Canada have not been a period of economic optimism. There is much talk about global competitiveness, about the dangers to our standard of living, about the need to be tough to survive in the world, and about the finite nature of our natural resources. Thousands of jobs are lost, entire industries disappear, and people go through wrenching changes as part of what is called "global economic restructuring."

As noted earlier, much of the criticism of schools, not only in Canada but in many other countries, is related to fear that each country will suffer economically unless it can create and maintain very high education levels. Whether these fears are accurate is, however, debatable.

The Canadian economy has changed greatly in the past 30 years, although generally these changes have occurred rather slowly. Over the long term, though, the changes are very significant. For much of its history, Canada was an agricultural nation. In 1911, agriculture accounted for 35 percent of employment in Canada, but by 1981 it provided only 5 percent of the jobs. Manufacturing, which grew significantly in the first half of this century, has also been declining in relative importance as services (e.g., banking, transportation, personal and public services) have grown. These trends have important implications for education.

The economic assumptions of the critics, however, are often simplistic (Levin, 1995b). One assumption is that increasing the education level of the population will result in economic growth. But the Canadian population is vastly more educated today than it was 30 years ago, and has more schooling per capita than most other countries, and yet our economic situation does not appear to have improved by any commensurate amount. Education is an important element in a country's economic development, but it is only one element. The economy must also be able to provide jobs for educated people. For fifteen years, Canada has had relatively high levels of unemployment, especially among young people, including those with a good education. For example, in 1991, 19 percent of 1986 postsecondary trade and vocational graduates and 7 percent of 1986 university undergaduate degree recipients were unemployed. About 40 percent of the 1986 college and university graduates in all fields rated themselves as underemployed in 1991 (Barr-Telford, Bowlby, & Clark, 1996). In some areas, demand has exceeded the supply of people with appropriate training, but in other areas—including law, medicine, and, at times, engineering, nursing, and teaching—the supply has exceeded the demand, leaving highly educated people unemployed or underemployed, and prompting some of them to emigrate.

In some areas, employing highly educated people may be associated with a loss of jobs as these people find ways to replace labour with technology. Employment in agriculture is a good example. More educated farmers may use more machinery and hire fewer workers. In industry, too, jobs are being replaced by machinery. Canada has always exported considerable numbers of highly educated people because there are no jobs for them here, or because they can earn more elsewhere. Moreover, the long-term level of unemployment in Canada has been rising over the past four decades. In the 1950s, unemployment rates averaged just over 4 percent; in the 1980s, they averaged 10 percent and remained high in the 1990s.

Another frequently cited trend is that all jobs will require a high level of education and that there will be no work for the high-school drop-out. The need to have workers who can operate advanced equipment is often mentioned as one of the forces behind the demand for higher skills. However, analysts are divided on this matter. While some believe that overall skill requirements in the economy are increasing, others believe that the labour market is being divided into two segments. One sector is characterized by stable, high-paying jobs that require advanced levels of education; a second, larger sector is characterized by boring or dangerous work, poor pay, and very limited benefits for a large segment of the population.

The fact that the equipment found in this second sector is sophisticated does not mean that the operator is highly paid to use it. The retraining of secretaries in the use of computer equipment and the greater automation used in retail sales and restaurants are two situations in which automation has not led to higher pay or more independence at work. Many of the new jobs created in Canada in recent years have been low-skill, low-paying, part-time jobs with few or no benefits, and women are most likely to hold such jobs. When analyzing changes in jobs, it is vital to move past glib generalizations about, say, service jobs versus manufacturing jobs, and to consider how specific occupations and industries are changing (Osberg, Wien, & Grude, 1995).

Direct job skills are not the entire picture. Schools are also frequently told by employers that students need to learn to be punctual, polite, independent, and reliable. Indeed, schools justify some of their discipline practices by referring to labour force demands. But jobs are changing in other ways as well. For example, a large number of jobs involve working in teams or working co-operatively with others. As the demand for workers with these abilities increases, schools may need to pay more attention to developing related skills. The Conference Board of Canada has developed an "employability skills profile" that focuses on three key areas: academic skills (communicating, thinking, learning); personal management skills (positive attitudes and behaviour, responsibility, adaptability); and teamwork skills (work with others) (Conference Board of Canada, 1992). This list is quite different from the standard high-school curriculum.

Two other labour market issues are worth noting. First, it is very difficult to predict labour force requirements more than a few years in advance. The market for jobs is itself affected by many developments, including the overall state of the economy; changes in technology; changes in the economies of other countries; changes in prices of commodities such as grain, oil, or lumber; and political developments such as trade agreements or wars. Canada, like other countries, has a history of labour market forecasts that turned out to be wrong; indeed, forecasts that assume that present trends will continue indefinitely are almost certainly wrong.

Second, the Canadian economy, and hence the labour market, is highly regional. The economy can be booming in British Columbia and slumping in Nova Scotia at the same time. Aboriginal communities have remained economically depressed through all the ups and downs of the southern economy. The requirements for skilled workers and the overall availability of jobs can be quite different from one region to another, with obviously different implications for schools.

Although preparation for work is by no means the only task of schools, it is certainly a major expectation, and one that is held strongly by students. Schools have long been criticized for failing to pay enough attention to the large proportion of students who do not proceed to postsecondary education. Current knowledge about the economy does not clarify how schools can best discharge this responsibility. Should schools put more emphasis on preparing for work through vocational programs or co-op education? Or is this the responsibility of employers? Is the best strategy to provide an overall grounding in many areas, without much specialization in any, in the belief that this will give students the most flexibility? The answers are not obvious. Many analysts believe that most skills, general and specific, are acquired either formally or informally on the job rather than in schools. This suggests that education has its impact, if any, in helping people get a job, rather than in helping them do the job once obtained. Or perhaps formal education helps people learn on the job, suggesting an emphasis on "learning to learn" rather than on particular skills.

Poverty

One of the most powerful, yet often neglected, influences on schooling is poverty. Family income is a very strong predictor of how well children will do in school. A great deal of research shows that poverty is related to lower achievement in school, to a greater risk of dropping out, and to lower eventual occupational status and income. Completing high-school and going on to postsecondary education in Canada are highly related to the education and income of parents; the higher one's parents' income, the more likely one is to finish high school and attend university. These relationships are at least as strong as the relationship between measured ability and achievement. Indeed, given the very clear link between poverty and later social costs and problems, and given the considerable documentation on poverty in Canada, it is remarkable that so little policy attention in education has been given to the issue (Levin, 1995b).

Poverty has always been an issue in Canada, as the data on family incomes provided in Chapters Five and Seven illustrate. Over the past decade, the proportion of Canadian children under 16 who live in low-income families has fluctuated between 15 percent and 20 percent, making a total of more than 1.1 million children in such situations (Ross, Scott, & Kelly, 1996a). The proportions are substantially higher in some provinces, notably Newfoundland, Saskatchewan, and Manitoba. Even during the good economic years of the mid-1980s, poverty remained a reality for many Canadians. Increasing child poverty is also related to marriage breakdown. As noted earlier, women are being required to carry more of the financial responsibility for children while still facing major inequities in pay and work benefits, frequent difficulty in getting fathers to provide child support, and a shortage of quality, affordable day care. Increasing child poverty is also related to higher levels of unemployment, and the decline in the availability and value of social supports such as employment insurance and social allowances. However, being prepared to work hard by no means guarantees a reasonable income. Many low-income families do have two working parents. In Aboriginal communities, poverty has been prevalent since treaties were signed and reserves created; it is no accident that Aboriginal communities, with the highest poverty levels in Canada, also have disproportionately high levels of suicide and disease.

Poverty creates many problems for schools. As discussed in Chapter Seven, students may come to school with fewer of the skills that the school expects. Students may be preoccupied with physical and emotional needs, making it more difficult for them to concentrate on academic tasks. It may, as well, be harder for students to see the relevance of schooling in their lives when they live with so much hardship and success seems such a distant possibility.

There is a danger of schools using poverty as a rationalization for their own failure to help students. Educators and policy-makers may assume that students from poor families cannot learn; failure thus becomes both expected and accepted. However, this is clearly a false and insidious presumption, and one that perpetuates inequality. Because poverty tends to be concentrated geographically, some schools have large numbers of students from low-income families while others have few or none; this increases the danger that some schools will become places of failure, while others will generally be places of success. There is convincing evidence that education programs that address problems of poverty can result in dramatically increased success rates for students (see, for example, Slavin et al., 1994; Means & Knapp, 1991). In particular, success has come from efforts such as preschool programs that help parents provide educational support to their children, and school programs that stress high expectations while providing high levels of support.

Technology and Schools

Changes in technology are among the most apparent in Canadian society. When one compares our world today with the world of 50 years ago, the first differences that typically spring to mind are technological — cars, airplanes, video, computers, and so on. The technology used in education, and therefore of most relevance to schools, has also changed dramatically. When public schools first began, print was the only information technology available. Teachers either spoke to students or the students read. Today the situation is very different. Video, whether broadcast by television, videotapes, satellites, or other means, has had a tremendous impact on the way in which people obtain information. Video differs greatly from text: it is regarded as more emotional, more wide-ranging, less subtle, and more immediate in its impact. Students are, of course, intimately acquainted with video by the time they reach school.

Computerization is the second major technological development that has enormous implications for education. Computers not only provide vastly increased access to information, they also have the capacity to change the way in which people handle and store information. To mention just a few examples, they allow people to communicate almost instantly with other people almost anywhere in the world, at a fraction of the cost of telephones. They allow individuals ready access, from almost anywhere, to vast amounts of information. They provide the means for individuals to rearrange information to suit their needs, and to store it for ready retrieval. Like video, computers have the capacity to allow much more individualized learning, and much more learning at locations other than a school.

Both video and computers have the potential to be widely used in education. In theory, very high-quality programming could be produced and made widely available to students on video, or by computer, or both. Students could then use or watch the material at their own pace, as many times as they wished, whenever (and almost wherever) they wished. Some of the organizational constraints in schools, discussed in earlier chapters, could be overcome in this way. Both technologies are widely used for training and education purposes in many workplaces. Yet neither technology has been used very extensively in schools (Riffel & Levin, 1997). Postsecondary institutions do make use of video for long-distance education purposes, but video continues to play a small role in schools and is typically being used for purposes supplementary to traditional instruction. Computers, on the other hand, have become a much more significant part of schools than video. Every school now has at least some computers, and most Canadian students have the opportunity to work with computers from primary grades onward. Some curriculum materials have been made available for the computer, although the quality of the materials is quite uneven. Again, though, computers are typically used to supplement or enrich instruction rather than as an alternative form of instruction.

The original rationale for bringing computers into schools had to do with preparing students to deal with computers in the workplace. However, schools historically have not played a major role in preparing the public to understand technology. The major technologies of today, such as electricity, automobiles, and digital electronics, or, for that matter, video technology, are widely used by people who know very little about how they work and who did not learn about them in school. Indeed, schools have traditionally been highly sceptical of technological change. For many years after the development of the ballpoint pen, for instance, schoolchildren were still required to learn to write with fountain pens. Schools also had a difficult time deciding what to do about pocket calculators.

Although there are some interesting experiments underway in schools all across the country, it seems unlikely that schools, as they are now constituted, will play a leading role in the technological development of society. Whether changing technology will play a major role in education remains to be seen.

Values and Ideology

Because we project onto schools our hopes for society generally, views and criticisms of schools are heavily influenced by the prevailing climate of opinion in a society. Changes in this climate have had important implications for schools. For example, earlier in this chapter it was noted that ideas about school reform tend to follow economic cycles. In the 1960s, the economy was buoyant and proposals for schools stressed greater openness, freedom, and liberalization. As economic conditions have worsened over the past fifteen years, more conservative ideas about schooling have come to the fore.

Thinking about education is significantly affected by other economic and social developments. One example of such a change is the emerging conception of rights in Canada. The whole idea of individual rights is a relatively new one, going back only two or three centuries. It is an idea that has had important effects on schools, whether through the *Charter of Rights and Freedoms*, through the development of individual protections in collective bargaining agreements, or through a general shift in people's view of what they are entitled to. Recent constitutional debates in Canada have also brought to the forefront the issue of collective rights, which are claimed in Canada particularly by francophones, ethnic groups, and Aboriginal peoples. Some of the most heated debates in education in Canada in recent years have been around how to accommodate group entitlements, whether of the groups mentioned in the *Charter* or others.

Another shift in thinking that has been important for schools has been the change in the common conception of government. After World War II, and well into the 1960s, government was seen by many people as a good way to address social problems. The extension of education, and the development of pensions, family allowances, employment insurance, and medicare are all examples of Canadian governments acting to try to solve, or at least ameliorate, severe social problems.

In the last fifteen years in Canada, as in other countries, faith in government has declined significantly. So, it might be added, has public faith in most other institutions, including churches, business, and the professions. Figure 10.1, drawn from a series of Canadian public-opinion polls, shows the relative change in public trust in various Canadian sectors from 1980 to 1988. Schools still enjoy more public confidence than many other institutions.

There is, however, less public confidence today that major social problems can be solved by governments. Beginning in the late 1970s, claims were made that the free market was the best vehicle for addressing social problems. However, we have seen that the market has its own problems and limits, and is, like government, a very imperfect vehicle. Moreover, Canadian political traditions have always been more communitarian than those of the United States. This means that Canadians have tended to place more reliance on group or societal efforts, and somewhat less on the efforts of individuals.

The tendency to label all social developments as "problems" should perhaps be resisted. Changes can have positive impacts as well as negative ones, and it may take many years before a good picture emerges of the overall effect of a major economic or social change. Perhaps increasing public concern about the answers being suggested by large institutions is a good development that will cause people to think more about and take more interest in public policy decisions. Surely one of the outcomes of education ought to be to make people more inclined and better able to form their own opinions on important issues. The increased emphasis on both individual and collective rights, and on arguing against policies that are seen as harmful, could be regarded as an indicator of the success of past schooling, even though it may create problems for the schools of today.

Nonetheless, there is clearly less public confidence in pronouncements about government policies being able to solve educational problems, which means that schools will have a harder time maintaining public trust in their quality and integrity. Public willingness to take major steps in remedying social problems is also reduced to the extent that people no longer believe that such action will be effective.

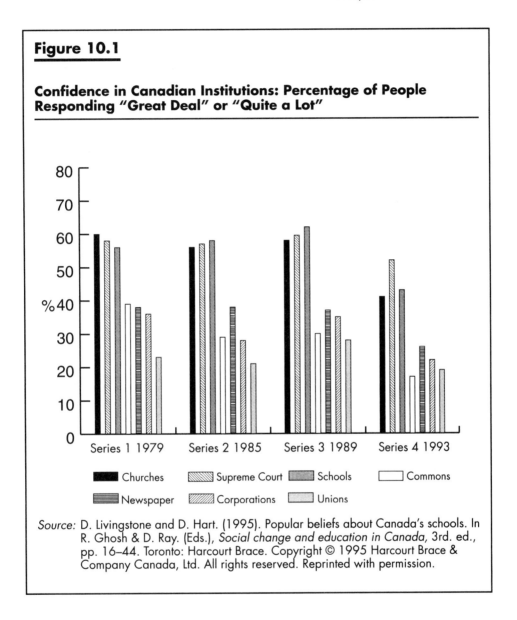

Figure 10.1

Confidence in Canadian Institutions: Percentage of People Responding "Great Deal" or "Quite a Lot"

Source: D. Livingstone and D. Hart. (1995). Popular beliefs about Canada's schools. In R. Ghosh & D. Ray. (Eds.), *Social change and education in Canada,* 3rd. ed., pp. 16–44. Toronto: Harcourt Brace. Copyright © 1995 Harcourt Brace & Company Canada, Ltd. All rights reserved. Reprinted with permission.

It is important to point out that public views about these broad issues do not simply arise spontaneously. Nowhere is the unequal distribution of power in society more evident than in the way in which ideas are handled. Almost all the major sources of news about public affairs — television, radio, newspapers, and magazines—are in private hands. Most of the organizations with the resources to mount extensive public-relations efforts are also in the private sector. There are far fewer important sources of public information that have as their wellspring a public agenda. The political agendas of those with wealth, then, are much more likely to be publicized broadly than are the political agendas of the poor and the dispossessed. Critics of the inequalities in Canadian society believe that the mood of disenchantment with government and institutions has served the interests of the wealthy and the powerful much more than it has served the poor.

System Complexity

To conclude this discussion of some of the many changes affecting schooling, it is important to point out that the changes are themselves interrelated. For analytic purposes, it is helpful to separate economic change from demographic change or political change. In reality, change in one sphere reverberates through all other spheres. Changing employment patterns affect incomes and family living arrangements, which in turn affect children's school experience, which affects the economy, and so on. The relationships are intricate and immensely complicated. As well, the major institutions of society are linked in many ways. Schools are affected by a whole array of decisions made by governments (at all levels), health-care organizations, social services, employers, labour unions, and numerous other groups. These relationships go beyond a school district or province, or even the country as a whole. Changes in political and economic circumstances in other countries may have important implications for Canadian society as well as for Canadian schools. Education is part of what might be called a worldwide ecology.

   Schools alone have not and will not be able to solve economic or social problems. Nonetheless, public schools are important institutions whose goals require them to be involved in the development of Canada as a whole. While schools may not be able to solve social problems, it is equally clear that they cannot ignore them, for students bring these issues into school. The pressures of changing demographics, changing economics, and changing values face every teacher and every school on a daily basis. In the past few years, educators have become increasingly aware of, and concerned about, the pressures being placed on schools by broader changes in Canadian society, such as those discussed in this chapter. In response, teachers and administrators see their ability to do their job being diminished by factors over which they feel they have little or no control. Current worries about violence in schools are an example of how wider social issues affect schools.

Proposed Reforms to Canadian Schooling

Given the diversity, complexity, and sometimes inconsistency of the social forces affecting schools, it is no surprise to learn that agendas for improving schools are also quite diverse. For example, an increasing literature in education policy and research argues that the improvement of schooling depends on increasing autonomy and professionalism (in the larger sense developed in Chapter Eight) of teachers. Schools and school districts interested in this approach have adopted practices such as school-based management, teaching portfolios, teacher-led action research, stronger teacher networks and increased collaboration both within and among schools, less hierarchical forms of school organization, and so on.

Another strong reform movement has been centred on helping schools cope with the increased diversity among students and families. Such ideas as inclusive education, multicultural education, and antiracist education, as well as the move to strengthen ties between schools and families, are expressions of the belief that schools can take steps to meet the needs of a wider range of students.

A third approach that has had some currency recently borrows from the private-sector focus on quality improvement. A number of schools and school systems have tried to apply principles of quality improvement to their work (Morgan & Murgatroyd, 1994). Though schooling is different in some very significant ways from private enterprises, as we have argued elsewhere in this book, the idea of paying ongoing attention to issues of quality could be a useful part of school reform.

Other examples could be cited, including advocacy for much greater emphasis on technology, a stronger emphasis on preparation for work, a movement to integrate schooling and social services (Mawhinney, 1993), or a belief that schools must be organized around more homogeneous religious, cultural, or ethnic communities.

The kinds of reforms being implemented by Canadian provincial governments, however, tend to focus on a few common elements related to curriculum, assessment, and governance. Many provinces have tightened curriculum requirements by, for example, increasing the emphasis given in elementary schools to reading, mathematics, and science, or increasing the graduation requirements in secondary schools. Accompanying stricter curriculum requirements has been a considerable expansion of provincial testing of students. Most provinces now have a program that tests all students at several grade levels. These testing programs are controversial, as noted in Chapter Nine; particularly contentious is the extent to which the results of testing are made public. Some see publication of school-by-school test results as giving parents more information to judge the quality of schools, while others worry that these results will be misleading and will penalize schools that are working in high-poverty communities.

Another general movement has been to reduce the numbers and powers of school districts. New Brunswick has abolished its school districts altogether, and several other provinces have reduced significantly the number of districts, apparently as a cost-saving measure. Even in provinces where districts have not been changed, provincial governments have been legislating greater powers for ministers and departments of education. For example, 1996 legislation in Manitoba gives the Minister of Education the authority to prescribe methods of instruction and student evaluation to be used by teachers.

Provincial governments in Canada appear to have been ambivalent about the role of parents. On the one hand, steps have been taken in most provinces to give parents a greater role in schooling. Most provinces have legislated some form of parent participation in local school councils, and several provinces now allow parents to choose the school their children will attend, even across district boundaries. Alberta has been the first Canadian jurisdiction to experiment with charter schools, which allow a group of parents or teachers to create their own school with a particular focus or emphasis that would then be directly funded by government and exempted from many of the regulations governing other schools. All these steps seem to imply a belief that parents should take over some of the responsibilities that have in recent years been held by professionals in schools. Other provincial moves, however, have tended to be in the opposite direction. As noted in Chapter Two, the legislation creating parents' councils almost always makes these bodies advisory only, without any real authority. And the increased authority being given to education ministers and provincial departments, coupled with more prescriptive curriculum and testing, seems to be in contradiction with a desire to empower parents and local schools.

Canada in Comparison with Other Countries

Although many educators feel that Canadian schools have been subject to a great deal of imposed change in recent years, in comparison with other countries the pace of change in Canada generally appears moderate. For example, the British government has made a dramatic series of changes in education in England and Wales, including giving much more power to school governing bodies (which include parents and community representatives), allowing individual schools to opt out of their school districts and be funded directly by the national government, instituting a national curriculum and testing program, publishing the academic results of individual schools, having compulsory external inspections of every school every few years, and giving parents the right to send their children to any school in the country (subject to the school's ability and willingness to accept them). New Zealand abolished its school districts and most of its national Department of Education and required each school, through a representative governing body, to draw up a school charter specifying goals and strategies. It has also implemented a program of parent choice of schools. Some states in the United States have adopted equally dramatic reforms, such as Kentucky, South Carolina, and Minnesota. The city of Chicago is another well-publicized example, in which local school councils, with a majority of parents, hire and fire school principals.

These reforms have embodied some of the same themes—more assessment, more parent control—and some of the same contradictions—between decentralization of some decisions from schoolboards to schools and greater centralization in other areas by governments—as are found in Canada. Other countries, however, such as France, Spain, and Sweden, have adopted quite different strategies, focussing on enhancing the professional status and training of teachers, and looking much more at improving education through altering instructional practices as well as relations among schools, parents, and communities (Kallen, 1996).

Several reasons can be suggested for Canada's relatively modest approach to change. Because of provincial control over education and the lack of a strong national presence, reforms occur province by province, and provinces tend not to want to be too different from one another in their basic approach to education. Canada also lacks a well-developed national infrastructure for spreading ideas about education, so that people in one province tend not to learn much from the experience of other provinces. Canadian preoccupation with constitutional, linguistic, and religious issues in education has sometimes diverted attention from other aspects of education policy. Another factor is the decentralized Canadian system in which school districts largely control implementation of provincial policy, and stakeholder groups such as teachers and school board associations have tended to be quite powerful. Perhaps most importantly, public-opinion data shows that Canadians continue to be reasonably content with their schools and less inclined than people in some other countries to believe that social problems are amenable to ready solution through new policies. In the United States, Plank and Boyd describe the mood as one of "antipolitics":

> The two most striking features of American school politics in the past decade have been an obsessive concern with the multiple "failures" of the educational system and a propensity to embark on a flight from democracy in the search for solutions. The consequence has been the growth of an *antipolitics* of education, in which disagreements about educational policy and practice are increasingly likely to be addressed in conflict over the institutions of educational governance rather than in open debate on the merits of alternative goals and strategies ... in the hope that new institutions will place braver, wiser, and nobler persons in charge of children's schooling" (1994, pp. 264–65).

Though some of this feeling also exists in Canada, so far Canadians have been less willing to abandon institutions and policies that are seen to have served us well, whether these are related to education or to other areas such as health care.

The Challenges of Improving Schools

Like most institutions, schools are better at maintaining the status quo than they are at making major changes. The tendency of any institution is to focus inwardly on its own operations, and to try to manage the outside world in a way that causes as little disruption as possible to business as usual. Although schools have been subject to all the criticisms and reform proposals already mentioned, many observers suggest that the major elements of schools have hardly changed at all. There are still groups of students who are organized by age and ability under the supervision of a teacher, who study a formal curriculum, and who are evaluated at the end of the year. In this sense, all the talk of reform seems to have made little difference (Cuban, 1990).

There are several reasons why this is so. The first is that many reform proposals may be mandated without enough thought given to whether they will work in practice (Sale & Levin, 1991). When these ideas collide with the everyday reality of classrooms and teacher–student/school–parent relationships, they turn out to be unworkable or not worth the trouble. Twenty years ago, schools experimented with what were called open-area schools, buildings in which most of the walls were removed, and students and teachers were asked to function in large groups. After a few years, the walls were reinstalled in most of these buildings. This was not because open area failed as a concept; the evidence suggests that open-area schools were about as successful as other schools (Walberg, 1990). Rather, open area embodied a particular view of learning that required major changes in teaching practice, and in teacher–teacher and teacher–student relationships. These changes needed a very large amount of time and energy to be implemented effectively. Moreover, the new settings made many parents uncomfortable. In the end, too many people felt that the change wasn't worth the trouble.

A second problem with changing schools is that people do not agree on what schools are for. Any particular change presupposes a certain view of the purpose and role of schools. Those who see schooling as being primarily about developing individuality may favour reforms that broaden students' choice, give more emphasis to issues of daily living, and so on. Those who regard schools as training grounds for the job market may want tighter discipline and more emphasis on mathematics, science, and work skills. Those who see schools as professional organizations may propose giving more authority to teachers, while those who value standardization and control may want provincial examinations instead. Since the formulation of school policy is largely a political matter, at any given time several of these agendas are likely to clash. Thus, schools are often asked to do things that are mutually incompatible. It is difficult for any organization to move decisively in two directions at the same time. No one should be surprised, then, to find that many changes in schools do not take root.

Finally, it is important to recognize that there are many things that we simply don't know how to do. If there were a straightforward way to teach every 6-year-old to read, schools would use it; but there isn't, at least as far as we know. Reading experts disagree, quite vehemently, about how reading should best be taught. What, then, are schools to do? The same is true of many of the other problems that face schools. There is no clear way to teach effectively in a classroom with 25 very different students; to provide challenging instruction for students who have different interests, motives, and needs; or to overcome the impact of poverty and violence that many children bring with them to school every day.

Some wag once said that "to every complex problem there is a simple, straightforward solution—and it's wrong." It would be comforting to think that the problems of schools could be solved simply through some change in school policy or teaching practice, but the world is not like that. We may hear a proposal about an educational reform, find it appealing, and think that it would really work. But in practice it turns out that the problems are multiple, complex, and interrelated, and that the solutions are more difficult to implement and less effective in practice than they seemed when first described.

Changing Thinking about Improving Schools

Thinking about school change and improvement has itself changed considerably over the last 30 years. In the 1960s and early 1970s, educators were startled by a series of studies that appeared to show that the inputs to schooling—numbers and qualifications of teachers, amount of money spent, class size, number of library books—were related only very weakly, if at all, to measurable school outcomes. Students' backgrounds, and especially the social and economic status of their families, seemed far more powerful than anything schools were able to do.

The reaction to this depressing view took the form of the **effective schools** movement. Researchers studied schools that seemed to produce better than expected results given the kinds of students enrolled. The intent was to examine variables that educators could influence rather than assuming that results were determined by the characteristics of students. A number of studies in the United States and England concluded that more effective schools did have certain definite characteristics, such as clear instructional goals, high expectations for what students could learn, a supportive climate, high levels of parental involvement, and strong leadership. Although the effective schools literature had its critics, it did help restore some faith among educators that schools could make a difference.

Over the last ten years, the research on school improvement has moved in several important directions. One body of work has continued to use large bodies of data to explore the factors that seem correlated with better student outcomes. A number of major studies have shown how complex the factors shaping school outcomes actually are.

A second strand of work has focussed on **school improvement**—on looking at the processes through which schools work to improve students' outcomes. Here, attention has been concentrated on how schools can improve themselves. This research has drawn attention to a number of factors, such as high-quality professional development for teachers, creating time and opportunity for teachers to try out new strategies, using research and data to learn about what works and what does not, and generally building a climate in schools that is supportive of change and of learning. The research on school improvement has also shown that the process of improvement takes a considerable amount of time, looks different in each school, and requires ongoing attention and support.

Emerging from the school improvement literature have been a number of large-scale projects that look at creating and sustaining school improvement in a large number of schools over a period of several years. In the United States these have included James Comer's School Development Project, Robert Slavin's Success for All, Henry Levin's Accelerated Schools, and a variety of other projects, largely funded by philanthropic foundations. In England the Improving the Quality of Education for All (IQEA) project had a similar focus, but was funded by participating schools. In Canada, consortia of schools and universities have worked on school improvement projects in Ontario and British Columbia, and in Manitoba the Walter and Duncan Gordon Charitable Foundation has funded a multi-year project to support lasting improvements in secondary schools.

The results of these studies and projects are sobering and heartening at the same time. They are sobering in that it is clear that there is no simple recipe for school improvement, and that change takes energy, commitment, and resources sustained over years. Because many partners, including students and parents as well as teachers, must be involved for change to be effective and lasting, the process of change is daunting. At the same time, the research gives ground for optimism that students' learning can indeed be improved, and that even in highly impoverished areas schools can help students succeed.

What Might We Do?

Some readers might find the analysis of schooling in this chapter depressing. Schools face important challenges in the form of social change, yet our experience indicates that creating meaningful and lasting improvement is quite difficult to do. To say that things are difficult and that we are not sure what to do, however, does not mean we should do nothing. In this final section of the book we suggest some strategies that educators and those interested in education might use to create a climate for the thoughtful improvement of schools. Because educators need to explain themselves, not just assert their opinions, they themselves need to put more care into their thinking—they need a more clearly articulated world view, better arguments, more evidence, and, most importantly, the disposition to change when they encounter persuasive views that are contrary to their own. And because of the growing pluralization of views, it is less likely that a single conception of education could be effective, let alone be imposed on everyone. While unsettling, the situation does suggest greater need and provides increased scope for the educational imagination.

Responding to change is an educational task in which educators and schools need to do the same things we say we want to do with students—define and debate problems, analyze data, develop and test strategies, and learn from our experience. True, there is no formal curriculum and no set of correct answers to be found in the back of the book. We will have to discover answers as we proceed, and to discard what does not seem to serve our purposes. But surely this is what real learning is about, and we should be excited by the opportunity to organize schooling in a manner that actually embodies the values we profess as educators. The absence of a single view of desirable change can be seen as an advantage that allows more options and possibilities. We need not wait to know the right way before we begin a journey.

What does this mean in specific terms? The four elements mentioned in the previous paragraph provide a set of possibilities:

Defining problems suggests that educators and their communities—parents, students, and the public generally—need more opportunities to talk about educational issues. Schools tend to shy away from conflict about ideas, yet different points of view provide the opportunity for everyone to learn. It is important to understand how students and parents think about schools and what their values, hopes, and aspirations are, and to compare those with the goals of staff. Disagreements and uncertainties can be explored so that everyone can understand one another's concerns.

It is also important to be able to talk more openly about issues we do not understand or do not know how to address. Educators, like other professionals, often feel that it is important to maintain an air of knowledge and certainty at all times. But this attitude may preclude the kind of open dialogue that today seems more important than ever. What does it mean to have truly public schools in the current era? How can we provide education that values both diversity and equity? We can only improve our ability to address these questions by debating them openly and accepting that our current knowledge and practices can benefit from thoughtful and sympathetic scrutiny. It is especially important to include in discussion those who may tend not to participate, or who may feel least able to contribute. The problems and challenges facing schools are different today; there is nothing wrong with admitting that we do not know how to address some of them. Admitting what we don't know is a critical step toward learning.

Analyzing data provides a way of testing our beliefs and assumptions. Much of the debate about education has proceeded in the absence of good evidence. Yet real learning must involve careful consideration of what is known. Schools can benefit from gathering and analyzing more information about their social context: Who are our students and their families? What is the social and economic structure of the community? What kinds of work do people do? What do they see as critical problems and important opportunities? In many of these areas, data already exist through sources such as Statistics Canada; in others, schools can gather data fairly readily through surveys of students and families (which might even be done by high-school students as assignments). These data provide additional opportunities to talk about important issues in the school and the community.

In Chapter One we suggested that schools all across Canada (and in many other countries) are very similar to one another. Given that we do not fully understand the changes taking place around us or their impact on us, experimentation seems an essential strategy, and this would seem to imply more diversity in the arrangements for schooling. It is vital to *develop and test strategies* for improved schooling. Learning occurs when people try a variety of different things to see how they work. Yet policies of conscious and deliberate experimentation organized to promote learning about education are rare. Much more frequent is the belief that a solution has been found and that the only need is to make everyone conform to it. The imposition of dogma—no matter whose dogma it is—inevitably leads away from learning, not toward it.

At the same time, experimentation is not very useful unless we *learn from our experience*. Schools have been, as noted earlier in this chapter, subject to many experiments. We have not, however, typically seen these as opportunities to learn. Instead, each new strategy has been treated as the answer—something to be done, not something to be learned from. Consistent and systematic use of research as a strategy for learning about what works in education is quite rare. A recent study by the OECD (Guthrie, 1996) concludes that

> virtually no central government has undertaken a serious effort to improve the effectiveness of its education system, at any level, through substantial investments in educational research or development of educational technology (p. 67).

Research is not only a matter for governments, however. Every teacher and every school can ask questions and collect data about the effects of different policies and practices. Limits of time mean that not everything a teacher or school does can be studied carefully, but schooling might very well benefit from a greater propensity to ask whether what we are doing is working and whether something else might work even better.

Schools can also benefit from looking at the research discussed on page 301. More is being learned all the time about effective teaching and learning practices, and about how to bring these into play in schools. Canadians such as Michael Fullan, Andy Hargreaves, and Ken Leithwood have been at the forefront of this research. The World Wide Web also provides ready access to a large number of school improvement projects all across the world, making it much easier than in the past to learn from what others have done.

Conclusion

The problems of maintaining a high-quality school system in a diverse, pluralistic, changing society are far from simple! Change affects schools in important ways that we may not understand very well. People have quite different views about how schools should be organized and operated. Governments are pushing change in particular directions without necessarily having a good understanding of what the results will be. Many teachers are feeling overwhelmed by all the changes that seem to be pressing on them, yet making lasting improvements in a well-established organization can be very difficult even when people agree on what the changes should be. All of this creates some dangers, for when people allow themselves to become preoccupied with unwanted changes, they lose the connection between themselves and the external world. People who are afraid of change also anticipate more and more threatening upheavals, condemning it in advance and, in a curious way, preparing themselves for the worst.

Seen from another perspective, however, this is a particularly exciting time to be involved in education. Teaching must be an optimistic endeavour. The whole idea of education rests on the possibility of betterment—on our belief that we can help the next generation create a better world. Could we ask for a more important and more exciting challenge? When people are questioning things, when long-established practices are open to scrutiny, when there is an acceptance that at least some things will need to be done differently, then there are also great opportunities for people with ideals and initiative. We have the opportunity to put our values into action in the service of education. Teachers, parents, and all those interested in schools can focus on the positive potential — the ability of people when motivated and supported to find ways of being in the world that are more conducive to creating and sustaining the kind of schools, and the kind of society, that most of us want.

Exercises

1. As a class exercise, brainstorm a list of all the forces outside the schools that are having an impact on what schools do. Organize your list in order of descending importance, and give reasons for your ranking.

2. Find a recent newspaper article that is critical of schools or proposes changes in schools. What assumptions underlie the article? How well supported are the proposals by evidence or argument? What alternatives might exist for dealing with the same issue?

3. Review one of the recent national or provincial reports on education. What are its main findings and recommendations? How do you rate the report's cogency and quality?

4. Review a few issues of a popular journal from the early 1970s (e.g., *Educational Leadership* or *Phi Delta Kappan*). What were the key issues at that time? Are they still current? If not, why not?

5. Interview an experienced teacher about the changes in policy and practice he or she has seen over the years. Which changes have had a lasting impact, and why? Which have disappeared with little trace, and why?

6. Obtain Statistics Canada demographic data on your province or school district. What are the key demographic features of the jurisdiction? How have these changed over the past ten or twenty years? What impact have these changes had on schools?

7. Interview a teacher or principal in a school that has a high proportion of recent immigrants or low-income families. What issues does the school have to consider as a result of these demographic factors? What steps do schools take to try to cope with these problems?

8. Obtain labour market data for your city or province. What occupations are most common, and how does this compare with Canada as a whole? What are the implications of these data for schools in your area?

9. Interview one or two teachers about the use of technology in schools. What do they see as the potential of computers and video for education? What do they see as the limitations of these technologies? Do you agree? Why or why not?

10. Talk with members of a school staff or parents to learn what mechanisms their school uses to raise and debate educational issues in the school and with the community. Is there an active process of studying and learning about emerging issues and problems? Why or why not?

11. Investigate the role that education research plays in affecting school policy and practice. Should the role of research in education be strengthened? If so, how might this occur?

Further Reading

For further information on emerging issues, readers should go beyond the literature in education to read material in other relevant fields, such as economic policy and social policy. Major Canadian organizations working in these areas, such as the Canadian Council on Social Development, the Canadian Labour Market Productivity Centre, and the Institute for Research on Public Policy, are good sources of material on the broad developments in Canadian society that have implications for schools. At the international level, reports on education issued by the Organization for Economic Cooperation and Development (OECD) often provide excellent overviews of emerging issues. Levin and Riffel (1997) offer a view of how schools understand and respond to change.

Popular news and business journals often carry material about education, but rarely with any depth of analysis. Better sources are some of the major practitioner journals in education, such as *Phi Delta Kappan, Educational Leadership*, and, in Canada, *The Canadian School Executive*. There is also a body of literature concerned with the future of education.

The literature on current and proposed reforms in education is enormous and quite international. Key writers on effective schools include Ronald Edmonds and Larry Lezotte in the United States. A highly influential British study is Rutter, Maugham, Mortimore, and Ouston's, *Fifteen Thousand Hours* (London: Open Books, 1979). Among Canadian authors, Michael Fullan, Andy Hargreaves, and Ken Leithwood offer insightful views on these issues. Many other writers in England, the United States, Australia, Europe, and elsewhere have also contributed important work on both school effectiveness and school improvement.

Information on the current status of reforms in Canada is best obtained through the various provincial governments (most of whom have World Wide Web sites), the Council of Ministers of Education, and the publications of the Canadian Education Association, as well as from the Web sites of many schools, districts, and reform projeccts. All of the major Canadian and international education journals carry articles about various aspects of education reform.

APPENDIX

Canadian Charter of Rights and Freedoms

Whereas Canada is founded upon principles that recognize the supremacy of God and the rule of law:

Guarantee of Rights and Freedoms

1. The *Canadian Charter of Rights and Freedoms* guarantees the rights and freedoms set out in it subject only to such reasonable limits prescribed by law as can be demonstrably justified in a free and democratic society.

Fundamental Freedoms

2. Everyone has the following fundamental freedoms:

> *(a)* freedom of conscience and religion;
> *(b)* freedom of thought, belief, opinion and expression, including freedom of the press and other media of communication;
> *(c)* freedom of peaceful assembly; and
> *(d)* freedom of association.

Democratic Rights

3. Every citizen of Canada has the right to vote in an election of members of the House of Commons or of a legislative assembly and to be qualified for membership therein.

4. (1) No House of Commons and no legislative assembly shall continue for longer than five years from the date fixed for the return of the writs at a general election of its members.

(2) In time of real or apprehended war, invasion or insurrection, a House of Commons may be continued by Parliament and a legislative assembly may be continued by the legislature beyond five years if such continuation is not opposed by the votes of more than one-third of the members of the House of Commons or the legislative assembly, as the case may be.

5. There shall be a sitting of Parliament and of each legislature at least once every twelve months.

Mobility Rights

6. (1) Every citizen of Canada has the right to enter, remain in and leave Canada.

(2) Every citizen of Canada and every person who has the status of a permanent resident of Canada has the right

> *(a)* to move to and take up residence in any province; and
> *(b)* to pursue the gaining of a livelihood in any province.

(3) The rights specified in subsection (2) are subject to

> *(a)* any laws or practices of general application in force in a province other than those that discriminate among persons primarily on the basis of province of present or previous residence; and
> *(b)* any laws providing for reasonable residency requirements as a qualification for the receipt of publicly provided social services.

(4) Subsections (2) and (3) do not preclude any law, program or activity that has as its object the amelioration in a province of conditions of individuals in that province who are socially or economically disadvantaged if the rate of employment in that province is below the rate of employment in Canada.

Legal Rights

7. Everyone has the right to life, liberty and security of the person and the right not to be deprived thereof except in accordance with the principles of fundamental justice.

8. Everyone has the right to be secure against unreasonable search or seizure.

9. Everyone has the right not to be arbitrarily detained or imprisoned.

10. Everyone has the right on arrest or detention

    (a) to be informed promptly of the reasons therefor;

    (b) to retain and instruct counsel without delay and to be informed of that right; and

    (c) to have the validity of the detention determined by way of *habeas corpus* and to be released if the detention is not lawful.

11. Any person charged with an offence has the right

    (a) to be informed without unreasonable delay of the specific offence;

    (b) to be tried within a reasonable time;

    (c) not to be compelled to be a witness in proceedings against that person in respect of the offence;

    (d) to be presumed innocent until proven guilty according to law in a fair and public hearing by an independent and impartial tribunal;

    (e) not to be denied reasonable bail without just cause;

    (f) except in the case of an offence under military law tried before a military tribunal, to the benefit of trial by jury where the maximum punishment for the offence is imprisonment for five years or a more severe punishment;

    (g) not to be found guilty on account of any act or omission unless, at the time of the act or omission, it constituted an offence under Canadian or international law or was criminal according to the general principles of law recognized by the community of nations;

    (h) if finally acquitted of the offence, not to be tried for it again and, if finally found guilty and punished for the offence, not to be tried or punished for it again; and

    (i) if found guilty of the offence and if the punishment for the offence has been varied between the time of commission and the time of sentencing, to the benefit of the lesser punishment.

12. Everyone has the right not to be subjected to any cruel and unusual treatment or punishment.

13. A witness who testifies in any proceedings has the right not to have any incriminating evidence so given used to incriminate that witness in any other proceedings, except in a prosecution for perjury or for the giving of contradictory evidence.

14. A party or witness in any proceedings who does not understand or speak the language in which the proceedings are conducted or who is deaf has the right to the assistance of an interpreter.

Equality Rights

15. (1) Every individual is equal before and under the law and has the right to the equal protection and equal benefit of the law without discrimination and, in particular, without discrimination based on race, national or ethnic origin, colour, religion, sex, age or mental or physical disability.

(2) Subsection (1) does not preclude any law, program or activity that has as its object the amelioration of conditions of disadvantaged individuals or groups including those that are disadvantaged because of race, national or ethnic origin, colour, religion, sex, age or mental or physical disability.

Official Languages of Canada

16. (1) English and French are the official languages of Canada and have equality of status and equal rights and privileges as to their use in all institutions of the Parliament and government of Canada.

(2) English and French are the official languages of New Brunswick and have equality of status and equal rights and privileges as to their use in all institutions of the legislature and government of New Brunswick.

(3) Nothing in this Charter limits the authority of Parliament or a legislature to advance the equality of status or use of English and French.

17. (1) Everyone has the right to use English or French in any debates and other proceedings of Parliament.

(2) Everyone has the right to use English or French in any debates and other proceedings of the legislature of New Brunswick.

18. (1) The statutes, records and journals of Parliament shall be printed and published in English and French and both language versions are equally authoritative.

(2) The statutes, records and journals of the legislature of New Brunswick shall be printed and published in English and French and both language versions are equally authoritative.

19. (1) Either English or French may be used by any person in, or in any pleading in or process issuing from, any court established by Parliament.

(2) Either English or French may be used by any person in, or in any pleading in or process issuing from, any court of New Brunswick.

20. (1) Any member of the public in Canada has the right to communicate with, and to receive available services from, any head or central office of an institution of the Parliament or government of Canada in English or French, and has the same right with respect to any other office of any such institution where

> (*a*) there is a significant demand for communications with and services from that office in such language; or
>
> (*b*) due to the nature of the office, it is reasonable that communications with and services from that office be available in both English and French.

(2) Any member of the public in New Brunswick has the right to communicate with, and to receive available services from, any office of an institution of the legislature or government of New Brunswick in English or French.

21. Nothing in sections 16 to 20 abrogates or derogates from any right, privilege or obligation with respect to the English and French languages, or either of them, that exists or is continued by virtue of any other provision of the Constitution of Canada.

22. Nothing in sections 16 to 20 abrogates or derogates from any legal or customary right or privilege acquired or enjoyed either before or after the coming into force of this Charter with respect to any language that is not English or French.

Minority Language Educational Rights

23. (1) Citizens of Canada

> (*a*) whose first language learned and still understood is that of the English or French linguistic minority population of the province in which they reside, or
>
> (*b*) who have received their primary school instruction in Canada in English or French and reside in a province where the

language in which they received that instruction is the language of the English or French linguistic minority population of the province,

have the right to have their children receive primary and secondary school instruction in that language in that province.

(2) Citizens of Canada of whom any child has received or is receiving primary or secondary school instruction in English or French in Canada, have the right to have all their children receive primary and secondary school instruction in the same language.

(3) The right of citizens of Canada under subsections (1) and (2) to have their children receive primary and secondary school instruction in the language of the English or French linguistic minority population of a province

> (*a*) applies wherever in the province the number of children of citizens who have such a right is sufficient to warrant the provision to them out of public funds of minority language instruction; and
>
> (*b*) includes, where the number of those children so warrants, the right to have them receive that instruction in minority language educational facilities provided out of public funds.

Enforcement

24. (1) Anyone whose rights or freedoms, as guaranteed by this Charter, have been infringed or denied may apply to a court of competent jurisdiction to obtain such remedy as the court considers appropriate and just in the circumstances.

(2) Where, in proceedings under subsection (1), a court concludes that evidence was obtained in a manner that infringed or denied any rights or freedoms guaranteed by this Charter, the evidence shall be excluded if it is established that, having regard to all the circumstances, the admission of it in the proceedings would bring the administration of justice into disrepute.

General

25. The guarantee in this Charter of certain rights and freedoms shall not be construed so as to abrogate or derogate from any aboriginal, treaty or other rights or freedoms that pertain to the aboriginal peoples of Canada including

> (*a*) any rights or freedoms that have been recognized by the Royal Proclamation of

October 7, 1763; and

(b) any rights or freedoms that may be acquired by the aboriginal peoples of Canada by way of land claims settlement.

26. The guarantee in this Charter of certain rights and freedoms shall not be construed as denying the existence of any other rights or freedoms that exist in Canada.

27. This Charter shall be interpreted in a manner consistent with the preservation and enhancement of the multicultural heritage of Canadians.

28. Notwithstanding anything in this Charter, the rights and freedoms referred to in it are guaranteed equally to male and female persons.

29. Nothing in this Charter abrogates or derogates from any rights or privileges guaranteed by or under the Constitution of Canada in respect of denominational, separate or dissentient schools.

30. A reference in this Charter to a province or to the legislative assembly or legislature of a province shall be deemed to include a reference to the Yukon Territory and the Northwest Territories, or to the appropriate legislative authority thereof, as the case may be.

31. Nothing in this Charter extends the legislative powers of any body or authority.

Application of Charter

32. (1) This Charter applies

(a) to the Parliament and government of Canada in respect of all matters within the authority of Parliament including all matters relating to the Yukon Territory and Northwest Territories; and

(b) to the legislature and government of each province in respect of all matters within the authority of the legislature of each province.

(2) Notwithstanding subsection (1), section 15 shall not have effect until three years after this section comes into force.

33. (1) Parliament or the legislature of a province may expressly declare in an Act of Parliament or of the legislature, as the case may be, that the Act or a provision thereof shall operate notwithstanding a provision included in section 2 or sections 7 to 15 of this Charter.

(2) An Act or a provision of an Act in respect of which a declaration made under this section is in effect shall have such operation as it would have but for the provision of this Charter referred to in the declaration.

(3) A declaration made under subsection (1) shall cease to have effect five years after it comes into force or on such earlier date as may be specified in the declaration.

(4) Parliament or a legislature of a province may re-enact a declaration made under subsection (1).

(5) Subsection (3) applies in respect of a re-enactment made under subsection (4).

Citation

34. This Part may be cited as the *Canadian Charter of Rights and Freedoms.*

REFERENCES

Abella, R. (1984). *Report of the commission on equality of employment.* Ottawa: Minister of Supply and Services.

Acker, S. (1994). *Gendered education.* Buckingham, UK: Open University Press.

Anderson, J. (1918). *The education of the new Canadian. A treatise on Canada's greatest education problem.* Toronto: J.M. Dent.

Anderson, J. (1986, October). Negligence by failure to provide make-up lesson. *Canadian School Executive (6)*4, 23–24.

Anderson, J. (1991a). Metal work class injury. *Canadian School Executive, 10*(10), 32–33.

Anderson, J. (1991b). Objective test for sexual assault. *Canadian School Executive, 11*(3), 29–30.

Anderson, J. (1992). Supervising students at recess. *Canadian School Executive, 11*(9), 33–34.

Anderson, J. (1995a). Teaching principal spanks student. *Canadian School Executive, 15*(3), 26–27.

Anderson, J. (1995b). Integration of autistic student. *Canadian School Executive, 15*(4), 25–27.

Apple, M. (1990). *Ideology and curriculum* (2nd ed.). New York: Routledge.

Assembly of First Nations. (1988). *Tradition and education: Towards a vision of our future.* Territory of Akwesasne, Hamilton's Island, Summerston, ON: Assembly of First Nations.

Baker, K. (1991). Yes, throw money at schools. *Phi Delta Kappan, 72*(8), 628–31.

Ball, S. (1987). *The micro-politics of the school.* London: Methuen.

Barber, B. (1984). *Strong democracy.* Berkeley, CA: University of California Press.

Barlow, M., & Robertson, H-J. (1994). Class warfare. Toronto: Key Porter.

Barman, J., Hebert, Y., & McCaskill, D. (1986). *Indian education in Canada: Volume 1: The legacy.* Vancouver: University of British Columbia Press.

Barr-Telford, L., Bowlby, G., and Clark, W. (1996). *The class of 86 revisited.* Ottawa: Human Resources Development Canada and Statistics Canada.

Barrow, R. (1981). *The philosophy of schooling.* New York: John Wiley.

Beck, K., Ogloff, J., & Corbishley, A. (1994). Knowledge, compliance, and attitudes of teachers toward mandatory child abuse reporting in British Columbia. *Canadian Journal of Education, 19*(1), 15–29.

Becker, H., & Epstein, J. (1982). Teachers' reported practices of parent involvement: Problems and possibilities. *The Elementary School Journal, 83*(2), 103–13.

Berla, N. (1991). Parent involvement at the middle school level. *The ERIC Review, 1*(3), 16, 17, 20.

Bernstein, B. (1971). *Class, codes and control.* London: Routledge & Kegan Paul.

Bernstein, B. (1975). *Class and pedagogies: Visible and invisible.* Paris: Organization for Economic Cooperation and Development (OECD).

Bezeau, L. (1995). *Educational administration for Canadian teachers* (2nd ed.). Toronto: Copp Clark Pitman.

Bezeau, L. (1996). *Educational administration for Canadian teachers.* Toronto: Copp Clark Pitman.

Blackmore, J., & Kenway, J. (Eds.). (1993). *Gender matters in educational administration and policy.* London: Falmer Press.

Blase, J. (1993). The micropolitics of effective school-based leadership: Teachers' perspectives. *Educational Administration Quarterly, 29*(2), 142–63.

Boyan, N. (Ed.). (1988). *The handbook of research on educational administration.* New York: Longman.

Bradley, J. (1992). A professional bill—now! *The Manitoba Teacher, 70*(3).

British Columbia. (1988). *A legacy for learners: The report of the royal commission on education.* Vancouver: Commission.

Canada. (1990). *A national stay in school initiative.* Ottawa: Minister of Employment and Immigration.

Canada. (1991). *Learning well ... living well.* Ottawa: Minister of Supply and Services.

Canada. (1996). *The report of the royal commission on aboriginal peoples.* Vols. 1–5. Ottawa: Minister of Supply and Services.

Canadian Education Association. (1995). *Study of exemplary secondary schools in Canada.* Toronto: CEA.

Canadian Education Statistics Council. (1990). *A statistical portrait of elementary and secondary education in Canada.* Joint publication of Statistics Canada and the Council of Ministers of Education, Canada.

Canadian Education Statistics Council. (1996). A statistical portrait of elementary and secondary education in Canada. Joint publication of Statistics Canada and the Council of Ministers of Education, Canada.

Canadian Teachers' Federation (CTF). (1992). *Teachers in Canada: Their work and quality of life.* Ottawa: CTF.

Canadian World Almanac. (1995). *Canadian world almanac, 1996.* Toronto: Global Press.

Celano, D., & Newman, S. (1995, February). Channel one: Time for a TV break. *Phi Delta Kappan, 76*(6), 444–46.

Christensen, C., Gerber, M., & Everhart, R. (1986). Towards a sociological perspective on learning disabilities. *Educational Theory, 36*(4), 317–31.

Clark, C., & Peterson, P. (1986). Teachers' thought processes. In M. Wittrock (Ed.), *Handbook of research on teaching,* (3rd ed). New York: Macmillan. 255–96.

Clark, L. (Ed.). (1968). *The Manitoba school question: Majority rule or minority rights?* Toronto: Copp Clark Pitman.

Claxton, G. (1984). *Live and learn.* Milton Keynes, UK: Open University Press.

Clifton, R., & Roberts, L. (1992). *Authority in classrooms.* Scarborough, ON: Prentice-Hall Canada.

Cohen, D., & Murnane, R. (1986). Merit pay and evaluation problems: Why most merit pay plans fail and a few survive, *Harvard Educational Review, 56*(1), 1–17.

Coleman, J. (1987). Families and schools. *Educational Researcher, 16*(6), 32–38.

Coleman, J., & Hoffer, T. (1987). *Public and private high schools: The impact of communities.* New York: Basic Books.

Coleman, P., & Collinge, J. (1991). In the web: Internal and external influences affecting school improvement. *School Effectiveness and School Improvement, 2*(4), 262–85.

Conference Board of Canada (1992). *Employability skills profile: What are employers looking for?* Ottawa: Conference Board of Canada.

Connell, R., Ashenden, D., Kessler, S., & Dowsett, G. (1982). *Making the difference: Schools, families and social division.* Sydney, Australia: George Allen & Unwin.

Connell, R.W. (1985). *Teachers' work*. Sydney, Australia: George Allen & Unwin.

Conway, J. (1993). *The Canadian family in crisis*. Toronto: James Lorimer.

Council of Ministers of Education, Canada (CMEC). (1994). Summary of significant initiatives in education in Canadian provinces and territories. Background paper prepared for the First National Consultation on Education. Toronto: CMEC.

Cousins, B., & Leithwood, K. (1993). Enhancing knowledge utilization as a strategy for school improvement. *Knowledge: Creation, diffusion, utilization, 14*(3), 305–33.

Craig, G. (1990). Lord Durham's report. In R.D. Francis & D.B. Smith (Eds.), *Readings in Canadian history: Pre-confederation*. Toronto: Holt, Rinehart and Winston. 312–21.

Crégheur, A., & Devereaux., M. (1991). Canada's children. *Canadian Social Trends, 21*, 2–5.

Cressy, G. (1994). Finding the common ground. In S. Lawton, E. Tanenzapt, & R. Townsend (Eds.), *Education and community: The collaborative solution*. The proceedings of an international conference linking research and practice. The Ontario Institute for Studies in Education, Toronto. 137–47.

Cuban, L. (1990). Reforming again, again, and again. *Educational Researcher, 19*(1), 3–13.

Cullingford, C. (1991). *The inner world of the school*. London: Cassell.

Curtis, B. (1988). *Building the educational state: Canada West, 1836–1871*. London, ON: The Althouse Press.

Curtis, B., Livingstone, D., & Smaller, H. (1992). *Stacking the deck: The streaming of working-class kids in Ontario schools*. Toronto: Our Schools/Our Selves.

Dampier, P., & Selman, G. (1991). *The foundations of adult education in Canada*. Toronto: Thompson.

D'Angelo, D., & Adler, R. (1991). Chapter 1: A catalyst for improving parent involvement. *Phi Delta Kappan, 72*(5), 344–49.

Davies, D. (1991, January). Schools reaching out: Family, school and community partnerships for student success. *Phi Delta Kappan, 72*(5), 350–54.

Dickinson, G. (1989). Principals and criminal investigations of students. *Canadian Journal of Education, 14*(2), 203–19.

Dickinson, G. (1995). The legal dimensions of teachers' duties and authority. In R. Ghosh & D. Ray (Eds.), *Social change and education in Canada*. Toronto: Harcourt Brace Jovanovich. 254–78.

Dickinson, G., & MacKay, A.W. (1989). *Rights, freedoms and the education system in Canada*. Toronto: Emond Montgomery.

Dolmage, R. (1995a). Accusations of teacher sexual abuse of students in Ontario schools: Some preliminary findings. *Alberta Journal of Educational Research, 41*(2), 127–44.

Dolmage, R. (1995b). One less brick in the wall: The myths of youth violence and unsafe schools. *Education and Law Journal, 7*(2), 185–207.

Dolmage, R. (1996). *So you want to be a teacher: a guide to teaching as a career choice in Canada*. Toronto: Harcourt Brace Canada.

Doyle, W. (1986). Classroom organization and management. In M. Wittrock (Ed.), *Handbook of research on teaching*, (3rd ed.) New York: Macmillan. 392–431.

Dror, Y. (1986). *Policymaking under adversity*. New York: Transaction Books.

Economic Council of Canada. (1992). *A lot to learn: Education and training in Canada*. Ottawa: Economic Council of Canada.

Epstein, J. (1986). Parents' reactions to teacher practices of parental involvement. *The Elementary School Journal, 86*(3), 277–94.

Epstein, J. (1991). Paths to partnership. *Phi Delta Kappan, 72*(5), 344–49.

Epstein, J. (1995). School/family/community partnerships: Caring for the children we share. *Phi Delta Kappan, 76*(9), 701–12.

Epstein, J. and Salinas, K. (1991). New directions in the middle grades. *Childhood Education, 67*(5), 285–91

Etobicoke Board of Education. (1996). *The formation and maintenance of school/business partnerships.* Toronto: Etobicoke Board of Education.

Fenstermacher, G. (1990). Some more considerations on teaching as a profession. In J. Goodlad, R. Soder, & K. Sirotnik (Eds.), *The moral dimensions of teaching.* San Francisco: Jossey-Bass. 130–51.

Fidkalo, W. (1992). Gender issues in mathematics, science, and computer literacy. *Canadian School Executive, 11*(8), 24–27.

Firestone, W., & Herriott, R. (1982, Spring). Two images of schools as organizations: An explication and illustrative empirical test. *Educational Administration Quarterly, 18*(2), 39–59.

Flaxman, E., & Inger, M. (1991). Parents and schooling in the 1990s. *The ERIC Review, 1*(3), 2–6.

Foster, W. (1986). *Paradigms and promises.* Buffalo, NY: Prometheus Books.

Fullan, M., & Stiegelbauer, S. (1991). *The new meaning of educational change.* Toronto: OISE Press.

Gaskell, J. (1988). Policy research and politics. *Alberta Journal of Educational Research, 34*(4), 403–17.

Gendron, F. (1994). Does Canada invest enough in education? *Education Quarterly Review, 1*(4), 10–25.

Gidney, R., & Lawr, D. (1979). Egerton Ryerson and the origins of the Ontario secondary school. *Canadian Historical Review, 60*(4), 442–65.

Giles, T., & Proudfoot, A. (1990). *Educational administration in Canada* (4th ed.). Calgary: Detselig.

Globe and Mail. (1991, December 1). Letter to the Editor. Boards must compete for existing space, p. A1.

Goguen, L., & Poirier, D. (1995). Are the educational rights of exceptional students protected in Canada? In R. Ghosh & D. Ray (Eds.), *Social change and education in Canada.* Toronto: Harcourt Brace Jovanovich. 310–22.

Goodlad, J. (1984). *A place called school.* New York: McGraw-Hill.

Goodlad, J. (1990). The occupation of teaching in schools. In J. Goodlad, R. Soder, & K. Sirotnik (Eds.), *The moral dimensions of teaching.* San Francisco: Jossey-Bass.

Goodlad, J., Soder, R., & Sirotnik, K. (Eds.). (1990). *The moral dimensions of teaching.* San Francisco: Jossey-Bass.

Gorton, R., & Schneider, G. (1991). *School-based leadership: Challenges and opportunities.* Dubuque, IA: William C. Brown.

Grant, G. (1988). *The world we created at Hamilton High.* Cambridge, MA: Harvard University Press.

Grant, J. (1984). The educational role of the federal government. *Interchange, 13*(4)–14(1), 25–40.

Greene, M. (1990). Opening spaces for the second chance. In D. Inbar (Ed.), *Second chance in education.* London: Falmer Press. 37–48.

Griffith, A. (1995, January). Coordinating family and school: Mothering and schooling. *Educational Policy Archives, 3*(1).

Guthrie, J. (1996). Evolving political economies and the implications for educational evaluation. In *Evaluating and reforming education systems* (pp. 61–83). Paris: OECD.

Haller, E., & Strike, K. (1986). *Introduction to educational administration.* New York: Longman.

Hanushek, E. (1989). The impact of differential expenditures on school performance. *Educational Researcher, 18*(4), 45–51.

Hanushek, E. (1994a, May). Money might matter somewhere: A response to Hedges, Laine, and Greenwald. *Educational Researcher, 23*(4), 5–8.

Hanushek, E. (1994b). *Making schools work.* Washington: Brookings Foundation.

Hargreaves, A. (1994). *Changing teachers, changing times.* New York: Teachers College Press.

Harte, A., & McDonald, K. (1996). Implications of the Charter for school discipline. *The Canadian School Executive, 15*(7), 3–6.

Hedges, L., Laine, R., & Greenwald, R. (1994, April). Money does matter somewhere: A reply to Hanushek. *Educational Researcher, 23*(3), 5–14.

Henchey, N., & Burgess, D. (1987). *Between past and future: Quebec education in transition.* Calgary: Detselig.

Henderson, A. (1987). *The evidence continues to grow: Parent involvement improves student achievement.* Columbia, MD: National Committee for Citizens in Education.

Henley, R., & Pampallis, J. (1982). The campaign for compulsory education in Manitoba. *Canadian Journal of Education, 7*(1), 59–82.

Hodgson, E. (1987). *Federal involvement in Canadian education.* Toronto: Canadian Education Association.

Holmes, M. (1986). The secondary school in contemporary western society: Constraints, imperatives, and prospects. *Curriculum Inquiry, 15*(1), 7–36.

Holmes, M., & Wynne, E. (1989). *Making the school an effective community.* London: Falmer Press.

Housego, I. (1989). Principals' evaluations of teachers in British Columbia school districts. *Alberta Journal of Educational Research, 35*(3), 196–216.

Houston, S., & Prentice, A. (1988). *Schooling and scholars in nineteenth-century Ontario.* Toronto: University of Toronto Press.

Hurlbert, E., & Hurlbert, M. (1992). *School law under the Charter of Rights and Freedoms* (2nd ed.). Calgary: University of Calgary Press.

Iran-Nejad, A. (1990). Active and dynamic regulation of learning processes. *Review of Educational Research, 60*(4), 573–602.

Jackson, P. (1968). *Life in classrooms.* Chicago: University of Chicago Press.

Johnson, J. (1995, February). Channel one: The dilemma of teaching and selling. *Phi Delta Kappan, 76*(6), 436–44.

Kallen, D. (1996). New educational paradigms and new evaluation policies. In *Evaluating and reforming education systems.* Paris: OECD. 7–23.

Kerchner, C., & Boyd, W.L. (1988). Chasing two rabbits: Market and bureaucratic failure in educational reform. *Journal of Education Finance, 14*(1), 57–75.

Kirkness, V. (1992). First nations and schools: Triumphs and struggles. Toronto: Canadian Education Association.

Laswell, H. (1950). *Politics: Who gets what, when, how.* New York: P. Smith.

Lawton, S. (1992). Why restructure: An international survey of the roots of reform. *Journal of Education Policy, 7*(2), 139–54.

Lawton, S., Hickcox, E., Leithwood, K., & Musella, D. (1986). *Development and use of performance appraisal of certified education staff in Ontario school boards.* Toronto: Ontario Ministry of Education.

Lawton, S., Tanenzapt, E., & Townsend, R. (1994). (Eds.) *Education and community: The collaborative solution.* The proceedings of an international conference linking research and practice. The Ontario Institute for Studies in Education, Toronto.

Leithwood, K., & Montgomery, D. (1982). The role of the elementary school principal in program improvement. *Review of Educational Research, 52*(3), 309–39.

Levin, B. (1990). Tuition fees and university accessibility. *Canadian Public Policy, 16*(1), 51–59.

Levin, B. (1994a). Education reform and the treatment of students in schools. *Journal of Educational Thought, 28*(1), 88–101.

Levin, B. (1994b). Rethinking resources in education. *The Canadian Administrator, 33*(4), 1–6.

Levin, B. (1994c). Students and educational productivity. *Phi Delta Kappan, 75*(10), 758–60.

Levin, B. (1995a). Changing basic delivery systems. In B. Levin, W. Fowler, & H. Walberg (Eds.), *Organizational influences on educational productivity* (pp. 195–213). Greenwich, CT: JAI Press.

Levin, B. (1995b). Education and poverty. *Canadian Journal of Education, 20*(2), 211–24.

Levin, B. (1995c). How schools respond to a changing labour market. *Canadian Vocational Journal, 30*(3), 8–20.

Levin, B., Fowler, W., & Walberg, H. (Eds.). (1995). *Organizational influences on educational productivity.* Greenwich, CT: JAI Press.

Levin, B., & Riffel, J.A. (1997). *Schools in a changing world: Struggling toward the future.* London: Falmer Press.

Lewington, J., & Orpwood, G. (1993). *Overdue assignment: Taking responsibility for Canada's schools.* Toronto: John Wiley.

Lightfoot, S. (1978). *Worlds apart: Relationships between families and schools.* New York: Basic Books.

Lindblom, Charles. (1980). *The policy-making process* (2nd ed.). Englewood Cliffs, NJ: Prentice-Hall.

Livingstone, D., & Hart, D. (1995). Popular beliefs about Canadian schools. In R. Ghosh & D. Ray (Eds.), *Social change and education in Canada* (3rd ed.). Toronto: Harcourt Brace. 16–44.

Lockhart, A. (1991). *Schoolteaching in Canada.* Toronto: University of Toronto Press. Published in association with Statistics Canada.

MacKay, A.W. (1984). *Education law in Canada.* Toronto: Emond Montgomery.

MacKay, A.W. (1995). The rights paradigm in the age of the Charter. In R. Ghosh & D. Ray (Eds.), *Social change and education in Canada* (3rd ed.). Toronto: Harcourt Brace Jovanovich. 224–39.

MacKay, A.W., & Sutherland, L. (1992). *Teachers and the law: A practical guide for educators.* Toronto: Emond Montgomery.

Maeroff, G. (1991). Assessing alternative assessment. *Phi Delta Kappan, 71*(4), 273–81.

Magsino, R. (1995). The family: Parents' and children's rights. In R. Ghosh & D. Ray (Eds.), *Social change and education in Canada* (3rd ed.). Toronto: Harcourt Brace Jovanovich. 290–304.

Malen, B. (1994). The micropolitics of education: Mapping the multiple dimensions of power relations in school politics. *Journal of Education Policy, 9*(5 & 6), 147–67.

Manicom, A. (1981, October). Reproduction of class: The relations between two work processes. Paper presented to the Political Economy of Gender Relations in Education Symposium. Toronto: OISE Press.

Manitoba. (1991). *Report of the Aboriginal Justice Inquiry.* Winnipeg: Attorney General of Manitoba.

Manzer, R. (1994). *Public schools and political ideas.* Toronto: University of Toronto Press.

Mawhinney, H. (1993). Discovering shared values: Ecological models to support interagency collaboration. In L. Adler & S. Gardner (Eds.), *The politics of linking schools and social services* London: Falmer Press. 33–47.

McEwen, N. (1995). Accountability in education in Canada. *Canadian Journal of Education, 20*(1), 1–17.

McLaren, P. (1989). Life in schools. White Plains, NY: Longman.

Means, B., & Knapp, M. (1991). Cognitive approaches to teaching advanced skills to educationally disadvantaged students. *Phi Delta Kappan, 73*(4), 282–89.

Melvin, J. & Juliebo, M. (1991). To retain or not retain: A critical look at retention procedures in North American elementary schools. *Canadian School Executive, 11*(2), 3–11.

Menzies, T. (1996). What do we know about school-based management and school councils? *Educators' Notebook,* 8(1).

Merttens, R., Newland, A., & Webb, S. (1996). *Learning in tandem: Involving parents in their children's education.* Leamington Spa, UK: Scholastic.

Metz, M. (1990). Real school. In D. Mitchell & M. Goetz (Eds.), *Education politics for the new century.* Basingstoke, UK: Falmer Press. 75–91.

Miles, K.H. (1996, Winter). Freeing resources for improving schools: A case study of teacher allocation in Boston public schools. *Educational Evaluation and Policy Analysis, 17*(4), 476–93.

Monk, D. (1990). *Educational finance: An economic approach.* New York: McGraw-Hill.

Morgan, G. (1986). *Images of organization.* Beverly Hills, CA: Sage.

Morgan, G. & Murgatroyd, S. (1994). *Total quality management in the public sector.* Buckingham, UK: Open University Press.

Nagy, P. (1996). International comparisons of student achievement in mathematics and science: A Canadian perspective. *Canadian Journal of Education, 21*(4), 396–413.

Nagy, P., & Lupart, J. (Eds.) (1994). *Is there a national role in education?* A publication of the Canadian Education Association and the Canadian Society for the Study of Education. Toronto: CEA.

National Advisory Board on Science & Technology (NABST). (1994). *Report to the Prime Minister on national standards in education.* Ottawa: NABST.

National Indian Brotherhood. (1972). *Indian control of Indian education.* Ottawa: NIB.

Nikiforuk, A. (1993). *School's out: The catastrophe in public education and what we can do about it.* Toronto: McFarlane, Walter & Ross.

No liability for volleyball accident. (1991). *School Law Commentary, 5*(10), 12.

Noddings, N. (1984). *Caring: A feminine approach to ethics and moral education.* Berkeley, CA: University of California Press.

Oakes, J. (1985). *Keeping track: How schools structure inequality.* New Haven, CT: Yale University Press.

Oakes, J. (1992). Can tracking research inform practice? Technical, normative, and political considerations. *Educational Researcher, 21*(4), 12–21.

Odden, A. (1990). Class size and student achievement: Research-based policy alternatives. *Educational Evaluation and Policy Analysis, 12*(2), 213–27.

Odden, A., & Clune, W. (1995). Improving educational productivity and school finance. *Educational Researcher, 24*(9), 6–10.

Olson, P. (1995). Poverty and education in Canada. In R. Ghosh & D. Ray (Eds.), *Social change and education in Canada* (3rd ed.). Toronto: Harcourt Brace. 196–208.

Ontario. (1968). *Living and learning: The report of the provincial committee on aims and objectives of education in the schools of Ontario.* Toronto: Ontario Department of Education.

Ontario. (1994). For the love of learning: Report of the royal commission on learning, Vols. 1-4. Toronto: Queen's Printer for Ontario.

Ontario College of Teachers. (1996). *Professionally speaking.* Toronto: Ontario College of Teachers.

Osberg, L. (1981). *Economic inequality in Canada.* Toronto: Butterworths.

Osberg, L., Wien, F., & Grude, J. (1995). *Vanishing jobs: Canada's changing workplace.* Toronto: James Lorimer.

Osborne, K. (1990). *Educating citizens: A democratic socialist agenda for Canadian education.* Toronto: Our Schools/Our Selves. 48–49.

Osborne, K. (1992, March). Give up the chase. *The Manitoba Teacher, 70,* 3.

Pajak, E. (1993). Change and continuity in supervision and leadership. In G. Cawleit (Ed.), *Challenges and achievements of American education.* Arlington, VA: ASCP. 158–86.

Pellegrini, A., & Horvat, M. (1995). A developmental contextualist critique of attention deficit hyperactivity disorder. *Educational Researcher, 24*(1), 13–19.

Plank, D., & Boyd, W.L. (1994). Antipolitics, education, and institutional choice: The flight from democracy. *American Educational Research Journal, 31*(2), 263–81.

Pratt, D. (1989, Summer). Characteristics of Canadian curricula. *Canadian Journal of Education, 14*(3), 295–310.

Radwanski, G. (1987). *Ontario study of the relevance of education, and the issue of dropouts.* Toronto: Ontario Ministry of Education.

Resnick, L. (1987). *Education and learning to think.* Washington, DC: National Academy Press.

Reynolds, C., & Young, B. (Eds.). (1995). *Women and leadership in Canadian education.* Calgary: Detselig.

Rich, J. (1984). *Professional ethics in education.* Springfield, IL: Charles Thomas.

Rideout, D. (1995). School councils in Canada. A cross country survey. *Education Canada, 35*(2), 12–18.

Riffel, J.A. (1991). Professional development. *Canadian School Executive, 11*(6), 28–29.

Riffel, J.A., & Levin, B. (1997). Schools coping with changes in information technology. *Educational Management and Administration, 25*(1), 51–64.

Riffel, J., Levin, B., & Young, J. (1996). Diversity in Canadian education. *Journal of Education Policy, 11*(1), 113–23.

Robinson, N. (1994). Education's publics. In S. Lawton, E. Tanenzapt, & R. Townsend (Eds.), *Education and community: The collaborative solution.* The proceedings of an international conference linking research and practice. The Ontario Institute for Studies in Education, Toronto.

Robinson, N., & Wallin, J. (1989, May). The quiet crisis in educational administration. *Canadian School Executive, 9*(1), 8–10.

Ross, D., Scott, K., & Kelly, M. (1996a). *Child poverty: What are the consequences?* Ottawa: Canadian Council on Social Development.

Ross, D., Scott, K., & Kelly, M. (1996b). Overview: Children in Canada in the 1990s. In *Growing up in Canada. National longitudinal survey of children and youth.* Ottawa: Human Resources Development Canada and Statistics Canada. 15–45.

Sadker, M., Sadker, D., & Klein, S. (1991). The issue of gender in elementary and secondary education. In G. Grant (Ed.), *Review of research in education*. Vol. 17. Washington: American Educational Research Association. 269–334.

Sale, T. (1992). *The financing of elementary and secondary education in Canada*. Working Paper No. 29. Ottawa: Economic Council of Canada.

Sale, T., & Levin, B. (1991). Problems in the reform of education finance: A case study. *Canadian Journal of Education, 16*(1), 32–46.

Saxe, R. (1980). *Educational administration today*. Berkeley, CA: McCutchan.

Schwartz, A. (1986). Teaching hatred: The politics and morality of Canada's Keegstra affair. *Canadian and International Education, 16*(2), 5–28.

Shack, S. (1993). The making of a teacher: 1917–1935. In R. Bruno-Jofre (Ed.), *Issues in the history of education in Manitoba*. Lewiston, ME: Mellon Press. 431–69.

Shakeshaft, C. (1989). *Women in educational administration* (rev. ed.). Beverly Hills, CA: Sage.

Shewan & Shewan v. Abbotsford (1987). 21 B.C.L.R. 93 (B.C.C.A.) at 98.

Shulman, L. (1987). Knowledge and teaching: Foundations of the new reform. *Harvard Educational Review, 57*(1), 1–22.

Shuttleworth, D. (1986, Summer). Parents-as-partners. *Education Canada, 26*(2), 41–42.

Slavin, R. (1987). Ability grouping and student achievement in elementary schools: A best-evidence synthesis. *Review of Educational Research, 57*(3), 293–336.

Slavin, R. (1990). Achievement effects of ability grouping in secondary schools: A best-evidence synthesis, *Review of Educational Research, 60*(3), 471–500.

Slavin, R. (1994). *Cooperative learning: Theory, research and practice* (2nd ed.). Boston: Allyn & Bacon.

Slavin, R., Madden, N., Karweit, N., Dolan, L., Wasik, B., Ross, S., & Smith, L. (1994). "Whenever and wherever we choose ...": The replication of Success for All. *Phi Delta Kappan, 75*(8), 639–47.

Sleeter, C. (1986). Learning disabilities: The social construction of a special education category. *Exceptional Children, 53*(1), 46–54.

Smith, D. (1996). Parent-generated home study in Canada. *The Canadian School Executive. 15*(8), 9–11.

Smith, W. (1994). *Equal educational opportunity for students with disabilities: Legislative action in Canada*. Montreal: McGill University Office of Research on Educational Policy.

Smith, M., & Shepard, L. (1987). What doesn't work: Explaining policies of retention in the early grades. *Phi Delta Kappan, 69*(2), 129–34.

Snider, R. (1992). The machine in the classroom. *Phi Delta Kappan, 74*(4), 316–23.

Soder, R. (1990). The rhetoric of teacher professionalism. In J. Goodlad, R. Soder, & K. Sirotnik (Eds.), *The moral dimensions of teaching*. San Francisco: Jossey-Bass. 35–86.

Stahl, A. (1992). Personal and cultural factors interfering with the effective use of individual and group learning methods. *The Journal of Educational Thought, 26*(1), 22–32.

Statistics Canada. (1986). *The distribution of wealth in Canada*. Ottawa: Minister of Supply and Services.

Statistics Canada. (1990a). *The aboriginal population survey*. Ottawa: Minister of Supply and Services.

Statistics Canada. (1990b). *Income distribution by size in Canada, 1990*. Ottawa: Ministry of Industry, Science and Technology.

Statistics Canada. (1991). *Education in Canada: A statistical review for 1989–90*. Ottawa: Ministry of Industry, Science and Technology.

Statistics Canada. (1992). *Employment, earnings and hours.* Cat. No. 72-002. Ottawa: Minister of Supply and Services.

Statistics Canada. (1995). Income distribution by size in Canada. Cat No. 13-207. Ottawa: Minister of Supply and Services.

Statistics Canada. (1996). *Growing up in Canada: A national longitudinal survey of children and youth.* Cat. No. 89-550-MPE, no. 1. Ottawa: Human Resources Development Canada.

Sullivan, B. (1988). *A legacy for learners: Report of the royal commission on education.* Vancouver: Province of British Columbia.

Sussel, T. (1995). *Canada's legal revolution: Public education, the Charter, and human rights.* Toronto: Emond Montgomery.

Symons, C. (1992). The ecology of achievement: A case study of John Norquay Collegiate. M.Ed. thesis, University of Manitoba.

Symons, T.B. (1975). *To know ourselves: The report of the commission on Canadian studies.* Ottawa: Association of Universities and Colleges of Canada.

Tabin, Y., and Coleman, P. (1993). From dollhouse to the schoolhouse: The changing experience of women principals in British Columbia, 1980–1990. *Canadian Journal of Education, 18*(4), 381–97.

Tardif, C. (1990). French language minority education: Political and pedagogical issues. *Canadian Journal of Education, 15*(4), 400–12.

Tepperman, L. (1988). *Choices and chances: Sociology for everyday life.* Toronto: Holt, Rinehart & Winston.

Thiessen, D., Bascia, N., & Goodson, I., (Eds.). (1996). *Making a difference about difference: The lives and careers of racial immigrant teachers.* Toronto: Garamond.

Tinder, G. (1991). Political thinking: The perennial questions (5th ed.). New York: HarperCollins.

Tite, R. (1994). Detecting the symptoms of child abuse: Classroom complications. *Canadian Journal of Education, 19*(1), 1–14.

Travers, W. (1986). *An introduction to educational research.* New York: Macmillan.

Vaillancourt, F. (1992). *Private and public monetary returns to schooling in Canada, 1985.* Working Paper No. 35. Ottawa: Economic Council of Canada.

Veenman, S. (1984). Perceived problems of beginning teachers. *Review of Educational Research, 54*(2), 143–78.

Walberg, H. (1987). Learning and life-course accomplishments. In C. Schooler & K.W. Schaie (Eds.), *Cognitive functioning and social structure over the life course.* Norwood, NJ: Ablex. 203–29.

Walberg, H. (1990). Productive teaching and instruction: Assessing the knowledge base. *Phi Delta Kappan, 71*(6), 470–78.

Walberg, H. (1991). Improving school science in advanced and developing countries. *Review of Educational Research, 61*(1), 25–69.

Walker, K. (1996). The Canadian copyright law and common educational reprography practices. *Canadian Journal of Education, 21*(1), 50–64.

Waller, W. (1932). *The sociology of teaching.* New York: Longman.

Wartella, E. (1995). The commercialization of youth. *Phi Delta Kappan, 76*(6), 448–51.

Wentzel, K. (1991). Social competence at school: Relation between social responsibility and academic achievement. *Review of Educational Research, 61*(1), 25–70.

Wilgosh, L. (1992). Integration of children with special needs. *The Canadian Administrator, 31*(4).

Williams, T., & Millinoff, H. (1990). *Canada's schools: Report card for the 1990s.* Ottawa: Canadian Education Association.

Willis, P. (1977). *Learning to labour.* New York: Columbia University Press.

Wilson, J.D. (1970). Education in Upper Canada: Sixty years of change. In J.D. Wilson, R. Stamp, & L-P. Audet (Eds.), *Canadian education: A history.* Scarborough, ON: Prentice-Hall. 190–213.

Wittrock, M. (Ed.). (1986). *Third handbook of research on teaching.* New York: Macmillan.

Wolfensberger, W. (1972). *The principle of normalization in human services.* Washington, DC: National Institute on Mental Retardation.

Wotherspoon, T., & Satzewich, V. (1993). *First Nations: Race, class and gender relations.* Scarborough, ON: Nelson Canada.

Ziegler, S. (1987). *The effects of parent involvement on children's achievement: The significance of home/school links.* Toronto: Toronto Board of Education.

Ziegler, S. (1992, January). Repeating a grade in elementary school: What does research say? *Canadian School Executive, 11*(7), 26–31.

Zucker, M. (1988). *The legal context of education.* Toronto: OISE Press.

INDEX

Reader Reply Card

We are interested in your reaction to *Understanding Canadian Schools: An Introduction to Educational Administration,* Second Edition, by Jon Young and Benjamin Levin. You can help us to improve this book in future editions by completing this questionnaire.

1. What was your reason for using this book?

   ❑ university course ❑ college course ❑ continuing education course
   ❑ professional ❑ personal ❑ other _____
   development interest _____

2. If you are a student, please identify your school and the course in which you used this book.

3. Which chapters or parts of this book did you use? Which did you omit?

4. What did you like best about this book? What did you like least?

5. Please identify any topics you think should be added to future editions.

6. Please add any comments or suggestions.

7. May we contact you for further information?

   Name: _____

   Address: _____

   _____

   Phone: _____

(fold here and tape shut)

MAIL ➤ **POSTE**

Canada Post Corporation / Société canadienne des postes

Postage paid
If mailed in Canada

Port payé
si posté au Canada

Business Reply

Réponse d'affaires

0116870399   01

0116870399-M8Z4X6-BR01

Larry Gillevet
Director of Product Development
HARCOURT BRACE & COMPANY, CANADA
55 HORNER AVENUE
TORONTO, ONTARIO
M8Z 9Z9